D0212158

TRADITIONAL
FESTIVALS

a multicultural encyclopedia

TRADITIONAL FESTIVALS

a multicultural encyclopedia

VOLUME I

CHRISTIAN ROY

A B C · CLIO

Santa Barbara, California · Denver, Colorado · Oxford, England

Library of Congress Cataloging-in-Publication Data

Roy, Christian, 1963-
Traditional festivals : a multicultural encyclopedia / Christian Roy.
p. cm.
Includes bibliographical references and index.
ISBN 1-57607-089-1 (hardback : alk. paper)—ISBN 1-85109-689-2
(ebook) 1. Festivals—Encyclopedias. I. Title.

GT3925.R69 2005
394.26'03—dc22
2005010444

07 06 05   /   10 9 8 7 6 5 4 3 2 1

This book is also available on the World Wide Web as an e-book.
Visit http://www.abc-clio.com for details.

ABC-CLIO, Inc.
130 Cremona Drive, P.O. Box 1911
Santa Barbara, California 93116–1911

This book is printed on acid-free paper.
Manufactured in the United States of America

To Lionel Rothkrug,
for first suggesting that I be entrusted with this project
that owes much to his groundbreaking work
on the history of religious mentalities

CONTENTS

Preface, xi

TRADITIONAL FESTIVALS
a multicultural encyclopedia

VOLUME I   A–L

A

Adae (Akan), 1
Akitu (Mesopotamia), 5
Anna Perenna (Rome), 8
Annunciation (Christianity), 9
Apaturia (Greece), 13
Argei (Rome), 14
Ascension (Christianity), 15
Ashura (Islam), 19
Assumption (Christianity), 23

B

Bear Festival (Japan), 27
Beautiful Festival of the Valley (Egypt), 30
Busk (American Southeast), 35

C

Candlemas (Christianity), 41
Caristia (Rome), 45
Carmentalia (Rome), 46
Carneia (Greece), 47
Carnival (Christianity), 48
Cherry Blossom Festival (Japan), 56
Chiao (China), 58

Christmas (Christianity), 61
Conception and Birth of the Virgin Mary
    (Christianity), 72
Corpus Christi (Christianity), 77
Cowherd and Weaving Maid
    (China, Korea, Japan), 81

D

Day of Assembly (Islam), 85
Days of the Dead (China, Korea,
    Japan), 87
Days of the Dead (West), 92
Dionysia (Greece and Rome), 100
Divali (Hinduism, Jainism, Sikhism), 109
Dong Zhi (China), 115
Double Nine (China, Korea), 116
Dragon Boat Festival
    (China, Korea), 116

E

Easter (Christianity), 121
Eid (Islam), 129
8 Monkey (Mayas), 133
Eleusinian Mysteries (Greece), 135

Elevation of the Cross (Christianity), 139

Epiphany (Christianity), 143

F

Feast of Fools (Christianity), 151

Floralia (Rome), 155

Fordicidia and Parilia (Rome), 157

Fornacalia and Quirinalia (Rome), 158

G

Games (Greece), 161

Games (Rome), 167

Ganesha Chaturthi (Hinduism), 178

Geerewol (Wodaabe), 180

Gion Festivals (Japan), 183

Gurpurb (Sikhism), 186

H

Hanukkah (Judaism), 189

Holi and Vasant Panchami (Hinduism, Sikhism), 192

Hollyhock Festival (Japan), 197

Holy Week (Christianity), 198

I

Inti Raymi and Huarachicu (Incas), 205

Izcalli (Aztecs), 211

J

Janmashtami (Hinduism), 213

K

Kasuga Festivals (Japan), 217

Kathina (Buddhism), 218

Kermis (Christianity), 221

Khoiak and Heb-Sed (Egypt), 223

KI.LAM (Hittites), 229

Kokuzahn (Voodoo), 231

Kukulcan Festival (Mayas), 232

Kunapipi (Australia), 233

L

Laba (China), 237

Lag ba-Omer (Judaism), 238

Lantern Festival (China, Korea), 240

Lent (Christianity), 244

Liberalia (Rome), 250

Lugnasad (Celts), 251

Lupercalia (Rome), 254

VOLUME II   M–Z

M

Mahashivaratri (Hinduism), 257
Martinmas (Christianity), 261
Matralia (Rome), 264
Matronalia (Rome), 265
Matsuri (Japan), 267
Matzu's Birthday (China), 270
Mawlid (Islam), 273
May Day (West), 276
Mid-Autumn (China, Korea, Japan), 282
Midsummer (West), 286
Midwinter (Iroquois), 291
Mi'raj (Islam), 295

N

Naadam (Mongolia), 299
Naked Festivals (Japan), 302
Navaratra and Dusshera (Hinduism), 304
Naw Ruz (Zoroastrianism, Bahá'ism), 311
New Fire Ceremony (Aztecs), 315
New Yam Festival (Ewe), 317
New Year (China, Korea), 319
New Year (Islam), 326
New Year (Japan), 327
New Year (West), 332
Nineteen-Day Feast (Bahá'ism), 338
Noumenia (Greece), 340
Nyepí (Hinduism), 341

O

Òsun Festival (Yoruba), 346

P

Palm Sunday (Christianity), 349
Panathenaea (Greece), 353
Pardon (Christianity), 355
Paryushana and Dashalakshana
   (Jainism), 356

Passover (Judaism), 358
Potlatch (Pacific Northwest), 364
Powwow (North America), 369
Presentation of the Virgin Mary
   (Christianity), 372
Protection of the Mother of God
   (Christianity), 375
Purim (Judaism), 377

Q

Quinquatrus (Rome), 381

R

Rain Festivals (Aztecs), 383
Ramadan (Islam), 384
Reed Dance (Southern Africa), 388
Ridván (Bahá'ism), 391
Rogations (Christianity), 393
Rosh Hashanah (Judaism), 395
Rosh Hodesh (Judaism), 398

S

Sabbath (Judaism), 401
Sacred Heart (Christianity), 406
Saint George (Christianity), 408
Saint Lucy (Christianity), 411
Saint Nicholas (Christianity), 415
Samhain (Celts), 420
Saturnalia (Rome), 424
Sekku (Japan), 427
Seven-Five-Three (Japan), 431
Shalako (Zuñi), 432
Shavuot (Judaism), 438
Situa (Incas), 440
Spring Dragon (China), 442
Spring Festival of Cybele and Attis
   (Rome), 443
Sukkot (Judaism), 446

Sun Dance (Plains Indians), 450
Sunday (Christianity), 453

T

Terminalia (Rome), 459
Thaipusam (Hinduism), 462
Thargelia (Greece), 465
Thesmophoria (Greece), 466
Tisha be-Av (Judaism), 470
Transfiguration
    (Christianity), 472
Tu bi-Shevat (Judaism), 474

V

Vaishakha and Vaisakhi (Hinduism,
    Buddhism, Sikhism), 479

Venus Verticordia and Virile Fortune
    (Rome), 484
Vestalia (Rome), 485

W

Water-Splashing Festival (China,
    Thailand), 487
Whitsuntide (Christianity), 489

Y

Yom Kippur (Judaism), 501

APPENDIXES

*I: Main Hindu Festivals and
Buddha Day in North India 2001–2031,* 509

II: Main Muslim Festivals 2001–2050, 518

III: Main Jewish Holidays in Israel 2001–2050, 519

IV: Main Moveable Feasts of the Western Church 2001–2050, 522

V: Gregorian Dates of Orthodox Easter 1875–2124, 523

VI: Dates of Chinese Lunar New Year's Day 1995–2020, 525

*VII: Comparative Table of Main Festival Entries
for Each Cultural Area by Time of Year,* 526

VIII: List of Full Festival Entries by Cultural Area, 529

Index, 531

About the Author, 549

PREFACE

SINCE THE BEGINNING of time, and despite the advent of modernity as the reduction of the latter to the linear progress of secular history, the life of most human societies has usually unfolded within the sacred cycle of a strict succession of festive observances. Interrupting daily routine, they temporarily loosen and rearrange the social fabric—the better to reaffirm its underlying pattern of beliefs and assumptions, hopes and fears, founding myths and redemptive visions. The fact that festivals provide an important key to understanding the cultures that produce them is borne out by news reports I read as I was completing the entries in this encyclopedia in the spring of 2003. They told about the massive pilgrimage of a million Iraqi Shiites to Karbala, the holy site of the event commemorated by the Muslim feast and fast of Ashura, long banned as an expression of Shiite identity under the regime of Saddam Hussein—and this only days after his dictatorship's downfall, amid the devastation of a war torn country where all social order had otherwise broken down! The bloody terrorist attacks targeting other major pilgrimage sites at the following year's Ashura celebrations also sadly illustrated their highly sensitive—and therefore politically strategic—social function. The stakes can be so high precisely because a particular culture's sense of its timeless underpinnings, whether conscious or unconscious, comes to the fore on such festive occasions. For that identity is then acted out in real time, through rituals that lift partici-pants beyond time to a renewed awareness of their place in the scheme of things—whether in terms of social structures, of the seasonal cycles of nature, or of their own ultimate destiny as spiritual beings. These levels of meaning usually coexist in the ceremonies and customs of traditional festivals—understood here as regularly occurring sets of actions aimed at making present and effective a certain dimension of human beings' belonging to a sacred cosmic order, as reflected in the ever-recurring cycles of time. Yet as a way for humans to "come home" to an original state outside the immediate demands of daily life—be it only to secure optimal conditions for their satisfaction—festivals also normally represent a certain release from customary practical strictures. This suspension of "normal" time is what makes them stand out as the archetypical manifestation of that "play element in culture" to which the Dutch historian Johan Huizinga (1872–1945) has devoted a classic study:

> The sacred act is "celebrated" on a "holiday"—
> *i.e.*, it forms part of a general feast on the occasion of a holy day. When the people foregather at the sanctuary they gather together for collective rejoicing. Consecrations, sacrifices, sacred dances and contests, performances, mysteries—all are comprehended within the act of celebrating a festival . . . Whether we think of the Ancient Greek festivities or of the African religions today we can hardly draw any sharp line between the festival mood in general and the holy frenzy surrounding the central mystery. (*Homo Ludens* 1955, p. 21)

Every traditional festival is at once "a popular festivity and a mystic ceremony" and belongs, as such, at some level at least, among "the only true festivals that religious festivals are, unlike secular, social festivals, since no contingent caprice attaches them to some day or other that is not specially meant for them, that has nothing essentially festive about it," as Marcel Proust appropriately noted at the outset of his vast novel cycle *Remembrance of Things Past* (freely translated from *À la Recherche du Temps Perdu, Tome 1: Du Côté de chez Swann* 1919, pp. 106, 130). For it was no coincidence that its narrator's personal quest for "privileged moments," when his life fleetingly came together as a meaningful whole—connecting these dots of real presence into a vivid unified pattern beyond time and space—seemed to take him back precisely to childhood memories of springtime church festivals, as a touchstone of authenticity. This in turn brings to light how festivals do play a similar role in the collective psyche of communities, united as they are at such "privileged moments" in the recollection, reenactment, or anticipation of—and always participation in—"timeless" moments that stand out amid the flow of time. As long as it is structured by such peak experiences of heightened vitality, social time can be said to follow the sacred rhythm of tradition, in contrast to the homogeneous tempo of modern mundane life, with its agenda of arbitrarily set dates for public events—including deliberately invented "traditions." Traditional festivals are defined here as opposed to such modern celebrations, as religious feasts are by Proust, though "pagan" impulses directly attuned to the seasonal rhythms of nature are given as much weight as the intimations of eternity woven into these or overwriting them in "high" or "world" religions—"revealed" or not.

This illustrated encyclopedia offers a survey of more than 150 traditional festivals chosen from a wide range of eras and areas, that cover the major feasts of all world religions, as well as high points in the sacred calendars of ancient civilizations and representative samples of the seasonal rites and celebrations of lesser known, indigenous local cultures. For this book is not simply meant to account for current festive customs, but also to provide insights into the festive patterns that structure all human societies—albeit more clearly and pervasively in the past than at the present time. The discussion of the festivals of extinct or remote societies may throw light on those still to be found in our own, by tracing their distant lineage or suggesting certain telling parallels with them—or with others that have made their mark in history. Full entries typically combine a variety of approaches—from traditional theology to cultural anthropology, and from folklore studies to social theory—to describe the content and context of a festival, including its historical development and geographical variations, wherever this is possible. They all aim to give a sense of what a traditional festival means to the people who celebrate it (or used to), while contributing to an understanding of the broader cultural dynamics and spiritual principles involved in its key features.

On the one hand, every entry is a self-contained portal to the cultural universe disclosed from the vantage point of a particular festival. Yet on the other hand, wherever they arise, connections are also made with the parallel universes of other entries—not only to fill out the immediate cultural context, but also to point out common patterns and related instances of festive behavior, whether it is done explicitly in the text or implicitly in the list of cross-references provided for each. Thus, should s/he be inclined to venture beyond the levels of casual browsing and the handy retrieval of information, the attentive reader ought to be able to "connect the dots" and see patterns emerge among, say, the New Fire Ceremony of the Aztecs of Mexico and comparable ones embedded in countless other festivals of new beginnings the world over; or among the

Aztec rain festivals, those of the Pueblos of New Mexico, and Whitsuntide folklore from Britain to the Balkans; among African New Yam festivals and the Native American Green Corn Ceremony as examples of the taboos surrounding first fruits also echoed in some Jewish festivals; among the scapegoating rituals found in other Jewish feasts, as in ancient Greece and Rome, in contemporary Japan as in pre-Columbian Peru; among winter gatherings and gift exchanges from Celtic Ireland to the Pacific Northwest and from China to French Canada; among rowdy Carnival behavior at New Year celebrations and commemorations of the dead as well as at spring festivals from Rio to Morocco and from Rome to Mexico.

Festivals and their various phases or combinations can often be known by a number of different names. All the names mentioned within the text of full entries appear in bold therein, even those of modern celebrations that, without being traditional, still have pre-modern connections or parallels and regardless of whether the festivals in question also have their own full entry in this book. Highlighted throughout it, just like the more than 150 full entry names (if "twin" entries for joint festivals are counted), over 700 additional or alternate festival names are thus listed in "blind entries" that simply refer the reader to the main entry heading under which they occur and are explained—sometimes quite incidentally; it should therefore be kept in mind that a given blind entry may actually point to a festival that is not synonymous or obviously connected with it.

The reader can get an overview of the festivals covered in the general list in the Appendixes, where the full entries are grouped by religion or by cultural area, and in a graph showing at a glance the relative places of the main festivals discussed within the cycle of a single year's seasons, from solstice to equinox to solstice. If balance has been sought in the number and length of entries between religious and cultural areas, no worldwide "neutral" coverage could be approached within the limited format of this encyclopedia, and difficult choices had to be made in the selection of festivals to be discussed. I opted to aim at near exhaustiveness in those areas where it was within reach, as in the festive cycles of China or in the "religions of the Book," at the expense of those marked by an overwhelming proliferation of festivals to choose from or by a relative dearth of readily available up-to-date studies, as in the cases of India and Africa, in which I settled for a selection of the best known, best documented festivals, without pretending to adequately cover the sheer variety or the full territorial distribution of all those to be found in these parts of the world. An effort was made, however, to provide examples for a fair sampling of the many deities or social groups around which a festival may focus.

For each festival, a brief list of written, audio-visual, or digital materials dealing with it has been provided in order to facilitate further research on that specific topic. Directly relevant works may thus not always be particularly recent or widely distributed; but at least the reader can get an idea of what to look for through the channels available for such specialized bibliographical investigation. Though this reference work does not really emphasize calendar systems, it does include as appendixes tables of dates for the major feasts of Hinduism, Judaism, Christianity, Islam, and China and in the early twenty-first century—or at times beyond.

References

Johan Huizinga. *Homo Ludens.* Boston: Beacon Press, 1955, p. 21.

Marcel Proust. *À la Recherche du Temps Perdu, Tome 1: Du Côté de chez Swann, 1e Partie.* Paris: Gallimard, 60th edition, 1919, pp. 106, 130.

ACTIAN GAMES
See Games (Rome)

ADAE (AKAN)
The Akan peoples of West Africa, who are concentrated in Ghana but are also found in parts of Ivory Coast to the west and Togo to the east, renew their connection with their past and present leaders once every three weeks in **Adae** ceremonies, held alternately on a Wednesday and a Sunday. Most of them also perform the *Odwira* **New Year** purification ceremonies and national festival in conjunction with either one of the last two **Adae** of the local Akan calendar.

Connecting with Revered Ancestors
The 378-day Akan year is made up of nine 6-week cycles called **Adae**. This is also the name of a ceremony that is celebrated twice during each cycle: first as an **Awukudae**, or Wednesday **Adae**, and then as an **Akwasidae** on the third Sunday thereafter, when the rites are more elaborate. The ritual is intended primarily to honor departed rulers and invoke the blessings of their spirits by recalling their names and deeds (although nature spirits are also recognized in the Brong version of **Adae** in Ghana's Northern Region). Most of the ceremony takes place in the resting or sleeping place of these rulers, which is where the Akan word *adae* comes from. Here, a lineage whose heads hold political office keeps all the stools of those who died while in power—provided they have proven worthy. Akans believe that they each have a *sunsum* (a part of the soul that wanders out of the body during sleep and joins the world of shadows after death) and that it is normally tied to his or her special white stool. However, they blacken the stools of their dead rulers with soot and egg yolk to preserve them as shrines. On an **Adae**, the current successors of those rulers may call their spirits by name to these shrines to dwell there again.

All families commemorate their dead in a similar fashion on the **Adae**. However, they only permit a select few senior members of their lineage to follow its head into the stool house. While the chief offers water, food, meat, and eggs to his ancestors to ensure his tribe's prosperity and the soil's fertility, the queen mother does the same in her own stool house. No work or travel are allowed on the **Adae** except in connection with the ceremonies. All the articles needed for the ceremony are gathered and brought home, along with firewood, the day before.

This day is called *Dapaa*—either *Benada Dapaa*, for a Tuesday, or *Memeneda Dapaa*, for a Saturday. Children born on these days are named **Dapaa** or **Adae**. This reflects the Akan belief that each day of the week is matched by a different kind of *kra* (a breath-like life-force in the soul that flies back to God as a bird at death).

The Typical Adae

The day of preparation for **Adae** is **Dapaa**, when all dwellings and their surroundings—as well as the stools and calabashes needed in the ceremonies—are tidied up. Drummers are heard playing in every chief's house from sunset until late at night. The following morning, the principal "divine drummer" gets up early to greet the chief with ceremonial songs. Then, the chief has a meal of mashed yam or plantain. Before the chief and his party proceed to the stool room or house, whatever ritual food remains is taken out and sprinkled in the courtyard to feed the dead courtiers and attendants. No salt is used (since the Akans believe the spirits cannot stand it), and a bell is rung to signify that the spirits are eating. The chief's attendants go back and forth to the stool room, returning with the blood of sheep they slaughter and prepare as additional offerings to the spirits in the stools. They use the blood to mark their master's chest and forehead. At the same time, the queen mother makes an offering of *fufu*—a cassava or yam paste—on the spot. Finally, the head attendant pours rum on the stools; any leftover rum is passed around among those present. The chief's subordinates and subjects then come to wish him "**Adae** morn" in the main courtyard, where he sits in state while a court poet recites the deeds of past chiefs. The celebrations go on until dusk, accompanied by the beating of drums and the blowing of horns. The offerings are only removed from the stools late in the evening; and any pieces of fat are left there even longer.

The Great Adae

The ninth Adae is the "Great **Adae**" or *Adae Kese.* At this ceremony, the chief carries the sacrificial sheep to the stools himself. **Adae** Kese ushers in the **New Year** under various names. The dates also vary from place to place between July and October, although several Akan states—such as Akim, Akwamu, and Ashanti—hold this ceremony in January.

This is when a number of Akan peoples—such as the Akuapem and the Brong—carry out the *Odwira* ceremony (pronounced "Oh-je-rah") of "purification" of the shrines of ancestral spirits and "cleansing" of the nation's defilements. In most states, it tends to overlap in timing and content with the yam harvest and associated rituals—hence the misnomer "**Yam Custom**" by which it was long known to Europeans.

In the Akuapem town of Aburi in Ghana's Eastern Region, the two-day **New Yam Festival** of thanksgiving for **first-fruits** (centering on a fetish of the sky god Ntoa which aboriginal clan heads brought from Nkoranza in Brong country before the arrival of Akwamu and Akim settlers) even takes the place of **Odwira** on the ninth **Awukudae**. Like **Odwira**, it is preceded by forty days of *adaebutuw* or "turning over of the **Adae**," when the ancestors are left alone in the stool house, and there is a ban on all loitering and noise-making in the streets. Even funeral ceremonies are scaled down to a minimum, as a barely tolerated transgression that should be atoned for by sacrificing a sheep.

The point of these restrictions is to avoid disturbing dead ancestors and living elders who may reside elsewhere but often return to their ancestral villages for the duration of the festival. These lesser chiefs have their own **Odwira** ceremonies in the villages, usually on different dates than those held in the state capitals. Like all able-bodied men and women, the elders are required to attend the state events. At this great national festival, where all the social ties binding different groups—living or dead, human or divine—are renewed, recently enstooled chiefs swear allegiance to the paramount chief. How-

A chief, carrying a golden staff, takes part in Yam Custom, or Great Adae, celebrations at the village of Akropong Akuapem. The festival attracts village chiefs from all over Ghana. (Margaret Courtney-Clarke/Corbis)

ever, the paramount chief leaves all secular state functions to his second-in-command for the seven-to-twelve days the festival can last.

The festival is observed by a ban on eating yam. Both the royal family and the paramount chief abstain from the **new yam** until completion of purification rites that the chief leads at the stool house and over graves of past chiefs.

The ban on eating yam may be lifted earlier for the common people. In Akropong, the Akuapem capital, for instance, fresh tubers are paraded on the second day. There, the official **Odwira** date is the day after the ninth Wednesday **Adae**. It occurs in September or October—as does Aburi's **Yam Festival**. The difference is that there, **Adae** Kese is considered a day of general mourning, especially for those departed in the past year. It is also when people who may have died since the previous Monday are buried. Though there is much drumming and drinking on this day, Thursday is the primary feast day. At the royal palace, feasting is open to subjects and foreigners alike; in every private home, food and drink are made available to all comers, and a procession takes a ritual meal to the dead at their shrine outside of town. Yet after nightfall, a hush falls over Akropong, and people are warned to stay indoors since none but a privileged few are entitled by birth or office to cast eyes on the shrines of the nation's revered ancestors, which are taken out in a solemn procession to the river and back to the stool house. An actual washing of the sacred stools of the state in the nearby stream is the "cleansing" that gives **Odwira** its name. When it is over, volleys of muskets are fired to give the all-clear.

African Durbars

Akuapem's **Odwira** culminates in Friday's great **durbar**. This Persian word for "court" was used in India for "any formal assembly of notables called together by a governmental authority" (*Encyclopedia Britannica* 1999) and gained currency in other British colonies, including those in West Africa. For on **Odwira**, Akan paramount chiefs convene such ceremonial assemblies to which lesser chiefs and all their subjects come to pay homage to their lord, while he in turn renews his oath of office to them and to the national government, amid the extravagant praise of minstrels and the frenzied drumming, dancing, and marching of courtiers and gunners.

In Akwamu, the **durbar** takes place in January on the ninth **Akwasidae**, or Sunday **Adae**, which is the third and most important day of the week-long local **Odwira**. It is better known there as Apafram. Saturday is called "*Odwirahuruda*"—"the day that brings in the **Odwira**"—and is marked by mourning for national heroes and offerings at the shrine holding their relics.

On the Sunday **durbar**, there is a morning parade of warriors in battle array, a midday cleansing of the paramount chief, and a blessing on behalf of various gods that he gives to the crowds with the same water, all of which precede an afternoon rally of state executioners. The latter become possessed by the fetishes they carry in a procession around town all the way back to the **durbar** site. There, a clearing is made in the crowd for wild acrobatic and military displays by *Asafo* ("war people") companies. These are hereditary militias formed by the neighboring Fante on the model of European units in the seventeenth century and adopted by the Akan peoples. The paramount chief, dressed in full regalia, will then, as elsewhere, renew his pledge to serve the public good before passing out rum to his assembled chiefs and subjects.

In contrast to the custom in Akuapem, it is on the evening after the **durbar**—rather than on its eve—that people huddle in silence inside the houses of Akwamu, at the approach of the "messengers of death"—the executioners on their way to the shrine of past rulers in the foothills to the south. At the royal palace, a vigil is kept, while townspeople hold their breath as these initiates perform a vital ritual that will determine Akwamu's fortune over the coming year. The chief executioner loudly calls upon the male and female **Odwira** spirits in turn, and shouts of relief fill the air when they are heard responding in the distance each time. A gunshot gives the signal for the stampede of the executioners from this oracle of the **Odwira** festival to the palace. Everyone then rejoices over clear indications that the festival's spirits have agreed to join living mortals in their celebrations of the past year and their welcoming of the **New Year**.

See also Busk; Kokuzahn; Shavuot; New Yam Festival

References

R. E. G. Armattoe. "Akwasidae," in *African Affairs: Journal of the Royal African Society* (Vaduz, Liechtenstein: Klaus Reprints Ltd., 1963), Vol. 50, October 1951, pp. 61–63.

Kwabena N. Bame. *Profiles in African Traditional Popular Culture: Consensus and Conflict, Dance, Drama, Festival, and Funerals.* New York: Clear Type Press, 1991.

Robert B. Fisher. *West African Religious Traditions: Focus on the Akan of Ghana.* Maryknoll, NY: Orbis Books, 1998.

A. A. Opoku. *Festivals of Ghana.* Accra, Ghana: Ghana Publishing Corporation, 1970.

▶ ADHIK MAAS

See Navaratra and Dusshera

▶ ADULTS' DAY

See New Year (Japan)

▶ ADVENT

See Christmas

▶ **AGONES**

See Games (Rome)

▶ **AGRANIA, AGRIONIA**

See Dionysia

▶ **AH-DAKE'-WA-O**

See Busk

▶ **AKITU (MESOPOTAMIA)**

Akitu is the earliest **New Year**'s festival for which we have written records, as well as one of the oldest Mesopotamian festivals, dating back to the middle of the third millennium B.C.E. Although it was initially observed on a semiannual basis, due to a local system of six-month equinox years, it sometimes came to be celebrated with more emphasis on one of its two dates in some of the region's city states. Thus, in Babylonia, it started on the new moon closest to the spring equinox to honor the sky god Marduk; the **Akitu** nearest the fall equinox in Assyria honored the high god Ashur; and **Akitus** were held on both dates each year in Uruk to honor the sky god Anu. In each case, there would be a procession to a temple called "**Akitu** house" along a canal out in the fields, cultic dramas reenacting the creation of the cosmos by the god being honored, and the sacred marriage of a god and goddess to ensure the land's prosperity.

Development

Which gods were involved depended on the current political fortune of the particular Mesopotamian city state that had them as patrons, since each would reenact with an **Akitu** festival a god's original triumphal entry to take possession of it. Each city had a calendar of its own, with months named after local religious festivals. That of Nippur, which was the religious center of legitimate authority for the region and where all its local practices converged, eventually became the standard calendar. This calendar incorporated the dates that originated in Ur for the **Akitu** festivals. One of these Ur Akitus was celebrated in the first month (lasting about a week) and the other in the seventh month (lasting eleven days) when the equinoxes occurred. In the Nippur calendar, one **Akitu** was celebrated in the fourth month (for five different deities!) and the other in the twelfth month, but the names of both months sounded like those of the Ur months for the **Akitus**. These imported festivals were absorbed by pre-existing agricultural festivals after which these months were named in Nippur, and they lost their connection to the moon, whose god, Nanna, was the one Ur worshipped (though the original Ur dates were still observed much later in the **Akitu** festivals of Babylon and even Hellenistic Uruk).

In its Nippur version, **Akitu** provided a model for other cities in Sumer and then Mesopotamia (the culture that succeeded Sumer in a larger area between the Rivers Tigris and Euphrates, which is now at the heart of Iraq), since each city also wanted to show its god the respect due it in a triumphal welcome (the equivalent of a medieval prince's **royal entry** into one of his cities), in return for which the god would rule the city justly and grant it a happy fate. Thus, there was an **Akitu** for Urash in Dilbat and one for Belit in Sippar. In some cities, other deities beside the local patron, such as the more broadly regional goddess Ishtar, might also be welcomed into the city at times of the year that did not conflict with their chief god's **Akitu**.

In the course of the second millennium B.C.E., Babylon became the political capital of Mesopotamia, and its god Marduk incorporated the attributes of the agro-pastoral god Tammuz he largely supplanted in the new state religion. In the process, the semi-annual **Akitu** festival held previously by the Akkadians (whose kingdom held sway in the region from the twenty-fourth to the twenty-second centuries B.C.E.) in honor of Tammuz (who emerged with the spring shoots and rose again with fall harvests after his death in summer droughts) became strictly a spring event. It even absorbed a fall **New Year**'s festival called **Zagmuk**. It filled the gap between the end of the solar and lunar years with a dozen-day celebration tied to the spring equinox (just like the twelve days of **Christmas** that follow the winter solstice in European tradition). Having started out as a sowing and harvest festival, it came to prominence in Babylon as the proper occasion for the crowning and investiture of a new king. On this occasion, the reigning monarch's divine mandate was renewed in connection with the sky god Marduk's victory over Tiamat, the goddess of salt water. As a spring festival, **Akitu** thus bound together the renewal of nature's fertility, the reestablishment of the king's divine authority (formerly a fall ceremony), and the securing of the people's favorable destiny over the coming year—especially the scorching summer heat—while putting an end to the sterility of the winter months when the world seemed old and worn out.

Seasonal Ordeals of Gods and Kings

In Babylon, the year's most important festival began with ritual preparations on the first three days of the month of Nisan. On the fourth day, a high priest, the *sheshgallu,* recited the creation epic *Enuma elish* (which was written down in the late twelfth century B.C.E.) in praise of Marduk (also known simply as Bel or Lord), who was the city's patron and head of its pantheon. Meanwhile, the king went to Borsippa to fetch an effigy of that city's patron, the sky god's son Nabu. He brought back the statue of this god of vegetation and of writing in a solemn ritual procession that arrived the next day by barge. In the interval, residents and pilgrims roamed the streets of Babylon looking for Marduk, whose captivity inside a mountain (like that of Tammuz, his predecessor as supreme god) explained the land's desolate

condition in the winter. The shrines of Marduk and Nabu were purified on the fifth day, when the king would enter the great Esagila temple to be greeted by a priest, who proceeded to lead him to Marduk's shrine. There, the priest stripped the monarch of his regalia, slapped his face, and pulled his ears. As part of this royal penitential rite, the king had to kneel before the god and assure him he had not neglected his duties toward his city Babylon and his temple Esagila. Only then could he be reinvested with the insignia of Marduk's kingship and partake again of his divine powers. It has been suggested (Cohen 1993, pp. 440–441) that this ceremony of the humbling of the king, which normally occured after his arrival from the **Akitu** house, was put on the fifth day because that was when time was available for it in the midst of the festivities associated with an **Akitu** of Nabu. The latter went on until the eighth day, followed by an abridged **Akitu** of Marduk which went on for another three and a half days (since the **Akitu**s of Borsippa and Babylon seem to have been combined due to the growing regional importance of the cult of Nabu in the first millennium B.C.E.).

After Nabu's own triumphal entry on the fifth day, mock battles were staged to reenact his struggle to avenge and free his father from his enemies. The enemies were represented by two small figurines, one made from tamarisk and the other from cedar. These were decapitated and burned on the sixth day. On the eighth day, Nabu could serve as a scribe to register the decrees of an assembly of all the gods, whose statues were arranged and carried following a strict hierarchy. The king would "take Marduk by the hand" (i.e., escort him) first to the temple's courtyard and then to his Throne-of-Destiny on the Sacred Mound to proclaim the solar sky god's sovereignty over all the other gods for the beginning of the **New Year** on **Zagmuk**. Then, he would "take Marduk by the hand" again to lead a grand procession of the gods, who went in battle order to the Euphrates in carriage boats to fight the forces of chaos. There, real boats awaited the royal party to take it upriver to the **Akitu** house (*Bit Akitu*), or "House of Offerings," north of the city, for a "banquet of the gods," which celebrated Marduk's triumph and the resulting prosperity of his Babylonian kingdom.

Ritual Dramas of Divine Victory and Sacred Marriage

As part of the ritual drama of this "banquet of the gods," the story of the *Enuma elish* (meaning "When on high . . .") was reenacted, either with the gods' statues or by humans, including the king who represented Marduk. It related the story of the sun god Marduk's victory over the titanic powers of chaos, which were unleashed by his great-grandmother Tiamat (turned sea dragon in her wrath) against her unruly divine progeny, and the resulting creation of the universe out of her carcass. With Marduk's enthronement as head of the gods, at which Babylon's gods annually renewed their consent to be governed by him, the dominance of the city's royalty was also reaffirmed as the earthly representation of the order of the universe created by its national god.

However, there was a period during the second half of the thirteenth century B.C.E. when Assyria defeated Babylon and took over its **Akitu** along with the statue of Marduk, only to cast him in a less glorious role: that of one who abused his commission in the cosmic battle by trying to claim for himself the legitimate supreme leadership of Anshar, the true hero of the *Enuma elish* in this alternate reading, allowing him to be identified with Ashur. In this version, Marduk appears to have been made to go through an ordeal and admit to having wronged Assyria's national god, before being allowed to return to his captors' capital and rejoin the assembly of his divine peers.

At the conclusion of their banquet in Babylon, the king, in the role of Marduk, would normally consummate his "sacred marriage" or hi-

erogamy with a priestess of royal blood, representing the god's consort Zarpanit—"she of the city Zarpan." Since the days of Sumerian civilization, what made kings divine were the marital relations they had with the goddess of the land they ruled at the beginning of a new year. This assured that she would ease this delicate transition and bestow her protection beyond it, bringing some seasonal regularity to the unpredictable environmental conditions of the region.

On the festival's eleventh day, the gods' statues were brought back by road to the Esagila from the **Akitu** house—whose main purpose was probably just to provide a city's primary god with a "home away from home." This journey gave him an excuse to reenter the city in the same glory as on the mythical day he first took possession of it.

Judgment and Celebration

Another assembly of the gods would take place in Babylon's Shrine of Destinies on the last day of **Akitu**. It represented the one held after Marduk's initial victory, when the gods decided to create humans as servants to work for them and to reward or punish them accordingly. For this was when the gods ratified what had been decreed about the kingdom's fate over the coming year at the previous assembly. It was followed by a final banquet of the gods. (Soon after **Rosh Hashanah**—the Jewish New Year festival of God's enthronement and "**Judgment Day**," which is probably derived from **Akitu**—a similar ten-day interval separates God's decree from its final ratification on **Yom Kippur**.)

In addition to this ritual drama, many sacrificial offerings were made; they stemmed from agrarian rites that were used for **Akitu** when it was celebrated in the month of Nisan—whether as a spring festival or as the **New Year**—on which this public, political dimension had come to be overlaid. This solemn state affair thus also had a lighter counterpart in popular feasting and street celebrations. They included joyful songs and dances that were fostered by the "sweet sounds" of lyres, harps, tambourines, and other instruments, as described in the allusions of ancient texts to such occasions where the festive spirit of the Babylonians (like that of the Sumerians before them) had always found an outlet in fun and games. Once **Akitu** was over and a new year had begun, gods and men returned from Babylon to their native cities and regular functions, reassured that they might get the kind of treatment they expected from each other to prosper in their respective spheres.

    See also Christmas; Corpus Christi; Naw Ruz;
    New Year (West); Purim; Rosh Hashanah;
    Yom Kippur

References

Mark E. Cohen. *The Cultic Calendars of the Ancient Near East.* Bethesda, MD: CDL Press, 1993.

Joachim Marzahn. *The Ishtar Gate, The Processional Way, The New Year Festival of Babylon.* Mainz am Rhein, Ger: Philipp von Zabern/ Staatliche Museen zu Berlin: Vorderasiatisches Museum, 1995.

Svend Aage Pallis.*The Babylonian Akîtu Festival.* Copenhagen, Dk: Det kongelige danske Videnskabernes Selskab, "Historisk-filologiske meddelelser XII, 1," 1926.

﹚ AKWASIDAE

See Adae

﹚ 'ALÁ

See Nineteen-Day Feast

﹚ ALL HALLOW'S EVE, ALL SAINTS, ALL SOULS

See Days of the Dead (West)

﹚ AMBARVALIA

See Rogations

﹚ AMBROSIA

See Dionysia

﹚ ANALIPSIS

See Ascension

﹚ ANANTA-CHATURDASHI

See Paryushana and Dashalakshana

﹚ ANASTENARIA

See Dionysia

﹚ ANNA PERENNA (ROME)

During the late Roman Republic, the festival of **Anna Perenna** was celebrated on March 15 to honor an ancient Italian divinity. This was a kind of **New Year's Day** in the calendar used at the time of Rome's foundation. Its name refers to the perennial course of the years.

Marking the First Full Moon

Like China's **Lantern Festival** or the archaic **Little New Year** of Japan, the mid-month holiday, or ides of March, had initially marked the first full moon of a **New Year**, when **Anna Perenna** was offered "public and private sacrifices for prosperity throughout the year and for years to come." This is the translation of a passage in which the fifth-century grammarian Macrobius accounts for her name: "*ut annare perennareque commode liceat*" (*Saturnalia* I, 12: 6, p. 85). Romans continued to offer these sacrifices, even under the new official calendar starting on the calends, or first day, of January.

Expelling the Old Year

On the eve of **Anna Perenna**, or March 14, the people of Rome would first expel Mamurius Veturius (just as the Hebrews used to drive away a scapegoat on **Yom Kippur**, ten days after their **New Year**). This mythical blacksmith was invoked by the Salian priests of Mars at the end of the ancient hymn they sang on March 19 as well as on October 19. But in the first context, he represented the old March of the dying year with its waning vital powers. A man was given animal skins to wear in order to impersonate

Mamurius Veturius and thus become a human symbol of the degeneration and vulnerability associated with wintertime. To drive out the perils concentrated in his person, a wild procession would form, and citizens, who lined the streets all the way beyond the city limits, would beat the poor man with long white rods. This ritual was supposed to clear the ground for a new incarnation of Mars as an archaic god of vegetation (as opposed to his later military features), who was reborn every spring.

Merrymaking to Welcome Spring

Welcoming spring on the day of **Anna Perenna** proper meant that couples of all ages would go a mile out of Rome on the Via Flaminia to lie on the grass near the Tiber river and drink all day among makeshift tents. For girls who had reached marriageable age, this was an occasion for romance with boys, regardless of which they would eventually marry. The idea behind this very old custom was that maidens should first pay their dues to the general fertility of springtime in the hope that it would rub off on them as young wives. For married people, the outing was an opportunity for casual, uninhibited merrymaking. It included dancing around the wine supply, loudly counting the cups of wine each person would gulp down in turn and asking the gods for as many happy returns of **Anna Perenna** as the cups they were able to drink. They would also sing and act out all the tunes and skits they could recall from the ancient Roman equivalents of the music-hall. A famous mime composed for the occasion by Laberius (106–43 B.C.E.) was even entitled *Anna Perenna*.

> **See also** Lantern Festival; Naked Festivals; New Year (Japan); New Year (West); Thargelia; Yom Kippur

> **References**
> Sir James George Frazer. *The Golden Bough. A Study in Magic and Religion.* One-Volume Abridged Edition. New York: Macmillan, 1985.

Macrobius. *The Saturnalia.* Tr. Percival Vaughan Davies. New York: Columbia University Press, "Records of Civilization" No. 79, 1969.
Ovid. *Fasti.* Tr. A. J. Boyle and R. D. Woodard. London and New York: Penguin Books, 2000.

▶ ANNUNCIATION (CHRISTIANITY)

The feast of the **Annunciation** on March 25 commemorates the Christian belief in the miraculous conception of Jesus Christ by the Holy Spirit in the Virgin Mary's womb, when the Archangel Gabriel came to her to announce that she had been chosen to play this pivotal role in God's plan to redeem mankind through the Incarnation of his Only-Begotten Son. It also recognizes that Mary had the option to refuse but that she made an historic choice to bear the child. Christians view Mary not only as heir to the providential history of the people of Israel, but as representative of the whole human race. The meeting of God's gracious election and the response of human free will in the person of Mary is the object of this joyous feast.

In Greece, the **Annunciation** has an especially exuberant character as both a religious and a civic celebration, which it also was in much of the rest of Christendom when celebrated before the Renaissance as the Roman **New Year**. The added dimension for Greeks is that they celebrate the same day as their national holiday, commemorating the start of the country's war of independence in 1821.

In Nice on the French Riviera, March 25 is also the traditional date of a lively folkloric spring festival known as *Lou Festin dei Cougourdoun* or "The Feast of the Gourds"— named after its displays of handcrafted gourds.

Place in the Calendar

Sermons for March 25 as the feast of the **Annunciation** have been found going back to the mid-fifth century, but for another couple of centuries before that its place in the calendar

A group of girls dressed as saints hold up cardboard plates with the various honorific names of the Virgin Mary during an Annunciation ceremony in Victoria, Seychelles. (Zen Icknow/Corbis)

to the Gospel narrative of the parallel conceptions six months apart of Jesus and John the Baptist, the latter's coming first when his father the priest Zechariah was designated to perform a Temple ritual of **Yom Kippur** in September. The feast of the **Conception of Saint John the Baptist** is thus set on September 23. Still, the most straightforward reason for putting the **Annunciation** on March 25 was to mark the conception of Christ exactly nine months before his birth, set on December 25 in the fourth century.

This would imply that the **Annunciation** may have been celebrated on March 25 for nearly as long as **Christmas**, if not longer. But in Eastern Christianity, the **Nativity** of Christ was initially celebrated as part of **Epiphany** on January 6, so that, in the Armenian Church, in the absence of a distinct **Christmas**, the same reasoning based on the nine months of Mary's pregnancy gives an April 7 date for the feast of the **Annunciation**.

By the end of the seventh century, when the Greek-born Pope Saint Sergius I ordained processions from Saint Peter's basilica to the church known today as Santa Maria Maggiore on the occasion of Marian feasts, this one was known in Rome as the **Annunciation** of the Lord, and Latin liturgical texts spoke of the Incarnation of the Word of God in Mary. It was later called the **Annunciation** of the Blessed Virgin Mary until 1969, when the Catholic Church made it a feast of the Lord again, along with the **Purification of the Virgin Mary** on February 2, **Candlemas**, henceforward known as the **Presentation of the Lord in the Temple**, which is the name it had always had in the Eastern Church, where, on the other hand, the **Annunciation** has remained a Marian feast.

As far back as 1042, March 25 also used to be the date for **Mothering Day** in England, when mothers would be offered an almond and spice "Simnel Cake." Today, this celebration occurs on the fourth Sunday of **Lent** in the Anglican calendar.

was uncertain and it was celebrated on different dates, depending on local usage. The March 25 date seems confirmed as the oldest because of a tradition from the third century that linked three key events to what was the official spring equinox at the time: the Creation of the world, the **Annunciation** to Mary, and the Crucifixion of Christ. In 656, the regional Council of Toledo in Spain adopted December 18 for the **Annunciation** in order to avoid the difficulties of celebrating a joyous feast in March when the **Lent**en fasting season occurs, thus making of the **Annunciation** a logical prelude to the **Nativity of Christ** on December 25. However, this decision was overturned at the more universal Council in Trullo, held in Constantinople in 692. There are complicated arguments accounting for the final choice of date with reference

In the Eastern Church, there are two cases in which the **Annunciation** is not celebrated on March 25: if it happens to coincide with **Good Friday** or with **Holy Saturday**. It is then observed concurrently with **Easter** Sunday. However, in the Roman Catholic Church, the **Annunciation** is postponed to the following Sunday if **Easter** falls on March 25 or 26, while **Good Friday** remains an acceptable day for marking the **Annunciation**. Such overlaps have been eliminated in those Orthodox jurisdictions using the Gregorian calendar for fixed feasts such as the **Annunciation**, since the date of **Easter** is still calculated in a different way that usually makes this movable feast fall at least a week later than it does in the Western Church.

An Angel's Good Tidings and a Woman's Response

The liturgical texts of the **Annunciation** are mostly based on the Gospel account of Saint Luke (1:26–38) and on Chapter Eleven of the apocryphal Book of James, as is its iconography, which is among the oldest to be associated with a particular Christian festival. Thus, the classic iconography of the feast of the **Annunciation** is first found in the second-century Roman catacomb of Priscilla.

Angelos is a Greek word for "messenger"— for someone who *announces*. The **Annunciation** of the *good news* of God's birth amidst mankind, called *Evangelismos* in Greek, is therefore the epitome of an angelic apparition. As one of the highest angels, Gabriel, who brought this announcement from God to Mary, has been depicted either with a staff as in the East or presenting a lily to the Virgin (but not with wings initially, since angels were not yet portrayed with wings in order to avoid confusion with pagan winged personifications of qualities such as glory and victory). This is one of the reasons that the lily, which had long been a pagan fertility symbol, has come to symbolize chastity.

Yet staff and lily were initially one, since early Greek icons portrayed Gabriel as a herald or ambassador like the *keryx* of classical times, who would hold a wand (called *kerykion* in Greek or *caduceus* in Latin) that made his person inviolable. This olive branch ending in two shoots decorated with garlands or ribbons thus became a symbol of peace in the hand of Greece's Hermes and Rome's Mercury—messengers of the gods. Now often confused with the serpent-entwined staff of Asclepius—the Greek healer god—it remains an emblem of the healing professions.

Unfamiliar with the background of the Byzantine iconography for the **Annunciation**, thirteenth-century Western painters (eventually imitated by many of their Eastern colleagues) turned the stylized rod into a three-petalled flower, offered to Mary as a tribute to her virginal purity, rather than wielded to transmit a message of peace from on high. In Mary's response of selfless obedience to God, Christian tradition holds that human freedom was fittingly reaffirmed, since it opened the way for Christ to liberate mankind through communion in his divinity.

Greece's Independence Day

In view of the theological role that human freedom plays in the feast of the **Annunciation**, it is also fitting that this day has become the national holiday of a country where this ideal has been championed since antiquity, namely Greece. For it was on March 25, 1821, that, after four centuries of oppressive Ottoman Turkish rule, the white and blue flag of the Greek liberation struggle was first raised at the Monastery of Aghia Lavra in the Peloponnese by Bishop Germanos of Patras. On this Greek Independence Day, all public buildings, houses, and shops are decked with flags throughout the country as well as in all foreign countries where there is a substantial Greek population. (On a March 24 evening, the author has even boarded a Montreal city bus to find its Greek driver had decorated the inside with white and blue balloons and streamers and was offering seasonal red candies to all passengers.) Churches and church squares are adorned with bay and myrtle, small paper flags, patriotic slogans on colored paper bands, and pictures of the Greek head of state and of heroes of the Greek Revolution. All local authorities, including guilds and trade unions, with their respective banners, are represented at the **Annunciation** and thanksgiving service held in great pomp at the main church of every town. People—especially womenfolk—who have traditional Greek costumes will wear them at this service and later that day at a colorful parade (where schoolchildren march through the streets led by their teachers), at the laying of wreaths at a monument to soldiers killed in action, and at a dance that is often held in the main square.

However, since the **Annunciation** always falls during **Lent**, there is a limit to the amount of celebrating that can go on for the Greek national holiday. The Orthodox Church allows only a slight relaxation in the Lenten season's vegetarian diet in honor of this feast; fish may be eaten, which, in Greece, will usually be fried or boiled salted cod with garlic sauce. On this day, the shepherds of Crete take their flocks to the mountain pastures for the fair season. In many parts of the country, children take off the red "March thread" they have been wearing around their wrist for good luck—a custom known in various local forms in the Balkans since ancient times and even in other festive contexts as far away as Tibet. They hang it on a tree for the swallows to take away, as these messengers of spring are supposed to come back from the south for the **Annunciation**.

Lou Festin dei Cougourdoun

The fact that the **Annunciation** naturally doubles as a festival of spring is also well illustrated by the Nice custom of "The Feast of the Gourds"—*Lou Festin dei Cougourdoun* as it is still called in the local dialect of the Occitan language. There, the word *festin* does not refer to a lavish banquet as it does in French, but to a homely country fair on the occasion of a local patronal feast. This one is held in connection with the Franciscans' Church of the **Annunciation** near the Roman ruins on the hill of Cimiez. It used to begin in the early morning, when lay brotherhoods of penitents from the various quarters of Nice led the faithful in processions that collected in front of the Church of Saint Ann before proceeding to the Church of the **Annunciation**—forming a mystical pilgrimage from the Virgin's mother to the Virgin as Mother. Some rest was in order to recover from this uphill journey out of town, so celebrants took the opportunity to relax, eat, dance, and play games on the convent grounds. There, stalls were put up to sell gourds of various shapes and sizes that had been emptied and dried over the winter either to be carved into utensils or made into funny-sounding musical instruments for the next year's **Carnival**. Today, the gourds are mostly turned into hand-painted heads wearing traditional fisherman's red hats, as a form of typical folk art. One of the traditional treats sold at other stalls is the *chaudèu*, an orange blossom- or anice-flavored bun on which an eggshell is held fast by a cross of dough. This is a reminder of the feast's fading connection with **Lent**. For in Nice, each Sunday's *festin* of this period of penance prior to **Easter** used to have a specific theme, like the *festin* of reproaches, when married couples would vent the winter's pent-up grievances, and the *festin* of reconciliation, when they would make up. As for the connection with the **Annunciation**, it has also grown looser, since the city now puts on what has largely become a celebration of local folklore on just any early spring weekend that suits its schedule, although it still does feature an outdoor mass.

See also Candlemas; Carnival; Christmas; Conception and Birth of the Virgin Mary; Easter; Epiphany; Holy Week; Lent; Matzu's

Birthday; Midsummer; New Year (West); Yom Kippur

References

The Festal Menaion. Tr. Mother Mary and Archimandrite Kallistos, Ware. London: Faber and Faber, 1977.

George A. Megas. *Greek Calendar Customs.* Athens, Greece: [*s.n.*], 1963.

Leonid Ouspensky and Vladimir Lossky. *The Meaning of Icons.* Tr. G. E. H. Palmer and E. Kadloubovsky. Crestwood, NY: Saint Vladimir's Seminary Press, 1982.

▶ **ANODOS**

See Thesmophoria

▶ **ANTHESTERIA**

See Dionysia

▶ **AN.TAH.ŠUM**^{ŠAR}

See KI.LAM

▶ **AOI (NO) MATSURI**

See Hollyhock Festival, Matsuri

▶ **APAFRAM**

See Adae

▶ **APATURIA (GREECE)**

The **Apaturia** were an ancient Greek festival, held throughout Ionia except for Ephesus and Colophon according to Herodotus (I, 147), and as a three-day holiday that has been dated from either the nineteenth to the twenty-first or the twenty-sixth to the twenty-eighth of the month of Pyanopsion (October–November) in Athens, where it originated. An equivalent annual festival of Apollo in Dorian states was called **Apellai**. This was also the name of another festival in Sparta, featuring rites of passage similar to those of the Ionian **Apaturia**, that granted ephebes (adolescent boys) the status of manhood in the Spartan system of education: the *agoge,* as part of an assembly held on the seventh of each month.

Men's Coming of Age in Athens

The **Apaturia** were an unofficial celebration of relationship through a "common father" (the likely meaning of its name), when over thirty marriage-based clan groupings known as phratries or fraternities who made up Attica's citizenry would gather to discuss their affairs and induct new brothers (*phratores*) into them. The older brothers would have a common dinner called *Dorpia* on the first day, after which they would drink offerings of wine contributed by the fathers of children being initiated. (The word for this sacrifice, *oinisteria,* was also used for another libation ephebes would offer to the hero Heracles on the occasion of haircuts—including one on the third day of **Apaturia**, when they were followed by a ritual drinking binge.) Various sacrifices—to Zeus Phratrios and to Athena Phratria in particular—were made on the second day. These were referred to as *anarrhusis,* after the "drawing back" of the necks of the animal victims.

The third day, called *Kureotis,* owed its name to the *koureion,* the shaving or shearing of ewes and goats brought by the relatives of the candidates for admission—which became official once the *phratores* ate the meat and offerings of the hair of citizens' sons were made. These offerings were normally made to deified heroes and originally next to a river where peasants had once met for mating feasts. They symbolized cutting the boys off from the world of childhood and occurred in the year they turned sixteen. As part of his second introduction to his father's phratry, each boy's qualifications for Athenian citizenship would then be scrutinized—mostly in terms of pedigree. The second introduction marked legal puberty, in contrast to an optional first introduction of children born since the last festival, when their fathers or guardians took an oath stating they were legitimate before their names were put down in the register. This ceremony was accompanied by a sacrifice called *meion,* about which little is known.

A fourth day called *Epibda* was sometimes counted as part of **Apaturia**.

Marriage as Women's Rite of Passage

A *meion* was also made when a young man's bride was introduced to his phratry. In that case, it was part of a wedding feast called a *gamelia,* which was a sort of female counterpart to the *koureion*—except of course that young women did not obtain citizenship but only recognition of their male children's legitimate claim to the birthright of freeborn Athenian men. A bride offered her hair on the eve of the wedding, because it was considered her passage into womanhood, even though there was no public rite entrenched in tradition comparable to the boys'.

Originally, the *gamelia* ceremonies might have been celebrated collectively on the same day as the young men's coming of age; the sacrifices made on behalf of young women on the last day of **Apaturia** continued to be called matrimonial offerings, while private feasts of the goddess Hera, patron of married women, were also known as *gamelia*. However, the month of Gamelion (around January) came to be favored for weddings in Attica.

See also Inti Raymi and Huarachicu; Liberalia; Seven-Five-Three

References

Mark Golden. *Children and Childhood in Classical Athens.* Baltimore, MD: Johns Hopkins University Press, 1990.

Marilyn A. Katz. "Women, Children and Men," in Paul Cartledge, ed., *The Cambridge Illustrated History of Ancient Greece.* Cambridge, UK: Cambridge University Press, 1998, pp. 100–138.

H. W. Parke. *Festivals of the Athenians.* Ithaca, NY: Cornell University Press, 1977.

▌APELLAI

See Apaturia

▌APOKREOS

See Carnival

▌APOLLINARIAN GAMES

See Games (Rome)

▌APOSTLES' FAST

See Lent

▌APPEARANCE DAY OF SRILA PRABHUPADA

See Janmashtami

▌APRIL FOOLS' DAY

See New Year (West)

▌ARAFAT (DAY OF), ARBAIIN

See Ashura

▌ARBOR DAY

See Tu bi-Shevat

▌ARGEI (ROME)

Because it was celebrated on May 14—an even day of the month—the festival of **Argei** was an anomaly in the calendar of ancient Rome. Usually, only odd days were set aside for religious festivals. It is also not clear what the object of the festival was, even though its practices (which are are fairly well known) suggest the expulsion in effigy of evil spirits from the city.

Dunking Dummies

Twenty-seven or thirty shrines (*sacraria*) scattered throughout the city were visited by a procession several weeks before the **Argei** festival. The purpose of the procession may have been to bring puppets made from rushes and/or reeds to each neighborhood shrine. These twenty-seven whitewashed, bulrush-plaited effigies of old men were also called *argives*. They may then have been gathered again in a second, undocumented procession during the festival on March 16 and 17, when the pontiffs and the vestal virgins threw them into the Tiber from the old Sublician bridge (entirely made of oak for obscure religious reasons).

The Greatest of Purifications

Plutarch refers to the festival of **Argei** as "the greatest of purifications." This makes it quite likely that the purpose of the reed figures was to channel and absorb the evils from every corner of Rome. These spirits, which were believed to exist in the form of unsettled, homeless spirits of the air, were regarded as malignant wanderers who envied the living and longed for homes. They were thought to be particularly active on the three odd days of the calendar immediately before **Argei** (the ninth, eleventh, and thirteenth of May). This time was known as the **Lemuria** in recognition of the nocturnal household rituals practiced to drive away these spirits, who were called *lemures*. Once they had been caught in the plaited dummies, the *lemures* could then be expelled from the city on the fourteenth and washed out to sea by the Tiber. This ritual expulsion of evil seems to derive from a practice that was common among the ancients of driving away a scapegoat—that is, a victim singled out to be loaded down with the community's sins and misfortunes. Indeed, the mythical hero Hercules is credited with convincing the Romans to stop scapegoating men and sacrificing them to Saturn in this way and to start using dummies instead for such rites.

After settling their business with the dead on May 14, the Romans turned back to the daily business of the living, for on May 15, they celebrated the dedication of the temple of Mercury, god of trade and communications.

See also Days of the Dead (West); Dionysia; May Day; Naked Festivals; Saint George; Situa; Thargelia; Vestalia; Yom Kippur

References

William Warde Fowler. *Roman Festivals of the Period of the Republic. An Introduction to the Study of the Romans.* Port Washington, NY: Kennikat Press, 1969.

Sir James George Frazer. *The Golden Bough. A Study in Magic and Religion.* One-Volume Abridged Edition. New York: Macmillan, 1985.

Robert Graves. *The Greek Myths.* London: Penguin Books, 1960.

▶ ASAKUSA SHRINE FESTIVAL

See Matsuri

▶ ASCENSION (CHRISTIANITY)

The feast of the **Ascension** commemorates the conclusion of the earthly career of Jesus Christ, when he is supposed to have parted from his disciples and risen to heaven. According to the main accounts, which are reported at the beginning of the Acts of the Apostles and at the end of Luke's Gospel, Christ ascended to heaven on the Mount of Olives near Jerusalem in front of the disciples, forty days after his resurrection from the dead, which is the central event of the Christian faith, celebrated on **Easter** Sunday. The feast of the **Ascension** is therefore held forty days later, on a Thursday in May or June. This place in the calendar gave rise to the popular old English name for the feast—**Holy Thursday** (which should not be confused with the **Holy Thursday**, also known as **Maundy Thursday**, that is part of **Holy Week**).

History

For over three centuries after the particular event it commemorates, the **Ascension** seems to have been celebrated as a secondary theme in the feast of **Pentecost** which occurs on the fiftieth day after Easter. Only in the fourth century did it begin to be detached from **Pentecost** as an independent feast (just as the **Nativity** was a theme of **Epiphany** that came to acquire an independent existence as **Christmas** around the same time).

The **Ascension** likely began to gain a separate status in the second third of the fourth century, after the Roman Empire, having embraced Christianity, sponsored the reconstruction of Jerusalem, a city that it had previously destroyed in the process of suppressing Jewish rebellions. At that time, churches were built on all the sites that could be connected with the life of Jesus Christ. Pilgrims from all corners of the Empire began to flock to these new shrines, creating a mass market for souvenirs of the sites and events from what then became known as the Holy Land. This in turn encouraged the multiplication of new or specialized celebrations for many of them.

One of the earliest examples of the classic iconography of the Ascension was found in Monza in Lombardy on a sixth-century *ampulla*—that is, a small round bottle used by pilgrims to take holy water or oil from a place associated with a sacred event. As such objects were spread everywhere by returning pilgrims, so was the awareness of the events in question and of the need to celebrate them in more specific and elaborate ways, despite the concerns of some of the early church fathers about such innovations.

A pilgrim from Gaul to the Holy Land in the 380s, named either Etheria or Egeria, left us her travel narrative. It includes the first known account of a feast of the **Ascension** on the fortieth day after **Easter**, though she also mentions the Ascension being commemorated on the afternoon of **Pentecost**.

The **Ascension** was celebrated separately from **Pentecost** throughout Christendom, by the first third of the fifth century, when sermons were written for the feast by the most authoritative church fathers. Among them, Saint Augustine of Hippo even went so far as to say of the **Ascension** that "this is the festival which confirms the grace of all the festivals together, without which the profitableness of every festival would have perished . . ." (Farrow 1999, p. 9). For Christians believe that, with Jesus Christ, "the dignity of human nature has ascended to heaven above the angels"—to the angels' great astonishment, concurred the mid-fifth-century Pope Saint Leo the Great, whose words appear in the fifth lesson of the Latin mass of the **Ascension** (de Mahuet 1948).

Theology

The **Ascension** brings to a conclusion the whole process of salvation held in Christianity to be accomplished in the passion, death, and resurrection of the Son of God, who then ascended to be enthroned on the right hand of the Father. Moreover, since this is the day when Jesus is said to have left the earth in the flesh, the paschal candle—which in the Western Church is lit during the main **Easter**tide services—is extinguished. This ritual follows the reading from Saint Luke (24:51) at the **Ascension** mass (often followed by an afternoon procession) and is done because the flame representing the Savior must disappear with him.

The Christian Church does not mourn Christ's departure from the midst of men, but joyfully celebrates his universal kingship during **Ascension**tide (the ten-day period between **Ascension** Thursday and **Pentecost** Sunday). In the East, the festivities begin with the repetition of the **Easter** Sunday liturgy on Wednesday night as the triumphal close of the **Easter** season and the climax of the incarnation of the Word of God, which had started to become manifest with his humble birth in human form. This is probably why early Christians long celebrated the **Ascension** in a cave in Bethlehem above the site of the **Nativity**, instead of on the Mount of Olives near Jerusalem where he was taken up, as if to underscore the unity between the first day and the final day of the earthly life of Jesus. According to Saint Paul in his letters to the Philippians (*Jerusalem Bible* 1968, 2:8–11), Christ was not content to be born as a poor lowly human, "he was humbler yet, even to accepting death, death on a cross. But God *raised him high* and gave him the name which is above all names so that all beings in the heavens, on earth and in the underworld should bend the knee at the name of Jesus and that every tongue should acclaim Jesus Christ as Lord, to the glory of the Father."

The Church understands itself as the community where this acknowledgment of Christ as Son of God takes place through the Holy Spirit, and Eastern Christians will therefore collectively kneel to receive it ten days after the feast of **Ascension**, at **Pentecost** vespers. For the Father's promise of a final parting gift, as repeated on his behalf by Jesus on the day of his **Ascension**, was to be fulfilled ten days later with the sending to his disciples of the Holy Spirit as the Paraclete, or Comforter, at **Pentecost**.

The feast of the **Ascension** looks back to the full revelation of the second person of the triune God in the life of Jesus Christ and looks forward to the full revelation of the third person of this Trinity in the life of the Christian Church through the Holy Spirit. "The inner link between Christ and the Church is expressed in the icon by the whole structure of the composition linking together into one whole the group on earth with its consummation in heaven" (Ouspensky and Lossky 1982, p. 196). To underscore this central idea of the feast's liturgy—the ecclesial union of above and below—an icon of the **Ascension** often appears within the dome of old Greek churches, representing heaven for the faithful below.

The feast of the **Ascension** points beyond history to Jesus Christ's triumphant return from heaven at the end of time. This Second Coming to earth in glory is prefigured by a luminous cloud (an Old Testament sign of the presence of God) that hid him from the sight of his disciples as he withdrew into the bosom of the Father—which Orthodox liturgical texts for the **Ascension** insist he had actually never left. According to Greek Church Fathers, this opened to human beings the possibility of the mystical process known as "deification," which has remained a central tenet of Orthodox faith. It finds liturgical expression in Eastern Church matins for the **Ascension** (cathism II, tone 3), proclaiming at the outset of the feast that "the supereternal and beginningless God who mysteriously deified human nature by assuming it has raised himself to heaven today . . ."—lifting up mankind along with the Son of Man.

Folklore

Being thus on a level with Christ in a mystical way, Orthodox Christians no longer repeat the paschal greeting "Christ is risen!"—though Rumanians like to replace it with "Christ is ascended!" on this finale of the **Easter** season, when they also repeat their **Easter** custom of giving red eggs to friends and guests. In the coastal regions of Greece, this is the day for the first swim, when some people used to take water from forty different waves (representing the forty days since **Easter**) to sprinkle it in their house as they recited, "As Christ rose to heaven, so may slander, disease, the evil eye and all other evils rise from our house and disappear" (Megas 1963, p. 126).

Similarly, since the Greek word for the **Ascension**, *Analipsis,* means "taking away," herbs and mud gathered on that day are supposed to take away skin diseases. On the other hand, Greek shepherds fear that their ewes' milk will be withdrawn as Christ was drawn up to heaven. This is why they make sure not to keep a single drop of the milk they draw on the **Ascension**. Instead, it all goes into making cheese for the local priest, as well as yogurt and other dishes for guests at a huge meal. Thus, the **Ascension** is really the greatest feast day of the Christian calendar for Greek shepherds. There is also a belief among Greeks that, as on **Christmas** Eve, the sky may be seen bursting asunder at midnight, so the pure of heart who staid up have a chance of witnessing the seasonal miracle of a light ascending to heaven. When Venice was a republic, the **Ascension** (known as the *Festa della Sensa*) was one of the highlights of its festive calendar the occasion for the annual ceremony of the city's Marriage to the Sea. This commemorated the gift of a ring by Pope Alexander III to Doge Sebastiano Ziani in 1177, in recognition of the latter's mediating role in his dispute with Holy Roman Emperor Frederick Barbarossa, and as a token of Venice's independence from both secular and ecclesiastical world powers as well as of its dominion over the sea. To renew the city's union with

Departure of the Bucintoro towards the Lido for the ceremonies of Ascension Day, by Francesco Guardi (1712–1793). (Erich Lessing/Art Resource)

its watery domain, its ruler, the Doge, would set out with dignitaries on a gilded ceremonial galley, surrounded by several thousand small vessels, to the island of Lido, where he would cast a ring into the sea to take it as his bride—which made him its lord and master. A mass would follow at the church of San Nicolò di Lido before the seaborne procession went back to the city. This ceremony, often depicted by Venetian painters, and now reenacted every year in historic dress and boat replicas, has parallels in Southeast Asia, where Javanese princes act as gods in symbolic weddings to the sea goddess.

See also Christmas; Easter; Epiphany; Holy Week; Transfiguration; Whitsuntide

References

J. de Mahuet. "Ascension," in dom Fernand Cabrol and dom Henri Leclercq, eds. *Dictionnaire d'archéologie chrétienne et de liturgie.* Paris, Fr: Librairie Letouzey et Ané, 1948.

Douglas Farrow. *Ascension and Ecclesia. On the Significance of the Doctrine of the Ascension for Ecclesiology and Christian Cosmology.* Grand Rapids, MI: Wm. B. Eerdmans Publishing Company, 1999.

Jerusalem Bible. Garden City, NY: Doubleday and Co., 1968.

George A. Megas. *Greek Calendar Customs.* Athens: [*s.n.*], 1963.

Leonid Ouspensky and Vladimir Lossky. *The Meaning of Icons.* Tr. G. E. H. Palmer and E. Kadloubovsky. Crestwood, NY: Saint Vladimir's Seminary Press, 1982.

Terisio Pignatti. "Venetian Festivals and Amusements," in *Apollo,* No. 102, 1975, pp. 208–215.

▶ ASCENSION OF BAHÁ'U'LLAH, ASCENSION OF THE BAB

See Ridván

ASH WEDNESDAY
See Lent

ASHURA (ISLAM)

Islam's oldest annual festival is **Ashura**, which is celebrated on the ninth and tenth of the month of Moharram. Modeled on the Jewish feast of **Yom Kippur**, it also comes ten days after the **New Year.** The interval may have been chosen to shift the focus away from pagan observances associated with the **New Year**. **Ashura** is an occasion for Sunni Muslims to fast and practice charity. There is also a **carnival**-like **Day of the Dead** among Sunnis of the Maghreb.

Shiite Muslims—that is, Muslims loyal to the lineage of Imam Ali as the Prophet Mohammed's designated successor in leading the Umma—have added a strong penitential dimension to **Ashura**, in mourning for the martyrdom of Hussein, grandson of the Prophet Mohammed, as they mark its anniversary on this day.

The Original Fast

The common idea of **Ashura** in both branches of Islam is that of expiation, which is derived from the great **Day of Atonement** in the Jewish calendar. It was referred to as *asor* in the Bible's Book of Leviticus (*Jerusalem Bible* 1968, 16:29), and "**Ashura**" is the Arabic form of the Aramaic word derived from this term. It means "tenth," because **Yom Kippur** falls on the tenth day of the first month of the year; as does **Ashura** in the Islamic calendar.

When he came to Medina after his daring escape from Mecca in 622 known as the **Hegira**, Mohammed observed the Jews there fasting for **Yom Kippur**. But he somehow got the mistaken impression from his conversations with them that it was in commemoration of their forebears' safe crossing of the Red Sea and of God's judgment on the pursuing army of Pharaoh that was drowned in it. As it happens, these are the events remembered on

Passover, not on **Yom Kippur**, though some allusions to the flight from Egypt in the latter festival's prayers may have been at the source of his confusion. In any case, it is on the basis of such a garbled account of the meaning of *asor* that Mohammed decided Muslims had all the more reason to fast, given their own flight across the desert and providential escape from pagan pursuers. He therefore took up for the *Umma*—the community of believers—the Jewish custom of fasting from one sunset to the next, as opposed to just during daytime as is the case with other fasts.

Then came the Battle of Badr in mid-March 624—a stunning victory for the fledgling Muslim community of Medina over the twice as numerous, better equipped, and seasoned warriors of pagan Mecca. As a result of his deteriorating relations with the Jewish community, on whose practices he had at first patterned the emerging ones of the Umma, Mohammed had just changed the *qibla*—the geographical orientation of prayer, which is marked by a niche in the wall of a place of worship—from Jerusalem (as found in ancient churches) to Mecca, only a few weeks before. (The anniversary of this crucial turn is celebrated during the **Night of Sha'baan** from the fourteenth to the fifteenth of that month; it is spent in prayer after a day of fasting.) He now similarly downgraded **Ashura** to an optional fast and made of the current Arab month of **Ramadan**—the one when he had first received the Koran now seen as such a sign of salvation and judgment from God—the main period of fasting for Muslims. To further distinguish **Ashura** from the Jewish festival of the tenth day of the **New Year**, its date was changed. Some traditions go so far as to place the day of fasting on the ninth of the first month of Moharram. For most, however, it was eventually set on the tenth day of the new, wholly lunar Islamic calendar, under the name **Ta'sua**.

A couple of months prior to his death on June 8, 632, the Prophet Mohammed made a pledge to fast on the ninth and tenth of Mohar-ram of that new Arab year (not yet dated from the **Hegira**). Once he had done so, he declared that **Ashura** was the best fast—better even than **Ramadan.** He is also believed to have said that the fast of **Ashura** takes away the sins of the past year as well as those of the coming year, whereas only the latter are removed by the fast of the **Day of Arafat**—named after the valley where pilgrims to Mecca converge on the ninth of Dhul-Hijja, the last month of the Islamic year, to prepare for the Great **Feast of Sacrifice:** *Eid-al-Adha.*

A North African Carnival and Day of the Dead

After *Eid-al-Adha* comes the **New Year**, soon followed by **Ashura**, a day commemorating the one when Noah left the ark to repopulate the world at the end of the Flood. This new begin-ning after the atonement of sins is celebrated on the twentieth of Moharram as the **Bianu** festi-val of the southern Sahara's Tuareg nomads, in a kind of **Saturnalia** that overlaps with the solemnities of **Ashura** and the **New Year**.

Likewise in the Maghreb, the seasonal re-newal of creation is marked on **Ashura** by col-orful customs that go back to pre-Islamic agrarian rituals (possibly in honor of Near Eastern fertility gods like Adonis and Tammuz), in which mourning for the year gone by is mixed with a joyful welcome to spring. The many variants of the **carnival** known as *farja* almost always include the mock trial, execu-tion, and funeral of an elderly man or woman dressed in animal skins or woven plants, while a traditional impersonation of a huge beast, such as a camel, a lion, or a mule, is intended to both scare and amuse the crowds in turn. Along with animal sacrifices, actual weddings are per-formed in Morocco or else they are depicted with dolls or dummies representing **Ashura** and her bridegroom Ashur (the name by which the month of Moharram is known in the re-gion). Many customs involve fire—such as

jumping over bonfires, throwing firecrackers in them, or tossing embers into rivers—and wa-ter—like pouring water into ashes or bathing or soaking both the living and the dead (since in Morocco the dead are honored by having water thrown on their tombs to clean them). Elsewhere in the Maghreb, the dead are hon-ored merely by laying myrtle leaves on their graves. There is also much alms-giving, whether it is in the guise of an official tithe (called the *zakat* and originally paid in grain) or of offerings to the Koranic school pupils who go from door to door singing to collect donations for their teachers—much as the chapter school pupils of medieval Europe did before their own **Yuletide Feast of Fools.** Cer-tain foods—such as donuts, cakes, or porridge, but especially eggs and poultry—will be eaten on this festival. Not surprisingly, the optional fasting that is recommended on this day tends to be lost sight of in the lively bustle of its fes-tive atmosphere. Nevertheless in Tunisia, on **Ta'sua** (**Ashura**'s Eve) people refrain from hav-ing their customary couscous fare; they kill a chicken instead, and before eating it, they may nibble dry fruits and unleavened cakes. Also, women rub kohl on their eyelids, since this is a sign of mourning appropriate for a fast.

The Shiite Day of Mourning for Martyrs

The Shiite rites of exacerbated mourning on **Ashura** may well have originated in agrarian precedents, such as those so well preserved in the Maghreb. Yet a pietistic interpretation rife with political overtones soon displaced all other aspects of this festival. For Shiites, it com-memorates the martyrdom of Muhammed's son, the third Imam Hussein, called the "Prince of Martyrs," at the Battle of Karbala, 110 kilo-meters southwest of Baghdad, on the tenth of Moharram 61 A.H. (October 10, 680 C.E.). (At one time, Sunni Muslims under the Umayyad Caliphs used to commemorate this battle as well—but as their dynasty's victory over Hussein.) The Shiite dynasty of the Fatimids (910–1170) made it a day of mourning for Imam Hussein, when princes and their officials dressed accordingly, and no meat or pastries were allowed to be eaten by their subjects. After the fall of the Fatimids, their Egyptian base came under the Sunni rule of Saladin's Ayyubid dynasty (1171–1258), and joy returned as the dominant note of **Ashura** there. Today in Egypt, as in other Sunni countries, it coexists with the fast recommended by Mohammed, in addition to being the customary local day for giving legal alms (*zakat*)—one of the five pillars of Islam.

In Iran, **Ashura** has long been central to the national consciousness, since it provides a link between that country's Zoroastrian past and its adoption of the Shiite version of Islam in the person of Imam Hussein. Iranians claim Hussein married the daughter of the last Sassanid Emperor of Persia, defeated by Arab armies at the battle of Nahavend in 632. During the first nine days of Moharram, other imams may also be remembered in Iran, along with all Shiite martyrs, providing inspiration to recover a sense of sacrifice for the Umma's sake and of personal spiritual commitment. In mosques as well as in specially erected private courtyard enclosures and their permanent public equivalents (called *hoseynieh*), which are all shrouded in black fabric, preachers sermonize and recite stories of the martyrdom of Hussein or of some other imam in elegies called *rowzekhani* during that period. People in their audience, dressed in black with faces covered in ashes, beat their chests and cry bitterly as they call out: "Hoseyn! Hoseyn! Hoseyn!" This even goes on nonstop from the evening of the ninth to the morning of the tenth, when all this somber exaltation culminates in the *sinezani*, a famous procession of black-shirted flagellants, who strike their chests with their fists, flog their own backs with chains, or cut themselves with sabers. This event is sometimes opened by blood-soaked performers displaying the wounds of the martyrs of Karbala, while participants with no special part to

play go bareheaded with their shirts open and often dirt on their faces. Each delegation from either a neighborhood or a guild is signaled by a distinctive banner. The procession stops in front of every mosque and holy tomb, until noon when all its paraphernalia are put down on the ground as a sign of mourning, and people go back whimpering to their starting point—the sad picture of the defeated heroes of Karbala.

Also specific to Iran is the *tazieh* (which means "consolation" in Farsi). This may be seen as a rare Muslim example of a passion play (similar to the kind put on in Europe about Christ's Passion) about the martyrdom of an imam, usually Hussein or one of his seventy-two companions, who almost all died at the hands of Caliph Yazeed's minions.

It is only since the accession of a Shiite dynasty—the Safavids—to the Persian throne in the sixteenth century that these **Ashura** rites could be carried out openly, in spite of the reluctance of religious leaders to allow such extravagant displays of piety. Later, under the Qajar dynasty in the nineteenth century, they were even encouraged to take on spectacular proportions. Yet by the time of the last shah of the Pahlavi dynasty in the mid-twentieth century, they had become an outlet for religious opposition to their leader's westernizing regime, and his attempts to control the rites went as far as an outright ban of these observances. They could no longer be suppressed, however, and were instrumental in the demise of the monarchy in the Iranian Revolution of 1979.

Ashura fit in well enough, however, with the ideology of systematic martyrdom promoted by the fundamentalist Islamic Republic that followed and was used to justify Iran's protracted war with Iraq. In the latter country, the public observance of this feast (known there as **Arbaiin**) was banned after the massacre of pilgrims on the road to Karbala in 1977, until the American invasion in 2003, whereupon a million of its long-repressed majority Shiites were finally able to make the pilgrimage to their holy

Iranians shout religious slogans and beat themselves with iron chains inside Tehran's bazaar during the Shiite version of the Muslim festival of Ashura on March 1, 2004. (Damir Sagolj/Reuters/Corbis)

place—which they did on foot through the rubble left by the fall of Saddam Hussein's secular dictatorship.

During the same period, **Ashura** penitential rites have also been used for political ends among the Shiite populations of Lebanon—especially by the moderate Amal militia. The festival was first introduced in that country by Iranian students of religion in the early twentieth century. It was then limited to urban centers like Baalbek, Nabatiyah, and Saïda, and marked with collective laments and public readings on the lives of Ali and his descendents. But it gradually came to include bloody processions of penitents who hit their own skulls with sabers to share in the suffering. This type of event expanded spectacularly from the 1970s onward as a militant expression—through the potent symbolism of martyrdom in the context

of civil war—of the previously voiceless identity of a Lebanese underclass of Shiite peasants and displaced persons. Other minority Shiite communities in the Middle East and South Asia (except in India where self-mutilation is banned), as well as in the West (for example, in Montreal for the first time in 2005), make a point of holding processions and assemblies on the occasion of this feast, when a popular slogan proclaims: "Every day is **Ashura**, every place is Karbala!"

See also Carnival; Day of Assembly; Days of the Dead (West); Eid; Feast of Fools; Holy Week; New Year (Islam); New Year (West); Passover; Ramadan; Saturnalia; Thaipusam; Yom Kippur

References

Jerusalem Bible. Garden City, NY: Doubleday and Co., 1968.

Mahmoud Ayoub. *Redemptive Suffering in Islam: A Study of the Devotional Aspects of Ashura in Twelver Shi'ism.* The Hague: Mouton, 1978.

Vernon James Schubel. *Religious Performance in Contemporary Islam: Shi'i Devotional Rituals in South Asia.* Columbia: University of South Carolina Press, 1993.

Steven M. Wasserstrom. *Between Muslim and Jew: The Problem of Symbiosis under Early Islam.* Princeton, NJ: Princeton University Press, 1995.

Edward Westermarck. *Ritual and Belief in Morocco.* Foreword by Bronislaw Malinowski. New Hyde Park, NY: University Books, 1968.

▶ ASS (FEAST OF THE)

See Feast of Fools

▶ ASSEMBLY (DAY OF)

See Day of Assembly

▶ ASSUMPTION (CHRISTIANITY)

The **Assumption** is the Western name for a feast day on which many Christian churches commemorate the miraculous translation to heaven of the body of the Virgin Mary upon her death. Eastern Christians refer to this event as the **Dormition of the Mother of God** and hold a two-week fast to prepare to celebrate it on August 15.

History

The traditional story of Mary's passing from earthly life to eternal glory was first recorded in an apocryphal text entitled *De Transitu Mariae* around the turn of the fifth century. The cult of Mary was then about to blossom, since she would be officially proclaimed the Mother of God (incarnate as her son Jesus Christ) in 431 at the Council of Ephesus. Ephesus is the Ionian port where Saint John the Evangelist likely took

Mary after Jesus entrusted his mother to his beloved disciple's care at the time of his Crucifixion, and many assumed she died there some time in the second half of the first century. It was also a major center of the cult of the moon goddess of fertility Artemis, who used to be invoked at the full moon of mid-August to protect vines and fruit trees from hail—just as it was claimed Christ's apostles had decreed prayers to Mary for blessings on vines and fruits on her feast day, which is around the same time. And yet, since most pilgrims went to Jerusalem to visit the holy sites, Mary's grave was soon conveniently located in the Garden of Gethsemani in that city. By 451, a church was built on it and dedicated to her **Dormition** or "falling asleep" on August 15. That same year, when the Eastern Roman Emperor Marcian requested to have Mary's body transferred to Constantinople, Patriarch Juvenal of Jerusalem answered by pointing out that the body was in heaven, so that the monarch had to be content with having her tomb and her shroud.

In the absence of any relics of Mary's body (often taken as evidence that it was indeed removed from this earth), by 590 her clothes had become the object of a cult in Constantinople's church of Blachernes. This was the year the Emperor Maurice made the observance of a major feast in honor of Mary on August 15 official throughout the Empire. (There is actually a possibility it originally celebrated her entire life, since the **Dormition** was not yet specified.)

Such a feast had also been observed previously on January 18, following an Egyptian usage that was also prevalent in Gaul in the West in the second half of the sixth century. But a 676 inscription from this same area (now France) is the first to explicitly link August 15 to the feast of the **Dormition**, as it was still known in the West. Unlike the Greek-born Pope Saint Sergius I, whose reign (687–701) saw the introduction to Rome of the four major Marian feasts of the **Nativity of the Virgin**, **Candlemas**, the **Annunciation** and the **Dormi-**

tion, there were many Western Christians who hesitated to follow Eastern Christians in affirming the nearly instant bodily resurrection of the woman they saw as the Mother of God. This may be why they preferred to talk of the "**Assumption**." First recorded in Gaul in 790, this term distinguishes the passive raising of Mary's dead body—to be revived in a glorious afterlife—from the active "**Ascension**" of a resurrected Christ. In the tenth century, there were even those who talked of a double "**Assumption**": that of Mary's soul on her **Dormition**, and that of her body upon the general resurrection at the end of time, which it would have been awaiting in an uncorrupted state at a secret burial site.

Theology and Liturgy

Though there was a general consensus by the fourteenth century about Mary's bodily resurrection, the papal bull entitled *Munificentissimus Deus* issued by Pope Pius XII on November 1, 1950, proclaiming the dogma of the **Assumption** was not welcomed by the Orthodox Church (to say nothing of Protestant denominations). For the Eastern Church felt that these hidden mysteries and pious conjectures were not meant to be proclaimed explicitly—like the good news of the public death and glorious resurrection of Jesus Christ—but to be approached instead with discreet, respectful veneration—much as it is in Orthodox services for the occasion. Thus, when the French Catholic hierarchy at the time consulted the émigré Russian Metropolitan Vladimir about the Orthodox stance on the **Assumption**, he referred them to these texts since "right doctrine" and "right worship" (the two meanings of "orthodoxy") are experienced as one and the same in the liturgy the Eastern Church. In the words of the Orthodox lay theologian Vladimir Lossky, "the significance of the Incarnation of the Word thus appears at the end of Mary's life on earth," two weeks before the close of the

Church calendar with its yearly cycle of feasts. For, he writes:

> the glory of the age to come, the last end of man, is already realised, not only in a Divine Hypostasis [or Person: Christ as the Word of God] made flesh, but also in a human person made God [Mary insofar as she partook by grace of her son's divine nature]. This passage from death to life, from time to eternity, from terrestrial condition to celestial beatitude establishes the Mother of God beyond the general Resurrection and the Last Judgment, beyond the Second Coming which will end the history of the world. The feast of August 15th is a second mysterious **Easter**, since the Church therein celebrates, before the end of time, the secret **first-fruit** of its eschatological consummation. This explains the soberness of the liturgical text which, in the office of the **Dormition**, permits a glimpse of the ineffable glory of the **Assumption** of the Mother of God. (Lossky 1982, p. 213)

Customs

This sobriety permeates the whole of Eastern Christians' lives for a two-week period known as "Our Lady's **Lent**" prior to and in preparation for this feast. Indeed, this day is itself actually a day of strict fasting on a par with **Christmas** Eve, **Good Friday**, and the **Beheading of Saint John the Baptist**, which occurs two weeks later, on August 29, when Eastern Christians emulate the fasting life of this ascetic prophet in the desert.

In Greece, the beginning of Our Lady's **Lent** on August 1 is marked by customs such as the cleansing of all copper pots, and offerings of fruit at church altars. After the first of each day's early afternoon invocations to the Mother of God, the priests distribute these offerings to their fasting parishioners. It must be said that the season's abundant harvest of fruit and tomatoes makes it relatively easy and not altogether unpleasant to follow the strict vegetarian diet that the Orthodox Church prescribes for such fasts.

When the day of the **Dormition** does arrive, a Blessing of Herbs and Seeds takes place at church services in many Eastern Christian countries. In Armenia, following a taboo on the **first-fruits** of a harvest (to be found the world over—e.g., as at African **New Yam Festival**s), no grapes are eaten until they are taken to church to be blessed on the Sunday closest to the **Dormition** and distributed to the faithful as they leave. Seeing this feast as their name day (at least as important as a birthday in many cultures), women named Mary then have parties in vineyards or in their gardens. According to the Armenian rite of the Blessing of the Grapes, "through this blessed fruit we shall receive in our spirit the intelligible grace of [God's] blessing, earning pardon and remission of our mortal sins; to be also worthy of partaking from the Tree of Life" (Guroian 1999). The Tree of Life is identified with Mary as the vine of salvation's wine in **Dormition** hymns, since in her son Jesus she is believed to have borne the fruit of immortality that takes away the bitter taste of death that is associated with the fruit of the Tree of the Knowledge of Good and Evil.

On the Ionian islands of Patmos and Corfu, a symbolic bier for Mary is decorated with flowers and carried through the streets in a solemn candlelight procession, on the model of the *Epitaphios* of the dead Christ on **Good Friday**. Copied on the matins of **Holy Saturday** (when Christ is buried), the August 17 service for the Burial of the Mother of God is a theologically doubtful recent addition to the Orthodox liturgical calendar.

In Greece, the **Dormition** is also the time for annual mass pilgrimages to miraculous icons of Mary on the Aegean islands of Tinos and Paros.

In Ethiopia, the thirteenth day of the **Dormition** fast (observed there by everyone over six or seven years old) and the ones before traditionally saw the whip-cracking festival known as **Buhe**. In the wet season, whips make an ex-plosive sound in the humid air, and the countryside would echo with that of shepherds cracking theirs for fun. There were even organized battles of men, young and old, who lashed out at each other in teams until one of them could no longer stand the pain. The whip cracking would go on into the night around the bonfires dotting the countryside, where people ate some of the *dabo* (whole wheat bread) specially baked for shepherds on **Buhe**.

In the West, on what was called **Our Lady's Herb Day** in Central Europe since at least the tenth century, Mary's victory over death used to be made manifest through aromatic herbs and flowers, which people brought to church to be incensed and blessed so they could bind them into a sheaf and keep them all year to ward off disease, disaster, and mortality (following the same principle as the "odor of sanctity" that wafts from the uncorrupted bodies of many deceased holy persons when they are exhumed).

At Dunkirk in northern France, while August 15 also has the quality of a memorial service and a blessing, its importance lies in commemorating the miraculous discovery of a statue of the Virgin Mary in 1403 in the course of the construction of city walls. A shrine was built to house this statue—called Our Lady of the Dunes—by a brook near the spot. Every year, a procession of fishermen and their wives in traditional Flemish dress takes the statue from there to Minek Square for the blessing of the sea—greeted by the howling sirens of all the ships in port. A rescue ship then goes out to sea with a number of seamen's widows on board to launch wreaths of flowers in memory of the victims of maritime disasters.

In the south of France, in Nice, a blessing of the sea also takes place on the **Assumption** (as well as on the feast of **Saints Peter and Paul** on June 29).

In France as a whole, August 15 is often the occasion of a large family meal—if only because it is one of several religious holidays that have remained enshrined in the civil calendar as statutory holidays, whether or not people are mindful of their religious meaning.

In Scotland on what is called there **Saint Mary's Feast of Harvest**, a magic bannock cake is handmade from sun-dried new grain, kneaded on a sheepskin and baked on a rowan-wood fire around which family members walk sunwise after each eating a piece in order of seniority. The embers are later also carried in the same clockwise direction as the sun in a pot around the farm and fields while an invocation of Mary's blessing is recited.

In the Balearic Islands—a Spanish archipelago in the Mediterranean—popular celebrations of the **Assumption** often feature masked dancers. In Italy too, this date still sees, alongside Christian celebrations, many ancient local harvest rituals of thanksgiving, such as the erection of a thirty-meter straw obelisk in the square of Fontanarosa near Avellino east of Naples. A little to the north, there is a sunset procession of tractors covered with straw decorations marking the **Wheat Festival** of Foglianise near Benevento.

August 15 is also the date for the traditional exhibits of the work of the *madonnari*—street artists who use colored chalks to reproduce religious paintings of the Madonna on the pavement. They then display their skills on the square outside the church of Santa Maria delle Grazie in Curtatone near Mantua in Lombardy.

In European folklore, the **Assumption** marked the start of **Our Lady's Thirty Days** (until the **Elevation of the Cross** on September 14), a period of relief when beasts and plants became wholesome again, purified of the threat of pestilence of the **Dog Days** of summer. The ancients attributed the latter to the combined heat of the sun and of Sirius, the sky's brightest star, which is in the constellation of the Great Dog, since they rise together from about July 3 to August 11. According to Plutarch's treatise on Isis and her son and husband Osiris, Egyptians in Ithiyiapolis—modern El-Kab south of Thebes—then burned this good god's evil brother: his murderer Seth, in the guise of human scapegoats (a practice also noted by Julius Caesar among the Gauls on **May Day**), before scattering their ashes in the wind to purify the air. In contrast to the **Dog Days** (*caniculares dies* in Latin), the auspicious thirty days that began on August 17 were also sometimes known as the **Cat Nights**.

> ***See also*** Annunciation; Ascension; Christmas; Conception and Birth of the Virgin Mary; Easter; Elevation of the Cross; Games (Rome); Holy Week; Lent; Lugnasad; May Day; New Yam Festival; Shavuot

References

Paul E. Duggan, *The Assumption Dogma: Some Reactions and Ecumenical Implications in the Thought of English-Speaking Theologians. A Doctoral Dissertation in Sacred Theology with Specialization in Marian Studies.* Dayton, OH: International Marian Research Institute, University of Dayton, 1989.

Vigen Guroian. *Inheriting Paradise. Meditations on Gardening.* Grand Rapids, MI: Wm. B. Eerdmans, 1999.

Vladimir Lossky and Leonid Ouspensky. *The Meaning of Icons.* Tr. G. E. H. Palmer and E. Kadloubovsky. Crestwood, NY: Saint Vladimir's Seminary Press, 1982.

Akalou Wolde Michael. "Buhe," in *University College of Addis Ababa Ethnological Society Bulletin,* No. 7 (1957), pp. 57–64.

On the Dormition: Early Patristic Homilies. Tr. Brian J. Daley. Crestwood, NY: St. Vladimir's Seminary Press, 1997.

Plutarch's De Iside et Osiride. Tr. J. Gwyn Griffiths. Cardiff, Wa: University of Wales Press, 1970.

ATEMOZTLI, ATLCAUALO
See Rain Festivals

ATONEMENT (DAY OF)
See Yom Kippur

AWUKUDAE
See Adae

B

▶ BACCHANALIA
See Dionysia

▶ BAEKJUNG
See Days of the Dead (China, Korea, Japan)

▶ BAHÁ
See Nineteen-Day Feast

▶ BAISAKHI
See Vaishakha and Vaisakhi

▶ BANK HOLIDAYS
See Lugnasad, Samhain, Whitsuntide

▶ BASANTI PUJA
See Navaratra and Dusshera

▶ BAYRAM
See Eid

▶ BEAR FESTIVAL (JAPAN)
The largely assimilated remnants of Japan's aboriginal Caucasoid Ainu people can now only be found in the country's northernmost Hokkaido Island (where they number some twenty-four thousand), as well as on the Sakhalin and Kurile Islands annexed by Russia at the end of the Second World War. The most im-

portant ritual in the Ainu religion centered on the sacrifice of a bear, typical of similar rites among many cultures of the Northern Hemisphere's higher latitudes.

An Ancient Circumpolar Bear Cult

According to legend, this sacrifice began when a hunting party discovered a bear that had taken care of an abandoned child and was then pursued and shot as a deity deserving worship by offerings of food, wine, and prayer sticks to accompany the soul to the other world. Today, it survives in a folkloric guise, but remains a classic example of a circumpolar bear cult that dates back to distant prehistory—since the bear was the first being to be worshipped as divine, by Neanderthal Man—and that is most developed among a range of cultures scattered around the Arctic Circle from Lapland to Labrador.

The original ritual of the Ainu was the sacrifice of a bear as an incarnation of "That Divine One Reigning in the Mountains," considered the most important of the spirits ruling the natural world. "The very essence of Ainu religion consists in communion with the greater powers, and the people imagine that the most complete communion they can possibly hold with some of their gods—animals and birds, to wit—is by a visible and carnal partaking of

Ainu men capture a bear and then threaten it with bows and arrows as part of the Ainu Bear Festival. The Ainus are the aboriginal people of Japan. (Hulton-Deutsch Collection/Corbis)

their very flesh and substance in sacrifice. At the time of offering, the living victim is said to be sent to his ancestors in another place" (Batchelor 1908, p. 249). Thus, the Ainu word for "sacrifice," which is *Iyomande,* has the meaning of "sending away." Hence the festival's name: **Kamui Omante** or "sending off of the bear."

Sending Off an Honored Guest

The black bear used in this ritual has traditionally been captured in the mountains and raised—even suckled—like one of the children of a chosen family. When it has gotten big enough to risk hurting its siblings, it is then placed in a special log cage for several months and fed a special diet of fish and millet porridge, until the time has come to release this spirit from its animal body and allow it to go back to its divine parents in their mountain. The ceremony's host convenes the entire village to the sacrifice of this little visitor. Prayer sticks ending with a cluster of shavings are then fashioned and stuck in the ground, first around the hearth of the household that adopted the bear, and then at the place of sacrifice—alongside *ok-numbani,* "the poles for strangling." Men approach the cage, followed by women and children who entertain the bear with singing and dancing. Once they are all seated in a circle around it, one of them comes up to it to explain to the god that it is about to be sent back to its parents, asking it to come again to be hunted and honored with its own sacrifice.

Lovingly raised by village elders, the animal is now usually spared in the reenactments of this sacrifice, which are usually held some time between December and February as part of a **Snow Festival**. It is chained to a pole in the center of festival grounds, where it can witness rare performances of Ainu folk dances performed in traditional costumes on what is today no more than a tourist attraction and secular celebration of Ainu identity.

However, when live bears were used in the ceremony, an actual sacrifice occurred after the bear, held with two ropes, had been taken out of its cage and walked around the circle of the people, who teased it with small bamboo *hep-ere-ai,* or "cub arrows," the tips of which were blunted by clumps of shavings like those of the prayer sticks. (This kind of bear baiting, though it eventually became more recreational than religious in focus, has been known in Europe from the Etruscans down to Elizabethan England, and was only banned by an act of the British Parliament in 1835.) The crazed beast was then tied to a decorated pole and held down by half a dozen strong men, who choked it between the two long thick poles, as an expert marksman shot an arrow through its heart in a way that prevented the blood from spilling on the ground. The bear's head and hide, still attached in one piece, were then taken inside and set on a makeshift altar among the prayer sticks and valuable gifts such as sacred wine arrayed by its adoptive family near the east window. In the **bear festivals** of mainland Siberian peoples of the Far East such as the Koryaks and Gilyaks, the victim is cut the same way and also oriented eastward (the favorable direction of the rising sun and benevolent spirits). These peoples also observe the same ritual as the Ainus, who symbolically fed the bear with a serving of its own meat and a helping of its own stew, along with wine or beer. He was then asked in a speech to tell his parents: "I have

been nourished for a long time by an Ainu father and mother and have been kept from all trouble and harm. Since I am now grown up, I have returned. And I have brought these prayer sticks, cakes, and dried fish. Please rejoice!" (Campbell 1988, p. 154).

Everyone Eats Everything

Once the bear had been fed, humans could begin their own feasting too, although laughter and tears alternated for the departing deity's adoptive mother and her predecessors of former years. After he had had a second bowl of stew, the host announced that "the little god is finished; come, let us worship!" He then ceremoniously shared the bowl's contents among the guests. Some of the men also drank the blood for strength and smeared it on their clothes, and other parts of the beast were eaten. The only part not consumed was the head, which was set among the skulls left from previous feasts upon the *ke-omande-ni,* "the pole for sending away." The Ainu festival went on until every bit of the bear had been consumed—a requirement that is found at other rituals of its kind.

American and European Parallels

In addition to the neighboring Lamut and Asian Eskimos around the Sea of Okhotsk, this ritual was practiced in the Arctic Northeast of the distant American continent, among the Innu, East Cree, and Attikamek of Labrador and Quebec.

Equally far away in the opposite, western direction, the ancient Finns (who were related to Siberian peoples, possibly even the Ainus) used to have a similar "bear feast" whenever they killed one of these animals. However, they only treated the bear's bones like a friend once they had eaten the flesh, as they buried the bones with various objects and asked the creature to tell other bears about the honors it had received from humans. The rationale was the same for the Finns as for the Ainus at the other end of

Eurasia—witness the seventeenth-century report by the Lutheran bishop Isak Rothovius: "When they kill a bear they hold a feast, drink out of the bear's skull and imitate its growling in order to ensure plenty of game in the future" (*Mythologica* 2003, p. 254).

See also Games (Rome)

References

J. Batchelor. "Ainus," in James Hastings, ed. *Encyclopedia of Religion and Ethics,* Vol. I. New York: Charles Scribner's Sons, 1908, pp. 239–252.

Joseph Campbell. *Historical Atlas of World Mythology.* Vol. I: *The Way of the Animal Powers, Part 2: Mythologies of the Great Hunt.* New York: Harper & Row, 1988.

William Fitzhugh and Chisato O. Dubreuil, eds. *Ainu. Spirit of a Northern People.* Vancouver: University of British Columbia Press, 2000.

A. Irving Hallowell. "Bear Ceremonialism in the Northern Hemisphere," in *American Anthropologist* (new series), Vol. 28, No. 1, January–March 1926, pp. 1–175.

Mythologica: A Treasury of World Myths and Legends. Vancouver, BC: Raincoast Books, 2003.

▶ BEAUTIFUL FESTIVAL OF THE VALLEY (EGYPT)

Once a year for the two millennia preceding the first century C.E., the Amon of Karnak was taken in effigy to the royal temples of the "city of the dead" across the Nile from that religious metropolis of Egypt, using ceremonial boats that were then carried overland through the funerary complex in a popular procession.

Amon's Nile Journeys

Throughout ancient Egypt, it was common practice to take out the idol of a god on his or her feast and have him or her visit the other gods' temples in a ceremonial boat. Such a boat, like a portable throne, was thought of both as the "powerful image" (*shm*) and the "upholder of beauty" (*wetes neferu*) of a deity—that is, as a magical actualization of timeless resurrected life—for the boat was raised up on the shoulders of priests, as on the life-giving waters of the Nile, floating above them like a permanent embodiment of their seasonal overflow.

In the Theban region, the god whose comings and goings were most often and most festively observed was Amon-Rê. The governors of Thebes—the name the Greeks gave Nuwe, meaning "the city" of Amon—made it the capital of a united Egypt when they founded its Eleventh Dynasty four thousand years ago, having combined the attributes of Amon as the god of their hometown of Tod to the south with those of the local goose deity of Thebes. Thereafter, based on the east bank of the Nile in Upper Egypt, a sacred royal domain (known as the Palladium of Thebes in modern times) stretched over ten square kilometers on both sides of the Nile River around Karnak and held many temples of national significance.

In this national center of his cult, the god Amon had a double significance: as "unknowable" (the first meaning of the hieroglyph for his name) or "source of all things"; and as this hidden source's "manifested light," or Rê, the sun above as well as the "breath" within each particular thing. The revelation of the supreme deity's creative activity, normally confined within a closed sanctuary, was publicly acted out several times a year in solemn journeys along well-defined paths, using slender boats whose gilded wooden cabins were actually duplicates of the temple's inner sanctum. The same term: *pr wr,* or "the big house," was used for both, as well as for the southern half of Egypt, corresponding in turn to the hidden world of the hereafter—that is, to the divine locus of the mysterious eternal life that such tabernacles were felt to hold within them. The god's actual image remained hidden behind the heavy curtains of the boat's cabin throughout the processions. In this way, his very inscrutability was allowed to become both tem-

The Sacred Bark of Amon-Ra at Abydos, Egypt. (Roger Wood/Corbis)

porarily manifest and mobile beyond the fixed confines of the temple's dark recesses, much as the sun radiates energy from an inaccessible source as visible light that cannot be directly gazed at.

Amon's boat was carried on a platform by specialized priests, who often sang as they walked, holding it up on transversal bars. Since the Middle Kingdom at least (that is, from the mid-twentieth century B.C.E.), thirty-two of them would take Amon's ship along symbolic itineraries of cosmic import at certain turning points of the cycles of nature, enshrined in the Theban calendar in use under the New Kingdom (that is, over roughly the second half of the second millennium B.C.E.). Thus, after the vital Flooding of the Nile that gave its name to

the season of Akhet had been welcomed with the **New Year** in the Coptic month of Thoth (around July 19), the river's power to wash over the land all the way to the sea was enhanced by such a ritual boat journey that began in the middle of the next month of Paophi (meaning "that of **Opet**"). The great **Opet** festival took its name from the shrine called *Ipet-Resyt* to which the Amon of Karnak, his consort Mut, their son Khonsu, and Rê's personification as Montu, god of weapons (though not of war), were taken for a few weeks, to visit the harem of the Amon of Luxor to the south of Thebes.

A Procession to the Western Land

But even more popular in the region was the procession that took Amon's court upstream

again in late May or in June. This occurred at
the time of the new moon of the month of
Payni, which meant "that of the Valley," since
the months, initially numbered from one to
four within each of the three Egyptian seasons,
were to be named by Christian Copts after the
main festivals formerly celebrated during them
by the Copts' pagan ancestors. Payni was thus
associated with the **Beautiful Festival of the
Valley**, which differed from most other festivals
in that it straddled both sides of the river,
rather than unfolding just along the eastern one
(which was the side of the rising sun and thus
of the living). To be sure, from about 1000
B.C.E. until well into the Roman era, Amon of
Luxor, or Imenipet—who was "the Unknowable" and therefore aniconic (or imageless)—
crossed the river every ten-day week to pay
homage to the gods buried opposite his shrine
at the mound of Djemê—where creation first
arose from the ocean of primordial chaos. Since
the time of Ramses III, the sacred mound was
enclosed within the temple compound he built
in the second quarter of the twelfth century
B.C.E. at Madînet Habu, in front of the entrance
to the Valley of the Queens. As the initial spot
of the renewal of the sun's cycle, Djemê was
considered sacred, and it held the creative principles revealed in Rê by Amon as universal
monarch before the world even existed: the *Ke-
matef* or "He who accomplishes his instant,"
and the ten *Baîs* or sparks of manifested energy
emanating from divine thought to provide the
basic structure of material life. Cosmic order
was thus reinforced by regular crossings to
Djemê, as the still-active repository of all the
divine energies otherwise latent in the material
world.

In contrast, the yearly procession of the
Beautiful Festival went there directly from Karnak to the north and then continued inland toward the setting sun along the Amentit range. It
made its return journey northward through the
necropolis—the "city of the dead" (made up of
royal mortuary temples and the houses of

priests, soldiers, craftsmen, and laborers in
their service)—almost up to the Valley of the
Kings, before crossing back the Nile River to
Karnak.

At both crossings, a bridge of ceremonial
barges welcomed the portable boats, which special galleys, manned by officials who vied for
this honor, would tug—all the way upstream to
the canal opening across from Luxor on the
first leg of the journey, while the crowds followed at some distance on the shore. Thus, imi-
tating the sun's cycle, the Amon of Karnak
reached the southernmost symbolic point of
the cycle of earth and water. Along with jars of
perfume and quarters of meat, the **first-fruits**
of the year's harvest were offered by the
pharaoh on behalf of mortals to his fellow god
Amon in a kind of intimate dinner. This was
depicted as such on the wall of the inner shrine
where it took place at Madînet Habu, while a
calendar of Egypt's festivals on its southern
outer wall details the make-up and recipes of
the offerings required on each occasion. This
mythical point of Amon's first arising and of
the original world of the Cycle of Light is where
the vast procession gathered on the first divine
station of its journey by land. The boats of
Amon and his court were proceeded by stan-
dard-bearers, fan-bearers, censers, royal guards,
instrumental musicians, and choral singers—
pious ladies playing sistrums to soothe the gods
with jangling sounds—and assorted clergy
singing hymns in their praise—not to mention
acrobats and other entertainers to cater to the
crowds of townspeople, while vendors set up
their booths along the way to attend to their
needs. Bystanders would throw themselves in
front of the boat to make petitions to the god in
the form of questions about issues in their personal lives, which he would answer by making
the priests who carried his boat take a step
ahead for "yes" or back for "no." Oracles could
also come forward on the same occasion, like
the one who confirmed the exceptional occurrence that a woman would take up the male

role of pharaoh in 1473 B.C.E. This allowed the Regent Queen Hatshepsut (who also maintained she was literally sired by Amon) to take the reins of power—and male attributes of power such as a ceremonial beard—as a "king." The first, highly successful, female ruler of a historical state, she reigned for twenty-two years thereafter.

There were an impressive number of other similar boats for all the statues of divine manifestations and immortalized ancestors. Carrying branches, soldiers marched in front of the royal family's escort as it visited the mortuary temples of its forebears, though their actual tombs were hidden in the cliffs' recesses to the south and north. The wealthier among their faithful subjects in the Valley had been conceded their own "dwellings of eternity," along the accessible eastern slopes, dug into the limestone, sometimes with several chambers to hold the mummies of many generations of a single family underneath a brick chapel.

Stations along the Way

To allow the boats to be laid down and their priestly carriers to rest awhile and feast on the offering, stations were provided at strategic points, such as royal temples on the procession's way. From raw brick, these stations gradually evolved into permanent structures of limestone, granite, or sandstone. Although they are long since ruined, they were originally meant to testify to the Egyptian monarchy's endless continuity over time—proof that it partook of divine eternity. They were thus called "temples of millions of years."

Ramses II, who ruled Egypt for most of the thirteenth century B.C.E., dedicated the great pillared hall of his jubilee temple—the Ramesseum—to the liturgical observances appointed for that station of the boat procession. Though the common people and resident foreigners were not admitted within the sacred precincts where these took place, the workers of the Western Valley's necropolis would surely have

gathered outside for the ongoing related celebrations. After all, they had long been erecting their own smaller monuments along the joyous procession's lotus-strewn path.

One of them, kept at the Cairo Museum, shows the great state barge called "Powerful-is-the-Front-of-Amon," with a ram's head on the stern, being welcomed with incense by Ramses II and escorted by his vizier Pa-Sar, then in charge of the Theban necropolis, toward the "Great Meadow" (*Sekhet aât*) of the Valley of the Kings. It is tucked behind the colonnaded temple built by Queen Hatshepsut in the mid-second millennium B.C.E. at Deir al-Bahri—the centerpiece of an ambitious building program meant to shore up her authority and legitimacy as a pharaoh.

An Egyptian All Souls

This station came after ten to thirteen days of solemn ceremonies and popular celebrations that echoed with the singing of pilgrims from Thebes and all of Egypt as they responded as a chorus to the love-praise of Amon when the procession reached its northernmost point. The nights were dotted with the hundreds of lights of small oil lamps, papyrus wicks, and brasiers—those of the banquets held in honor of Hathor (who was Amon's heavenly mother as identified with the Western Summit crowning the Valley of the Kings), and of all these royal embodiments of the solar deity—living, resurrected, or still to be born. All along the Theban mountain's eastern face, after each royal station in the boat procession, ordinary families would have first gathered in the open funerary chapels of departed relatives and friends to decorate their statues with lotus wreaths, also offering them food and drink along with floral bouquets soaked in frankincense and terebinth resin "that makes divine." They ate and drank a lot themselves, and the wine helped them reach altered states of consciousness in which they could feel closer to their departed loved ones. Often, wistful verses about the cycle of life closed these votive offerings, leading up to a happy commemoration of the dead, in advance of the yearly return of their spirits at the end of the Season of the Flood, during **Khoiak**.

See also Days of the Dead (West); Khoiak; New Year (West); Shavuot

References

A. Rosalie David. *The Ancient Egyptians: Beliefs and Practices.* Portland, OR: Sussex Academic Press, 1998.

Henri Frankfort. *Ancient Egyptian Religion: An Interpretation.* Mineola, NY: Dover Publications, 2000.

Donald B. Redford. *The Ancient Gods Speak: A Guide to Egyptian Religion.* Oxford: Oxford University Press, 2002.

Ramona Louise Wheeler. *Work Like an Egyptian: A Modern Guide to Ancient Time and the Egyptian Horoscope.* Holicong, PA: Wildside Press, 2003.

BEFANATA
See Epiphany

BEGINNING OF THE MONTH
See New Year (China, Korea)

BEHEADING OF SAINT JOHN THE BAPTIST
See Assumption, Conception and Birth of the Virgin Mary

BELTANE
See May Day

BÉNICHON
See Conception and Birth of the Virgin Mary

BESTA BERRI
See Corpus Christi

BHAI BIJ, BHAI TIKA, BHRATRI DWITIYA
See Divali

BIANU
See Ashura

BIG SUNDAY
See Kunapipi

BIJOYA
See Navaratra and Dusshera

BINDING OF THE YEARS
See New Fire Ceremony

BIRTH OF BAHÁ'ULLAH, BIRTH OF THE BAB
See Ridván

BIRTH OF THE MOTHER OF GOD
See Conception and Birth of the Virgin Mary

BISKET
See Vaishakha and Vaisakhi

BLACK FRIDAY
See Christmas

BLACK SABBATH
See Tisha be-Av

BLOWING THE HORN (DAY OF)
See Rosh Hashanah

BLUTRITT
See Rogations

BOHAG BIHU
See Vaishakha and Vaisakhi

BON
See Days of the Dead (China, Korea, Japan)

BOOK DAY
See Saint George

BOXING DAY, BOXING NIGHT
See Christmas

BOYS' FESTIVAL

See Sekku

BRIGHT WEEK

See Easter

BRUMALIA

See Saturnalia

BUDDHA'S BIRTHDAY, BUDDHA DAY

See Vaishakha and Vaisakhi

BUHE

See Assumption

BULL RUN

See Games (Rome)

BURI DIALI

See Divali

BURIAL OF THE SARDINE

See Carnival

BURNING OF CLOTHES FESTIVAL

See Days of the Dead (China, Korea, Japan)

BUSK (AMERICAN SOUTHEAST)

The most important festival of the Native American cultures of the Southeastern United States is the **Busk**. Celebrated in late July or August, this **Green Corn Ceremony** of purification traditionally involved discarding old utensils, extinguishing fires, fasting, and refurbishing structures. It was both a celebration of thanksgiving to the Breath-Maker or Creator for the **first-fruits** of the harvest and a **New Year** festival of new beginnings, when grievances were laid to rest and a **New Fire** was kindled, from which all household fires were rekindled.

Purification and Pacification

The Creek Confederation of mostly Muskogean-speaking tribes that had settled in the greater part of Alabama and Georgia at the time of European contact were united by a major festival that each town celebrated over four to eight days around the same time every year during the "Everything Grows Moon" (July–August), albeit on a slightly different date determined locally by the ripening of the late corn crop. It is called the **Green Corn Ceremony**, and white traders came to know it as "**Busk**," which is a corruption of the Creek word *puskita* for "a fast." It is said to have been dreamed by a man in ancient times as a way to bring to an end all fighting and warring. During this **Great Peace Ceremony**, war-like deeds are acknowledged and all transgressions are forgiven—somewhat as in Iroquois **Midwinter** ceremonies. Young people are initiated as members of the square ground in related rites that further foster social unity within a town, just as the tribal bonds uniting various towns are renewed sometimes by celebrating the **Busk** together. In any case, it was only held in "white" towns dedicated to peacetime activities and ceremonies, as opposed to the "red" towns devoted to military functions and observances. As Joseph Campbell has pointed out:

An appreciative comment on the **Busk** by the naturalist and explorer, Benjamin Franklin's friend John Bartram (1699–1777), published by his son William, illuminates the spiritual aspect of the annual fast, which in its psychological sense might be likened to an eight-day compression of **Ash Wednesday**, **Lent**, **Good Friday**, and then **Easter**. "When a town celebrates the **busk**," Bartram wrote, "having previously provided themselves with new clothes, new pots, pans, and other household utensils and furnitures, they collect all their worn-out clothes and other despicable things, sweep and cleanse their houses, squares, and the whole town, of their filth, which with all the remaining grain and old provisions, they cast together into one common heap and consume it with fire. After having taken medicine, and fasted for three days, all the fire in the town is extinguished. During this fast they abstain from the gratification of every appetite and passion whatever. A general amnesty is proclaimed, all malefactors may return to their town, and they are absolved from their crimes, which are now forgotten, and they are returned to favor." (Campbell 1989, p. 239)

Old items had to be destroyed and absolutely everything used in the **Busk** had to be brand new to contribute to the renewal of the world, the seasons, and the agricultural cycle. As for the Green Corn Medicine in question, it was prepared while the ritual ground was swept clean, and a layer of white sand was sprinkled over it. English traders and later anthropologists named this medicine the "Black Drink" because the liquid itself is very dark in color, though a white froth formed on the surface when the Indians shook it before consuming what was to them the "White Drink." Its very whiteness betokened the spiritual presence breathed into it through a straw. This caffeine-laden mixture of seven to fourteen herbs was otherwise known to strangers as "Carolina Tea." The main ingredient was *assi-luputski*—Creek for "small leaves" of Yaupon holly or *Ilex vomitoria*. It is also known as *Ilex casseina*, from *casseena*—the word used by the Timucua allies of the Spaniards in Florida whom the Creeks had helped English Carolina colonists exterminate in 1704. Like other cultures north of the Gulf of Mexico, the Creeks knew the right mix and temperature needed to maximize a caffeine "high" along with diuretic and vomitive properties. In conjunction with fasting (and even skin-scratching), the drink thus acted as a purgative at every level—both physical and spiritual, at the same time as it favored an altered state of consciousness, more open to higher powers. Purification was also achieved

by scratching the skin. The White Drink was only prepared in a ritual context—whether as a gift of good will to allies, enemies, and strangers alike or as a peacemaking tool for deliberations within or between clans and tribes, fostering male bonding.

Women only ever drank small amounts—never enough to throw up. In some cases, most of them were deemed unfit to enter the consecrated ground, along with children, animals, and any other beings who had not followed marriage laws and the taboo on unconsecrated **first-fruits**. Sentinels made sure only initiated warriors came in to observe the strict fast of a couple of days, when they purged sins from their bodies with White Drink and another strong vomitive known as *passa* made from button-snake root. The people kept out were given green tobacco to chew on so as to afflict their souls, while they were allowed to relax their own fasting after noon if they happened to be female, very young, or very frail. Women would also be in charge of preparing food from old provisions for the general breaking of the fast, but all traces of it had to disappear before noon. They would also prepare the new maize for the subsequent feast, but no one could touch it before it had been consecrated by the head priest or *Mico*.

First-Fruits and New Fire

Just as with the **New Yam festival**s of West Africa that revolve around such a taboo, all home fires had to be completely extinguished and their ashes swept away thoroughly with all rubbish before the ritual of thanksgiving for the new crop was carried out by the priest. He would have first cleaned out and purified the ceremonial public fireplace, often set atop one of the pyramidal mounds typical of Southeastern cultures. In some cases, he would plant some fresh green branches on it before kindling the new fire by the friction of two pieces of wood and placing it on the altar underneath. A specially appointed fire-maker might also light

A lithograph of Jemez Indians performing the Green Corn Dance. Celebrated in late July or August, the Green Corn Ceremony of purification traditionally involved discarding old utensils, extinguishing fires, fasting, and refurbishing structures. (Corbis)

the **New Fire** in the middle of four logs laid crosswise to point to the four directions. The Mico would take out a little of each of the new crops—not just corn, but beans, squash, and all wild plants as well, rubbing them with bear oil and offering them together with some meat as **first-fruits** and an atonement for all sins (except maybe murder) to the fire as Little Brother of the Sun and life force of the people. This **New Fire** would then be given out to the women to rekindle their home fires with, and they could now bake the new fruits of the year over it, to be eaten with bear oil.

At different points in the endlessly varied proceedings, men and women might rub ash, white clay, or analogous mixtures over themselves and then bathe as purification, and do the same with the new corn as a kind of blessing. There were dances throughout, performed by various clans and specialized groups until a mad final climax, which might be preceded by a mock battle of the warriors. This ceremonial violence has allowed L. R. Farnell to draw a par-

allel between the **Busk** and the ancient Athenian **Thargelia** festival of **first-fruits** in honor of the sun god Apollo, famous for the custom of taking unpopular "losers" as scapegoats through which evil was expelled from the community at the delicate time of the new harvest.

Variants and Distribution of a Mississippian Institution

But the sun is actually more central to the theology of all of the peoples primarily influenced by Mississippian culture, as it is the Breath-Maker animating all living things and represented on earth by a sacred fire. It was rekindled at dawn in some versions of the **Busk** among the Creeks, and the Mico faced the rising sun to make his offerings, setting copper plates with mythological designs on sand altars so they could reflect it as the image of the Breath-Maker. While the Natchez, who belonged to the Creek Confederation, had an equivalent **New Fire Ceremony** with the same Mexican roots as the widespread cultivation of maize, beans, and squash, the neighboring Muskogean-speaking Choctaws and Chickasaws, who did not belong to this political entity, celebrated the **Busk** itself.

Likewise, though the Cherokees were not even Muskogean but Iroquoian, their civilization was similar to the Creeks' in almost every respect, so that they too celebrated a **Green Harvest Festival** of **first-fruits**. They had a theory that disease was the natural world's revenge for humans' contempt and indifference toward animals, and could only be contained by plants, herbs, and trees as mankind's faithful friends. In such a view, dances are done and prayers and offerings are made in thanks for all of the foods and medicines that are gifts from the plant kingdom, as well as for the air we breathe as a gift from the Breath-Maker. For many centuries, Cherokee towns, like those of their Creek neighbors, were built around large central square grounds as the place devoted to just these kinds of ritual ceremonies, gatherings, and prayers. An annual festival is celebrated on these sacred grounds in North Carolina by the Cherokees who managed to buy back their ancestral lands after they were seized by the American federal government. But even for those Cherokees the authorities scattered or resettled in the Indian Territory that became the state of Oklahoma in 1907, the **Green Corn Ceremony** is still a time for coming together to renew family ties and honor traditional ways.

Due to the extensive early disruption of their own way of life, it is hard to say whether the Cherokees' original neighbors, the Tuscaroras, used to follow the **Busk** ceremonial in full or in part before they had to flee their North Carolina homeland in the eighteenth century. The Tuscaroras eventually joined their distant Iroquois cousins in New York State as the sixth nation of their famous confederation. But the fact remains that the August **Green Corn Ceremony** called *Ah-dake'-wa-o* has somehow become part of the ritual calendar of the Iroquois

as far north as the Kanesatake Mohawk reserve at Oka near Montreal in Quebec, Canada.

At the southernmost tip of the range of cultures in which it figures, the **Green Corn Dance** is still performed today by the thousand or so Seminoles left in Florida. It normally begins while the White Drink is being consumed—failing which, the new corn partaken of the next day is sure to make one sick over the year. A day's fast would follow (so as not to pollute the sacred food still present in the system) before the great feast on the third day. Until recently, Seminole medicine men would join in the dance and open their deerskin medicine bundles of sacred objects on the annual occasion of this festival. They might also perform incisions—especially on the arms—to purify people and protect them over the coming year, relying on dreams sent by mostly animal "spirit helpers" to dispel the fear of spirits who might otherwise turn against humans.

Like the Creek people of which they were an offshoot, and along with the Choctaws, Chickasaws, and Cherokees, the Seminoles were counted among the so-called Five Civilized Tribes who had largely espoused a Western lifestyle by 1830. But that did not prevent the Indian Removal Act from coming into effect that year or from being enforced over the next decade or so, when they were sent packing along the infamous "Trail of Tears" to an alien prairie habitat in and around Oklahoma. It is now mostly there that the **Green Corn Ceremony**, once central to the basically Mississippian cultures of the American Southeast and best exemplified by the **Busk**, may still be found in a variety of altered forms.

See also Easter; Holy Week; Lent; Midwinter; New Yam Festival; New Year (West); New Fire Ceremony; Thargelia

References

Joseph Campbell. *Historical Atlas of World Mythology.* Vol. II: *The Way of the Seeded Earth, Part 2: Mythologies of the Primitive*

Planters: The Northern Americas. New York: Harper & Row, 1989.

William C. Sturtevant. ed. *A Creek Source Book.* New York: Garland Press, 1987.

John Witthoft. *Green Corn Ceremonialism in the Eastern Woodlands.* Ann Arbor, MI: University of Michigan Press, 1949.

▶ CALÈNA

See New Year (West)

▶ CALENDS OF JANUARY

See Saturnalia

▶ CALUMET

See Powwow

▶ CANADA DAY

See Midsummer

▶ CANDLEMAS (CHRISTIANITY)

In the West, it has been the tradition on February 2 that the candles set aside for use over the year in churches or for religious purposes be blessed with holy water before a solemn candle-light procession. This is why this day has been known as **Candlemas** (and by similar terms in other languages) for about a thousand years. These rites were performed in honor of the **Purification of the Virgin Mary** (that is, in commemoration of the day she went to the Temple of Jerusalem after giving birth to Jesus in order to present him and be restored to ritual purity). They are accompanied by many folkloric customs of pagan origin, like those of **Groundhog Day,** though the latter has always remained a purely secular seasonal observance.

Timing and Meaning

Being temporarily considered unclean due to the raw, earthy messiness of childbirth, Jewish women could not be admitted into consecrated space for a forty-day period after having a baby. In compliance with this religious law, as well as with the one demanding concrete acknowledgement that any firstborn belonged to God, Mary went to the Temple in Jerusalem with her husband Joseph to introduce the child Jesus into the community of God's people by making the customary sacrifice of two pigeons. In this event, echoed in the Orthodox Blessing of Infants when they are forty days old and more widely celebrated as a yearly liturgical feast forty days after the **Nativity of Christ**, the Christian Church sees the chosen people represented at the Temple by Symeon the Elder and Ann the Prophetess, who both recognized the infant Jesus as the Messiah they had been waiting for all their lives. This day has therefore long been known in the Anglican Church as the **Presentation of Christ in the Temple**, and to Catholics too since the liturgical reforms of 1969. The same idea is conveyed by the more succinct names for this feast in the Eastern Church: the "**Meeting of Our Lord**" (by Ann and Symeon, that is), called *Hypapantí* in Greek and *Srétenye* in church Slavonic.

The scribe Symeon's song of praise for this day of fulfillment, known from the Latin translation of Luke's Gospel (2:29–32) as the *Nunc Dimittis,* provides much of the material for the day's liturgical texts, and is also part of both the Catholic mass and the Orthodox divine liturgy. It says: "Now, Master, you can let your servant go in peace, just as you promised; because my eyes have seen the salvation which you have prepared for all the nations to see, a light to enlighten the pagans, and the glory of your people Israel" (*Jerusalem Bible* 1968). This light is revealed when the lawgiver willingly submits to the law, just as he would freely lower himself by taking baptism from John in the Jordan, as celebrated at **Epiphany** as the "**Feast of Lights**" on January 6 by the Eastern Church. But believers also hold that divine light had actually begun to shine in the world when God became incarnate in lowly human form through the **Nativity of Jesus Christ**.

Following this common theme of the self-emptying (called *kenosis* in Greek) of the Word of God, the **Nativity** sequence of celebrations, which opened with the four-week **Advent** period in the West and the forty-day Short Lent before **Christmas** in the East, comes to a close with the feast of the **Meeting of Our Lord** on February 2, forty days after **Christmas**. This is the reason for the Greek saying: "*Hypapanti* drives away all festivals with the distaff" (Megas 1963, p. 57), since the holidays are over and a more regular work schedule resumes until the **Easter** cycle. Because the observance of the **Nativity of Christ** began as part of **Epiphany** on January 6, it was on February 14 that the **Meeting of Our Lord**, as the fortieth day after **Epiphany** (*Quadragesima de Epiphania*) was initially celebrated "with the greatest joy, just as at **Easter**," by the time Egeria (formerly known as Etheria), a pilgrim from Gaul to the Holy Land, gave us the first historical record of it in her travel diary in 386—the earliest surviving prose text by a woman in the West. The feast was moved to February 2 by 542, when

Emperor Justinian established the festival throughout the Roman Empire. Yet on its Eastern frontier, February 14 has been kept as the date of this feast in the Oriental Orthodox Armenian Church.

Roman Remnants

In the West, where it was long a Marian feast (or feast of the Mother of God) rather than a feast of the Lord, **Candlemas** took over from some well-established fertility rites. This explains the large amount of folklore surrounding this festival. The very name of the month of February referred to seasonal purification in ancient Rome, which was accompanied by rites intended to appease the spirits of the dead at the end of winter as well as to usher in springtime fertility. It was probably no coincidence that the same North African Pope Gelasius I, who instituted this Christian festival in the West at the end of the fifth century, also took steps at the same time to ban the Roman people's continued observance of the **Lupercalia** on February 15. Calling for the use of goat-skin strips called *februa* to dispel evils and bring on fertility in women, this pagan festival of purification could not be better countered—or indeed outdone—than by a Christian feast devoted to the restored purity of a miraculously fertile virgin mother. The Roman Church started calling it the **Purification of the Virgin Mary** in the eighth century, and after the blessing of candles was introduced by the late ninth century, it became "**Candlemas**" in the eleventh.

The actual procession with candles seems to have been first suggested by the Roman matron Ikalia in the middle of the fifth century, when the faithful held candles during the feast's services in Jerusalem. Candles were already conspicuous at an ancient Roman festival of the dead, the February **Parentalia,** and were even used to evoke the dead in Rome's **Shrove Tuesday** parades during the Renaissance. But candlelight processions were held in honor of the Virgin Mary on February 2 instead, and they accompanied the Church feast on this date as it spread to other European countries from Spain to Britain, mostly around the turn of the second millennium. Since the Reformation, Protestant pastors in many of those countries have often endeavored to suppress these processions, just as they have also tried to ban the lighting of a large candle to burn through part of the night, but it is a **Candlemas** custom still observed in some English homes. Protestant denominations objected to the superstitious use of the light of candles to ward off evil spirits, and, when King Henry VIII nonetheless authorized the keeping of the feast in his British realm, it was with the understanding that this was not its purpose, but that the custom only symbolized the proclamation of Christ as the light of the world.

Candlemas observances had practically vanished in Protestant countries by the middle of the eighteenth century. The Catholic faithful, who continued to take part in such **Candlemas** processions, often wore black or purple as a sign of penance before purification; and the children would ask for money as they sang seasonal tunes on the way to the day's highpoint— the formal blessing that purified the candles in order to make them fit to be used at church (and incidentally at home for the power of their wax as well as their light to dispel evil).

A Celtic Variant: Saint Bridget's

Celtic people had long been accustomed to celebrating one of their four major yearly festivals, called **Imbolc**, on February 1. It involved collecting the purifying water that came down from the sky as dew. It was thus easy for their many descendants in the west of Europe to relate to the sprinkling of holy water on candles during the feast of the **Purification of the Virgin** on February 2, to the point of generally naming it after these candles.

However, the February 1 feast of **Saint Bridget** (452–525) remained a distinct and more prominent festivity in Irish, Scottish,

and Manx folklore. It traditionally involved various observances aimed at securing protection for crops, beasts, and people alike over the coming year. The namesake of Ireland's patron saint, the goddess Brigit, had fulfilled a similar function in the ancient Celtic winter purification rites of **Imbolc**. One of the few specifics that have come down to us is the washing of feet, hands, and head—which people may have done for one another. This would explain the "mutual cleansing" suggested by the Celtic roots of the name of this pagan festival.

In Ireland, the evening of January 31 was one of the year's handful of universally observed "set-nights," like **New Year**'s Eve, "**Old Christmas**" Eve on **Twelfth Night** or **Epiphany**, **Shrove Tuesday** as **Carnival** before the start of **Lent** on **Ash Wednesday**, All Hallows' Eve or **Halloween**, and **Christmas** Eve proper. Some milk would be put aside by the housemistress over a week before the first of February, at a time of year when milk was not easy to come by, so that freshly made butter could be part of the **Saint Bridget**'s Eve dinner. Otherwise, it would not be worthy of the holy woman. This custom may also reflect the requirements of **Imbolc**, since we know they involved tasting food in a certain order. In any case, on **Saint Bridget**'s Eve, an Irish house would be thoroughly cleaned, barnyard animals would get fresh straw in their stalls, and a good fire—or at least candles—would be lit. The idea was that everything should be nice and fresh to welcome **Saint Bridget** at dinner in the guise of a large sheaf of wheat, fashioned into roughly human shape under "**Saint Bridget**'s coat" (the *brat*). The saint's protective power remained concentrated in whatever piece of clothing the *brat* had been made from, once it had been left outside during all of **Saint Bride**'s (or Bridget's) night. Sometimes on **Saint Bride**'s Eve, people would dress up as for a **Carnival**, and walk in a procession with a puppet depicting the holy woman, called a "Biddy."

Pancake Sunday and the Christmas Season

In France, **Candlemas** remains—if nothing else—a day for eating crepes, whether in church halls or at home. The crepes are usually served with apple cider from Normandy or Brittany. Turning these thin pancakes over in the pan with a piece of gold (such as a ring) in one's hand is considered to bring good luck. In the past, it might have been rolled into the first crepe to be flipped and carried in procession to be put on top of the cupboard of the eldest person of the household, from which the previous year's gold piece would be taken from the remains of its crepe and given to the first poor person to come along. There even used to be a collection for the poor of the parish among the Acadians of the Canadian province of Prince Edward Island.

In the French-Canadian countryside, **Candlemas** also used to mark the very end of the festive season (*Temps des fêtes*) following **Christmas,** when people would visit each other for family parties. Leftover eggs and dairy products would therefore go into the making of large amounts of pancakes on this happy send-off of the winter holidays, anticipating *Mardi Gras.* Generally speaking, in French **Candlemas** folklore, the remainder of the previous year's wheat harvest is entirely used up in crepes, or alternatively in donuts, as a way to secure an abundant and healthy harvest in the coming year, by symbolically completing the cycle of the sun—also represented by the golden color and round shape of the dishes involved.

In Spain though, many regions have a tradition of family barbecues on **Candlemas**; in Mexico, it is the person who found a bean or a baby Jesus in his or her share of the **Epiphany** cake who is supposed to organize and pay for the **Candlemas** party centering on *tamales*— another kind of crepe. Also underlining the links between the end of the old year and the beginning of the new year, in much Northern European folklore, the failure to take down all **Christmas** decorations by **Candlemas** was believed to invite bad luck.

Because of the feast's association with the child Jesus, it was chosen as the **World Day of Orthodox Youth** in 1992. No doubt on account of an underlying parallel between the early stages of Christ's life, of human life, and of the yearly cycle itself, there was long a custom in Scotland of small-town children presenting gifts to their teachers on **Candlemas**. Much as with related seasonal rites of social inversion from **Saint Nicholas** Day to **Epiphany** elsewhere in Europe, they had a little party afterwards, where they would elect a **Candlemas** king—and sometimes a queen as well. For each of the six weeks of his reign, this **Candlemas** king was entitled to claim an afternoon of games or recess for his classmates and had the royal prerogative of canceling punishments at his discretion.

Groundhog Day and Weather Forecasting

That same six-week period, which lasted until **Saint Patrick**'s Day on March 17, was one when the Irish would closely watch the skies for indications of future weather, just as they observed the behavior of hedgehogs on **Saint Bridget**'s for the same purpose.

Though in some Slavic Orthodox churches, there is a service of the Blessing of the Candles, which the faithful can then take home, in Greece, the popular name of the feast of the **Meeting of our Lord** is not "**Candlemas**," but *Miliargousa*—the "Miller's Holiday." This is because the windmills stay idle on this day.

Cretans maintain that the windmills would not work even if the miller did try to use them. Whereas other Greeks and Eastern Christians think the weather remains what it was on this day for forty days—or at least to the end of the month—the inhabitants of the island of Crete believe that clear weather on this day means the winter will be long. This ancient folk belief about **Candlemas**, if it was not inherited directly from the Celtic folklore of **Imbolc,** may have been taken by the Roman legions to the Germanic tribes of Northern Europe, who related it to the hibernation patterns of certain animals—such as the badger, the wolf, and the hedgehog—which they credited with an ability to gauge how much winter weather was left before spring. German and British immigrants took it to North America, where it became the premise for **Groundhog Day** customs as a divination ritual based on whether or not the rodent sees its shadow. If it does, it will hibernate through another six weeks (forty days framed by two extra ones) of cold weather. The towns where **Groundhog Day** is still celebrated with the most fanfare and media attention are Punxsatawney, Pennsylvania, and Wiarton, Ontario.

Based on the same principle as the Cretan belief about **Candlemas, Groundhog Day** is a living example of the connection ancient peoples made between this point of winter (about midway between solstice and equinox, as in other Celtic festivals beside **Imbolc**) and the coming spring—evident as far away as China (with a festive calendar also structured around these four midpoints between our current seasonal markers). It is no mere coincidence that Chinese **New Year** celebrations tend to start around this time by early February, as the **Spring Festival**.

See also Carnival; Christmas; Days of the Dead (West); Easter; Epiphany; Holi and Vasant Panchami; Inti Raymi; Lugnasad; Lupercalia; New Year (China, Korea); New Year (West); Saint Nicholas; Samhain

References

Bill Anderson. *Groundhog Day: 1886 to 1992. A Century of Tradition in Punxsutawney, Pennsylvania.* Punxsutawney, PA: Bill Anderson, 1992.

The Festal Menaion. Tr. Mother Mary and Archimandrite Kallistos Ware. London: Faber & Faber, 1984.

Jerusalem Bible. Garden City, NY: Doubleday and Co., 1968.

Stewart A. Kingsbury, Mildred E. Kingsbury, and Wolfgang Miede. *Weather Wisdom: Proverbs, Superstitions, and Signs.* New York: Peter Lang, 1996.

George A. Megas. *Greek Calendar Customs.* Athens: [s.n.], 1963.

Séamas Ó Catháin. *The Festival of Brigit: Celtic Goddess and Holy Woman.* Blackrock, Ireland: DBA, 1995.

Sean Ó Súilleabhìn. *A Handbook of Irish Folklore.* Detroit, MI: Singing Tree Press, 1970.

The Pilgrimage of Etheria. Tr. M. L. McClure and C. L. Feltoe. New York: Macmillan (Ann Arbor, MI: University Microfilms International, 1978).

▌ CANICULARES DIES
See Assumption

▌ CAPITOLIA
See Games (Rome)

▌ CARÊME
See Lent

▌ CARISTIA (ROME)

The Roman festival of Caristia was also known as *Cara cognatio* (or "Dear Relatives"). It came on the day after **Feralia,** marking the end of **Parentalia,** nine days devoted to making peace with dead relatives. On February 22, Roman families turned from the dead to the living and put aside their quarrels amid good cheer, bringing concord to the home. No outsiders were allowed to take part.

Minding the Lares

As the poet Ovid wrote about this festival, "It is sweet of course to turn from dead kin and tombs / And direct one's gaze toward the living / And view what line remains after so many lost / And enumerate the generations" (*Fasti* 2:619–622, p. 45). But a plate had to be laid out for the meal to be shared with the familiar deities or benign ancestor spirits known as *Lares,* who protected the household and its fields. The day before the festival, their mother Tacita would have been invoked in magical rites by an old woman so as to prevent any slander against the family and especially to preserve the reputation of maidens. There originally used to be one *Lar familiaris* for every Roman homestead, but by the time of the Empire, domestic chapels like those found among the ruins of Pompeii would depict Lares dancing in pairs with their tunics hitched up, as they poured wine into cups.

From a National to a Clerical Fathers' Day

Also, the first Roman Emperor Augustus Caesar had combined the cult of his own *genius* or individual protecting deity (also known as his *Fortuna*) with that of the Lares when he restored the *collega compitalicia*—associations which sponsored their own crossroad shrines and festivals (such as **Compitalia**). Thus, when night fell on Caristia, the family members who had gathered would each take a great cup of wine and spill it onto the ground as they made this double toast as a solemn prayer: "To your health, Lares! to your health, Father of the Fatherland [*Pater Patriae*], excellent Caesar!"

Many early Christians would endure martyrdom rather than toast or salute, let alone worship in any way, the Emperor's *Fortuna* on these and other occasions. Witness the earliest story of a saint's martyrdom, that of **Saint Polycarp** on January 26, 155, which provided the model for this pious genre, down to the identification of its date with that of the saint's eternal birthday or ***dies natalis.*** In order to displace the pagan practices still current in Rome around February 22 (like the ancestor-worship of **Feralia**) long after the Empire became Christian, the date of Caristia was later chosen for the **feast of the See of Saint Peter** in honor of the bishop of Rome, heir to Caesar's universal authority as Holy Father (*pappas* in Greek—hence pope) of the Catholic Church,

and eventually to his temporal power in the Eternal City after the fall of the Empire in the West in 476.

See also Days of the Dead (West); Matronalia

References

William Warde Fowler. *Roman Festivals of the Period of the Republic: An Introduction to the Study of the Romans.* Port Washington, NY: Kennikat Press, 1969.

Simon Hornblower and Antony Spawforth, eds. *The Oxford Classical Dictionary.* 3rd revised edition. Oxford: Oxford University Press, 2003.

Ovid. *Fasti.* Tr. A. J. Boyle and R. D. Woodard. London: Penguin Books, 2000.

▶ CARMENTALIA (ROME)

Carmentalia was an ancient Roman festival dedicated to a goddess of childbirth, held on January 11 and 15. If little is known of its origins and exact nature, historical records reveal a few instances when the key role of women in it gave them unaccustomed leverage at some turning points of Roman politics.

Maternal Privileges

The Arcadian goddess Carmentis or Carmenta was said by Romans to owe her name to the rhymed prophetic songs or *carmina* (plural of *carmen* and Latin for "divine incantation" and later "song") that she inspired. But this old divinity of childbirth who protected women was no longer very important by the time of the Empire, when no one seemed to remember just why the Senate had added a second day (January 15) to her festival of Carmentalia, which was originally celebrated on the eleventh only. Some said it was so that one could ask for the safe delivery of baby boys or baby girls, but there is no indication of any such gender specialization on the two festival days.

We do know from the Roman historian Titus Livius (64 or 59–7 B.C.E.) that the matrons had been granted the privilege of going to Carmenta's shrine (situated between the Capitol and the Tiber) on two-wheeled wagons called *carpenta*. This was an enduring reward for having offered their gold jewels so that the dictator Camillus could pay what he still owed the Delphic Apollo from the booty of Veii, since the god had granted Rome a victorious end to her ten-year long siege of this Etruscan city—her great rival in Italy—in 395 B.C.E. This privilege was abolished during the Second Punic War by the Oppia Law of 215 B.C.E., but it had to be restored ten years later. Some authors say this was as a result of a pressure tactic of systematic abortions on the part of the women of Rome.

Portents of Childbirth

This would have constituted a striking inversion of the life-fostering energies of Carmenta, which were normally disturbed by the mere introduction into her shrine of dead materials such as leather. Among the ancient rites performed there by her priest at **Carmentalia** were prayers that included obscure invocations of *Porrima* and *Postuerta*. The poet Ovid (43–17 B.C.E.) took these names to refer to prophecies of times past and times to come, while the scholar Varro (116–27 B.C.E.) thought these attributes referred to the positions of the fetus at birth, which determined whether it came out of the womb safely head-first or unsafely feet-first.

See also Matralia

References

Cyril Bailey. *Phases in the Religion of Ancient Rome*. Westport, CT: Greenwood Press, 1972.

Georges Dumézil. *Archaic Roman Religion, with an Appendix on the Religion of the Etruscans*. Tr. Philip Krapp. Baltimore, MD: Johns Hopkins University Press, 1996.

Ovid. *Fasti*. Tr. A. J. Boyle and R. D. Woodard. London: Penguin Books, 2000.

▶ CARNEIA (GREECE)

The Dorian festival of Apollo Carneios, protector of herds, was celebrated in most of the Peloponnese with sacrifices, military contests, and a race to catch a "jack-in-the-green."

A Portrait of Dorian Camps

Though this festival was common to Dorian-speaking Greeks, we only know its date in the calendar of Sparta, where it took place from the seventh to the fifteenth of the month of Karneios (in late July and August). This was a time sacred to all Dorians on account of their common cult of Apollo Carneios.

In Argos, both Apollo and his priest were called *hagetor*—that is, "leader of the host"—of Dorian Greek tribes who took over most of the Peloponnese over 3,000 years ago. Elsewhere, the priest was called *karnos* or *karneio* (likely meaning "ram")—the name of the prophet-priest of Apollo who led the host and was unjustly killed by the Dorian descendants of Heracles. He would thus have been commemorated in this festival to appease divine anger, or he might actually have been a local fertility god displaced by the Dorians' own sun god Apollo.

During the nine days of **Carneia** in Sparta, a sacred truce was observed during which no military action might be undertaken. Instead, the Spartans experienced this festival as an "image of the military life," everything being done "by word of command" by nine groups of three *phratries* or brotherhoods. Each occupied a place called a *skias,* where they lived in "something like tents" (probably huts made out of branches), according to Demetrios of Skepsis (Farnell 1907, p. 260). There, young and old feasted together naked all the while, as they formed competing choirs (whose leaders wore palm crowns) to sing and dance as well as test their athletic skills in celebration of past victories and achievements.

The **Gymnopaidiai** or **Festival of Naked Youths** in honor of Apollo Pythaeus, Artemis and Dionysus seems to have formed part of the celebrations of **Carneia** in Sparta, and unmarried men were not allowed to attend. From about the Twenty-Sixth Olympiad (676 B.C.E.)

onward, poets and artists from all over Greece would gather in Sparta for a contest on the occasion of **Carneia**, since the sun god Apollo was the patron of the arts.

Racing Against Death

It was perhaps to commemorate the Dorians' legendary crossing to the peninsula that Spartans also carried model rafts in procession; at the same time (in a custom also attested in Cnidus and on the island of Thera), *staphylodromoi* (young grape-cluster-runners) pursued the garlanded priest who would have first prayed for blessings on the city. These would only come if the five-man teams of unmarried *Karneatai* chosen in each tribe every four years caught the running man—thereby effecting a transfer of magical energy from him as vegetation spirit to the samples of vines the runners held. Allowing the priest to get away was a bad omen, tantamount to letting the power of growth go by after the harvest without laying hold of it for future crops.

If this was a typical agrarian ritual to secure the fertility of the vintage and the harvest (with many equivalents in European folklore, as well as a similar race once held on one of the last days of the **Shalako** festival in Zuñi, New Mexico), military rites reinforced its power, as they staged the mythic struggle of the forces of nature's bounty over the demons of scarcity. Thus in Cyrene, a Dorian colony in Libya, there was a war dance of hoplites—heavily armed infantrymen.

For the warrior hero is someone who has been victorious over death and thus stands for invincible life, like Heracles when he arrived just in time to wrest Alcestis from the clutches of Hades (that is, death and the underworld), because her husband Admetus, king of Pherae, had been granted the privilege of getting someone to die in his stead on Apollo's intercession, and Zeus would not let this unnatural trading of places be carried out. This allowed Euripides to imagine in his play about Alcestis (verses

449–452) that hymns were sung in her praise "both in Sparta when the Karneian month rolls around in its season/ and when the full moon risen/ stays high all night, and in/ shining, happy Athens, glittering and bright" (*Alcestis* 1974, p. 31).

See also Games (Greece); Shalako

References

E. H. Binney. "The *Alcestis* as a Folk-Drama," in *Classical Review,* Vol. XIX, No. 98, 1905.

P. E. Easterling and J. V. Muir, eds. *Greek Religion and Society.* Cambridge: Cambridge University Press, 1985.

Euripides. *Alcestis.* Tr. Charles Rowan Beye. Englewood Cliffs, NJ: Prentice-Hall, 1974.

Lewis Richard Farnell. *The Cults of the Greek States.* Vol. IV. Oxford: Clarendon Press, 1907.

Michael Pettersson. *Cults of Apollo at Sparta: The Hyakinthia, the Gymnopaidiai and the Karneia.* Stockholm: Svenska Institutet i Athen and Göteborg: P. Åström, 1992.

▶ CARNIVAL (CHRISTIANITY)

The word "**carnival**" probably comes from the Latin *carnem levare,* meaning "to take away meat," or perhaps simply, *carne vale,* which translates as "goodbye, meat!" It stands for a fond, often boisterously self-indulgent goodbye to meat and all the other carnal pleasures that Christians are traditionally supposed to abstain from during the **Lent**en season of ascetic preparation for **Easter**. **Carnival** allows them to give in with wild abandon to the unruly passions that any established order usually frowns on and which church discipline is then about to repress with a vengeance. Prior to modern attempts to channel them into more genteel, officially organized urban attractions, **Carnival**s were structured around rituals of social inversion and scapegoating. These were pagan remnants of archaic agrarian observances (the reason they were later banned in Spain under the right-wing Franco dictatorship). **Carnival**s often dramatized the competition between the bountiful powers of a new spring and the constraining forces of winter, together with the last hurrah of the chaotic remnants of old life as the fertile ground for revitalized order.

Place in the Calendar: East and West

In Greece, **Carnival** is called *Apokreos*—"away with meat." The **Carnival** season begins three weeks before **Lent**, when its commencement used to be announced from atop a hill by a villager, with drumbeats by the town crier or with the firing of guns in cities. The first week was therefore known as *Propsoni*, from the verb "to announce," and was the one when fatted pigs were killed so they could be eaten during the second or **Meatfare Week** (when even regular fasting is banned), on the big family meals of Thursday, Saturday, and Sunday.

This is when **Carnival** activities really get under way, with after-dinner masquerades, including satirical plays on a variety of themes. Among the most common are mock weddings and the moot trial of a man accused of having killed a pig, who is pardoned just when he is about to be hanged.

The climax of the sanctioned licentiousness and merrymaking of the Orthodox **Carnival** season comes on **Cheesefare** Sunday, after a week without meat has already passed. Similarly, in prerevolutionary Russia, peasants managed to stuff themselves with pancakes (since all dairy products had to be consumed before the onset of full **Lent**en fasting) so much that many died each year. In Greece, firecrackers go off until vespers, and then large bonfires are lit—especially in the north. Neighbors greet each other with gunshots after the big meat-free dinner, when dances are often disrupted by marauding bands of maskers.

Though officially part of **Lent**, the next Monday is really an extension of **Carnival**, with mummers staging the funeral of King **Carnival** in some places. However, it is generally an open-air holiday when people go outdoors—be

it in the country or in their backyards—to have special **Lent**en-fare meals, dance, and fly kites. These are all ways of greeting spring and dismissing winter, as is the custom after which **Clean Monday** is known. This is when pots and pans are cleaned the next day with hot water mixed with ashes.

In the West, the **Carnival** season generally begins on **Quinquagesima** Sunday—the one before **Lent**. **Ash Wednesday** is included in it in some parts of Spain—a holdover from the time over a thousand years ago when it had not been made the official start of **Lent** yet.

Carnival normally reaches its final climax on **Shrove Tuesday**, when one used to get "shriven"—that is, absolved after confessing one's sins, having no doubt committed more than one's usual share over the last couple of days alone. In France, where **Carnival** is often limited to this single day, it is called *Mardi Gras*—"**Fat Tuesday**," and is the last opportunity to consume meat and poultry products.

However, in New Orleans, the **Mardi Gras** season extends ten days back as the culmination of a **Carnival** season that itself begins on January 6 with **Epiphany**, as it does in Guadeloupe, as well as in most Catholic German lands.

German-Speaking and Low Countries

The Rhineland is different from other Catholic countries since November 11 (at eleven past eleven o'clock) marks the start of Cologne's elaborate *Karneval* for instance. Though characteristic Napoleonic costumes arose as a satire of French invaders in the early nineteenth century, this celebration was first recorded in 1234. The equivalent *Fastnacht* was observed even earlier in Mainz and other southwestern German cities; in Bavaria and Austria, it is known as *Fasching*.

The celebration of these German **carnival**s starts on the Thursday before **Lent**, but it reaches fever pitch on the last three days, as a time when everyday rules are turned upside

The three-day Binche Carnival, held near Mons (Belgium) just before Lent. During the Carnival, festivities are led by "Gilles," men dressed in high, plumed hats and bright costumes. (Charles & Josette Lenars/Corbis)

down. Thus, the keys of the city could be handed over to a council of fools, or to women, who were solemnly invested with full powers.

Surviving practices include satirical plays, speeches, and newspaper columns, along with noisy costumed parades and masked balls, and all manner of overt excess. These are also observed in the German-speaking area of Belgium in Eupen and Malmédy, as in most other **Carnival**s still thriving in that country, like those in nearby Stavelot and in Aalst in East Flanders—where bloody panties are even thrust at bystanders.

Yet the tone is strangely different in Belgium's most famous **Carnival**: that of Binche near Charleroi. Going back at least to the fourteenth century, it has become highly formal-

ized over later ones. This is especially true of the **Shrove Tuesda**y procession of the *Gilles*. The Gilles societies are comprised of hundreds of native sons and longtime male residents, who save and prepare all year for the privilege of solemnly stomping in step through the streets for nearly twenty-four hours at a stretch. Like quaint clowns in eerie masks, they dress in one-of-a-kind, elaborate, and costly **Carnival** outfits, with meter-high ostrich feather headdresses worn only in the afternoon. This famous event remains primarily a ritual of collective belonging, and little effort is made to welcome the many outsiders who come to witness it. Though it has spawned many cheap imitations in other Belgian towns, the genuine article is jealously guarded by the locals, who are not allowed to collaborate in such exports, since doing so would demean this unique bond between them.

Despite the uncharacteristic decorum strictly maintained throughout, there is no mistaking the features of archaic agrarian rites: the rhythmic gait with heavy wooden clogs to a steady drumbeat as a dance to trample the ground so as to awaken its fertility and chase away evils—with the help of a ritual rod—and the spreading of fruitfulness through an ongoing offering of bread—which has been replaced by the throwing of at least 300 oranges by the Gilles to the crowd ever since railways have made it possible to import them all the way from Spain.

Food Fights and Seasonal Scapegoats

In Spain, as in Portugal and parts of Southern France, things were a lot rowdier when not only oranges and lemons, but lupines (as in ancient Rome's **Floralia**), flour, eggs, mud, and a variety of unsavory fluids were thrown at passersby with the same implicit symbolism. Such life-giving aggression might include pitched battles using wax lemons, plaster eggs, corncobs, and beans (blown through straws) as projectiles, as well as brooms and wooden spoons as hand-held weapons. Verbal abuse and obscene gestures, mostly under the cover of bawdy humor (evident in cross-dressing), did not exclude actual street brawls in the popular quarters of Spanish cities like Seville, where women would deliberately provoke them.

True to the inner logic of the primitive crowd psychology thus ritualized, all the energies of life and death were first exercised and then exorcized under the rule of a temporary **Carnival** king. This was usually a kind of colorful dummy who no doubt stood in for a former human scapegoat like the one who used to be sacrificed at the end of the year-end Roman **Saturnalia** after having presided over all its excesses and social inversion. In some places, a real scapegoat was even appointed to be the butt of the public, as in Oviedo until as late as 1867. Elsewhere in Spain, the poor, customarily dealt with in a kindly manner until the end of the eighteenth century, would suddenly find themselves fair game for all manner of derision and cruel taunts, in a perverse twist of social inversion. As a rule, the **Carnival** king took all the credit and all the blame for the unleashing of passions—listed in detail by a monk who denounced all the sins indulged in by *Don Carnal* (as he was known in Spain) in the sermon closing the **Carnival** and opening **Lent**.

In modern times, a similar practice has been revived since 1981 in a Vaucluse valley, in a lively parody of French central administration and Provençal village life, when all of the bad blood between members of the community and any resentments at broader social or natural conditions may be freely vented at the moot trial of *Caramantran* (a name derived from a phrase meaning "entering **Lent**") at the end of the Murs **Carnival**. In order for the community to put behind itself all its pent-up frustrations and the guilt of their unruly release, the final outcome is invariably the same—the **Carnival** king's execution by any combination of methods: gunshot, fire, water, reflecting the range of nature's violent energies. Being scapegoated as

the embodiment of unruly passions as well as of their past and coming repression, the king is also mourned as both their short-lived liberator and a redeemer from the personal guilt incurred by all under his brief rule. For it is marked both by dangerously antisocial freedom and by the community's renewed "partnership in crime"—sealed by the collective murder of a scapegoat. In Murs, all can then partake in the *crespeou*—a communal meal having as a centerpiece a large omelet that uses up all the eggs soon to be forbidden for the duration of **Lent**. In the English-speaking world, **Mardi Gras** is also known as "**Pancake Tuesday**" for similar reasons.

The pig often had an important role to play in the **Carnival**. In Madrid, a rowdy ceremonial, immortalized in the Goya painting *Burial of the Sardine*, was held until the outbreak of the Spanish Civil War in 1936. However, it did not owe its name to the fish that was about to become standard **Lent**en fare, but to a certain pig bone. It was also out of pig's bladders that the balloons formerly used to hit people at the Nice **Carnival** and to this day by the *Clovis* clowns of the Rio **Carnival** were originally made.

In Renaissance Rome, the stately **Shrove Tuesday** parades still culminated with an archaic sacrifice reminiscent of the all-important **pig feasts** of Oceanian cultures, when six carriages took live pigs up the fifty-meter high Monte Testaccio. The city's thirteen quarters each led a magnificent fierce bull in procession to tether it to one of the carriages. The raging bulls would stampede behind the carriages (draped in red to excite them) when they were suddenly sent careening downhill and over a cliff, to crash on the rocks at the bottom. There, thousands waited to thrust spears into the mass of broken wood and torn limbs, providing the meat for a massive early morning **Ash Wednesday** feast.

Cats have often been favorite scapegoats, especially during **Carnival**. In Renaissance Venice, this was a favorite time for the "Cat Game," in which men shaved their heads and used them to crush a cat that had been spread-eagled on a plank or a pole. (The nasty Fascist character played by Donald Sutherland gives a memorable demonstration of this Italian game in Bernardo Bertolucci's 1975 family saga *1900.*) In Denmark, where **Fastelavn** (pronounced "Festalawn") is now limited to **Fat Sunday** as a time for children to dress up and go trick-or-treating for seasonal cream cakes (*fastelavnsboller*), they also play a game of "killing the cat in the barrel" with a stick, although the animal is now made of paper. In Brazil, the sacrifice of a cat traditionally marks the climax of **Carnival** in Bahia. There, as in Rio, "making a cat's skin speak" means playing the *cuica*, since cat hide is supposed to be used in the making of this seasonal instrument—an open-ended drum with a metal stick in the middle to produce a high squeaky sound when it is rubbed with a wet cloth. Just as the *cuica* accompanies *baterias* or percussion ensembles in Rio, the similar (though closed) *petadou* is part of the traditional *vespa* ensemble of sculpted gourd instruments of the Nice **Carnival**. They are both relatives of the *Rummelpott* used on **Martinmas** or **New Year**'s Eve in Northern Europe as the eerie yet comical voice of the underworld.

From Venice to Nice: The Eagle and the Bat

It has also been reported that, since rabbit skins were in short supply, some 300 cats from the popular quarters of Nice were used to make the costumes of the forty bat impersonators who flapped their wings on the famous float called *Ratapignata* (the Nissart word for "bat"), which forever changed the character of the city's official **Carnival** in 1875. There, an organizing committee had been set up in 1873 by the local bourgeoisie and some wealthy winter residents, who wanted to attract more of the latter, since they had become wary of recent revolutionary movements ensuing from France's defeat at the hands of Prussia in 1870.

In the spirit of Victorian charity events, they decided to award prizes to allegorical floats and flower-covered carts at the various parades, as well as to cavalcades and masquerades. Originating in Renaissance Florence and further developed in Venice, such events had been features of the **Carnival** in Turin, capital of the Kingdom of Piedmont-Sardinia, to which Nice had belonged until 1860. They had become part of its **Carnival** after being first put on in honor of a royal visit in 1830. Some of the county's residents longed for Nice to return to the House of Savoy—which now ruled over a united Kingdom of Italy. This conservative, largely upper-class separatist party rallied around the committee's decision to award the first prize to an allegorical float depicting Caterina Segurana—the popular heroin of the city's resistance to a siege by France's Turkish allies in 1543. But the more lower-class French party, which was loyal to the newly founded Third Republic and was supported by the winter residents, bitterly contested the neglect of a widely favored, albeit unorthodox and fanciful, float on the theme of the bat.

The black bat symbolizes the inversion of the red imperial eagle of Savoy heraldry on Nice's coat-of-arms, since it hangs upside down by day and takes its flight under cover of night, in the dark realm of subconscious drives as opposed to the bright daylight of organized social life. The bat would endure as a kind of mascot of Nice's "wild side"—that of a native folk culture often overlooked by the cosmopolitan patrons of the Riviera's tourist industry and looked down upon by those who catered to them. It managed to find officially sanctioned expression at the **Carnival** after the 1875 *Ratapignata* affair, which forced that year's organizing committee to step down. From then on, the float parade would be given over to the grotesque fantasy and outrageous satire favored by the popular imagination, with stock characters developed by dynasties of float designers and master-builders. (One example is the

Babau dragon that started embodying the now-suppressed Paillon River in 1882—just when it was covered over by a new boulevard.)

By contrast, genteel allegory would be reserved for the "flower battle"—as the parade of flower-covered floats along the beachfront is known. While today scantily clad local beauties (succeeding the daughters of Nice's good families) throw flower bouquets at the spectators, this flower battle used to be more vigorous and less one-sided. It first broke out between the decorated carriages of the gala *corso* in which Nice's notables paraded before King Charles-Felix in 1830, and included not only flowers, but also rock candy *coriandoli* and flat, almond-shaped sugar *confetti*. Over the years, the **Carnival** battlefield expanded, and there was an arms race of sorts. The winter tourists at their windows and on their balconies and the locals on the streets below would confront each other—at first with "noble" missiles: flowers, candies, and cigars, and then with all manner of ammunition—dry vegetables like peas, soot or sawdust, eggs (which were often rotten), and especially flour (also often gone bad). There came a point where, replacing the original candies, plaster confetti became the weapon of choice in a total war from which there was no safety, so that one needed to go out in a dustproof overcoat with a protective wire mesh mask, armed with a large bag of confetti and a shovel. In 1892, paper confetti were invented by an engineer from Modane in Savoy (ceded to France along with Nice in 1860), recycling paper used in raising silkworms, and replaced the heavy plaster confetti, the use of which was now limited to certain days and events.

Today, the streets get white from the flour used liberally and aggressively in the wild neighborhood **carnival**s that have recently made a comeback in Nice (much as in Rio) with homemade floats and costumes, off the tourist-beaten track of the city's official **Carnival**. In the latter, aside from confetti, innocuously nonsticking colored foam sprays now largely replace all other projectiles along the course of both the flower and float parades. As highly organized spectator events, these have provided the model for other modern urban **Carnival**s that often started out as genteel bourgeois affairs, from that of the Viareggio beach resort near Pisa since 1873 to the Quebec Winter **Carnival** held continuoulsy since 1955 after some late-nineteenth-century precedents.

In 1998, after nineteen years of interruption, the *Gran Veglione*—an exclusive masked ball on a chosen theme, first held in Nice in 1873—was revived. The Venice **Carnival** that was a prototype for this Italian-style event was also revived for the benefit of tourists as of 1980. However, it now lasts only ten days, which is a far cry from the two months it took up before it died out at the end of the eighteenth century. It grew out of the Baroque taste among the ruling classes for exhibiting oneself as an allegory. The mask came to denote not so much the vertical inversion of social roles among the increasingly separate classes as the ability to escape them horizontally within their top ranks and to take liberties in the pursuit of private fantasies under the cover of conventional anonymity. This was now symbolized by a small domino mask for the eyes—white for men or black for women—and it was enough to pin one of these to one's hat in order to get away with unconventional behavior.

Brazil's Character Unmasked

Masks became all the rage in much of Europe and even in some colonies such as Louisiana, where the masked balls started under French rule in the 1740s remain the oldest component of the New Orleans **Mardi Gras** (followed by other European imports like pageants from 1827 and by the torchlight parade of King **Carnival** from 1857). However, masks were banned in Portugal in 1689, and this original focus of most modern **Carnival** traditions was long missing from those of Portuguese-speaking countries like the Cabo Verde islands and above all Brazil.

There, as in the rest of Latin America, **Carnival** instead evolved from the *Entrudo*—the Iberian food fight described earlier. In addition, so much water was used for it in Rio de Janeiro that it put the city's water supply at risk. One could not go out without an umbrella to avoid the dousing, which was accompanied by pelting with wax lemons that entire families—along with their slaves—would spend weeks making just for this occasion.

This was even true at the Imperial Palace in Rio de Janeiro, though eventually the tide began to turn. In contrast to the premodern disorder, both masked balls and competitive allegorical float parades (featuring a "Float of Criticism" about topical issues as well as beauties in risqué disguises) had already begun being organized by the bourgeoisie's *sociedades carnavalescas* in the middle of the nineteenth century. In 1888, Emperor Pedro II attended the Nice **Carnival** as part of his tour of Europe, and his Princess Regent Isabel was inspired by it to organize Brazil's first parade of flower-decorated carriages to celebrate the abolition of slavery she had decreed in her father's absence.

Similarly, on January 1, 1890, a Battle of Flowers patterned after that of the Nice **Carnival** by Francis Rowland was first organized in Pasadena, California by members of the Valley Hunt Club from the East Coast and the Midwest who wanted to celebrate the mild winters of their new home. This was eventually renamed the **Tournament of Roses**.

Meanwhile in Brazil, a military coup had made that country into a Republic, and urban middle-class propriety soon seemed to prevail over the festive excess of **Carnival**, as traditionally indulged in by both the landed gentry and the rural populace. For Black slaves too had begun to express their heritage under cover of their masters' *Entrudo* in the *lundu*—joining tribal dances and syncopated percussions.

Even the urban working classes then formed their own groups or *blocos* to sing and dance to the accompaniment of batteries of pots and pans, which used to be thrown out as part of the Iberian *Entrudo*. Recent, mostly Portuguese immigrants to southern Brazil turned the *ranchos de reis*—**Yuletide** processions dramatizing that of the Three Wise Men to the Christ Child for **Epiphany**—into the secular, satirical *rancho carnavalesco* accompanied by brass and string polka bands and waltz ensembles. Their European *modinhas* (or sentimental ballads) were eventually put to African rhythms to give the samba.

The first-known samba *Pelo Telephone* ("By Phone") was recorded in 1917. Soon the Rio suburbs took it up as the music for low-end *ranchos,* who were accompanied by enlarged rhythm sections due to lack of money for other instruments. The modern **Carnival** *bateria* was born. *Blocos* grew and organized, their largely illiterate members composing new songs in bars, until at the 1929 **Carnival** one of them stood out in the middle of a chaotic parade by its marching order, uniform costumes, and unified musical program. The idea of this first "samba school" caught on like wildfire, and others like it multiplied, vying for popularity in contests that became official along with the **Carnival** in 1935, since state authorities had come to appreciate its populist potential. Favored by the common people, the increasingly well-organized samba schools of the peripheral underclass with their itinerant miniature musicals came to compete seriously with the **Mardi Gras** costumed saloon-car parade of the *sociedades* and increasingly racy society masked balls, not to mention the ranchos of working-class districts.

A breakthrough came in 1948, when the samba schools' parade first extended over two days at the climax of **Carnival**. Both the samba schools and the underprivileged groups that invested endless energy and creativity (along with their meager resources) to maintain them had long been repressed, and even compelled to go underground or to seek sanctuary in official places of Afro-Brazilian pagan worship. They came to be recognized as bearers of the national character of a dynamic, multiracial Brazil, now embraced (and idealized) in all its diversity by the intellectuals, and they were supported as such by the urban middle class after about 1960. This was when Rio de Janeiro was replaced as federal capital by Brasilia, built from scratch to reflect this modern spirit by the famous Brazilian architect Oscar Niemeyer.

As if to confirm the convergence of Brazil's public identity with the **Carnival** as the scene of its egalitarian self-image—on which the poorest citizens temporarily take center stage, Niemeyer (who happened to be a Communist) would also design Rio's Sambadrome, a stadium holding over 50,000 people built in 1983 especially for the great competition of the samba schools. Each one slowly circles it as a kind of mobile Las Vegas revue in its own right that takes about an hour and a half to complete, so the whole show can last more than twenty hours—from one afternoon to the next —on the last weekend before **Lent**. The city of Rio de Janeiro also organizes about 100 balls and 50 free parades for **Carnival**.

Many feel this channeling of **Carnival**'s chaotic energy into well-organized events at well-defined venues and times goes against the original spirit of street-level spontaneity it epitomizes. They prefer to look for it in the less publicized, less tourist-oriented urban festivals of Brazil—not so much to the west in its other megalopolis São Paulo, as in those of the otherwise very poor Nordeste, in Recife or above all in Salvador de Bahia. This is where Brazilians go when they want to plunge headlong into no-holds-barred, old-fashioned **Carnival** madness as it sweeps through all the streets of a city, rather than look at a glittery parade going by on its predetermined path between rows of spectators.

In Bahia, this traditional spirit has been galvanized by a technological innovation first introduced in 1950. The orderly *corso* of expensive convertibles in which the rich liked to show

off in fancy costumes as they threw streamers and confetti on less fortunate onlookers was then thrown into disarray when a radio technician and a small garage owner burst in driving a 1929 Ford they had rigged up with electric instruments connected to the battery. The crush of the frenzied crowd suddenly swarming around the jalopy carried it along without anybody noticing the motor had given out. The next year, a third player joined the original two in a Chrysler van equipped with a small generator, two amplifiers and eight fluorescent lamps; the *trio elétrico* was born. This name was kept for other customized musical trucks that would multiply and expand in size and power from 1952 onward. Today, they may be fifteen meters long, four meters high, and hold a recording studio—complete with air-conditioned bar and washrooms for the show going on on the rooftop stage with tropical props—as thousands of light-bulbs blaze, and dozens of speakers blare the demonic rhythms that keep in thrall the entranced throngs furiously jumping up and down in their wake. The phases and traits of the contagious possession taking hold of an electrified crowd in the procession of Bahia's electric gods has been compared point by point to the unfolding of the **Dionysian** rituals described in Euripides' play *The Bacchae*, to show the ancient roots and perennial wellsprings of **Carnival** celebrations.

See also Ashura; Candlemas; Christmas; Dionysia; Epiphany; Feast of Fools; Floralia; Games (Rome); Holi; Lent; Lupercalia; Martinmas; Midsummer; New Year (West); Purim; Saturnalia; Thargelia; Yom Kippur

References
Daniel Crowley. *Bahian Carnival*. Los Angeles: Museum of Cultural History, UCLA, Monograph No. 25, 1984.
Umberto Eco, V. V. Ivanov, and Monica Rector. *Carnival!* New York: Mouton Publishers, 1984.
Albert Goldman. *Carnival in Rio*. Photos by Douglas and Lena Villiers. New York: Hawthorn Books, 1978.

Maria Julia Goldwasser. "Carnival," in Mircea Eliade, ed. *The Encyclopedia of Religion*, Vol. III. New York: Macmillan, 1987, pp. 98–104.

Samuel Kinser. *Carnival, American Style: Mardi Gras at New Orleans and Mobile*. Photos by Norman Magden. Chicago: University of Chicago Press, 1990.

Annie Sidro. *Carnaval à Nice*. Nice: Serre Éditeur, 1993.

CASK-OPENING
See Dionysia

CAT NIGHTS
See Assumption

CERIALIA, CERTAMEN
See Games (Rome)

CHALANDA MARZ
See New Year (West)

CHEESEFARE WEEK
See Carnival, Lent

CHERRY BLOSSOM FESTIVAL (JAPAN)

Japan's most famous festival may be the **Cherry Blossom Festival** called *Hanami* or "**Flower-Viewing**." It celebrates the weeklong flowering of the cherry trees in the early spring.

A Festival of Fleeting Beauty

Japanese people experience this as the best illustration of their typical aesthetic and spiritual sensibility, summed up in the phrase *mono no aware* by the literary scholar Motoōri Norinaga (1730–1801) to refer to the sadness that is inevitably bound up with the experience of beauty, because nothing lasts. This Buddhist sense of impermanence is joined to Shinto communion with nature in the joyous,

yet solemn, way the Japanese relate to the short-lived, overwhelming beauty of the pink and white cherry flowers. There are two hundred varieties of cherry trees now growing in Japan. And yet this national symbol is not indigenous to the country. Cherry trees were first introduced over a thousand years ago. They are in bloom at different times in different places, depending on the latitude and the particular variety growing there. The seven-day **Flower-Viewing** Festival can accordingly be held as early as March in the South and as late as May in the North. For these two months, huge crowds of Japanese people travel by car, by bus or by train to gather in whichever stretch of the archipelago happens to be the current scene of this fleeting, yet ever-recurring wonder of nature. This is especially true during the so-called **Golden Week**, when most people in Japan get several days off in a row connected to a weekend, so as to bridge three successive holidays: the first is April 29, which is Emperor Hirohito's birthday and is still observed even after his death in 1989 as **Greenery Day** (*Midori no Hi*) to perpetuate his concern, as a marine biologist, for the natural environment; the second is **Constitution Memorial Day** (*Kenpo Kinen Hi*) on May 3; and finally comes **Children's Day** (*Kodomo no Hi*) on May 5, preceded by another statutory holiday on May 4, which was enacted in 1985 to bridge the latter two.

Floral Pilgrimage Sites

A favorite station on **Hanami**'s floral pilgrimage is Mount Yoshino on Honshu Island. Tradition holds that this is where a Buddhist monk planted the first cherry trees in Japan. Over 100 thousand wild cherry trees now grace the mountain's slopes. A long time ago, it was only the Emperor and his retinue that used to go there from nearby Kyoto, the former capital. But nowadays, people of all classes go by the thousands in the early morning, when the mountain is still shrouded in fog, and the smell

A troupe of women dancers wears traditional Japanese kimonos at the Cherry Blossom festival in Kyoto, Japan. (Jack Fields/Corbis)

of the flowers is said to be particularly subtle and heady. Many artists over the centuries have depicted Mount Yoshino at this time in the spring, as it seems to be floating in mid-air. At the local temple of the Shingon sect of Buddhism, priests burn green leaves in order to get the attention of the *kami*—Japanese deities of the land and the elements.

In Kyoto itself, the Heian shrine is one of the many sacred precincts where people gather to meditate in silence as they gaze at the cherry trees in bloom in the park. They come in such numbers that each person has a time limit of an hour to do it. People who have an inauspicious horoscope can write it on a strip of paper and tie it around a blooming bough, in the hope that the cherry tree will cancel the ominous predictions and bring good fortune instead. All through the cherry blossom season (from

around late March to early May), the Kodai-ji temple is splendidly illuminated from dusk till about half past nine.

Dignified Secular Entertainment

Not all **Hanami** observances are particularly religious or magical in character, but they tend to be rather formal and always highly aesthetic. Each year, novice geishas (called *miko*) perform elaborate ceremonial dances (called *miyako, kyo,* and *kitano*) in honor of the cherry tree (called *sakura*) on the main stage of Kyoto's Kabureno Theater, which is decorated with pink trees. During intermission, the audience is offered tea and is shown around the garden's cherry trees. In fields and parks in town and country, friends, relatives and neighbors—often joined by passersby—gather for cheerful picnic lunches under the blossoming trees.

Sometimes dressed in their best kimonos, they may get up afterward to perform very dignified classical dance figures with fans to recorded or broadcast traditional melodies. These picnics on the grass under the cherry trees began as a way to mark the beginning of the agricultural calendar and have been popular in all walks of life from the seventeenth century onward. They may now also be organized in the Japanese gardens of botanical gardens in the West; thus, at the one in Montreal, Japanese lunchboxes are even prepared for the visitors who reserve a place in advance, though apple trees in bloom have to stand in for the cherry trees.

See also Sekku

References

Isamitsu Kitakoji, and Jack and Dorothy Fields. *Cherry Blossoms.* Tokyo: Kodansha International, 1973.

Wybe Kuitert with Arie Peterse. *Japanese Flowering Cherries.* Portland, OR: Timber Press, 1999.

Manabu Miyoshi. *Sakura, Japanese Cherry.* Tokyo: Board of Tourist Industry and Japanese Government Railways, 1934.

▶ CHIAO (CHINA)

A chiao or "offering" (formerly known as *chai* or "retreat" in medieval times and also known as *hui* or "gathering") is a Taoist community festival centering on penitential observances and liturgical rites of cosmic renewal in a local Chinese temple.

Renewing the Cosmos and the Community

Normally, a *da-chiao* (great offering) should be held at the transition between one sixty-year cycle and the next. The cosmic significance of the number sixty is that it is the product of the number twelve (after the twelve animals or branches affecting each year in turn in an astrological cycle) and the number five (that of the five elements and the sum of two, the first even,

feminine or *yin* number, and three, the first odd, masculine or *yang* number). However, the sixty-year schedule is rarely observed nowadays, either due for instance to religious persecution causing a community to miss the appointed time and hold its **chiao** many years late, or on the contrary because economic prosperity allows temples to hold them at shorter intervals—of ten years for example in many Hong Kong temples. The end of an old cycle and the beginning of a new one is a proper time to reaffirm the integrity of the community that unites people with each other and with their protective deities. The same holds true for the dedication of a temple after it has been built or renovated, so that it is very common to have a special "construction offering"—*chien-chiao*—on such occasions. Other kinds of **chiao**s may be celebrated to be delivered from a drought, in thanksgiving for relief from an epidemic, or to exorcise the spirits of disease causing such disasters, like the "plague expulsion ritual" performed every three years in the southern Taiwanese town of Tungkang, where they are literally sent packing on a drifting boat. In addition to these external agents of evil and peril, the community must rid itself of its own inner impurities and restrictive old energies as well, down to the ritual confession of individual sins. Only then can the blessings of peace—*p'ing-an*—from above be bestowed on it by the Great Triad of heavenly powers, which it is the job of priests to bring down through rituals to restore the harmony of the community and rekindle its spiritual energies.

Preparation

These rituals could take fifty days or longer in ancient times, but today they are more likely to last either nine, seven, or most commonly five or three days, due to the high cost of putting on such elaborate affairs. (Sometimes, two extra days are added before the **chiao** proper for an exorcism of fire and water at the start of a new era, so as to pacify the volatile spirits of these two elements that can so easily turn destructive in accidents and bad weather.) It is the board of directors of a temple which decides the time is coming to hold a **chiao**, and sets up different committees (under a general planning committee) to take charge of the tasks involved in its organization, such as finances, equipment, venue, catering, travel, traffic control, and of course the rituals themselves. Preparations begin at least a year in advance (or in the larger temples several years ahead) of the lucky date selected by fortune-tellers or a medium. For instance, special symbolic objects have to be collected, and the main Taoist temple needs to be refurbished while many temporary additional shrines are erected for the occasion. This construction work is among the biggest expenses, along with the priests' wages. To finance this whole operation, each household on the temple's territory is taxed, and prominent community members make large donations in exchange for fancy honorific titles and getting listed as such in temple records. Also, shelf space around the temple's sanctuary is rented out on the basis of size and location to the sometimes thousands of visiting deities whose statues are brought over from other temples to witness the local rituals, and get recharged by the extra boost of beneficent power they imbibe there. The entire community gets involved through volunteer work, which in itself works miracles in renewing social bonds of cooperation, by allowing people to gain personal prestige within it and project civic pride beyond it, to start a new cycle on the right foot in the spirit of the **chiao**.

To this same end, certain meritorious acts are called for in the weeks preceding a **chiao**. They may include the repayment of debts, moral as well as financial, demonstrations of filial piety, purification through a vegetarian diet, and penitence through charity. As the time for the rites approaches, temple guards will be on the lookout around the sacred precinct, ready to deny access to anyone wearing leather, woolen, or white objects, because of their association with death.

Welcoming Heavenly Guests

All classes of spiritual beings are invited to attend the ceremonies—aside from human dignitaries and foreign visitors: they range from ancestors and souls from the underworld that may find rest on this occasion, to the liberated Buddhas and bodhisattvas who join up with Taoist and folk deities and the immortal founders of Taoist sects. At a larger **chiao** like a sixty-year one, an endless succession of gods or goddesses, impersonated by devotees in solemn poses and lavish costumes, may be carried on a float that is pushed in a procession. In any **chiao**, wealthy families set up special shrines to host these celestial dignitaries, while the small images from country shrines are put on a platform before the main temple. Yet rich and poor, clergy and laymen all address their petitions to them in similar fashion: they take a bundle of five, twenty-one, or any lucky number of joss sticks, put the lower end to their chest, their forehead, and sometimes their head, and point the burning end in each of the five directions (including the zenith) before sticking them in the sand of the incense-burners, where they shine like hundreds of dots of light among scented clouds of smoke.

Every day of the festival begins with an announcement (*fa-piao*) and an invitation (*ch'ing shen*) to all these gods and spirits to come down and take part in the festival. This welcome, part of a liturgy that goes back largely to the early days of organized Taoism, is offered by the specially enlisted professionals of the Way or *Tao shih* (pronounced "dawshr"), the hereditary priests of the spiritual lineage of the second-century patriarch Chang Tao-ling, founder of the Way of the Celestial Masters or *T'ien-shih Tao*. Called "Blackheads" (*wu-t'ou*) after their headgear as opposed to the "Redheads" (*hung-t'ou*) of enthusiastic folk religion, they are trained in the rituals described in the vast collection of sacred literature known as *Tao tsang*. A high priest and at least four other priests (up to twelve or fourteen in larger temples) with four or five liturgical musicians are each paid a fee to perform their office in the local temple, wearing elaborate red vestments.

During a service, the head priest (*tao-chang*) stands in the main courtyard of the temple with two cantors: one on his right who leads the alternating singing as the representative of *yang* forces, and an assistant on his left representing *yin* forces. The chanting of canons of repentance is associated with the first day. It is also taken up by the Purification of the Sacred Area—a succession of exorcism rites behind closed doors, where the priest sprinkles holy water everywhere, writes sacred formulas in the air, wields a ritual sword to cut down evil, before the attempted stealing of the gods' incense-burner by a demon is acted out—often by a professional actor playing the part of the devil catcher Chung K'ui.

Between Heaven and Hell

Held on the first or second evening in most cases, to recall pre-Taoist rites of seasonal renewal for fire and water, *fen-teng* is the Consecration of **New Fire**—brought inside the temple for the Great Triad of deities. At the end of the day, toward midnight, talismans symbolizing the five life-giving cosmic elements will be placed in the five directions of the temple, in a key ritual aimed at renewing the community by implanting these five energies in it as microcosm, once the master has drawn them from primordial inner space into his own body with meditation.

Starting on the second day, the master uses the same method to ascend to the heavens so as to draw into himself and channel to the community the powers of the three supreme deities. These audiences with the threefold Tao are spread out over the morning, midday and evening. It is also at night that the focus shifts to ancestors and the dead in general. Aside

from burning huge stacks of spirit paper money as an offering to facilitate their journey, they are invited to join in the last day's feast by paper lanterns that are either hung atop bamboo poles—to attract the land ghosts, or attached to small rafts and lit up before being released on the waves of the sea or of a river that leads them out to it—to call up the sea ghosts.

On the third or final day, a special rite of homage to the Jade Emperor (chanting his scripture) precedes the *Tao Ch'ang* ceremony, that completes the renewal of the cosmos by bringing all Three Pure Ones of Taoism (that is, in addition to the Pure August One just mentioned, the August Ruler of the Tao, and the August Old Ruler representing a deified Lao-Tzu) into a compact with the local people. Their names and petitions, with an account of the festival, appear in a memorial presented first to a host of heavenly worthies inside the temple, and then to the Jade Emperor outside.

A great banquet is then offered to the souls of the underworld, each family having brought dishes for display on tables set up on temple grounds or a nearby field. Row upon row of goats and pigs (some of the latter fattened over years to weigh close to a ton) also rest on tables or on special wooden frames, while ducks may be dressed up with masks as the same gods whose statues stand on temple roofs to guard against evil curses, and cakes and fruits are artfully arranged in piles alongside impeccably aligned bottles of wine, beer, and lemonade. In the evening, the priests, in addition to their prayers for the well-being of the country and for world peace, for enough rainfall in the countryside and for the city's protection from typhoons, come out to bless these offerings and chant the scriptures of salvation (*tu-jen ching*) in the hope of giving rest to the hungry ghosts who have just partaken of them, and of ultimately releasing them from hell, into a better life. Yet in ancient times, after this rite of universal salvation (*p'u-tu*), all hell would break loose as hundreds of beggars scrambled for the food left physically intact by the ghosts' banquet.

Nowadays, individual families pay caterers to organize this final banquet for their own benefit after the spirits have enjoyed it and all the deities have been thanked and sent back to their sacred homes. But in case gods or men are ever in doubt that the proper ritual of renewal has recently been offered for the entire community, each family receives a yellow certificate to this effect to put up over its home altar. All can then relax and enjoy an evening **carnival** with festive entertainment ranging from crassly pornographic sideshows, through classical opera, to ritualized Punch-and-Judy shows where the puppets have been consecrated as gods, and are often handled by Taoist masters, to reflect the cosmic play of good and evil, reality and illusion.

All through the **chiao**, but especially before people sit down to partake of the final banquet, mediums (that is, Taoists of the Redhead persuasion) are also on hand to allow people to communicate with heavenly powers or with the spirits of dead relatives or even of historical characters. These specialists of kung-fu (in the full sense, encompassing a whole range of "meritorious action" aside from the better known martial arts) do this by falling into a trance, often induced by whirling dances and various forms of self-laceration under the spirits' control. In the midst of their speaking in tongues, they may then allow the spirits to answer through them the public's questions about whether they liked the offerings they got at the **chiao** and will be kind to the mortals over the new cycle it ushers in. Though the Redhead mediums can also give people private consultations for anything that ails them in body or in soul, including business concerns and political problems, their public seances are most popular. Proceeds from these Redhead sideshows are very helpful in complementing the community-based financing of the more formal and elaborate Blackhead liturgical affair that takes center-stage at a **chiao**.

See also Days of the Dead (China, Korea, Japan)

References

John Lagerwey. *Taoist Ritual in Chinese Society and History.* New York: Macmillan, 1987.

Julian F. Pas and Man Kam Leung. *Historical Dictionary of Taoism.* Lanham, MD: Scarecrow Press, 1998.

Michael Saso. *Taoism and the Rite of Cosmic Renewal.* Pullman: Washington State University Press, 1990.

▶ CH'I CHIEH, CHI CH'IAO T'IEN
See Cowherd and Weaving Maid

▶ CHILDERMAS, CHILDREN'S CARNIVAL
See Feast of Fools

▶ CHILDREN'S DAY
See Sekku

▶ CHILDREN'S FESTIVAL
See Lantern Festival

▶ CHILSEOK
See Cowherd and Weaving Maid

▶ CHOAI
See Dionysia

▶ CHONGJIU, CHONG YANG
See Double Nine

▶ CHOYO NO SEKKU
See Sekku

▶ CHRISTMAS (CHRISTIANITY)
Christmas is a festival of light in two senses: as the church feast of the **Nativity of Christ**—the transcendent Light of the world entering it as a lowly human being, and as the pagan celebration of the winter solstice—when sunlight starts growing back in strength just after having

reached its lowest ebb. The two meanings of **Christmas** are intertwined in the host of seasonal observances that have developed around it in the many cultures of the Christian world, as varied as the local backgrounds out of which they grew, yet united by certain recurrent themes from ancient nature religions as well as from theology.

Advent

Christmas is preceded by **Advent**, a preparatory period instituted by the church in the sixth century. It already existed in Gaul and Spain at the end of the fourth century, in the guise of three weeks of ascetic preparation, initially aimed at converts who were to get baptized at **Epiphany**. At that time, this feast was still second only to **Easter**, because the feast of the **Nativity** was just getting detached from it to become **Christmas**. The Roman Church gave **Advent** a less ascetic, more festive liturgical character as the new **Nativity** celebration developed. The old pagan term *adventus* came to be understood in a new eschatological sense, to refer to the advent of Jesus as the promised Messiah, not only through his humble human birth as foretold at the **Annunciation** to the Virgin Mary, but also in view of his Second Coming in glory at the end of time. These remain the themes of the four **Advent** Sundays before **Christmas** and used to be those of the *Regem venturum* ("Future King") nightfall services of the novena preceding the feast. The services from December 17 to 23 were known for the *O* antiphons addressing Christ by a different name or attribute each day, from *O Sapientia* (Oh Wisdom) on the seventeenth to *O Emmanuel* on the twenty-third.

In Northern European folklore, it was the custom to plant four candles—one every Sunday—in the braided **Advent** crown. In France, **Advent** was traditionally a bad time to get married, to do the laundry, to go out with friends at night, when will-o'-the-wisps and ghosts were roaming; but it was the proper time to clean the house, stables, and sheepfold, and to renew the furniture and utensils, as used to be the case in Finland too, and it still is in Sweden on the occasion of the **Advent** feast of **Saint Lucy** (*Sancta Lucia*) more specifically.

In the Eastern Church, the initial ascetic focus of **Advent** has remained: it is not even called "**Advent**," but the "**Christmas Lent**"—a forty-day fast like the one before **Easter**. Yet a joyful mood prevails during the five days of prefeast celebration before the **Nativity of Christ**. Thus, Orthodox services do not emphasize the Second Coming as in the Latin West, but the precondition for this ultimate fulfillment in the first blossom of the Incarnation of God, leading up to the redemption of mankind at **Easter** in the resurrected life of Christ as the New Adam.

Midnight Mass

At the origin of the feast's English name (*Cristes Maesse* is first recorded in 1058), Roman Catholic services for **Christmas** are unique in that the mass is celebrated four times: with a vigil mass and a night mass on **Christmas** Eve, and a dawn mass and a day mass on **Christmas** Day. "When peaceful silence lay over all, and night had run the half of her swift course, down from the heavens, from the royal throne, leaped your all-powerful Word." Owing its timing to this passage about the Exodus, as applied to Christ in the Book of Wisdom (*Jerusalem Bible* 1968, 18:14), the midnight mass that bridges the two days is the focus of popular traditions playing on the anticipation of the wondrous occasion of a joyful gathering of the whole community in the middle of the deepest winter night. This brings about a transfiguration of the cold and dark by the sheer overflow of human warmth and fellow feeling, often underlined by feasting and gift-giving once the family is back home—which used to be welcome relief after a long day of fasting. The emotional appeal of midnight mass has endured in secularized Western societies: for many people, this is the only mass they attend all year, be it only as a quaint prelude to their private family gatherings.

Christmas Meals

As for the special **Christmas** meals, their main course depends on local custom. For Estonians, it was long vital to have blood-pudding heated with lard on **Christmas** Eve, or major trouble might ensue over the coming year. Their Finnish cousins however used to have rice porridge (still favored in Denmark) and stockfish after coming back from the outdoor sauna that night, but now they mostly have cold cuts. Pork was the favorite dish in Russia and still is in Europe from Greece to Germany, as well as in French Canada, whose *tourtière* meat pies and *cretons* mince stand out in the midst of English-speaking North America with its **Christmas** turkeys. Yet pork was originally preferred in England too, where **Christmas** turkeys appeared in 1542, after the species was introduced from America; but they only became popular at the turn of the next century—partly in imitation of King James I, who did not like pork. In France, customs vary: if Parisians have oysters, caviar and *foie gras*, turkeys are also eaten in Burgundy, and geese are preferred in Alsace—as they are in Denmark, along with ducks. Among traditional desserts are fruitcakes, because they are a promise of plenty in the **New Year**. This also goes for Britain's plum pudding, eaten at lunch on **Christmas** day.

In Poland, the **Christmas** meal takes place long before midnight mass, at the end of a day of fasting that can only be broken when the first star appears. On a pattern also found in Southern Europe (though the symbolic number there may also be thirteen or seven), but mostly through much of Eastern Europe, the Polish dinner consists of twelve traditional dishes, supposed to stand for the Twelve Apostles. It starts with the solemn breaking of a **Christmas** loaf, said to evoke the Last Supper, which the father passes to all family members standing around the table (one place being left empty for Christ), so each of them can make three wishes. Sometimes, he may instead break an unconsecrated host previously blessed by the local priest for him to distribute to the family, giving each member his best wishes as he does. In the Serbian version of this family blessing as part of a final meat-free meal, a piece of the **Christmas** loaf is put aside for the first **Christmas** visitor as a bringer of good luck—like the first **New Year** visitor elsewhere (and much as departed relatives used to be symbolically included in this family gathering in Russia). Also, whoever finds the coin hidden in the bread will be blessed over the year—which is reminiscent of Greek **New Year** and Western **Epiphany** customs about the King of the Bean. As a rule, the actual feasting, including meat aplenty, does not follow the **Christmas** Eve vigil as in the West, but only the **Christmas** morning liturgy.

The Christmas Crib

In Eastern and Western **Christmas** services alike, the faithful sing, "Glory to God in the highest, and on earth peace, good will among men!" This is the song of praise of the host of angels that suddenly appeared to the shepherds at Bethlehem after one brought them "news of great joy, a joy to be shared by the whole people. Today in the town of David a savior has been born to you, he is Christ the Lord. And here is a sign for you: you will find a baby wrapped in swaddling cloths and lying in a manger" (*Jerusalem Bible* 1968, Luke 2: 10–14).

This sign is the basis of the religious and folkloric practice of the **Christmas** crib, reproducing the scene of Christ's birth in a cave outside Bethlehem, where it probably originated, so that pilgrims brought home this image on small flasks of holy water or oil called *ampullae*. Local imitations are thus attested as early as 248 by the theologian Origen, and in a sermon of December 20, 386, Saint John Chrysostom mentions how he is looking forward to finding the Lord lying in his crib in every Christian home. He was the bishop of Constantinople, where there was a tradition of building a grotto in every church on the day of the **Nativity**, with a child lying on a mattress inside it to represent the Christ Child. In Rome since at least 435, the crib was long confined to the Church of Santa Maria Maggiore—first called until the ninth century *Sancta Maria ad Praesepe,* which means "Saint Mary's of the Crib" in Latin; it was built there in the context of a permanent reproduction of the original cave in which Christ was born, since a fragment of the latter was kept as a relic. Saint Francis of Assisi put up the first actual manger filled with straw as a *presepe* in the nearby forest in Greccio in 1223, in combination with an actual ass and ox to represent the ones held by custom to have kept the Christ Child warm with their breath. He even put an altar in it to celebrate **Christmas** mass, since he wanted the people to better understand its meaning with the help of these props. **Christmas** cribs are therefore still set up in all of Assisi's churches, streets and squares, while the shepherds of Abruzzi and Calabria used to come down to play fifes and bagpipes as they sang a *cantata dei Pastori* about their Bethlehem colleagues in front of Roman churches on **Christmas** Eve.

Since the sixteenth century, evolving from three-dimensional sculptures on church altars, **Nativity** scenes have been put together in a variety of forms and combinations of live and crafted figures, primarily in Catholic countries—Sweden being a belated exception. Monasteries sometimes had such scenes for all feasts of the church year and might even set up "**Lent**en cribs," while princely courts allowed ever more detailed depictions of popular life and exotic costumes to crowd out the **Christmas** story itself. Such local flights of fancy had a free rein with the Catholic Counterreformation's successful use of the crib as a propaganda tool for the Roman church, once the Council of Trent (1545–1563) authorized departures from the canon in the characters shown as present in Bethlehem at the **Nativity**; it was soon thereafter that the first modern crib with movable characters was displayed in Prague by Jesuits. But in Southern Germany for instance, the En-

lightenment's repression of folk piety banned cribs from churches in the eighteenth century, allowing them to find pride of place in countless individual homes instead by the nineteenth century. This in turn gave rise to a flourishing church crib industry, as in Austrian Tyrol, while the Polish city of Cracow is known for its crib contest.

Yet with a host of popular traditions as well as historic centers of artistic **Nativity** scene production like Naples and Sicily, Italy is rivaled only by Southern France in this respect, especially since the development there in the seventeenth century of *pastorales*—**Nativity** plays (also known in Spain and related to Mexico's *posadas* or caroling quests led by Joseph and Mary impersonators), and in the late eighteenth century of *santons*—crib figurines made of clay (like the first man by God in Genesis). They both drew on the loving depiction of characters of traditional Provençal life, which proliferated in an endless variety of types and sizes. Since 1803, they are all displayed in an early December or January santon fair in booth upon booth along Marseille's main thoroughfare, the Boulevard de la Canebière. (Other **Advent** fairs in France are more similar to the older *Christkindlmarkt* or "Market of the Christ Child" found in many Germanic cities from Strasbourg to Vienna where the first one is recorded in 1278, often taking the form of a temporary "village" of booths displaying **Christmas** items and foods amidst a fairy-tale array of colored lights and decorations—the likely prototype of the **Christmas** lighting of commercial streets and shop-windows in all Western or Westernized urban centers.) Santons were not so prominent until well into the twentieth century in the long distinct County of Nice, which has however since 1942 made a specialty of "mechanized cribs"—whole landscapes with moving parts and crowds of santons (not unlike the ones that have been a family tradition for generations in a number of Czech towns).

A priest holds the crib in procession during the midnight mass celebrating the birth of Christ at St. Peter's Basilica, December 25, 2003, in Vatican City, Italy. (Franco Origlia/Getty Images)

Nice had used to be better known for its **Nativity** scene puppet shows, gradually supplanted in the last century by live pastorales like those of the rest of Provence. Both kinds of **Christmas** plays present variations on a common theme: typical representatives of all walks of preindustrial life (shepherds, merchants, notables, common people) receive the news of the Savior's birth and rush to the scene, thereby foiling the Devil's schemes as all forget their quarrels and mutual shortcomings to gather in wonder around the Christ Child in the crib.

Christmas Carols

Such a striving to realize—however fleetingly— "peace on earth, good will toward men" was institutionalized in medieval Europe's twelve-day **Christmas** truce, as well as in Greek Constantinople, where no one was to be arrested or put in jail on **Christmas** Day, no matter the crime. On the way to and from the morning liturgy at the basilica of Saint Sophia, the Emperor was welcomed and acclaimed at six different places by official representatives of the Eastern Roman capital's boroughs. Twelve poor people were invited at his festive luncheon along with officials and foreign guests, as living symbols of Christ's Twelve Apostles. During all twelve days of **Christmas**, from morning till late at night, the city's children went from door to door singing seasonal songs and wishes called *kalandai*. These were probably the first **Christmas** carols (though the word refers to the **calends of January**: the Roman **New Year**). Accompanied by adults playing instruments, Greek children might expect a tip when they threw in a flattering couplet for their host. Today, a Greek housewife gives them buns, chestnuts, and walnuts when, in town and country, they come singing *kalandai* from the break of day on **Christmas** Eve.

The demand for treats was more insistent in seasonal children's processions elsewhere in Europe. These collections were often made before **Christmas**, sometimes during all of **Advent**. The related terms *aguinaldo* and *guignolée* for this collection were used in Spain and France respectively. **Christmas**time food drives are still called *guignolées* in French Canada, as heirs to an old tradition of more adult caroling collections on behalf of the poor of every parish on the night of December 23. In the northern Spanish province of Asturias, older boys and unmarried girls might tag along with the tambourine-playing children singing *villancicos* (carols) from homestead to homestead, but they rarely got any of the sausages handed out to the *bona fide* youngsters. In the neighboring Basque Country straddling Spain and France, aside from money, children got chicken, ham, and eggs for the **Christmas** lunch, as well as apples and nuts they could eat in the meantime, when they went from door to door between seven and nine in the evening on December 24: *Eguberri,* the "New Season" or winter solstice in Basque. They were led by **Olenzaro**—Yuletide as personified by a pipe-smoking, black-faced coal man, who has been enjoying a revival in the guise of a regional Father **Christmas** handing out small gifts to children in an informal parade in most towns and many villages, largely due to the spread of Basque language-schools since the 1970s. And yet the traditional Basque songs for this occasion describe this unattractive character as a dim-witted, gluttonous drunkard, who used to be invoked to frighten children—when it was not the sickle as his main attribute, symbolizing the cutting away of the old to make way for the new, like the scythe of Saturn as Father Time often depicted in modern **New Year** imagery. It was often in effigy that **Olenzaro** was carried from house to house by youngsters, and sometimes expelled or burned in a lighthearted festive mood, like a

Carnival king embodying the old year. Though folklore depicts him as a messenger of Christ's birth, the charcoal-maker coming down from his mysterious workplace in the wild mountain forests points to the much older solar symbolism of new light coming out of pitch darkness like fire from embers—or a revived sun when the night is longest. Likewise, in much of Spain, there is a practice echoing classic **Midsummer** solstice customs: that of lighting bonfires called *hogueras* with torches and jumping over them in the belief this will keep illness at bay, the more so the higher the flames get.

In Russia, December 24 was the culmination of the winter solstice festival of the Slavic solar deity Koliada (a name possibly derived from both an old Russian word for something circular and the Greek word *kalanda*), starting around December 12. In time, its focus shifted from ancestor-worship and it came to acquire Christian trappings, such as the large eight-pointed wooden star of Bethlehem with an icon in the center that children and young people might carry on a stick as they did the rounds of a *kolyadovanye,* singing their wishes for wealth and a good harvest at every house in hopes of getting small gifts of food or money. In the former Russian colony of Alaska, every night between **Christmas** and **Epiphany** (that is, from January 7 to 19, since the Julian calendar is still followed), Orthodox Christians of all ages go "starring" from house to house or, in some cases in Western Alaska, from village to village, singing traditional songs in English as well as Slavic and Native American languages, talking about the holiday, and socializing at each stop. In the capital Juneau, they go starring to nursing homes and those of some church members, following two stars—one made in Juneau and the other in Western Alaska.

A similar questing pattern typified Russia's *ryazhen'ye* during the **Christmas** holidays or **Sviatki** (as well as on **Cheesefare Week** before **Lent** and in other Eastern Slavic lands), except that youngsters grouped in brotherhoods were rewarded for their mostly animal disguises. For instance, a bear or a goat might ritually resurrect somebody who played dead (at a time when the recently departed were kept in a shack outside the village until they could be buried in the spring), and aside from the "bull's game" and "goats' parades," there was much drinking to licentious songs and lewd gestures, all of which was no doubt meant to stir up and spur on the fertility spirits of new life still dormant under the frozen earth. In Rumania, adults may still wear goat masks and carry a decorated Morning Star, much like the Russians do, as they go from house to house to carol (*colindat* in Rumanian), and perform **Nativity** plays that seem to go back as far as ninth-century Constantinople.

Christmas Mummers

In Northern Europe, the Renaissance masque—an allegorical short play with masked actors—developed from **Christmas**time banquets at medieval courts, where the guests ended up joining on the dance floor the traveling mummers' troupes which had been entertaining them in bird masks or other animal costumes. Similarly, formal pageants of music and dancing evolved from rowdy year-end street entertainment, as in Philadelphia, where the latter was channeled into the official, century-old, competitive **carnival** of the **New Year**'s Day Mummers' Parade, featuring a succession of comics, fancy costumes, string bands, with fancy brigades to provide indoor entertainment.

Closer to the archaic origins of these seasonal revels, informal mummers still follow the Hooden Horse or the **Christmas** Bull over the Twelve Days of **Christmas** in some localities in Wales and the west of England, where the animal's wooden or skeletal head is mounted on a stick. The beasts can thus roam the streets and invade houses, bringing them fertility and luck and driving away lost souls. A hobbyhorse that would chase people with whips tipped with inflated bladders also used to figure in the mum-

mering practices brought from these same areas of Britain by the early settlers of Newfoundland. A province of Canada since 1949, this North Atlantic island is one of a handful of places in the world (another one being the tiny South Atlantic island of Tristan da Cunha) where they have survived in some form to this day, in remote outports. But leaving aside a few contemporary revivals in university towns, modern life and mass entertainment have been more successful in nearly stamping them out than legislation dating back to the sixteenth century in England and to 1861 in Newfoundland—after somebody died as a result of the rowdy excesses of mummering. "To mum" (from Momus—court jester of the Greek pantheon) means both "to mutter" and "to be silent"—two ways of concealing one's identity, aside from the bags and scarves worn on their heads by the outrageously costumed bands of cross-dressing revelers going from door to door (except for houses where there had been a death during the year), asking to be let in. They would have to admit who they were if someone succeeded in recognizing them as they loudly horsed around through the house demanding a drink before starting their performance. In the Middle Ages and since pre-Christian times, this would be a seasonal play about the death of winter and the old year (though mummering is also known at **Easter** and **Halloween**). This theme is echoed in the death and resurrection of the Turkish knight in his fight with **Saint George** the dragon slayer in the traditional mummers' plays long preserved in Newfoundland, and related to the **Carnival** *Fastnacht-spiel* and its Jewish equivalents on **Purim**. (In Ethiopia, this kind of festive inversion is brought to a violent pitch at the seasonal free-form hockey-like game of *ganna* that gives **Christmas** its common name in Amharic, since it is only played that January 7 afternoon in the Julian calendar, so roughly that injuries usually result by the end of the day, when victors abuse their defeated opponents with offensive limericks.) Over the years, these brief formal mummers' plays were eventually replaced on the island by more informal step dancing, accordion playing, and singing. If **Boxing Night** (December 26) was the high point of the mummering season, the afternoon of **Old Christmas** (January 6) at its tail end was set aside for "little mummers"—youngsters who would go their rounds in daylight and receive molasses cookies and **Christmas** candies.

The Winter Solstice

In the fifth century, Saint Cesarius (470–553), bishop of Arles in Provence, seems to have been alluding to similar pagan Winter Solstice practices when he denounced the seasonal habit of some supposed Christians of dressing up in cattle remains and wearing animal heads. There is little doubt that the date of December 25 for the **Nativity of Christ** was established around 330 largely in order to counter—or at least channel—not only these Celtic seasonal rites, but the ones current in Rome on this traditional date of the winter solstice. Since a decree by Emperor Aurelian (who saw himself as a solar epiphany) in 273, it officially marked the pagan holiday of the **Nativity of the Invincible Sun** (*Natalis Soli Invicti*), celebrating the start of the sun's victorious northward progress from its southernmost point on the horizon, as well as the birth of the Persian god Mithra from a stone as the bringer of light in Mithraism—an Oriental religion rivaling Christianity in popularity at that time. It also closely followed the Roman **Saturnalia** with their orgiastic social inversion and laborers' costume parades, and even **Hanukkah**—another **festival of lights** celebrated on the twenty-fifth day of the Jewish month of Chislev. Yet the fifth-century Pope Saint Leo the Great, at the end of his second "Sermon on the Feast of the **Nativity**," insisted that "the festival has nothing to do with sun-worship, as some maintain." He forcefully rejected "the pestilential notion of some to whom this our

solemn feast day seems to derive its honor, not so much from the **Nativity of Christ**, as, according to them, from the rising of the new sun. Such men's hearts are wrapped in total darkness, and have no growing perception of the true Light: for they are still drawn away by the foolish errors of heathendom, and because they cannot lift the eyes of their mind above that which their carnal sight beholds, they pay divine honor to the luminaries that minister to the world" (*A Select Library of Nicene and Post-Nicene Fathers of the Christian Church* 1997, pp. 131–132).

Still, unable to stamp out these practices, the early church not only learned to accommodate the general habit of celebrations on this date, but encouraged the faithful to see in the annual renewal of created light a symbol of the eternal dawn of uncreated Light, brought within easy reach by the coming of Christ, which thus freed mankind from bondage to the endless natural cycle of light and dark—life and death. There was good scriptural ground for depicting Christ as the true, though invisible, Light of the world, and to substitute the material sun of the solstice that comes and goes each year with the ever-unconquered spiritual Sun of Justice announced in one of the last verses of the Old Testament (Malachi 3:20 or 4:2, depending on the version). It is thus easy to see how seasonal symbolism is used to convey a theological truth in the Latin "O" antiphon (see above) for December 21: "Oh you Orient [i.e., Rising Sun], Splendor of the Eternal Light [of the Father], and Sun of Justice: Come enlighten those who sit in the darkness and shadow of death." It seems the Three Wise Men were already led by their very devotion to the heavens' natural lights to shift their allegiance to the Light without evening toward which the star of Bethlehem guided these fire-worshipping Persian kings, as they are referred to in the final prefeast matins of the Orthodox **Christmas** service.

A direct result of this double meaning of the solstice was the decoration of houses with

Christmas lights—usually candles (before electricity largely replaced them), whether they floated in water basins set in front of them, as in Spain, or they were set on window sills as elsewhere, often in combination with evergreen branches or with boughs of holly, bearing winter fruits. In northern Europe, shoots of quickblooming trees or flowers would be put in water in a warm room around the start of **Advent** in order to later produce the wonder of **Yuletide** blossoms—as harbingers of nature's springtime renewal. In Denmark, the flowering of the hyacinth used there is said to keep disease away from the house. In other places, setting evergreen decorations in the home before **Christmas** Eve and removing them after January 6 was thought to bring it bad luck. Foliage strewn with lights and small gifts already adorned ancient Rome at this time of year. As for the New Rome—Constantinople—the city's governor had the streets washed and decorated for **Christmas** with rosemary and myrtle and with columns decked with seasonal flowers.

The Christmas Tree

This came close to a kind of tree symbolism that the Western Church was not always so comfortable with, largely due to its age-old pagan association with fire from heaven—be it sunlight or lightning. But scattered attempts by Catholic or Protestant clergy to suppress the **Christmas** tree were no more successful than all those of the early Church against other **Yuletide** foliage. First recorded and depicted in Alsace in 1605, the **Christmas** tree was denounced as a revival of pagan tree-worship by the clergy of Strasbourg in the seventeenth century. Yet it was but an offshoot of the devotional plays of Paradise performed on church porches in Alsace in the Middle Ages on **Christmas** Eve as the day of Adam and Eve. In order to depict the Tree of Knowledge and the Tree of Life in the earthly Paradise, a tree that was still green was used. An evergreen fir tree soon came to be favored, which was thus decorated with red apples and white hosts, symbolizing the old mortal Adam and Christ as the New Adam respectively. It was likely Nuremberg merchants returning from the Strasbourg fair who popularized the **Christmas** tree throughout Germany, although its spread long met with some resistance in Catholic areas. There, it was seen as a Protestant practice, since Martin Luther is said to have decorated one with candles. Thus it was not until the second half of the twentieth century that it made a breakthrough in Catholic Italy, France, and Spain—as an American import.

The **Christmas** tree may have been first brought to the United States and Canada by German troops who fought in the British army in the War of Independence. It long remained confined to some German communities there as in Britain, where the one in Manchester had just begun to make it a local custom by the time Queen Victoria and her German Prince-consort Albert had a tree at Windsor Castle for **Christmas** 1841. (It was soon afterwards that the busy British civil servant and designer Sir Henry Cole asked an artist to create the first holiday card as a way to expedite seasonal greetings—an idea that was commercialized by merchants around 1868.) Czar Peter the Great had introduced the **Christmas** tree from Germany to the Russian nobility in the eighteenth century; it became part of the seasonal celebrations in Saint Petersburg in 1852, when one was lit up in front of Saint Catherine Railway Station. The habit of putting up **Christmas** trees in all public places seems to have first arisen in 1909 in Pasadena, California; imitated in New York City, it then turned into an unstoppable worldwide trend. The exception that confirms the rule is Greece, where it has recently been reversed in favor of boat models, as a reminder of sailors who used to spend **Christmas** at sea, but mostly as a way to save trees and preserve the forests.

The Yule Log

More entrenched in European folklore from ancient times than the **Christmas** tree, the **Yule** log now mostly survives in the shape of a **Christmas** cake devised to replace it by a Paris confectioner in 1875. *Yule* is an old Germanic word for the twelve-day gap or "loose end" between the start of the solar year and the end of the lunar year following the winter solstice, when the heavens also gaped, allowing the Wild Huntsman and his crew of lost souls to be seen and heard riding the season's storms. They take the form of gnomes called *tomter* in Norway, where people still visit their dead and decorate their graves on **Christmas**, and used to be wary of the pranks of those less welcome spirits (quite comparable in this to the *Kallikantzaroi* in the Balkans) over the twelve days to **Epiphany**—although the thirteen *tomter* of Iceland (perhaps still following the Julian calendar) concentrate their mischief before **Christmas**, starting on **Saint Lucy**'s on December 13. On the other hand, it is a scrawny, bearded *Jultomte* who traditionally puts the gifts at the foot of the **Christmas** tree in Scandinavian countries, where people still use the old pagan term *Jul* for the feast. Its equivalent *Joulu* also prevails in the Finno-Ugric languages of Finland and Estonia, which both once belonged to Sweden.

Nevertheless, it is in the folklore of some Balkan countries like Greece and Serbia, as well as in that of France and Britain, that the **Yule** log (as it is known on that island) long featured in customs that used to be remarkably pervasive, in endless variations. The log was often taken from a tree ritually cut down on **Christmas** Eve, or else was a choice log from the past year's supply of firewood (sometimes cut on **Candlemas** as the end of the previous **Christmas** season). It was burned in the hearth that night amid much ceremony, which could include aspersions of wine or oil, incantations, wishes, blessings, and the collaboration of the family's elder with a youngster, to parallel the replacement of the previous year's symbolic log with a new one. The **Yule** log was often kept in some form—either charred or ground to ashes—over the coming year to obtain protection from lightning, sorcery, human and animal diseases, and to promote the fertility of fields, animals, and people by contact with its remains. Spreading them or keeping the flame for all Twelve Days of **Christmas** was often vital: the number of sparks generated in the process was an indication of the positive results to be expected. Though its ashes might cure swollen glands, carelessly sitting on the chosen log could cause boils. Depending on local tradition, a range of tree species was favored: oak, ash, beech, olive, and fruit trees such as the pear tree—hence perhaps the latter's appearance as one of the gifts "my true love gave to me" in the famous **Christmas** carol.

The Twelve Days of Christmas

The twelve-day period bridging the twin winter feasts of **Christmas** and **Epiphany** is known by its Greek name of *Dodecahemeron* to the Church, which declared it festive at the synod of Tours in 567. It actually perpetuates pre-existing pagan winter holidays such as **Yule**, being a period of transition from one yearly cycle to another and, as such, a kind of supernatural microcosm of the year itself, with twelve days to match its twelve months. This has given rise to a variety of seasonal divination methods, be it about an unmarried girl's prospects for a wedding over the coming year, as in Russia and Greece, or about the weather of each one of its months, as in the West. There, many such pre-Christian observances have come to be associated with the saint who happens to be commemorated on a given day of the **Dodecahemeron**.

Whereas in the Eastern Church, the day after **Christmas** is dedicated to the Virgin Mary as the Mother of God and December 27 to **Saint Stephen**, this first deacon and first martyr of the Church is commemorated on December 26 in the West, while **Saint John** is honored on December 27. On his feast, called **Priests' Day**, Alsatians would begin preparing *Johannisminne*—

a schnapps-based orange liqueur; this was an auspicious day to start something new. **Saint Stephen**'s feast was **Deacons' Day** in medieval Europe, and was associated with death. Identifying with deacons and staging a mock martyrdom, boys in France and the British Isles would kill a wren—the king of all birds—as they sang from door to door, holding it up on a fir branch or a stick decked with holly or mistletoe. People would give them food in exchange for a feather, or else, for instance, a fisherman would be risking shipwreck. (In the long exclusively Irish copper-mining town of Butte, Montana, the **Day of the Wren** used to be observed under this name, even though children paraded a **Christmas** turkey's head instead.) **Saint Stephen**'s name means "crown" in Greek, and if his martyrdom defines the kind of spiritual kingship that Jesus Christ came to establish, it also overlaps with the ancient pagan pattern of the slaughter of the king at year's end.

The same ambiguity surrounds the commemoration of the **Slaughter of the Innocents** on December 28 (or 29 in the East), glorifying the children of Bethlehem whom the old king Herod had killed in a vain attempt to get at the newborn king Jesus. But just as the new year and daylight break free of a declining cycle, Jesus Christ escaped this darkest hour of peril and grew to invincible strength, while King Herod soon died. This reversal of the existing order to establish a fresh new one—often through the sacrificial shedding of innocent young blood—is a familiar feature of nature religions. This probably explains the social inversion of the **Feast of Fools** that was **Innocents' Day** on December 28 and January 1 in the Middle Ages, when the lower strata of society and of the human psyche ruled with complete abandon and irresponsibility for a day or more. Even though the feast of the **Holy Innocents** is still a day of merrymaking for children in Roman Catholic countries, in Rome itself it used to be a day of fasting and mourning. In England until the seventeenth century, children

were whipped in bed in the morning, so as to give them a sense of the pain felt for their sake by these early infant martyrs for Christ. The red berry sauce on the light-colored pudding still served on **Childermas** (as this feast is also known) symbolizes the blood they shed. In Ireland, this is known as "the day of the cross of the year"—*là crosta na bliana*—when it is best to refrain from any activity if one's endeavors are to be successful during the rest of the year—a taboo found in the **New Year** customs of many cultures around the world.

Boxing Day

The element of slaughter on the other hand may in part account for the fact that December 26 is the main traditional date for the foxhunt in the English countryside. In the towns of Great Britain and former colonies like Canada, the prevailing mood of this day is now the thrill of the hunt for bargains that brings crowds into the stores on their busiest day of the year, comparable only to what is known in the United States as **Black Friday**, when retailers' accounts leave the red the day after **Thanksgiving**. **Boxing Day** has its roots in the medieval custom of English feudal landlords giving their tenants utilitarian products—leather, linen, dried fish and meat, seeds to plant crops, and the like—in boxes when they went back to their cottages after **Christmas** festivities around the manor's church. It came to be somewhat resented as demeaning and fell into disuse, until it reappeared in a new urban setting in the nineteenth century on December 26. Upon returning from their **Christmas** day off, employees would each set a box at their workplace for the boss to put a little something in. Similar practices were long observed in the United Kingdom and its overseas possessions by servants, then by mailmen and milkmen, and finally by newspaper boys, until shopping outlets came up with the clever advertising ploy of slashing their prices on **Boxing Day**, as just such a belated "gift" to customers. **Boxing Day** discounts on **Christmas** cards, decorations, and gift wrapping are now part of the season—as the economic first seeds of the next year's cycle of holiday celebrations.

See also Ascension; Candlemas; Carnival; Days of the Dead (West); Easter; Epiphany; Feast of Fools; Hanukkah; Lent; New Year (Japan); New Year (West); Purim; Saint George; Saint Lucy; Saint Nicholas; Samhain; Saturnalia

References

R. J. Campbell. *The Story of Christmas.* New York: Macmillan, 1934.

Nina Gockerell. *Krippen—Nativity Scenes—Crèches.* Munich: Bayerisches Nationalmuseum, 1998.

Herbert Halpert, ed. *Christmas Mumming in Newfoundland. Essays in Anthropology, Folklore, and History.* Toronto: University of Toronto Press, 1969.

Jerusalem Bible. Garden City, NY: Doubleday and Co., 1968.

Claude Labat. *Olentzero. Le charbonnier qui ranime les braises du soleil.* Bayonne, France: Elkar, 2004.

A Select Library of Nicene and Post-Nicene Fathers of the Christian Church, 2nd Series, Vol. VII. Grand Rapids, MI: Eerdmans, 1997.

Tony van Renterghem. *When Santa was a Shaman. The Ancient Origins of Santa Claus and the Christmas Tree.* St. Paul, MN: Llewellyn Publications, 1995.

Herbert Henry Wernecke. *Christmas Customs Around the World.* Philadelphia, PA: Westminster Press, 1959.

▌ **CHRONIA**
See Saturnalia

▌ **CHRYSANTHEMUM FESTIVAL**
See Sekku

▌ **CHUN JIE**
See New Year (China, Korea)

▌ **CHUNG CH'IU**
See Mid-Autumn

▌ **CHUNG YUAN**
See Days of the Dead (China, Korea, Japan)

▌ **CHURCH NEW YEAR**
See Conception and Birth of the Virgin Mary

▌ **CHUSEOK, CHUSHU KANGETSU**
See Mid-Autumn

▌ **CIRCUMCISION**
See New Year (West)

▌ **CLEAN MONDAY**
See Carnival

▌ **COLACHO "BABY-JUMPING" FESTIVAL**
See Corpus Christi

▌ **COLD FOOD DAY**
See Days of the Dead (China, Korea, Japan)

▌ **COLOR (FESTIVAL OF)**
See Holi

▌ **COMING-OF-AGE DAY**
See New Year (Japan)

▌ **COMPITALIA**
See Caristia, Days of the Dead (West)

▌ **CONCEPTION AND BIRTH OF THE VIRGIN MARY (CHRISTIANITY)**

The first feast of the Catholic Church's liturgical calendar celebrates the Birth of the Mother of God, incarnate as Jesus Christ, on September 8. Alternatively known as the **Nativity of the Blessed Virgin**, it is complemented by another, lesser feast dedicated to Mary's conception by her parents, Joachim and Ann, coming nine months earlier: on December 8 in the Western Church, where Roman Catholics know it as the **Immaculate Conception**, and on December 9 in the Eastern Church, where it is called the

Native Indian women carry candles as they march to celebrate the day of the Immaculate Conception in Antigua Guatemala, on December 8, 2001. (Reuters/Corbis)

Conception of Saint Ann. The September 8 celebration of the **Nativity of the Virgin Mary** has more often been surrounded by folk practices, marking turning points in the agricultural and pastoral year, especially in the Alps.

Church New Year

The Catholic Church's liturgical year begins on September 1—a date adopted when Christianity became legal in the Roman Empire in the fourth century, on account of its administrative and popular observance as the **New Year**. It is traditionally known as the **Feast of Indiction**, after the fifteen-year taxation cycle used for property evaluation that started on that day since it was introduced by Emperor Constantine in 312 (a year before the Edict of Milan

recognizing the Christian religion), and continued being used in the West with a September 24 date in the Holy Roman Empire until the latter's demise in 1806. It is therefore still surrounded by **New Year** festive customs in some Greek islands like Carpathos and Rhodes, and especially in Ethiopia. In this East African country, celebrations start on the last feast of the old year: the **Beheading of Saint John the Baptist** on August 29 (actually mid-September in terms of the Gregorian calendar), with children caroling or bringing wild flowers to relatives for a piece of whole wheat *dabo* bread, and the slaughter of an animal in most homes. In 1989, the Ecumenical Patriarch of Constantinople Dimitrios I officially dedicated this day to Creation as a whole (much as the Jewish

New Year—Rosh Hashanah—commemorates Creation as an event), to promote environmental awareness among Orthodox Christians.

The Nativity of the Virgin Mary

A week later, the sun reaches the middle of the constellation of Virgo. This is likely why the date of September 8 had been favored for a while by the time it was made official by the Greek-born Pope Saint Sergius I in the late seventh century for the new, but already widespread, Christian feast of the **Nativity of the Virgin Mary**, Mother of God, except in the Coptic churches of Egypt and Ethiopia, where it falls on May 1 in their version of the old Julian calendar. At the first Council of Lyon in 1251, Pope Innocent IV gave new prominence to this mostly Eastern feast in the Roman Church by adding an octave of extra celebrations to it over the following week. The city of Lyon had been an early center of Marian piety in the West since the early twelfth century, when an altar was for the first time dedicated to the **Immaculate Conception** of Mary at the abbey of Ainay—much to the chagrin of no less an authority than Saint Bernard, who decried this innovation. Yet it became part and parcel of the powerful cult of Mary in Lyon, whose officials vowed to hold a yearly procession to the chapel of the **Immaculate Conception** of Fourvière on the hill above on the **Nativity of the Virgin Mary** if the city was spared from the plague of 1643—which it was. Except for a break between the revolutions of 1789 and 1848, the September 8 feast has been a cherished tradition in a city known a century ago as the one with the most statues of Mary.

Between Covenants

It is appropriate that the Birth of the Mother of God is celebrated on the heels of the church's **New Year**, since it marks the beginning of the final stage of God's providential care for His Creation: after the first Covenant with Noah and all creatures, and the Old Covenant with Moses and the chosen people of Israel, a New Covenant with all mankind in Jesus. In it, God as the Holy Trinity takes on human nature in the person of His Son Jesus Christ, so that, through this gift of adoption, human beings may in turn partake of divine nature. To this end, an opening first had to be prepared from the human side in order for the divine gift to be freely accepted. As the human being who, at the **Annunciation** (commemorated on March 25), will freely consent to give birth to the Son of God, the Blessed Virgin Mary comes at the culmination of this process of providential preparation through the history of the people of Israel in the Old Testament. From the start, her life is preordained for this vocation, just like the life of Saint John the Baptist also is for his own mission, as another transitional figure between the Old and New Testaments. Both Mary and her young cousin John were miraculously born of sterile parents, in a way that calls to mind Old Testament antecedents like the birth of Isaac to Abraham's ninety-year-old wife Sarah, which Christian tradition reads as prefigurations of the Resurrection of Jesus. But in Mary's case, the symbol is the doorstep to the real thing. As Orthodox Christians sing in the vespers of the feast, "mystery goes before greater mystery": "the sterile door is opened and the virginal Door comes forth" to "introduce Christ into the world" (Sticheria of Tone 8, in Ouspensky 1982, p. 146).

If the **Conception** and the **Nativity of John the Baptist**, as lesser festivals of the Catholic Church (held on September 24—or 23 in the East—and June 24, respectively), are based on solid Gospel accounts, the corresponding Marian feasts draw from apocryphal sources, chiefly the Book of James, where the relevant passages date back to the 130s. They tell how the righteous Joachim came to the Temple of Jerusalem one day to make his offering and was turned away by the high priest because he did not have any children. This added insult to injury, and a dejected Joachim went to hide his shame among the shepherds. As he was praying in the hills, so was his wife Ann in the garden of their Jerusalem home. The old spouses were simultaneously visited by angels announcing that Ann would bear a child whose name would be famous throughout the world. She promised to dedicate the child to God and ran out of the house to tell her husband the good news. She ran into him at the city gate as he came running down from the hills to tell *her* the good news. They fell into each other's arms, and nine months later Mary was born. Their passionate embrace against the backdrop of Jerusalem is depicted in the Orthodox icon of the **Conception of Saint Ann**, in a moving celebration of the holiness of marital love. The blessing and election of Mary as its "fruit most pure" has never required in the East the special exemption from a sexually transmitted original sin, which the Western Church saw fit to apply to the Mother of God.

Immaculate Conception

The doctrine of the **Immaculate Conception** (of Mary—not to be confused with her virginal conception of Jesus as most people do) arose in Europe in the eleventh century, shortly after the schism between the Roman Church and the Eastern Church. But this did not prevent the former from importing the feast of the **Conception** from the latter, where it was born in the eighth century. However, in a move that only deepened the rift between the Roman and Eastern Churches, the controversial teaching of the **Immaculate Conception** was made official after centuries of theological debate by Pope Pius IX in a definition published in his encyclical letter *Ineffabilis Deus* on the December 8 date of that feast in 1854. It "holds that the most Blessed Virgin Mary, in the first instance of her conception, by a singular grace and privilege granted by Almighty God, in view of the merits of Jesus Christ, the Savior of the human race, was preserved free from all stain of original sin." This was now declared to be an official dogma of the

Roman Catholic Church, "revealed by God and therefore to be believed firmly and constantly by all the faithful" (www.papalencyclicals.net/Pius09/p9ineff.htm).

The revised, reemphasized December 8 Marian feast which Catholics have since been calling the **Immaculate Conception** was observed with spectacular gusto in Lyon, France, the oldest site of this devotion, and even more nowadays, though for more mundane reasons. Two years earlier, around December 8, 1852, the inauguration of the golden statue of the **Immaculate Conception** on the new bell tower of the Fourvière shrine had been marked by the largely spontaneous, widespread illumination of the city with candles and lamps and by every available means, in a universal outburst of popular devotion by which clerical as well as civic authorities were taken aback. This was in stark contrast to the lukewarm observance of the official illumination decreed a few days before to celebrate the proclamation of the Second Empire of the Bonaparte Dynasty under Napoleon III on December 5. Times had changed since such illuminations could be decreed by state authorities on the occasion of a **royal entry** into a subject city. Apart from a handful of special religious occasions, the annual December 8 illumination in honor of the **Immaculate Conception** was the only one to stand the test of time from then on. It even became politicized in the anticlerical climate of the Third Republic around the turn of the twentieth century, when it came to sometimes fatal blows in scuffles with militant secularists intent on disrupting the celebrations. Generally speaking, December 8 became known as the "winter July 14"—the Catholic answer to the *Fête Nationale* instituted in 1880 by the Republic; the more lights could be seen, the larger the ranks of opponents to the secularist regime were deemed to be.

If the First World War, while reducing this polarization at a time of national peril, only caused a temporary scaling back of Lyon's illuminations, the Second World War triggered a more prolonged interruption from which they long seemed unable to recover, even after they started again in 1949 minus the procession. The clergy stopped supporting such quaint expressions of popular piety in the wake of the Vatican II Council, so that there was almost no trace left of the practice by the late 1980s, when a couple of fundamentalist groups helped initiate a minor comeback. But the illuminations were about to be reinvented by civic authorities in a very different spirit, with Mayor Michel Noir's *Plan Lumière* to wrap the city's monuments in sophisticated lighting as part of a secular **Feast of Lights** centering on the traditional date of the **Immaculate Conception**. In its present form, the *Fête des Lumières* was launched on the tenth anniversary of the plan on December 8, 1999, and is held over four days on the weekend closest to that date, attracting over a million tourists annually. Since 2003, people from all over the world can even send their own designs through the Internet to be projected onto Lyon's night sky by twenty huge light beams. Yet the display of the religious feast's humble candles is still encouraged by city hall, and the illuminated Fourvière basilica continues to stand out in the skyline above the lightshows distantly inspired by its ancient cult of the **Immaculate Conception**.

In Italy, the **Immaculate Conception** is the occasion for a fair in the Fornoli quarter of Bagni di Lucca in Tuscany, and near Naples, for a sausage and polenta festival in San Bartolomeo in Galdo, in addition to the procession of an elaborate float depicting the Madonna with angels and carried by a team of over a hundred men through the streets of Torre del Greco in thanksgiving for her role in saving that town from a volcanic eruption in 1861. In Central America, December 8 celebrations in Antigua Guatemala include a traditional dance called *Los Diablos,* done in demon and skeleton costumes, and going back to the Mayas. In Argentina, this religious feast is also a national holiday known as **Virgin Mary Day**.

Popular Devotion on Mary's Birthday

The September 8 feast of the **Nativity of the Virgin Mary** remains a more important festival in East and West alike and a joyful one in tone—not just for theological reasons. In Hungary, it is a day of rest for women. In Lanciano, in the Abruzzo region of Italy, it is known as the feast of the **Madonna del Ponte**; there, the women of the town's various quarters carry on their heads typical copper vessels containing seasonal produce, and decorated with colored ribbons and paper flowers. In Corsica, peasants and craftsmen from the entire island gather for its major fair over three days in the village of Casamaccioli in the Niolu Valley. It starts after the September 8 mass honoring the local Madonna statue and features the spiral-shaped, dancelike *Granitola* procession as well as an improvisational song contest between the men. Elsewhere in France, marriageable girls used to stick pins into wooden Madonnas so as to get the Virgin to heed their requests for a husband. If they threw two pins in the holy wells to which pilgrims came that day in many places, and the pins happened to form a cross as they reached the bottom, they were supposed to get their wish within the coming year. On France's northern coast, miniature ships as well as Madonna statues are taken to the sea in processions to bless it in French Flanders and Brittany, and a shepherds' feast ushers in the novena in honor of the Leaning Virgin of Brebières in Picardy on September 8. In many Greek villages that day, the privilege of carrying the icon of the Mother of God to the church in the procession is sold to the highest bidder every year. Sick children are sold to the Virgin Mary as "the slaves of Our Lady" so she will take care of her own and cure them by the time their parents buy them back from her a year later. It is thus to four centuries of healing miracles that the famous church of Our Lady of Health at Vialankanni in Tamil Nadu owes its prominence among a number of Marian shrines spread around India where

Catholics and Oriental Christians flock for the **Nativity of the Virgin**. In this case, it comes at the climax of a week of celebrations, surpassing those at the church of Saint Mary in Niranam, one of the shrines said to have been founded by the Apostle Thomas himself in Kerala.

Alpine Pastoral Customs

The period between the feast marking the end of Mary's earthly life—the **Assumption** on August 15—and that of her **Nativity** on September 8 formed an end-of-summer Marian period that covered critical points in the yearly cycle of Europe's peasant cultures, sometimes extending a full month to the **Holy Cross** festival of September 14, and therefore known as **Our Lady's Thirty Days**. Because it gets cold early in the Alps, it is on the occasion of the Virgin Mary's birthday that the cattle are ceremoniously brought from the pastures—where the beasts have been grazing all summer—down into the valleys, where the entire community is again reunited for the winter. In the preceding days in Bavaria, women weave splendid wreaths out of fir branches and decorate them with paper roses and little mirrors—meant to keep away demons over the long trek downhill. In other Alpine areas, cattle are also adorned with special decorations of flowers, branches and ribbons, following different rules. On the eve of what is called *la désalpe* in French-speaking areas, the shepherds of France's Hautes-Alpes region invite each other to eat lasagna and doughnuts and signal their imminent arrival to the people below with fires. In the Swiss canton of Unterwald, the shepherds have rosemary sprigs on their hats or in their mouths when the cattle's owners welcome them back to the villages with lavish feasts. These *bénichons* (the word for "blessing" in the local French dialects), lasting until the next morning, feature oratorical contests and cattle competitions.

It has been suggested that these folk customs may have been derived from a pre-Christian end-of-summer festival of the Germanic goddess Idun. She kept the golden apples of eternal youth but was kidnapped for a while by the giant Thiazi. This would have explained the sudden onset of the cold at this time of year. It seems nonetheless appropriate that Alpine shepherds come down from the hills on this feast of the Birth of Mary, just as Saint Joachim did when he first heard it announced by an angel after finding refuge among Jewish shepherds.

> ***See also*** Annunciation; Assumption; Corpus Christi; Elevation of the Cross; May Day; Midsummer; New Year (West); Rosh Hashanah

References

Gérald Gambier. *La merveilleuse histoire du 8 décembre à Lyon.* Châtillon-sur-Chalaronne, France: Éditions La Taillanderie, 2003.

Donald N. Levine. *Wax and Gold. Tradition and Innovation in Ethiopian Culture.* Chicago: University of Chicago Press, 1972.

Edward Dennis O'Connor, ed. *The Dogma of the Immaculate Conception: History and Significance.* Notre Dame, IN: University of Notre Dame Press, 1958.

Leonid Ouspensky and Vladimir Lossky. *The Meaning of Icons.* Tr. G. E. H. Palmer and E. Kadloubovsky. Crestwood, NY: Saint Vladimir's Seminary Press, 1982.

▶ CONCEPTION OF SAINT ANN, CONCEPTION OF SAINT JOHN THE BAPTIST

See Conception and Birth of the Virgin Mary

▶ CONSTITUTION DAY

See Cherry Blossom Festival

▶ CONSUALIA

See Games (Rome), Saturnalia

▶ CORPUS CHRISTI (CHRISTIANITY)

Shortly after the general adoption of **Trinity Sunday** a week after **Pentecost** in the early fourteenth century, the following Thursday (or Sunday in some countries) was chosen by the church of Rome for a joyous new feast of the Eucharist alone, free of the tragic setting of the sacrament's institution at the Last Supper on **Maundy Thursday**.

From Liturgical Act to Sacred Object

For the first thousand years of the Christian church, while it was still a single body, it seemed enough—as it still does in its Eastern half—that the Bread of Life was timelessly available on almost any day through the sacrament of the Eucharist, to be experienced by the faithful as the mystical union of God with mankind in which all could take part. The consecrated host representing Christ's body was initially important only in this liturgical context. Its ontological status did not become an issue until scholastic philosophy, seeking rational explanations for the mysteries of the faith, made it into one in the West by the twelfth century, by trying to keep track of how, when and for how long a piece of bread could actually become God. These Eucharistic controversies were resolved (until the Protestant Reformation at least) when the Roman Church adopted the doctrine of transubstantiation at the Lateran Council of 1215, proclaiming in the dogma of the Real Presence of God in the Eucharist that it was switched with the natural substance of the bread at a given point of the Mass. In a prime example of that "metaphysics of presence" typifying Western thought according to post-modern thinkers, the objective fact of the Supreme Being's presence among—yet above—other beings had gained center-stage, over against the existential act of the mutual—albeit asymmetrical—gift of Creator and creatures in the inscrutable mystery of the liturgical sacrifice.

In a parallel process, full participation in the sacrifice of the Mass was gradually curtailed, so that it came to be experienced more like a dramatization of the Passion to be watched from a distance. For the drinking of the wine standing for Christ's blood came to be restricted to the clergy (hence the flourishing of lay literature about the Quest for the Holy Grail as the original chalice containing it), while the rest of the faithful were now too intimidated most of the time to even take communion with the bread as Christ's body (except at **Easter** when it was mandatory). Looking at the latter with reverence and yearning, both during Mass and increasingly outside of this normal ritual setting, therefore became an attractive alternative to actual participation in the sacrament. An emerging subjective piety dwelt on the reserved consecrated host as a self-contained object of worship.

A New Feast of Private Devotion and Corporate Pride

The Blessed Juliana (1193–1258), Augustinian prioress of the abbey of Mont Cornillon near Liège, thus came to have visions in which a dark spot on a full moon was supposed to point to the lack of a feast in honor of the Eucharist in the church calendar. On this basis, Robert de Torote, bishop of Liège, ordered the festival celebrated in his diocese in 1246. It had already been adopted in many German and Slavic lands when one of its early promoters in Liège, Jacques Pantaléon, became pope as Urban IV, and decreed in the 1264 bull *Transiturus de hoc mundo* that the whole church should celebrate the *officium novae solemnitatis,* "the service for the new feast." There was still resistance to the observance of this "new feast" (or **Besta Berri** as it is still known in Basque-speaking areas of Spain and France) even in Liège and Rome, until Pope Clement V confirmed the bull at the Council of Vienne in 1311. Nevertheless, by the next century, Corpus Christi had virtually become, as a public event at least, the main feast of the Church—witness its French name of **Fête-Dieu** ("God's Feast") or the Hungarian **Urnap** ("Lord's Day").

This was even truer of the Roman Catholic Church after the Protestant bodies that left its fold also dropped the feast celebrating one of the dogmas they questioned. For in the context of the Counterreformation, it became a defiant proclamation of the core of the Roman faith and of Catholic identity, centering on an ever-more lavish display of pomp and luxury around the Eucharist itself in a splendid procession. First put on in Cologne in 1279 on the model of **Holy Week** precedents, in which the Eucharist was carried in a veiled chalice, the procession became general practice over the next century. Reliquaries were first used to make the consecrated host more visible, until a round glass monstrance was designed specifically for this purpose. It was itself set within an ornate ceremonial display prop designed by the best goldsmiths: the custodia, from the fifteenth century onward. Throughout Europe, the **Corpus Christi** procession of the Blessed Sacrament under a golden canopy, preceded by clergy and followed by rulers and magistrates, had soon become a public celebration of the corporate identity of all the bodies constituting the Christian community around the body of Christ as its triumphant king, from whom all sovereignty was derived, both spiritual and temporal. It thus resembled a **royal entry** into a subject city, as all orders of society from prince to pauper, and from guilds or professional corporations to religious and neighborhood associations, would appear and parade through the streets in full array, each at the rank that fit its importance within the community. They all proudly displayed their distinctive banners and symbols as they deliberately came together as an organic body politic—much like the faithful communed in the church as the mystical body of Jesus Christ.

Animal Symbolism and Agrarian Rituals

In Germany, the procession also wound its way out of town into the country. But there, certain **Rogation**tide rituals to secure good weather for the crops seem to have been absorbed or echoed in the practice of stopping at four different spots to bless the four directions in turn with the singing of the beginning of each of the four Gospels. The same association with stomping the ground—on horseback this time—is suggested in the story attributing the institution of the spectacular *Fronleichnam* ("Lord's Body") processions sponsored by Austria's Hapsburg dynasty to its founder Rudolf I. While he was riding, this late thirteenth-century German king had once come across a priest carrying the Blessed Sacrament, stepped off his horse to leave it to him, and declared he could no longer ride an animal which had carried the Lord Himself. In Brindisi on the heel of the Italian boot, it is still a splendidly caparisoned horse that bears the tabernacle in the **Corpus Christi** procession.

Rogationtide dragons and other processional giants and symbolic animals typical of summer festivals, originally tied to the regularity of the water supply and to fertility, started to figure more prominently in **Corpus Christi** processions in Spain at the end of the seventeenth century. However, monsters (such as the *tarasca* imported from Provençal festivals like the famous Aix *Fête-Dieu* procession later banned by the French Revolution) were sometimes rationalized there as allegories of the vices and heresies that church and state subdued. A century later, neo-classical taste and Enlightenment ideas had made such popular displays—smacking of paganism—appear too profane; like many of the peasant dances that had become fixtures of the feast, they were eventually forbidden or discouraged by royal authorities, with varying success.

From Mystery Plays to Modern Theater

Accusations of irreverence to the Sacrament while straying into secular social comment brought the same fate to the *auto sacramental* ("mystery play") as a short allegorical verse play illustrating a particular dimension or some implications of the mystery of the Eucharist. It had evolved from the tableaux depicting religious stories on floats within the **Corpus Christi** procession, with live characters who eventually performed them in dramatic form, until such carts formed a parade of their own to selected places in the city. The autos would be presented in sequence, much as the scriptural mystery plays had been on pageant wagons during the Middle Ages in the Netherlands and northern England—sometimes over several days on the occasion of **Corpus Christi**. Such dramatic cycles, like the York one that has come down to us in late-fourteenth-century manuscripts and is still performed at York Minster every four years, are not without literary merit. But whereas the genre was soon to disappear—usually along with the feast—in northern Europe as the Reformation set in, it would become a regular feature of **Corpus Christi** in the Iberian Peninsula by the end of the sixteenth century. There, it was taken from an unsophisticated form of pious entertainment to a high level of artistic achievement by the likes of the Spaniards Lope de Vega (1562–1635) and Pedro Calderon de la Barca (1600–1681), thereby providing an important formative nucleus for the emerging literatures of both Portugal and Spain.

Floral Symbolism and Baby-Jumping

In the latter country, tapestries and flags still hang from windows, balconies, and walls on the way of the procession, as fruits and flowers also used to. It is hard to tell whether they imitate or inspired an even clearer celebration of nature's summer bounty: the elaborately designed carpets of flowers, petals or dyed wood chips of many colors, evoking ancient triumphal processions and floral festivals, that are painstakingly assembled in front of each house on the Sacrament's passage and on wayside altars, there and elsewhere in Catholic Europe—from Brittany to Poland and from Italy to Alsace. It is sometimes largely as a **Rogation**-like plea for divine blessings on the coming harvest that **Corpus Christi** processions subsist in parts of rural Quebec—one of the places where they have been considerably toned down since the Vatican II Council made the Roman Catholic Church move away from the somewhat arrogant triumphalist stance long affirmed through this feast. This recent trend has not significantly affected the *Colacho* **Baby-Jumping Festival** of Castrillo de Murcia instituted in seventeenth-century Spain by the local lay brotherhood of the *Santisimo Sacramento de Minerva*. It was based on the belief that babies could only be protected from the effects of original sin on their chances for survival if their guilt was taken away on the heels of the devil jumping over them, whom someone still impersonates, waving a whip as he leaps over a mattress where babies have been lined up, as crowds of locals and tourists look on.

Precolumbian Survivals

Yet **Corpus Christi** generally remains a major celebration in former Spanish colonies. This is especially true in Peru, where it absorbed the **Inti Raymi** solstice festival of the Incas, or rather allowed it to continue in a Christian guise. Similarly, the *Qoyllur Riti* ("Star of the Snow") festival, held on the full moon before **Corpus Christi** on a peak fifty miles east of the former Inca capital Cuzco, perpetuates the worship of various mountain deities, in seamless conjunction with a mass pilgrimage of Indians from all over Peru and Bolivia to the site of a miraculous apparition of the Christ Child to an Indian herdsman in 1780. During the general procession from the glacier's edge to the valley, some men fetch glacier ice, which they bring back to Cuzco for the celebration of **Corpus Christi**.

See also Akitu; Easter; Holy Week; Inti Raymi and Huarachicu; Rogations; Sacred Heart; Whitsuntide

References

Ronald Hutton. *The Rise and Fall of Merry England: The Ritual Year, 1400–1700*. Oxford: Oxford University Press, 1994.

R. M. Lumiansky and David Mills. *The Chester Mystery Cycle: Essays and Documents.* Chapel Hill: University of North Carolina Press, 1983.

Alan H. Nelson. *The Medieval English Stage: Corpus Christi Pageants and Plays.* Chicago: University of Chicago Press, 1974.

Miri Rubin. *Corpus Christi: The Eucharist in Late Medieval Culture.* New York: Cambridge University Press, 1991.

▶ COWHERD AND WEAVING MAID (CHINA, KOREA, JAPAN)

This minor festival, called **Chi Ch'iao T'ien** in Chinese and also known as **Chilseok** in Korean and **Tanabata no Sekku** in Japanese, comes up on the seventh day of the seventh lunar month (**Double Seven**), in either July or August, in honor of the stars Altair and Vega. Separated by the Milky Way, they are identified respectively with the legendary lovers **Cowherd and Weaving Maid**, who are reunited once a year on a kind of Far Eastern **Saint Valentine**'s Day. This is a day to foretell the success of womanly pursuits and pray for it.

A Bridge of Magpies Over the Milky Way

Known in China as the Heavenly River, the Milky Way is said in Chinese folklore to have arisen when the Queen of Heaven waved a hairpin to put this obstacle between the celestial Weaving Maid (*Chih-nü*—or *Jingnyeo* in Korean, represented by Vega) and her chosen husband the mortal Cowherd (*Ch'ien-niu*—or *Gyeonu* in Korean, represented by Altair). He had been about to overtake the two goddesses as the fearsome queen was forcibly taking her granddaughter back home, pursuing them in a flying boat (the transformed horn of his magic buffalo), which also held the couple's son and daughter. The Queen of Heaven challenged him to cross the torrent if he wanted to see his wife again; but hearing this, the Phoenix was moved by the lovers' plight to intervene by sending all the magpies in the world to form a bridge between them (called *Ojakgyo* in Korean). Taken at her own word, the Queen of Heaven then relented, and allowed the family to reunite once a year over this bridge of magpies on **Chi Ch'iao T'ien**.

This story was first mentioned under the Western Han Dynasty (206–24 B.C.E.) in Ying Shao's book on *Uses and Customs* as something that occurred on the seventh day of the seventh month. It is traditionally said that if one witnesses the actual scene and prostrates while saying a wish for fortune, long life, or descendants, one of the three will be granted within three years. Alternatively, if a brick is thrown up in the air at the very moment when Heaven's gate is opened to allow the Weaving Maid to walk onto the bridge, it will fall back on the ground changed into gold. But should it rain on that night, the Heavenly River will swell to overflow and carry off the bridge, leaving **Cowherd and Weaving Maid** to wait another year for the chance for a brief encounter. Hoping to avert such a sad and inauspicious occurrence, women pray for clear skies on that night and leave cosmetics on the roof for Weaving Maid, asking her in return to give them lasting beauty, a child, or skill in needlework, at which maidens compete by moonlight to show they are marriage material. On this day for drying clothes and books in the sun, Korean wives and children also used to perform a sacrificial rite at the well to secure the water supply, as well as an ancestor memorial service in honor of the Big Dipper God for the prosperity of their homes.

Divination Techniques

In late Imperial times, Chinese women would buy a *moheluo* clay doll to promote childbirth, and children would go around carrying a lotus leaf, like this doll often did. But most popular customs about that day involved divination concerning productive needlework over the coming year, since the star Vega was one of the beings who spent eternity weaving the clouds in the sky. This elevated but thankless estate made sharing the hard but free life of an earth-bound peasant comparatively attractive to the Weaving Girl. Hearing the hapless lovers whisper through the grapevine on the one day when they were reunited held the promise of expert weaving.

There were also ways of telling this kind of fortune that were less dependent on other-worldly visitations, as they could easily be practiced at home under controlled conditions. One of them was called *pao chieh*, and used shadows at the bottom of a bowl of water. In the long version, having let some peas soak in the dark a month in advance of **Chi Ch'iao T'ien**, a woman would tie a red ribbon to the foot-high shoots that resulted by then and break off their ends with her hand while praying to **Cowherd and Weaving Maid**. She would then put them overnight in a bowl of water, in the hope of being able to see needle-like shadows in it before dawn the next day. In an alternate short version, women watched out for any shadows evoking flowers, birds, or beasts that might be thrown by needles floating on the surface of the bowl, literally foreshadowing the figures they hoped to realize in their own handiwork.

Another method, called *bu chieh* and attested under the Sung Dynasty (960–1279), was based on the regularity of the web that a spider would spin overnight in a box. In some places where **Ch'i Chieh** (as **Chi Ch'iao T'ien** was also known) was called the **Women's Festival**, they would meet at nightfall and offer wine, fruits, and melons to the two stars, before launching on a competition about who would first succeed in putting multicolored threads through the nine holes of a special needle. Under the Northern and Southern Dynasties (420–589 C.E.), women used seven-hole needles for the same purpose.

The Timeless Tale of the Seven Bathing Beauties

It was no coincidence that this number of holes in the needle matched that of the Seven Sisters Cowherd espied bathing in the Silver River when he went there on the counsel of his magic buffalo, as this incognito exile from Heaven knew very well that these weaving girls must have slipped away unnoticed from their celestial workplaces. When it was time to go back to the sky, one of them had to stay behind on earth, because Cowherd, following the plan of his faithful companion, had stolen her clothes, and was thus able to make her his wife. Interestingly enough, the same story of bathing beauties is told by the Toradja people of the central highlands of the island of Celebes or Sulawesi in Indonesia about an earthly prince and the same seven stars known in the West as the Pleiades, only to account for the origin of mankind as the offspring of heaven and earth.

But the Chinese versions of this motif of East Asian folklore, as told about **Double Seven**, do not emphasize its cosmological dimensions so much as its social overtones, from the dispossession of the orphan Cowherd at the instigation of a greedy sister-in-law to the obstacles to love marriages, especially across class barriers. This has contributed to make of the story of **Cowherd and Weaving Maid** and their yearly encounter a classic theme of Chinese letters, because of their touching loyalty, as evoked in a fine example of the genre like this famous poem by Qin Guan from the time of the Sung Dynasty:

> Purple clouds of many shapes go across the sky.
> Although the Heavenly River separates the
>   Cowherd from the Weaving Maid,
> It cannot prevent them from telling each other
>   their sorrow.
> They can only cross the river on one night
>   every year.
> The happiness they know then
> The happiness they know then is greater than
>   the whole world.
> Their love is as tender as water,
> Their rendezvous is as brief as a dream.
> At the time of parting,

How can they bear the pain as they look at the
way back?
But if they remain faithful to each other,
Do they really need to spend their life together?
(Freely translated from pp. 50–51 of Qi Xing
1987.)

See also Lupercalia; Sekku

References

Juliet Bredon and Igor Mitrophanow. *The Moon
Year: A Record of Chinese Customs and
Festivals.* Shanghai, China: Kelly and Walsh,
1927 (New York: Paragon Book Reprint Corp.,
1966).
Choe Sang-su. *Annual Customs of Korea: Notes on
the Rites and Ceremonies of the Year.* Seoul:
Seomun-dang, 1983.
Goh Pei Ki. *Origins of Chinese Festivals.*
Singapore: Asiapac Books, 1997.
Qi Xing. *Les Fêtes traditionnelles chinoises.* Beijing:
Éditions en langues étrangères, 1987.

▌**CUARESMA**
See Lent

▌**CULTURE DAY**
See Seven-Five-Three

▌**CYBELE AND ATTIS
(SPRING FESTIVAL OF),**
See Spring Festival of Cybele and Attis

D

DAEBOREUM

See Lantern Festival

DAHIHANDI

See Janmashtami

DAMBA

See Mawlid

DANO

See Dragon Boat Festival

DAPAA

See Adae

DASAIN

See Navaratra and Dusshera

DASHALAKSHANA

See Paryushana and Dashalakshana

DAY OF ARAFAT

See Ashura

DAY OF ASSEMBLY (ISLAM)

In Islam, the weekly **Day of Assembly** for collective worship is Friday; but unlike its equivalents the Christian **Sunday** and the Jewish **Sabbath**, this is not a day of rest.

Origins

The **Day of Assembly** was devised by the Prophet Mohammed in 621 C.E., when he was still based in Mecca but already had a large following in Medina—as we now know the oasis of Yathrib after the Arab form of the Aramaic name given to it by its substantial Jewish community. The new Prophet was then trying to reach out to the Jews as heirs to the first genuine monotheistic revelation, prefiguring the ultimate one: the Koran. One of his moves in that direction was to ask his disciple Mu'sab ibn 'Umayr to get the Muslims of Medina to have prayers in the middle of the day like the Jews, and to do them as a group once a week while the Jews were preparing for **Sabbath** the next day. Choosing Friday as the **Day of Assembly** for Muslims at once established a parallel with the weekly Jewish festival and a crucial distance from it, signifying at first respect for a potential ally, and later on rivalry with infidels who refused to follow the new dispensation.

Practices

The five daily prayers required of all Muslims ever since this early phase of emulation of Jewish practices do not have to be said in common as a congregation, with the exception of the one replacing the early afternoon *Dhur* on the **Day of Assembly** (*Yawm al-Jum'a* in Arabic) set

Muslims attend Friday prayers in Moulay Mohammed Mosque in the Libyan capital Tripoli on February 2, 2001. (Reuters/Corbis)

aside for this purpose. But since attendance is only optional for women because of their household duties, they may say their *Dhur* prayer at home as usual.

In this respect, the call of the *muezzin* or "mosque crier" to Friday public worship is no different from the standard calls to the five daily hours of prayer. This *adhan* (Arabic for "announcement") was originally a simple injunction to "come to prayer" shouted by someone outside the mosque, but Mohammed soon looked for a more dignified formula. In the first or second year of the Hegira (the Muslim era beginning on July 16, 622), after his disciple 'Abd Allah ibn Zayd reported a dream in which somebody called the faithful to prayer from a rooftop, Mohammed followed his future successor Omar's advice to entrust this task to a spe-

cialist. The first muezzin was the freed slave Bilal the Ethiopian. Muezzins initially did their calling from the highest roof near the mosque, then from the towers of churches and fortifications in conquered Christian areas, and within a century, from one built as part of the mosque itself (with a few exceptions in medieval Central Asia, Iran, and Iraq, where it stood apart) to serve as such a "beacon" or *minaret* in Arabic. The call to prayer also became more elaborate, to the point where it now goes: "God is most great. I bear witness that there is no god but the One God. I bear witness that Mohammed is the Prophet of God. Come to prayer. Come to salvation. God is most great. There is no god but the One God." The first sentence is intoned four times, and the last one but once—except by Shiites, who say it twice, as all Muslims do the ones in between.

The specifically congregational *Jum'a* prayer of Friday afternoon differs from the everyday *Dhur* in having only two units (*rakat*) instead of four. It comes after the sermon (*khutba*) by the *imam,* whom the congregation has elected to lead it in prayer. The *khutba* is meant to be listened to with undivided attention by the worshippers, once they have praised God, blessed the Prophet Mohammed and his companions, and made a supplication for all Muslims; it will be concluded in the same way. The sermon is in two parts, divided by a short break. It may deal with current affairs, issues of concern to the *Umma* (the global or local community of believers), or Koranic commentary, to educate Muslims in the faith and strengthen the bond of brotherhood uniting them in it.

It is therefore important to observe the **Day of Assembly** in a proper setting; in the absence of a mosque, a Muslim community has the duty to set up a place of worship on a stable footing with as little delay as possible. But of course, in a Muslim country, businesses will often close for a while on Friday afternoon in order to allow people to go to the mosque, in compliance with the Koran's injunction to the believers.

> O you who believe! when the call is made for prayer on Friday, then hasten to the remembrance of Allah and leave off trading; that is better for you, if you know. But when the prayer is ended, then disperse abroad in the land and seek of Allah's grace, and remember Allah much, that you may be successful. (*sura* 62:9–10)

This means that a Muslim is to return to the useful tasks at hand, not to take the remainder of the day off, as in the Judeo-Christian weekly day of rest. For both **Sabbath** and **Sunday** are based on the idea that God rested at the end of a week of work on the Creation, which is unacceptable to Islam because of its insistence on the omnipotence of God: how could the all-powerful Creator become weary so as to need rest from labor?

See also Ashura; Nineteen-Day Feast; Sabbath; Sunday

References

Karen Armstrong. *Muhammad. A Biography of the Prophet.* New York: Harper Collins, 1992.

The Koran. tr. M.H. Shakir, http://etext.virginia.edu/koran.html.

Azim A. Nanji, ed. *The Muslim Almanac: A Reference Work on the History, Faith, Culture, and Peoples of Islam.* Detroit, MI: Gale Research, 1996.

E. van Donzel, ed. *Islamic Desk Reference,* compiled from *The Encyclopedia of Islam.* Leiden, The Netherlands: E. J. Brill, 1994.

DAY OF ATONEMENT
See Yom Kippur

DAY OF BLOWING THE HORN, DAY OF JUDGMENT
See Rosh Hashanah

DAY OF MANKIND
See Sekku

DAY OF ORIGIN
See New Year (Japan)

DAY OF THE RAT (FEAST OF THE)
See Sekku

DAY OF THE WREN
See Christmas

DAYS OF THE DEAD (CHINA, KOREA, JAPAN)
Among days honoring the dead in the Chinese world, some have lost currency, like the **Burning of Clothes Festival** and **Cold Food Day** on the eve of **Qing Ming**—which on its part has

remained central. The same goes for **Chung Yuan**, also known as **Yu Lan Pen**, marking the midpoint of the seventh month, during which the gates of Hell are open. It has taken on a Buddhist coloring in the way it focuses on re-lieving the sufferings as well as appeasing the envy of the hungry ghosts caught there—dead relatives in particular. Aside from gravesite and home offerings, the latter festival, like its Japa-nese version called *Bon,* is associated with the launching of floating lanterns, while kite-flying is a spring custom typical of **Qing Ming**, the **Festival of Pure Brightness**, that puts dead an-cestors in a more unambiguously positive light by cleaning their graves, much as in Western **days of the dead**.

Lesser Festivals of the Dead

Traditionally in China, six major festivals stood out above the rest. They were divided between **Three for the Living** (**New Year**, **Dragon Boats**, **Mid-Autumn**) and **Three for the Dead**: the **Festival of Pure Brightness**, or **Qing Ming**, the **Festival of Hungry Ghosts**, or *Zhong Yuan Jie,* and the **Burning of Clothes Festival**, or *Shao Yi Jie,* which has now become uncommon. It used to be observed on the first day of the tenth month, as a way to send winter clothes to dead ancestors.

Usually held on the eve of **Qing Ming**—as the putting out of the old fire before the kin-dling of the new fire that ushers in spring re-newal (now used instead to burn spirit money on gravesites so the smoke brings good fortune to the dead), **Cold Food Day** or *Hanshi* has also declined in importance. Though it probably goes back to prehistoric times before agricul-ture, the story goes that it was Prince Wengong of Jin (in present-day Shanxi Province) who, during the Spring and Autumn Period (770–481 B.C.E.), first ordered that no fire be lit to cook food on that day in his realm. Food was thus prepared in advance the day before, to be eaten cold. This was meant to mark the prince's eternal gratitude for the selfless loyalty of his most faithful companion Jie Zitui during his wilderness years, when he struggled to claim his throne from a usurper, and his regret at how badly he repaid him when he refused to come out of the forest where he had fled from honors and riches to accept the gifts and thanks of the prince. Not to be outdone, the ruler had had the forest set on fire, assuming the hermit would at least want to save his mother—who was living with him. This plan literally misfired, as they did not come out, and only their charred remains were later found clinging to a willow tree. During the Sung Dynasty (960–1279 C.E.), there arose a custom of hanging "Zi-tui swallows" made from flour and dates on a willow branch in one's doorway, which children also offered to the village god, along with boiled eggs and imitation gold and silver ingots.

Qing Ming

The willows are in bud at this time of year, and have always been associated with the special at-mosphere of **Qing Ming**, the hundred-and-fifth day after the winter solstice (around April 5), when, in ancient times, everyone would go for a stroll in the countryside to "tread the green grass." Women too for once: on the way back, they would be sure to wear willow branch crowns like the men, or at least headbands, since "the girl who does not wear willow branches on **Qing Ming** is sure to grow old"—prematurely, according to the proverb. Willows were a springtime symbol of eternal youth on a day that is still universally observed by Chinese people to sweep the tombs of their dead rela-tives. This custom became prevalent in the form of a festival under the Tang Dynasty (618–907 C.E.), on the basis of a story about Emperor Kao Tsu, founder of the Han Dynasty in 206 B.C.E. Sorry that his parents could not see him and rejoice in his good fortune, he went back to his hometown to seek out their resting place. However, it proved impossible to locate it in a graveyard that had been a battleground during the years of civil war. Until, that is,

Family members honor the dead by cleaning graves and burning offerings during the Qing Ming Festival at the United Chinese Cemetery in Macau. (Michael S. Yamashita/Corbis)

someone came up with five-colored paper, used to write on for purposes of divination. The monarch threw a pile of these paper slips in the wind, calling onto Heaven to help him fulfill his filial wishes by marking his parents' grave as the one on which paper would land. Indeed, the tombstone to which the paper stuck turned out upon closer inspection to be the right one. Ever since then, people who clean grave sites and put flowers on them on **Qing Ming** (as most Chinese have continued doing even through the harshest antireligious repression) make sure they also place five-colored paper on them, to show they have paid their respects in prayers and offerings. The latter include glutinous red "grave cakes" as well as spring rolls—originally designed to hold the leftovers from **Cold Food Day**, and they are eaten there afterwards in memory of the deceased. In order to ensure a

man's material welfare in the beyond, his children also used to burn gold and silver ingots, servants, horses, sedan-chairs—in paper effigy, of course, like the special paper money used for the same purpose today.

These seasonal stories reflect the family values of the Former Han Period (202 B.C.E.–8 C.E.) of imperial formation, when Confucianism became the State creed. The name **Qing Ming** is said to go back to the same time, and to refer to the "clear and pure" weather of the third lunar month. It changes later, when the wind direction becomes unsteady, so that **Qing Ming** is the last and best time of the year to fly kites. They were invented during the Spring and Autumn Period for the purposes of military topography, as a way to survey enemy territory from a distance. During the Five Dynasties Period (907–960 C.E.), a certain Li Ye equipped a paper hawk with a bamboo tube and a silk ribbon. As it soared and glided in the sky, the wind made it sound like a *zheng,* a zither-like musical instrument; hence the name of this type of kite, *feng zheng.* Over the centuries, designs have come to include mythological figures, characters from classic plays, butterflies, goldfish, larks, dragonflies, eagles, bats, frogs, centipedes, and the like. Techniques have even been developed to make these kites fly in group-formations. Kite-flying is but the most aesthetic and spectacular feature of **Qing Ming** (though it is now practiced throughout the year—weather permitting); among other favorite outdoor activities on this day are swings, ballgames, cock fights, and dog races.

However, many of the social preconditions for the observance of **Qing Ming** as part of the ancestor-worship that was the cornerstone of traditional Chinese culture have been swept away by the Communist regime of mainland China. No productive land may be used for burials, and cremation is compulsory (with some exceptions for Muslim minorities) so as to limit land use even in public graveyards, where ashes are stored for no more than five years.

Chung Yuan

The **Chung Yuan** Festival, in the middle of the seventh month, is not just one of **Three for the Dead,** but also one of the **Three Yuan,** before *Xia Yuan* on the fifteenth day of the tenth month, and after *Shang Yuan* or *Yuan Xiao* on the fifteenth day of the first month, the Festival of **Lanterns,** and the last day of the **New Year** season. While the latter ushers in the half of the year that is dedicated to Heaven (like the first and fifteenth of each month), **Chung Yuan** opens the half dedicated to Earth (as are the second and sixteenth day of every month). While it lasts, the Chinese have always believed that the dead come back from the underworld; and this time, not just deceased relatives who demand to be revered with incense and fed from special banquet tables, but also the lonely hungry ghosts who do not have living descendents to

care for them, and so roam the earth seething with frustration. That is why the fifteenth was sometimes called the **Festival of Devils—Guijie.** The judge of Hell is also inspecting the human realm on this occasion to keep track of people's good and bad deeds for future reference—whenever they fall under his jurisdiction. Since the sixth century, the day has therefore been set aside for remembrance of the ancestors, to make sure their post-mortem trials are kept to a minimum and they can rest in peace.

Still, no one wants to take any chances during this whole late summer **Ghost Month** (from August 9 to September 8 in 2002) when the dead mix with the living, and may even be spotted by looking at their feet—which do not touch the ground. Weddings should not be celebrated while it lasts (as was also the case in the West for the same reason during its taboo month of **May**), and business deals should likewise be postponed to a more auspicious time. In Taiwan, most people try to refrain from risky activities like swimming, driving, and going outside after sundown, wary of the heavy traffic of souls out and about. To entertain the dead, operas are performed nonstop in Taoist temples while they can spiritually dine on offerings of meat (above all a sacrificed hog roasted on a spit), as well as fish, vegetables, canned food, and alcoholic drinks, dedicated to them by a Taoist or Buddhist priest, and which the living proceed to consume on the tables set up in front of the temple for this "**General Salvation** meal." Neighboring communities take turns hosting each other due to the vast quantities of food to be prepared, which contemporary governments, seeing this only as "waste" (the same reason invoked across the Pacific to suppress the Native American **potlatch** as a similar way to maintain bonds between communities), have tried to discourage by either limiting the event to a single day—thus making it impossible—or by banning it altogether. When it is held, the premises are left cluttered with *tou teng*—rice containers topped with symbolic objects like knives, umbrellas, and mirrors, that are known to ward off evil. Though the origins of **Ghost Month** are obscure, Taoists account for **Chung Yuan** as the birthday of *Yenlo Wang*, the Demon King.

Yet **Chung Yuan** took on a Buddhist flavor when it spread among the people in its current form in the first half of the sixth century, through the sponsorship of the Southern Liang Emperor Wu Ti (502–549 C.E.), a devout follower of the newly introduced Indian religion. It then became known as **General Salvation—** *Pudu,* or as the Festival of **Yu Lan Pen**—a name that has long been assumed to be a transcription of the Sanskrit word *Ullambana,* meaning "to be suspended upside down." However, the French scholar Jean Przyluski (1885–1944) has argued that it is more likely to be derived from another Buddhist term: *Avalambana,* which in India referred to certain offerings to all living beings but whose merits could also benefit the dead. It is mostly for this purpose that a **Yu Lan Pen** Society is set up in every Buddhist temple: putting fruits of every variety in basins to offer them in the ten directions—above, below, and the eight compass points. The *sutras* that are read all day in order to guide lost souls (*guhun*) out of Hell relate the story from the Buddhist canon on which a number of **Chung Yuan** practices are based. It is that of Maudgalyayana, a disciple of the Buddha known in Chinese as Mulian, who had a vision of his departed mother in Hell, fighting with hungry ghosts for food. The rice he spiritually sent her to appease her hunger turned into burning coals when it reached her. Turning to his master for advice, he was instructed to do these **Yu Lan Pen** offerings every year; they would go to feed the hungry ghosts and allow some relief to people's dead relatives who were caught in their realm. This answered to the priority always given to family ties in traditional Chinese culture, only in terms of Buddhism; for this imported religion's emphasis on indiscriminate universal compassion must otherwise have been a bewildering challenge to it.

Chung Yuan thus became another favorite occasion for displays of filial piety (as in the even more staunchly Confucian culture of Korea on its equivalent **Jungwon** or **Baekjung**—which entails serving a hundred different things on the table for a memorial service, aside from a ceremonial feast for farm laborers on this day off from harvesting). People who could afford it would evoke their forebears up to seven generations back by means of sutra readings in their homes, done by Buddhist monks and nuns. They gave them alms and gave charity to the poor as signs of gratitude and virtue. Joss sticks were lit and offerings were done on home altars, while sacrifices were also performed on ancestors' graves, including the burning of tin foil shaped to represent silver ingots, as a way to transfer wealth to their account, now done using mostly fake paper money.

These and similar practices are still observed today on both **Qing Ming** and **Chung Yuan** in Chinese homes and grave sites all over the world. But paper lanterns (at times houseshaped—not unlike the floating "**Lucy** houses" of Fürstenfeldbrück, Bavaria, on December 13) are specifically associated with **Chung Yuan** as a way to represent wandering souls and thereby try to do something to rescue them. They are launched onto a river or directly into the sea, so that unsettled spirits can easily spot them and grab a hold of them to find their way out of Hell and get to be reborn in a better place.

Japan's Bon Festival

This is one of the many customs of **Chung Yuan** that are also associated with its Japanese version, *Urabon* (from *Urabon-kyo,* the Japanese title of the *Avalambana-sutra*), also known as *O-bon* or **Bon** for short. The latter also happens to be the word for "tray," and it is on trays that offerings of food are made to the different categories of ancestors on temporary home altars built in bamboo a week early to welcome the ancient ones who then move into the top section, in hopes of getting their protection. The recently departed have to be appeased earlier still, as they are even more dangerous than the vindictive homeless dead. In modern Japan, the festival is most often moved from its traditional date on the full moon of the seventh lunar month to begin on the thirteenth of July (or August in some places like Kyoto) with welcoming fires (*mukaebi*) to greet the ancestors, and end on the sixteenth with seeing-off fires (*okuribi*), such as the giant multiple one tracing the Chinese character for "Great" (in honor of the Buddha) on the slopes of Mount Nyoigadake overlooking Kyoto. Joyful public dance parties take place outdoors along with fireworks displays on the nights of the fourteenth and fifteenth.

Living elders also get food offerings at the end of this festive period in Japan. As for children who have died without getting to know the Four Noble Truths of Buddhism, and who are therefore condemned to build and rebuild small stone towers on the edge of the River of Hell as demons keep tearing them down (a bittersweet fate that is reminiscent of that of unbaptized infants in limbo in Catholic doctrine), they have their own **Bon** festival on August 24. On this **Bon** of Jizô—a bodhisattva or compassionate saint who intercedes to bring them some relief, living children paint his effigy (as a bald old monk) on small stone slabs to invoke his protection and thank him for his care for their unfortunate peers.

> **See also** Days of the Dead (West); Dragon Boat Festival; Lantern Festival; May Day; Midautumn; New Fire Ceremony; New Year (China, Korea); Potlatch; Saint Lucy; Samhain

References

Jan Chozen Bays. *Jizo Bodhisattva: Guardian of Children, Travelers, and Other Voyagers.* Boston: Shambhala Publications, 2003.

Catherine Lang. *O-Bon in Chimunesu.* Vancouver, BC: Arsenal Pulp Press, 1996.

Stephen F. Teiser. *The Ghost Festival in Medieval China.* Princeton, NJ: Princeton University Press, 1988.

Judy Van Zile. *The Japanese Bon Dance in Hawaii.* Kalilua, HI: Press Pacifica, 1982.

DAYS OF THE DEAD (INDIA)
See Navaratra and Dusshera

DAYS OF THE DEAD (WEST)

Throughout the Western world, it is now mostly around November 1 that the living interact with the dead in the context of a public festival, because this is **All Saints**' Day for the Roman and Anglican Churches. If English-speaking peoples are haunted by the dead the night before on October 31 (**All Hallows' Eve** or **Halloween**), Spanish-speaking peoples tend to favor the following day of **All Souls** (hallowed or not) to visit their dead—or as in Mexico to be visited by them—on November 2. Yet these were not always the **days of the dead** in the Western Church, nor in the pagan cultures of classical antiquity previously; and the Eastern Church today also has a different set of **days of the dead**.

The Greek World

In ancient Greece, the three days before the last one of each month were devoted to the dead and to the gods of the underworld; while they lasted, criminal tribunals could not sit and no death sentence could be carried out. In Athens, the great yearly festival of the dead was the **Nemesia**. Named after the nymph Nemesis who saw to the "due enactment" (as her name translates) of the ritual death of sacred kings in order to ensure fertility, this ceremony to appease the angry dead took place toward September, on the fifth day of the month of Boedromion, concurrently with the festival of **Genesia**. This private commemoration of somebody's death on its anniversary, "known to all the Greeks" according to the historian Herodotus, had been set on this fixed date as a public remembrance day of all the dead as part of Solon's reform of the religious calendar in the sixth century B.C.E. At the end of the campaigning season in early winter, there was also an annual ceremony for the war dead, well known from a description by the historian Thucydides. The soldiers' bones were taken in a wagon procession in coffins—including an empty one for those whose bodies could not be recovered (comparable to the tomb of the unknown soldier, holding unidentified bones, that is wreathed in some of the Allied countries on **Remembrance Day** as the anniversary of their victory in World War I on November 11, 1918). The Dionysian festival of **Anthesteria**, toward the end of February, was devoted both to fertility and to the dead—more specifically the restless shades that then came out to haunt the living. Greeks still commonly believe they do during the first of three weeks of the **Carnival** season preceding **Lent**, and therefore dedicate the festive Sunday meal that concludes it with the prayer: "May God forgive the souls of the dead."

In the Greek Orthodox Church, there is no one special date set aside to honor the dead. Common days for commemorating the departed are scattered over the entire year, most of them on Saturdays, corresponding to the time when Jesus, after his crucifixion on the original **Good Friday**, was among the dead before his resurrection on **Easter** Sunday. For this reason, the Greek Church frowns upon the Russian custom of commemorating individual departed souls right after **Sunday** liturgy, the weekly feast of the Resurrection.

Nevertheless, throughout Orthodox Christianity, the first Sunday after **Pentecost** is devoted to **All Saints** following the ancient Antiochian custom of commemorating martyrs on this day, recorded by the fourth-century Church Father Saint John Chrysostom. Otherwise, aside from **Joyday,** the second Tuesday following **Easter** (plus a certain day in the interval in some Greek localities), the other days when the souls of the dead are commemorated are all Saturdays: the first Saturday of **Lent** along with the preceding two Saturdays, as well

as the last three Saturdays of **Advent,** the Saturdays of the two-week fast before the **Dormition of the Mother of God** on August 15, the **Soul Saturday** of Saint Demetrius toward the third week of October, **Holy** and Great **Saturday** on the eve of **Easter,** and **All Souls** on the eve of **Pentecost.** In all cases, the priest celebrates the commemorative service after the liturgy next to a table set with candles among the faithful. He blesses the consecrated bread and special cakes on the table.

These *colybes* are made with boiled rice or wheat, sugar or honey, raisins, and ground nuts. They may be related to the *panspermia* that were once distributed on the third and final day of **Anthesteria**, around the same time of year as the pre-**Lent Soul Saturdays.** Friends and relatives of the deceased, who bring these dishes, can consume them after the service, at church, at home, or on that person's grave. In the latter case, the priest will put the first share under the cross and some wine will be poured on the tombstone before a festive meal is partaken of on the premises. The role of wheat in these rites recalls age-old Greek agrarian precedents and the **Eleusinian Mysteries** of death and rebirth, initiation, and personal salvation, derived from them in late antiquity.

The Roman World

Testifying on behalf of the Latin Church in the early third century already that "as often as the anniversary comes round, we make offerings for the dead as birthday honours," Tertullian noted: "If, for these and other such rules, you insist upon having positive Scripture injunction, you will find none. Tradition will be held forth to you as the originator of them, custom as their strengthener, and faith as their observer" "The Chaplet, or De Corona," ch. III and IV). Yet in pagan Rome too, modest offerings of wheat, wine, salt, and flowers—along with prayers—were brought to the graves of dead relatives during the **Parentalia.** The nine-day commemoration, which had been extended over time to the dead in general, was opened in the name of the state with a funeral sacrifice by the great vestal at noon on February 13. It ended with the private festival of **Feralia** on February 21, when gifts were placed at the graves and the anniversary of the funeral feast was celebrated. During this period, temples would be closed and home fires would be put out, because the gods from heaven were to remain hidden while the shades of the dead came up from the underworld to consume the offerings on their graves. No weddings were to be performed during these unclean days when the dead roamed, as their souls might take over newly conceived bodies; it was therefore no time for a new human life to begin.

A trace of this ancient prohibition on weddings, initially aimed at widows and virgins alike, could be observed down even to the end of the nineteenth century as part of the customs of the famous Nice **Carnival**, held on about the same dates. Officially abolished in 1721, the *charavilh* (a local equivalent of the French *charivari*) was a way for the Abbots of Fools, who oversaw **Carnival** celebrations with full discretionary powers, to collect a tax from newly remarried widowers or betrothed widows; their unions were thus discouraged as being of doubtful fertility. This was done by making lots of racket in front of their house with various musical instruments and metal implements until they paid up, since there was no escape from all the noise and offensive singing: the doors were first blocked either with a fishing boat or with mock mortuary trappings, complete with bones and candles. In a related mock haunting practice imitated for a while in the late nineteenth century by the Nice **Carnival**, the Renaissance Roman **Carnival** used to culminate on **Shrove Tuesday** with a candlelight procession where everyone would try to put out the others' candles to the cry of "Death to him who has no candle!" Over two thousand years, the benign presence of the family dead during the Roman **Parentalia** seems to have evolved into the play-

ful evocation of the hereafter under the disguise of **Carnival** masks, wherever Rome left the legacy of mid-February memorials of the departed, mixing with the living.

But the atmosphere was long very different during the other major series of **days of the dead** in ancient Rome (if we neglect the **Compitalia** and little known **Larentalia**). Older than the nine relatively auspicious days of **Parentalia** according to Ovid, the **Lemuria** were three decidedly inauspicious days in **May**: the ninth, the eleventh, and the thirteenth. If the *parentes* were honored ancestors that people were glad to visit at their graves, the *lemures* were anonymous hungry ghosts floating through the air, whose visits to the living's homes were feared. To drive them out of the house, a man would have to get up in the middle of the night barefoot, do an obscene gesture with the thumb and fingers (still called "making the fig" in Italian), wash his hands, and throw beans over his shoulder nine times, which the restless spirit supposedly picked up behind him. This is how it was led out of the house, where the noise of a bronze utensil was enough to chase it away. The householder could safely turn back and sleep soundly. However, if any of the beans used germinated and if a woman ate the new beans from the plant, it was feared she would get pregnant with a wandering soul. It was probably due to such concerns about the interference of ghosts in human reproduction that, while the temples remained closed for the three days of **Lemuria** as they did for the novena of **Parentalia**, the taboo on weddings extended to the entire month of **May**. It survived until recently in some former Roman provinces like Provence in Southern France, where people were reluctant to get married in **May** till the twentieth century, for fear of misfortune and death.

All Saints' Day and Halloween

The Western feast of **All Saints** started out as the annual commemoration of the dedication by Pope Saint Boniface IV (608–615) of the Roman Pantheon as a church in honor of the Blessed Virgin and all martyrs. (This may be why the Greek word for a "temple of all the gods" gave the Spanish word *panteón* for a family vault in a cemetery—or for the cemetery itself in Mexico, Central America, and Andean countries.) The commemoration took place on May 13, 609, and was probably based on the original Eastern feast of all martyrs —eventually **All Saints**—on the first Sunday after **Pentecost**, known from the mid-fourth century when the Roman Empire became Christian. Yet May 13 had also happened to be the last day of the Roman **Lemuria** for lost souls. Nevertheless, the dead still used to be widely commemorated toward the spring equinox in late March (or mid-April in Ireland) even a couple of centuries after Gregory III, who was Pope from 731 to 741, decided to start observing the relevant rites on November 1, the date on which he consecrated an oratory at Old Saint Peter's Basilica to **All Saints**, known and unknown, living and dead, and so no longer just martyrs. Pope Gregory IV kept this widened scope for the feast: that is, the communion of all Christians beyond time, when he made the switch universal in 837.

The fact that outside of Rome, in areas of Europe where Celtic influence was still strong, the memory of this date of November 1 as that of the **New Year** lived on, might have been a reason why it was now made into that of a minor Christian festival. This day—called **Samhain** in Ireland—used to be a time when the boundaries between the Other World and the everyday world faded, so that all kinds of supernatural entities of pagan religion could manifest themselves to mortals. They were all lumped together as evil by the church, so that this now became a time of communication with the underworld, when demons lurked, and the dead also came into contact with the living. Hence the macabre, sinister trappings of **Halloween**, drawn from the Celtic heritage of Irish immigrants to the United States. Albeit reduced to mere fun and games, they are currently spreading all over the world as stock imagery under the irresistible marketing pressure of American popular culture—just as its version of **Christmas** customs did decades ago, on an increasingly comparable scale. In France especially, with the active encouragement of English teachers, newfangled **Halloween** observances were spreading for a while at the turn of the century, albeit with interesting small departures from their American model, such as an exclusive focus on lurid imagery as opposed to "cute" or merely fanciful disguises, and the invention of a special pumpkin-shaped **Halloween** cake lit from inside by a candle, called *samain* after the old Celtic term for the feast: **Samhain**.

All Souls' Day and Día de Muertos

The actual **Day of the Dead**—**All Souls**—was set on November 2, to follow **All Saints** (and perhaps in contrast to the nocturnal focus of "All Hallows' Eve"—**Halloween**) around the turn of the last millennium. Its observance was first spread by way of the monasteries by Saint Odilo (962–1049). This abbot of Cluny (the great Burgundian monastery spearheading the Gregorian Reform that recast the Western Church around the centralized authority of the Papacy) was supposed to have instituted the celebration of **All Souls** after hearing from a pilgrim returning from the Holy Land about the torments endured by the deceased in a volcanic place. By the end of the thirteenth century, this festival fulfilled a newly pressing need in most of Western Christendom to supplicate for the departed souls of the faithful. For their plight had become at once more dreadful and more open to negotiation due to another Catholic innovation going back to Saint Odilo: Purgatory (that is, the concept of an actual place where the souls of those who were not damned to Hell nonetheless suffered some of its pains for the length of measurable time necessary to purify them of their sins, so that God

Participants in a Día de Muertos pageant march in a mock funeral procession toward Mexico City's main square as part of celebrations honoring the dead that culminate on November 2, the feast of All Souls. (Reuters/Corbis)

would one day consider them fit to enter Paradise). It was even said that the restless souls burst out laughing with joy when they heard the tinkling of coins being collected for masses to shorten and alleviate their punishment on **Halloween** in Brittany. There, some parishioners would be appointed for this purpose and go from door to door all night as the church bells tolled, waking people up so they would pray for the dead and contribute for their repose. On that night, the dead might also expect to find the doors and windows of their former homes open to welcome them for a meal laid out for them inside on a white tablecloth, next to a fire in the hearth—so they could take in its warmth for the coming year. By now though, it is only in the Black Mountains of Armor that some families still set aside the "bread of the souls" (*barec an anaon*) on the dead's one night

out, though this used to be common practice throughout the Celtic areas of Western Europe.

Both **All Saints** and **All Souls** are devoted to communion with the dead in Italy, Portugal, and Spain. In these three countries, the cemeteries are then crowded with people who have come to offer their prayers and candles to dead relatives. In Spain and its former colonies, poor people also go from tomb to tomb offering to pray for the dead in exchange for food. Sharing food on their graves is a common way to associate them for a while with the activities of the living, which they are assumed to miss. Chestnuts play a special role, be it as honey and nut cakes made to look like them in Southern Italy, and called *pabassine,* or as actual chestnuts at the *castañadas* ("chestnut parties") seen throughout Spain, where cream-filled doughnuts called *buñuelos* are eaten too. Chestnut-shaped almond pastries called *panellets* are specific to Catalonia and the Balearic Islands, while in Aragon, Castille, and Navarra, people eat almond paste *huesos de santos* ("saints' bones") with yellow cream filling to represent the marrow.

The Spaniards brought their **Día de Muertos** (**Day of the Dead**) from Europe to Mexico. There, the descendants of the Aztecs, already notorious for their casual familiarity with death in all its forms, embraced the feast's customs and expanded upon them with a vengeance.

By early November in Mexico, all bakeries display *panes de muerto*—sugar-coated round breads decorated with shinbones and other symbols of death, cakes in which a tiny skeleton is hidden (like the lucky bean in the **Epiphany** "twelfth cake" in England and France), and all sorts of bone-shaped candies. But the most typical food of the season in Mexico is the *calavera,* a sugar (or more often nowadays a chocolate) skull, often decorated with chocolate and icing. The universal favorite is the actual-size variety—with the name of the person to whom it is offered written in sugar on a silver foil band on its forehead. Children especially look forward to theirs, among other gifts.

In the pre-Conquest calendar of Mexican Aztecs, the "Great **Feast of the Dead**"—*Hueymiccaihuitl*—was immediately preceded around mid-August by a "Lesser **Feast of the Dead**" (*Miccailhuitontli*) in honor of dead children (and immediately followed by the "**Falling of Fruit**"—*Xocotl Huetzi*). Since Spanish missionaries shifted the dates of these observances to the Christian feasts of **All Souls** and **All Saints** respectively, the latter is set aside on November 1 for dead little children (presumably more saintly—not having had time to commit any sin), as the **Día de Muertitos,** especially in small towns and Indian communities. Flower-decorated home altars set up to welcome them back hold as many candles as the family can remember *muertitos* ("dead little ones") or *angelitos* ("little angels"), along with their favorite foods and toys, plus the seasonal

toys that living children also get: tiny plastic bones, little coffins with a miniature skeleton as a jack-in-the-box, and the like. The word *calavera* is also used for all the sweets or change children ask of passersby (though this form of begging is being increasingly displaced by American-style **Halloween** trick-or-treating), as well as to refer to illustrated satirical pamphlets issued on this day to lampoon some of the more powerful figures among the living by depicting them as skeletons in the name of equalizing death—following in the footsteps of the graphic artist José Guadalupe Posada (1851–1913), creator of the genre and initiator of a lot of classic *Muertos* imagery. A lot of pointed social criticism gets to circulate freely under this **carnival** guise, as it never could to this extent in everyday life.

If political dissent surfaces in such urban practices, religious dissent is a feature of the widespread rural worship of *Santa Muerte*—"Saint Death," clearly of Spanish Catholic derivation, but which the Church disapproves of. In the countryside, certain rites recur in endless local variations, especially in Indian villages. There, the dead may be called in the graveyards to the sound of guitars and accordions played by villagers in colonial-style costumes, not to mention church bells pealing on October 31, as they will again on November 2, to invite them to leave their living relatives' homes and go back to their resting places. Throughout Mexico on November 1, crowds start streaming toward the nation's cemeteries to the cheerful, lively tunes of mariachi bands (who may offer to sing one for a departed person for a fee from the family), amid the loud bursts of firecrackers and fireworks, and the ghostly dances of people disguised as the roaming dead.

If the descendants of the Spaniards, like their European cousins, bring mounds of flowers to their dead relatives' resting places, the scene in the graveyards of predominantly Indian communities is somewhat different—especially in urban contexts (as opposed to the more serious and contemplative atmosphere of many country celebrations, more in tune with the pre-Hispanic origins of these celebrations). There, it is mostly food that is offered to the dead, being consumed by the living on the spot, with lots of strong drink (though a clay dog or dog-shaped bread is frequently put on the altar at home or at the cemetery—recalling the originally Mayan custom of killing a black dog and incinerating it with the body of the deceased so it could help his or her soul cross the river of death to heaven). Relatives and friends make macabre jokes, sing humorous songs, and may even dance among the graves. This merry party often degenerates into drunken confrontations where tempers flare, fights erupt, and accounts are settled. Many Mexicans die this way every year, adding to the numbers of the dead being celebrated on their own special day for fun and partying.

But the major difference between the Mexican and European **Days of the Dead** is not so much that one is tinged with sadness and the other exuberantly happy. In Mexico, the living do not just visit the dead at their current residence; they above all expect them to come over from their graves to visit their former homes. The paths leading home from the cemetery are marked with *cempazuchitl* petals (from the orange marigold known as "Indian rose" used in funerals in Mexico since Aztec times—as white chrysanthemums are in Europe), so the ghosts do not get lost on the way they take only once a year. It is a privilege for the living that they even bother to return at all, since as a popular saying goes, they must be better off "over there" in the beyond than "here" on earth; otherwise, they would come back for good. That is why they are induced to stay for a few hours of celebrations with an Altar of the Dead, especially set up in the home as a kind of landing pad for returning spirits. It is covered with an often richly embroidered cloth and decorated with *cempazuchiles,* tissue paper garlands of different symbolic colors (often cut to represent flowers,

birds, and cavorting skeletons), candlesticks, and incense burners—used to spread clouds of copal, so the pungent odor of this pine resin will guide departed spirits home like a beacon even as it wards off evil spirits. The returning dead also recognize themselves in family photographs, in sugar skulls bearing their name in icing, and in the hand-crafted skeletons called *calacas* representing their former occupations and hobbies on the three-tiered pyramidal altar. The wall behind the altar is frequently covered with pictures depicting various saints, among which the Virgin of Guadalupe has a place of honor. They may range from tacky color prints cut out from magazines to precious works of art handed down from generation to generation as family heirlooms. In the middle of these religious objects, the offerings for the dead are placed: cups and plates holding their favorite foods, beer bottles, cigars, their favorite objects—like a hat, a guitar, a deck of cards, along with glasses of water, because the dead are said to be always thirsty, as well as bread and salt—also offered as a sign of hospitality to the living in Rumanian folklore. And much as a white towel was used to welcome guests in a Karelian (Eastern Finnish) home, a washbasin, soap, towel, mirror, and comb are put at the disposal of a Mexican family's departed, so they can clean up when they come back home to visit those they have left behind, for twenty-four hours from around three in the afternoon on their appointed day—sometimes a special one set before the actual **Día de Muertos**.

To the sound of all the church bells, dead relatives come to the parties awaiting them at home in a precise order: a hierarchy based on factors like "reverse seniority." Thus in Oaxaca, known for its authentic **Muertos** observances, October 28 is set aside for people who died in accidents, took their own life, drowned, burned to death, or had any other kind of violent death, in that order. October 29 is for the unbaptized, and October 30 for other restless, lonely souls, before baptized children come home on November 1. From two o'clock the next day, the rank-and-file of adults who have died of old age, disease, and natural causes are first remembered at their graves before being entertained at home later that night—except for those who lost their life over the last year. This may be to ensure that surviving relatives have taken enough distance from the deceased, so that they do not feel the grief of the loss of someone only recently still present among them so much as the joy of having a chance to reunite with a family member who has gone off to another, better place. But aside from this exception that confirms the rule, in today's Mexico just as in the Europe of old, there is an underlying assumption that bad things can happen if the living fail to give the dead what is their due, in the form of prayers, food, or entertainment. Furthermore, tampering with the celebration of ancestral ties puts collective identity in jeopardy; this is why altars are also being put up in the public spaces of Mexico on *Los **Muertos**,* in schools, offices, and many supermarkets, as a statement of national pride and identity against the marketing onslaught of standardized **Halloween** customs, costumes, novelties, and paraphernalia from the United States.

The Huron Feast of the Dead

Further north in America, the great **Feast of the Dead** once observed mostly among the Hurons by early French missionaries also had a vital political dimension, insofar as it cemented a nation's inner peace as well as its foreign alliances. This was accomplished through lavish feasts and extravagant gifts comparable to those of the Northwestern **potlatch**, except that their main focus was the remains of the dead from natural causes. They were brought from all village cemeteries inside precious pelts for reburial in a central ossuary pit every decade or so, or else after a migration, toward May. The mixing of their bones (in which the sensitive as opposed to the rational souls of friends and rela-

tives still dwelled) around some broken kettles (hence the feast's Huron name: **Yandatsa** for "kettle"), placed in their midst so the objects' "souls" would serve them in the beyond, fostered the parallel intermingling of the living in an indissoluble unity. This might include Algonkian neighbors, like such Ojibwa groups as the Nipissing, trading partners of the Hurons who imported their **Feast of the Dead**. It was also a pivotal institution in the life of other Iroquoian peoples: the Tionontatés, the Neutrals (though they insisted on distinct individual burials in the common pit), and probably the Eries and Wenros. This great ten-day ritual is unique to the Ontario region, where it evolved from about 300 B.C.E. to its apogee and collapse upon European contact in the mid-seventeenth century. "It sums up the whole of Wendat [Huron] thinking, and by analogy, the thinking of all the peoples belonging to the social and spiritual universe of the Northeast, with Wendake [Huronia] as its geopolitical heartland" (Sioui 1999, p. 146).

> ***See also*** Argei; Assumption; Beautiful Festival of the Valley; Caristia; Carnival; Christmas; Dionysia; Easter; Eleusinian Mysteries; Epiphany; Holy Week; Lent; May Day; Navaratra and Dusshera; Potlatch; Samhain; Sunday; Whitsuntide

References

Catherine Chambers. *All Saints, All Souls, and Halloween.* Austin, TX: Raintree Steck-Vaughn, 1997.

Franz Cumont. *Lux Perpetua.* New York: Garland Publishing, 1987.

Jack Santino, ed. *Halloween and Other Festivals of Death and Life.* Knoxville: University of Tennessee Press, 1994.

Chloë Sayer, ed. *The Mexican Day of the Dead: An Anthology.* Boston: Shambhala Redstone Editions, 1994.

Georges E. Sioui. *Huron Wendat. The Heritage of the Circle.* Rev. Ed., Tr. J. Brierley. Vancouver: University of British Columbia Press and East Lansing: Michigan State University Press, 1999.

Tertcillian. "The Chaplet, or De Corona." Tr. Rev. A. Roberts and J. Donaldson, www.ccel.org.

DEACONS' DAY
See Christmas

DECENNIAL GAMES
See Games (Rome)

DECLARATION OF BAHÁ'U'LLAH'S MISSION, DECLARATION OF THE BAB'S MISSION
See Ridván

DEDICATION (FESTIVAL OF THE)
See Elevation of the Cross, Hanukkah

DEEPAWALI
See Divali

DELIA
See Thargelia

DEPOSITION OF THE MOST PURE VEIL OF THE HOLY MOTHER OF GOD OF BLACHERNES
See Protection of the Mother of God

DÉSALPE
See Conception and Birth of the Virgin Mary

DEVILS (FESTIVAL OF)
See Days of the Dead (China, Korea, Japan)

DHANTERAS
See Divali

DÍA DE LOS TRES REYES
See Epiphany

DÍA DE MUERTITOS, DÍA DE MUERTOS
See Days of the Dead (West)

DIES NATALIS
See Caristia

DIONYSIA (GREECE AND ROME)

In Greco-Roman religion, the many festivals of the ambiguous and lascivious wine god Dionysus could be referred to as **Dionysia**. They began as crude fertility rituals and later evolved into widespread mystery cults in answer to new spiritual needs and social conditions, since they favored ecstatic personal communion with the seemingly "foreign" god of all that could not be placed within the fixed scheme of things as they were soberly defined in ancient Greece and Rome. The best known of Greek **Dionysia** are those of Attica, such as **Oschophoria**, **Lenaea**, **Anthesteria**, the Lesser or Country **Dionysia**, and the Greater or City **Dionysia**, as part of which the theater developed. There were wilder **Dionysia** elsewhere in the Greek world, since this cult spread to its furthest reaches under a multitude of guises. **Bacchanalia** were first met with hostility in Rome, but would gain wide acceptance under the Empire. Dionysian feasts also left their mark on several Christian ones.

Winter Festivals for a Dark Olympian

In ancient Greece, many festivals of the cold season were devoted to Dionysus early on. The freedom from agricultural labor and the ready availability of its harvested fruits over this period made it well suited for the kind of heavy partying they often involved. At a deeper symbolic level, this was also the dark half of the year, the night of the cosmic cycle, when order, structure, and hierarchy gave way to elemental chaos and the powers of the underworld of shadows and instinctual drives. Likewise, the earth's recesses were the dark womb of springtime's abundant plant life, which Dionysus embodied. And yet, the name Dionysus was sometimes held to mean "twice the son of

Zeus"—the sky god by whose full revelation his mortal mother Semele (a name possibly related to *z'emlya*—the Russian word for "earth") was literally thunderstruck. Zeus then took their child from her charred remains and implanted him in his own thigh to carry him to term. Dionysus was thus born twice—once of a dead mortal, then as an Olympian god, fusing in himself heaven and earth. His divinity was unique in blurring all distinctions between the plant, animal, human, and divine realms.

Oschophoria

The first of his festivals in Athens was actually devoted to his half-sister Athena as well in the deme—or country district—of Phalera during the month of Pyanepsion, that is around mid-October. Organized by the *genos* or clan of the Salaminioi, the **Oschophoria** were the "Carrying of the Grape Clusters" on their vines from the temple of Dionysus to the shrine of Athena Skiras by a singing procession of twenty well-born adolescent boys or ephebes (led by two in drag), representing the ten tribes of Attica. They would also race along the same course holding these *oschoi* for the prize of the first taste of *pentaploa*—a special brew of five ingredients: wine, honey, barley, oil, and cheese. (Minus the latter and plus figs, they were also those displayed on the *eiresionai* branch at festivals such as the **Panathenaea**, **Pyanopsia**, and **Thargelia**.) At a banquet involving female "dinner-bearers" (*deiplophoroi*) in honor of the three daughters of Cecrops—the half-man, half-snake ancestral culture hero of Athenians to whom their civilized customs were traced, the young men would dance and make sacrifices and libations (wine offerings) to the liturgical cry of *Eleleu iou iou!*—strangely mixing joy in the first part (reminiscent of the Hebrew *Alleluia!*) and grief in the second part, in a way that was as typical of the spirit of Dionysian worship as the mixing of gender roles at the ambivalent common root of comedy and tragedy.

Two masked comedians marching. Terracotta figurines (second half of the first century B.C.E.), from Myrina, Isle of Lemnos, Greece. (Erich Lessing/Art Resource)

Country Dionysia

Country **Dionysia** were held at different times in all demes or villages throughout Greece (over the month of Poseideon or December in Attica), as a cheerful vintage thanksgiving holiday—whether or not they grew wine. It unfolded publicly along the lines of the private family celebration described in the earliest of Aristophanes' surviving comedies: *Acharnians,* performed in Athens in 425 B.C.E. at the Greater **Dionysia**—as opposed to which this festival, first called **Theoinia**, came to be known as the Lesser **Dionysia**. In this poetic account, it starts with prayer and a procession to the sacrifice, with the daughter as basket-bearer (*kanêphoros*) for the offerings such as cakes she carries on her head, followed by a slave carrying a large-size phallus effigy meant to stimulate the fertility of the fields and the wombs, while the master of the house sings a merry phallic song, and his wife looks at the procession from the rooftop. Slaves would also take part in such processions where the whole family—covered in foliage, smeared with wine, joking around—went about in carts with wine vases and fruit baskets to lead a goat to be sacrificed at the shrine of Dionysus.

There, a choir would stand around the altar to sing the god's praises and tell the story of his birth, sufferings, and death—at the roots of the dithyramb genre, which originally mimicked the dismembering and devouring of a bull in a dance-like trance of frenetic gestures, while its name refers to "him who entered life by a double door." In the seasonal game of *askoliasmos,* young men would hop with one foot at a time on greased wine goatskins while others tried to push them off. The fall of each contestant was greeted with general laughter, and the last one standing won the wine skin with its contents. Noisy bands of masked, disguised young men roamed country roads and village streets singing and dancing to the tune of flutes, and making obscene jokes at the expense of all they came across. Two of them would have mock quarrels as part of interludes called *komoi*—out of which the comedy genre evolved. From the fifth century B.C.E. onward, wandering actors toured the countryside to put on plays in wealthier demes on makeshift outdoor stages, drawing them from the established repertoire of larger towns. The older Country **Dionysia** only gradually made their way into the cities, but in time they would themselves almost altogether give way to the newer urban festivals of Dionysus.

Lenaea

Thus, the festival of **Lenaea**, held at first over two days, and eventually up to four from about the twelfth of Gamelion in late January or early February, seems to have been little more than the Country **Dionysia** transferred to the urban setting of Athens—or more precisely the suburban one of Limnae, where the Lenaeon temple was located. Possibly owing its name to the wine-

press (*lenos* in Greek), it was the destination of a procession with sacrificial animals, where a torch-bearer of Eleusis would tell the crowd to "call the god," whereupon it shouted "Iacchus, Son of Semele, giver of riches!"—as at the **Eleusinian Mysteries**. "Jokes from the car" in the parade on this occasion became proverbial.

On this first day, there were also wild dances by the—*maenads* ("mad ones") or *Lenai*—ecstatic female devotees of Dionysus after which this shrine and the festival may have been named. Part or all of this festival was also referred to as **Ambrosia** in honor of the drink of the gods, no doubt because plenty of wine was drunk on this as on all feasts of its god Dionysus, at a great banquet at public expense. A yearly bull representing him was cut into nine pieces in sacrifice to his mother Semele: one was burned and the others eaten raw by the worshippers. The priestly king archon provided actors and the city made seats available at a wooden theater built every year next to the Lenaion, until it crumbled during a performance in which the tragic playwright Aeschyles was involved in 478 B.C.E., to be replaced by a permanent stone theater of Dionysus in the heart of Athens under the administration of the statesman Lycurgus (338–326 B.C.E.). No less than fifty performers were involved in the dancing performance of dithyrambs—hymns to Dionysus by a choir of satyrs. Though they took on literary forms and dramatic structure over time, they remained popular spectacles, using ritual exclamations and hypnotic rhythms to draw everyone into the trance of collective enthusiasm. The latter word was first used in Greek to refer to "possession by the god," namely Dionysus, often induced in his devotees—female *Bacchae* and male *Bacchi*—by chewing ivy as the other plant in which he dwelled, aside from the vine. An ivy wreath and an incense tripod rewarded the best performance in contests called *agones*—involving dithyrambs only at first, until tragedies were added in the middle of the sixth century B.C.E., as were comedies by the middle of the fifth century B.C.E.

Anthesteria

Another **Dionysia**n festival of rustic origins was held in Athens (the oldest one there according to the Greek historian Thucydides) over three days from the eleventh or twelfth of the month of Anthesterion (February–March), to mark the start of spring and taste the wine stored the previous fall. The fermentation of the juice of crushed grapes seemed to distill the essence of the mysterious process of transformation of wintertime's dead nature into the flower of its springtime rebirth. The **Anthesteria** were thus a "Feast of Flowers" celebrating nature's revival.

The first day was a family festival called the "cask opening"—**Pithoigia**—offering the **first-fruits** of the wine harvest to Dionysus to dispel the danger inherent in all new things, and to turn the potential poison into a blessed source of pleasure and a wholesome *pharmakon*. Servants brought in the casks of the new wine to be used at the next day's banquet, opened them, poured it into vessels, and could taste it along with their masters, hence the saying: "Get out, slaves! The **Anthesteria** are over." Their first two days were also school holidays for children, who were crowned with flowers and received gifts such as miniature wine jugs (some of which have been found in the graves of infants who died well before **Anthesteria** age). On the first day, the wooden statue of Dionysus Eleutheros (originally from the Boeotian village of Eleutherai) was taken out of the temple of Dionysus Limnaeos—that is "of the marsh" south of the city. To symbolize this god's "foreignness" to Greek order and measure, he was brought from the seaside on a boat-shaped cart decorated with grape clusters and leaves to a chapel in the outer Ceramicus. This was the starting point of its solemn entry into the city as part of the procession of the following day—though it actually began at sunset, like all Greek festivals.

On this **Feast of the Pitchers** or *Choai*, children aged three and older also figured in this boisterous costumed procession with torches around the cart of Dionysus. As part of the various rites observed along the way, the wife of the king archon of Athens had to sit beside the god's statue as his bride for a day. The *basilinna* would first have sworn in—in the only rite ever performed inside the Marsh shrine—the *erairai* or ladies of honor appointed by the king archon, in view of secret ceremonies involving various offerings and the manipulation of sacred objects or *hiera* inside baskets. They culminated in the *bukoleion* or "ox stall"—the old royal residence (and home of Dionysus as sacrificial bull?) southeast of Athens' civic square or *agora*, with the sacred marriage of the figurehead "queen" to the god, symbolized by the statue. The king himself may have initially stood in for him to literally consummate his union with the city as "giver of riches." This attested the integration into Athenian civic order of the god of irrational transgression that had long been kept at its margins.

The merriment that went on outside all the while was but a foretaste of that of the **Pitcher Feast** itself the next day. It owed its name to the wine containers for which the State gave each citizen a fixed sum, as well as for the food of the great banquet it sponsored in the theater of the Lenaeon, though the head priest of Dionysus had to supply tables and seats. An unusual silence was to be observed between partakers in the peculiar "banquet" where people had to bring their own food on this "day of impurity" (*miara hemera*), due to the evil spirits and wandering souls that then roamed the earth. Still, there was a drinking contest where the king archon would reward with a wine skin, a cake, or a wreath the first person to silently empty a five-liter pitcher of wine at the signal given by a trumpet. Many of these containers have been found; miniature ones were given to children as toys. These *choai* are also often decorated with pictures of small children playing with toys and wreaths of foliage such as those they would especially wear the next day, as human embodiments of springtime renewal. There were also private parties, such as those of the Sophists—late-fifth-century B.C.E. professional philosophers who, on this occasion, received presents and fees for the rhetoric training they offered. When night had fallen, guests would take their pitchers and the wreaths of fresh flowers they had been wearing in the procession to the shrine of Dionysus Eleutheros, where a priestess would take the wreath and the remaining wine was poured as a libation.

During the **Anthesteria**, all shrines except that of the Marsh were encircled with a red rope to preserve their ritual purity from the souls of the dead freed from the underworld on these days. People smeared their own doors with tar and chewed *rhamnos*—whitethorn leaves (an aphrodisiac)—to keep the dead at bay. The third day was more specifically devoted to the dead, let out of Hades along with its nefarious spirits, the *Keres*. It was called the "**Feast of Pots**" or *Khitroi* after the earthen containers used for offerings to the dead and to the netherworld deity Hermes Chthonios, consisting mainly in *panspermia*: a hodgepodge of various plant seeds cooked together and also eaten as a meal, since no meat was allowed. The living and the dead thus partook in the same banquet to encourage the powers of the underworld to also give out their riches as abundant crops. To further stimulate the forces of life, there were seasonal games like boxing, a race with torches, drinking contests, or music competitions.

Young girls and sometimes children played a game of swings—called *aiora*. Their movement echoed that of the Athenian maidens who hanged themselves in imitation of Erigone. She had first called the curse of this wave of suicides on her land for as long as her father's death remained unavenged. Icarius had been killed and buried under a pine tree (like Attis in the myth at the basis of the **Spring Festival of Cybele**—which this cult seems to echo) by the shepherds to whom he had given the first trial jarful of a new drink the vine god Dionysus had taught him how to make. Unused to wine, they had thought themselves bewitched when they began to see double, and had turned on him. The story of the hanged girls probably derived from the seasonal appearance of the masks of the long-haired and effeminate Dionysus that were hung on a pine tree in the middle of a vineyard, so the wind would make them look upon all sides of it in turn in blessing. As for the swings also tied to its branches for girls to stand on, they were meant to dispel the mortal curses and bad omens they evoked. They were often placed above lidless jars buried in the ground as the gaping womb of the earth, so humans could capture its fertile power, which they in turn encouraged with their swinging motions. In the latter sense, similar swing games are also part of **Holi** celebrations around this time of year in India, as well as of several Chinese and Korean festivals. For Athens, the libations and other rites in honor of Icarus and Erigone took place in the village of Icaria on the northern slope of Mount Pentelicus, in a valley that is still called the place of Dionysus today, since this is where the "foreign" god was first welcomed in Attica. The swing game is best known from this region, but is also attested as far away as the Greek colony of Massalia—present-day Marseille in southern France. There were also variants of **Anthesteria** in other colonies in Asia Minor, often involving the expulsion of evils with a human scapegoat.

City Dionysia

It was also Icarius who was said to have introduced in Athens the sacrifice to Dionysus of a goat—the latter being his enemy, since it eats the vine plants, the Roman poet Virgil reasoned. Icarians were the first to dance around the slain beast and compete in hopping on the wine bottle made from goatskin. Dionysian dancers and musicians would come down from

Icaria for the Greater **Dionysia** (*Megala Dionysia*) of Athens, a springtime festival of the flowering vine held in March from the eighth to the fourteenth of the month of Elaphebolion. The sea was then safe enough to allow pilgrims to come from all over Greece—on a scale comparable to the influx for the **Panathenaea**. Vital like them as an affirmation of civic identity and political awareness, these relatively secularized City **Dionysia** still opened with a sacrifice for public health to the healing god Asclepios, and the official announcement at the *odeon*—or music theater—of the contestants in dramatic competitions to be held from the third day to the fifth and last day.

In the meantime, there would be processions of the newer gold and ivory statue of Dionysus Eleutheros between the marsh shrine and the theater of Dionysus, with *kanêphoroi* (as at the **Panathenaea**) bearing the tributes of allies, as well as sacrificial animals and dancers in animal skins and masks like those from Icaria. When the tyrant Pisistrates refounded the festival (some time between 534 and 531 B.C.E.), the Icarian head performer Thespis first played an articulate human character distinct from the rest of his troupe with its chanting of choral lyrics. Actors are therefore also known as thespians after him, since his innovation marked the birth of tragedy—a Greek word referring to the "song of the goat" which the tragic hero (either masked or chalk-faced—like the ancestral heroic spirits he evoked) replaced as a fictional human scapegoat. The prize for the best tragedy was even a goat (whereas a tripod rewarded the best dithyramb and a basket of figs with a wine amphora went to the best comedy). This is what allowed Aristotle to speak of the cathartic—that is, purifying—effect of watching heroes get torn apart by a tragic fate before dying on stage at the theater of Dionysus. No doubt as part of that collective process of dealing with life's traumas, the sons of actual heroes who had fallen in battle were paraded in full armor in the theatre prior to the performances.

The plays were shown under the direction of the head priest of Dionysus and organized long in advance by religious and secular officials along with designated private sponsors as part of Dionysian festivals, where poor citizens were given a special subsidy to pay their entrance at the theater. At the Greater **Dionysia**, three poets wrote, produced, and probably acted in three tragedies on a single theme, also providing comic relief in a satyr-play that handled heroic subject matter in a burlesque fashion (like the only surviving complete example: Euripides' *Cyclops*). The latter genre was introduced at this festival shortly after tragedy in the last third of the sixth century B.C.E. in order to deal with some of the original Dionysian content neglected by tragic authors as they treated other material. It was likewise developed from the dithyramb as a dramatic choral hymn to Dionysus by performers dressed as satyrs (goat-footed followers of the god), of which each of the city's ten tribes provided one chorus for the men's competition and one for the boys'. The god could just as well be represented by the goat as the animal that was slashed to pieces in his name and in imitation of his own fate as a boy at the hands of the Titans. He had then been revived and later temporarily transformed into a kid or a ram after Zeus's wife Hera, goddess of marriage, drove his foster father King Athamas mad, and had him kill his own son Learchus when he mistook him for a stag. The Greater **Dionysia** took place during the deer-hunting season, at a time when wine stock stumps looked like budding antlers or horns that needed the blood of the animals they called to mind to grow to maturity. Several elements in the costume of the *hypokrites* (the actor as "speaker from beneath" the mask—and the play of appearances) recalled the original animal victim he supplanted. The dramatic contests of Athens prompted a widespread demand for the founding of theaters, so **Dionysian** festivals could be held in this domesticated form in cities scattered across the

Mediterranean basin. Yet wilder versions kept featuring bloody rites.

Agrionia

On the island of Tenedos off the coast of western Anatolia, the victim was a male calf, and its mother was treated as a woman while it gave birth to this incarnation of the god, which was given to wear the same high-platform shoes or *cothurni* that actors would wear on stage later on. Along with the islands of Chios and Lesbos, Tenedos sacrificed a fawn to Dionysus Omadios—"the Raw-flesh-eater." Such *omophagia* (a Greek term for the eating of a sacrificial victim's raw flesh) also characterized the offering of a kid or a piglet to Dionysus Scyllitas ("the Ripper") on the island of Cos. Yet it was not known for human sacrifice, as were the other islands just mentioned, along with Crete and Patras, or Potniae near Thebes, where a child was eventually replaced by a goat.

The most notorious Dionysian festival of this kind was the **Agrionia** (from *agrios* for "wild" or "savage"), best known from its celebration at Orchomenus in Boeotia every other year well into the Common Era. The three daughters of Arcadia's King Minyas preferred to keep on doing housework rather than join other women in one of them, and, like many other legendary figures who tried to stand in the way of the sacred mania of Dionysian festivals, incurred the god's wrath in the guise of a fit of his brand of madness, in which one of them ate her own son. This is why it was originally the custom at this festival for the priest of Dionysus to pursue women of the accursed Minyan royal clan at night with a sword and slay any he caught. Similar **Agrania** were held on the basis of other versions of this story in two major centers of the enthusiastic cult of Dionysus: Argos and his native city of Thebes.

Trieterides

These were foremost among the many places in Greece where **Trieterides** were held in winter every couple of years. On such occasions, wearing fawn skins and ivy wreaths and waving *thyrsoi* (ivy-tipped fennel wands bound with vine leaves), female Bacchants would run and dance with torches through the hills at night, shouting "*Euoi!*" with wild motions in a state of trance induced by the rhythm of flutes and kettledrums, which endowed them with the ability to charm snakes, suckle beasts or tear them to pieces with their bare hands to eat them raw. In Delphi, home of the Panhellenic oracle of Apollo—god of light and order, these devotees of his nocturnal counterpart Dionysus, called Thyiads ("rushing distraught ones"), were joined on the slopes of Mount Parnassus by a delegation of their colleagues from Athens. A sacrifice was offered each winter at his grave near the tripod of Apollo's oracle at the exact moment when, on the Parnassus, the Thyiads awoke Dionysus Liknites—the "Cradle-child" which their namesake nymphs had been entrusted with there. This echoed his rebirth after having been put to death and laid out in the temple of Apollo, which symbolized the winter death and spring rebirth of vegetation. At the **Thyia** festival of Elis, women invoked him in the shape of a bull. Various festivals of Dionysus were observed in every corner of the Peloponnese, as in all islands of the Aegean Sea, and in over 150 cities in Asia Minor.

Hellenistic Heyday

To the north of Greece, Thrace and Macedonia were hotbeds of the cult of Dionysus, and Alexander's conquests favored its spread (sometimes as a compulsory state religion) from there to all of the eastern Mediterranean and the Middle East, where it melded with many local fertility and mystery cults. From the second third of the fourth century B.C.E., Alexander and his descendants grounded their divine kingship in their frequent claim to be a "New Dionysus"—that is, a violent, invincible god of insatiable appetites, whose conquest of the known world up to India dovetailed with the evangelistic zeal of the *thyasi*—religious societies that were open to all devotees of Dionysus regardless of gender, class, or ethnic background. For the ecstasy he brought was also a liberation from the strictures of social order for those otherwise confined to the bottom of the ladder, such as women and slaves. In an increasingly cosmopolitan and urban setting where uprooted groups of foreigners and freed slaves contributed to a demand for social moorings that traditional local allegiances could no longer provide, voluntary associations in view of personal salvation through transgressive experiences provided an answer to a widespread spiritual malaise. This revolutionary power could now be harnessed and channeled through Dionysian festivals by charismatic leaders for their empire-building purposes, rather than remain in latent conflict with the rigid rationality of ancient republics.

In these Hellenistic kingdoms, the frenzied whirling and tossing around of ecstatic maenads and thyiads could now move from the margins of civic life to center stage on public squares. In the port of Miletus in Asia Minor, according to an inscription from 276 B.C.E., private and public *thyasi* existed side by side, their clergy and functions were largely interchangeable, and the priestess performed rites such as *omophagia* on behalf of the city—leaving a mouthful of raw meat in a sacred basket to symbolize the older human sacrifice. This official status as part of civic life was remarkable for a secret cult of personal initiation into orgiastic mysteries. In the Hellenistic era, theaters became central institutions as they spread apace with the popularity of **Dionysia**. It was there that, during these festivals, the public benefactors (*evergetes*) who helped put them on were honored. The Dionysian space of the theater could even replace the public forum of the agora for political assemblies, like the ones held regularly in the theater of Megalopolis by the cities of Arcadia. Many cities that held Dionysian festivals had their own actors' guilds, which also traveled to other cities to offer their services for the local versions of these theatrical events. This allowed Greek literature to provide common points of reference for all the countries that were hellenized as a result of the conquests of Alexander the Great. In this way, the **Dionysia** were instrumental in laying the foundations of Western culture in the ancient world.

Bacchanalia and Backlash

And yet the backlash they provoked in Rome probably slowed their expansion for a couple of centuries. Known there under the name of Bacchus (meaning "bough") used mostly by tragic poets at the theater, Dionysus was like a Greek import—though he borrowed some traits of his more sedate local counterpart Liber Pater. His cult came to Rome from both the Greek colonies of southern Italy and the neighboring areas of Campania and Etruria. Until about 200 B.C.E., following the tradition of Boeotian **Trieterides**, the Roman **Bacchanalia** were celebrated in broad daylight three times a year with only respectable matrons as priestesses. Then a priestess of Campanian background, Paculla Annia, secretly changed the rites to hold them at night up to five times a month and admit men, with a twenty-year age limit for initiation. Ten days of sexual abstinence closed by a meal and a purifying bath preceded clandestine meetings and orgies involving collective delirium with wild contortions, loud cries, entranced prophecy, mad races to the Tiber River to plunge torches in it (though they remained miraculously lit), and taking initiates into caves in imitation of the descent of Dionysus into Hades to take Semele back to life. These practices are well known from the **Dionysia**n festivals of Asia Minor, but there is no proof they also included human sacrifice as Roman prosecutors alleged. They created a scandal upon their chance discovery in 186 B.C.E. and were seen by authorities as highly subversive of the stability and security of the Republic, threatening the unity of the citizenry along with its austere public morality.

The repression was swift and brutal throughout Italy, with 7,000 initiates facing execution—such a vast number that only active participants in secret rituals were actually put to death and the others were put in jail.

There were uprisings in certain rural areas, and the **Bacchanalia** partly went underground, while their public manifestations were strictly limited and severely regulated. This campaign provided a model for the later persecution of Christians by the Roman Empire, once it had taken over the Hellenistic kingdoms of the Near East and the cult of Dionysus was resurfacing everywhere—from the underclass to the Emperor as "New Dionysus" on the model of Alexander—as one of a number of Oriental religions competing to quench the spiritual thirst and address the social unrest of Mediterranean peoples in late antiquity. Having developed a rich theology of the wine-press in which the god was torn to pieces and yielded his blood as wine for humans to partake in his immortal life, it was the last of these new religions to give way before triumphant Christianity, which borrowed some of its symbolism. It also survived several centuries in covert forms, especially in wine-growing areas from Germany to Algeria. Traces of it abound in European folklore, be it on the Feast of **Saint Vincent** as patron of the vintage on January 22 (on the **Lenaea**) or above all during **Carnival** with its unleashing of carnal instincts and suspension of social order in the shadow of death (around the **Anthesteria**).

Dionysian Survivals in Modern Greece

Northern Greek **Carnival** folklore is particularly rich in **Dionysia**n survivals. Many villages of the east and north of Thrace have bawdy processions and plays by mummers called *Kalogheroi* (or *Kukeri* across the border in Bulgaria) who dress like wild men in animal skins, carry a phallic rod, and sometimes act out a premature birth like that of Dionysus Liknites. Another offshoot of the ancient cult of the god

Dionysus is still to be found in the same areas of Greece on the May 21 feast of **Saints Constantine and Helena**—favorite patrons of countless churches. Throughout the country, processions and folk dancing honor them on this occasion, and rams or bulls are often sacrificed to obtain their favor, before a feast that ends in games and dances. In the north, though, a number of small communities have strayed far enough from orthodoxy in celebrating pre-Christian rituals under the cover of venerating Constantine and Helena that they have been excommunicated by ecclesiastical authorities. They still follow annual firewalking dance ceremonies called **Anastenaria** that now attract a steady flow of tourists, and which clearly owe more to Dionysius than they do to Christ. They originated in eastern Thrace, a former center of the orgiastic cult of this god in present-day Bulgaria, from which the populations exchanged with Greece after the Balkan Wars of the early twentieth century spread it to their areas of resettlement in the Greek portion of Macedonia, another ancient Dionysian center. Prior to this, the most perfect form of the **Anastenaria** rites was to be found in the small Thracian village of Kosti, where the icons of Constantine and Helena (a son and mother like Dionysus and Semele—who perished by fire) were rescued from a burning church in the Middle Ages. This gave rise to the practice of dancing with these icons on burning coals, that may now be witnessed chiefly in the village of Aghia Eleni (Saint Helena) near Serres, and in the nearby ones of Meliki-of-Verres, Mavrolefki-of-Drama, and Langada-of-Salonica.

Yet such *pyrobasia* was already associated in ancient times with the cult of Dionysus, while its brotherhoods of trance specialists are also replicated in that of modern-day *Anastenarides*—from *anastenazo*: "to sigh," as they do with short, loud gasps when they lead the increasingly rapid dance around the fire with the icons. During the three to eight days of the festival, the portable icons of **Saints Constantine and Helena** dancing together are kept in the meeting hall of the brotherhood, where the sacred drum, flute, bagpipe, and one-stringed fiddle are permanently stored, along with the sacred axe, knife, and chopping block used to kill the sacred bull. As at any Dionysian ritual, wine and spirits flow, helping people to work themselves into a trance, so that some can walk barefoot or in their socks on the burning embers of the fire, and even trample them for several minutes at a time, while holding up the icon.

It is the icon that summons those who are clean to walk on the fire and remain unhurt. A dancer who has been chosen in this way may then become possessed by the spirit of Emperor Constantine (as a "New Dionysius"?), and after some inarticulate cries, start shouting: "Make your vows to the Saint!" and "Restore justice, lest the Saint destroy you!" The villagers obey these commands by pledging gifts to the church and by trying to recall any offense they might have given to another, so as to try and make up for it. Thus, the firewalking ceremony of the **Anastenaria** functions as a kind of group therapy where people sort out their relational problems and, like ancient priestesses of Dionysius, women can exceptionally assume a position of authority as channels for this healing spirit. If they are called to walk on the fire, they too can become Anastenarides, and get to ask the icon of Constantine to forecast the future by talking through them (as Dionysus used to do at Thracian oracles). The new Anastenarides who are inducted in this ordeal by fire can henceforth hang a lantern at their front door to show that they belong to the chosen few. The dancing of the **Anastenarides** goes on well into the night as they leave the square and, preceded by the musicians with their drums and flutes, take the saints' icon on the mountain roads in a torch-lit procession to visit its "brothers," the icons of Constantine and Helena in other villages.

Following an all-night service in honor of **Saints Constantine and Helena** at the church, the priest blesses the sacred bull and other ani-

mal victims the next morning. The Head *Anastenaris* then waves the saints' icon over the head of the bull in the sign of the Cross before slaughtering the beast in such a way that its blood splashes onto the church's foundations. The raw meat is shared among the villagers, while the leather is cut into strips that will be made into sandals, each household getting a new pair every year. Except for the sacrifice, the same routine is followed every day of the feast's octave over the following week. But on the feast itself, as in the most archaic dithyrambs of Dionysus, omophagia comes at the climax of his sacrifice as a bull following manic dances and mystic trances.

See also Argei; Carnival; Days of the Dead (China, Korea, Japan); Days of the Dead (West); Dragon Boat Festival; Eleusinian Mysteries; Games (Greece); Games (Rome); Holi; Liberalia; Midautumn; New Year (China, Korea); Panathenaea; Saturnalia; Thaipusam; Thargelia; Whitsuntide; Yom Kippur

References

J. K. Cowan. *Dance and the Body Politic in Northern Greece.* Princeton, NJ: Princeton University Press, 1990.

Lewis Richard Farnell. *The Cults of the Greek States.* Vol. V. Oxford: Clarendon Press, 1909.

Martin Persson Nilsson. *The Dionysiac Mysteries of the Hellenistic and Roman Age.* New York: Arno Press, 1975.

Sir Arthur Pickard-Cambridge. *The Dramatic Festivals of Athens.* Revised 2nd Ed. Oxford: Clarendon Press, 1988.

▶ DIVALI (HINDUISM, JAINISM, SIKHISM)

The word **Divali** is a common contraction of **Deepawali**, from Sanskrit *awali* for "string, line" and *deepa* for small earthenware oil lamps. The latter are placed in rows in front of temples and houses and set adrift on streams and rivers on what is one of the year's major festivals for Hindus as well as for Jains and Sikhs all over the

An Indian girl lights a deepa oil lamp on the eve of Divali, the Hindu festival of lights, when Hindus in India and around the world light lamps in their homes to symbolize the victory of good over evil. (Reuters/Corbis)

world. The lights commemorate the return of Rama, whom Hindus see as the seventh incarnation of the god Vishnu (the Preserver in the Hindu triad), to Ayodhya, to be enthroned after fourteen years of exile in Sri Lanka.

A number of different religious observances are featured in turn over the five days of **Divali**, which occurs in late October or early November, from the thirteenth day of the dark half of the Hindu month of Ashvina to the second day of the light half (from new to full moon) of the month of Karttika. The festival has special significance for the Vaishya caste of merchants be-

cause it also honors Vishnu's wife Lakshmi, goddess of wealth.

First Day: Dhanteras

Divali celebrations are ushered in by *Dhantray-odashi*, from *dhan* for wealth and *trayodashi* for the "thirteenth day" of Ashvina. More commonly known as the festival of **Dhanteras**, this is a day when people clean their houses and draw elaborate *rangoli* designs on the floor with powders of different colors. New utensils are also bought, as well as crackers, candles, toy-shaped candies, and small idols of Ganesha and

Lakshmi for the evening service or *puja* in honor of the goddess of wealth, marking the official start of **Divali** with the lighting of new *diyas* (the modern word for deepa lamps). The markets selling the prescribed items are brightly decorated, while, at home, women prepare pungent or sweet seasonal foods. All this is meant to invite the goddess into the house for the duration of **Divali**.

This day also marks the triumphant return of Rama to the capital of his ideal kingdom Ayodhya—long identified as a city in the state of Uttar Pradesh that has been the focus of bitter Muslim-Hindu strife ever since Rama's shrine was replaced by Babur's Mosque under this Moghul ruler in 1528. Hindus believe that Rama had previously rescued his wife Sita from the demon Ravana's kingdom of Lanka and defeated it with the help of his brother Lakshman and Hanuman's army of monkeys. They celebrate this victory of good over evil every year with fireworks, the bursting of crackers, and the lighting of lamps all over their houses.

Practitioners of Ayurvedic medicine joyfully celebrate this day as the one when its patron deity Dhanvantari first emerged from the churning of the primordial ocean with a container of the *amrita* drink of immortality. In southern India, the common observance of this day has been absorbed by the celebrations of the next, which now include consuming a preparation of dry ginger and jaggery (unrefined sugar) after that morning's special prebath massage with oil, flour, and turmeric. This concoction used to be offered to Dhanvantari on his birthday.

There is also a tradition of praying to Yama, Lord of Death, on this day to win his favors for long life. For it was on a thirteenth of Ashvina that Yama's servant once asked him to be spared from taking mortals away in the bloom of life, and he decreed that from that day on, anyone who observed the five-day festival of light would not die an untimely death.

The Nepalese equivalent of **Divali**, **Tihar**, is therefore also known as **Panchak Yama,** the "Five Days of Yama." His messenger is worshipped on the first of them as **Kag Bali,** the "Day of the Crow," when people set out offerings in dishes of sewn leaves to appease this bird of ill omen. Among the Tamils of southern India, **Divali** lights are supposed to guide the spirits of the dead who return to earth during this festival back to the realm of Yama.

Second Day: Narak Chaturdashi

The second day of **Tihar** is **Swan** or **Sho Puja,** when every dog in Nepal is worshipped as the guardian of hell's gates and is thus in a position to ease the soul's passage on its way to judgment by Yama. Children are warned to deal kindly with dogs, for though they are usually treated with disdain as scavengers, each one is now fed like a king for a day, garlanded with flowers, and decorated with a red *tika* mark of blessing on its forehead.

In most of India, this is the "Small **Divali**" or *Chhoti Diwali.* The eve of **Divali** proper is actually called **Narak Chaturdashi**—after the Sanskrit word for the "fourteenth day" and *narak* for "hell" and refers to the demonic, power-hungry king of Prag-Jyotishpur whom Krishna's wife Satyabhama killed on this day, when fasting paves the way to heaven. Satyabhama represents the role of women in the struggle against evil, having liberated Narak's 16,000 woman prisoners, who expressed their joy by lighting lamps and drawing rangoli in their homes. All Hindus celebrate the joyous entry of the rightful king by doing the same after an early bath.

In Bengal, where it is known as **Kali Chaudas,** this day is allotted to the worship of the great goddess Kali, as the aspect of spiritual power that is used for God's work.

Third Day: Lakshmi Puja

The next day is that of the new moon (*amavashya*) of Ashvina. In Nepal, it begins with *Goru Puja:* morning worship of the sacred cow as the visible form of the goddess of wealth Lakshmi, who is often replaced by money in offerings to priests, so that the three are actually interchangeable. People then take off the protective thread that friends or sisters (in the case of men) had put on their wrists on **Rakhi Bandhan**, which occurs on the full moon of Shravana (July–August), to tie it around the tail of a sacred cow as they pray to Goddess Lakshmi's animal to assist their souls to heaven when the hour of death comes.

At midnight on this day when it is believed Vishnu's fifth avatar Vamana defeated King Bali, who had taken over the world and enslaved Lakshmi, she herself makes her annual round of inspection of the entire globe. But she only visits those homes that have prepared for her visit by cleaning and decorating every corner, throwing open all windows and doors, and laying a path for her with diyas from the road to the front entrance and with rangolis from there to the treasure box, so she can protect the household's wealth. She is even asked to increase the extra nest egg that is placed in the box as part of the worship of her flower-decked image (which a gold or silver coin may stand for) in front of it.

During **Lakshmi Puja**, shopkeepers and merchants also worship their merchandise and their account books, closing the old ones and opening new ones afterwards to pray for renewed success.

Fourth Day: Navu Varsh

The fourth day (**Divali** proper) ushers in the **New Year** of the Vikram calendar. It is called **Navu Varsh**. As in other **New Year** customs in East and West, illuminations and fireworks signify the victory of divine forces over those of wickedness, as people make **New Year** resolutions, visit each other, exchange gifts, feast, and wear new clothes to the temple. There, they greet relatives and acquaintances at the service, if they do not give their wishes for happiness, health, and prosperity over the coming year by

phone or e-mail or on colorful **Divali** greeting cards.

Amid general rejoicing, villagers in Himachal Pradesh forget all grudges and embrace in the streets, having often run through them with torches and sparklers and gathered around a bonfire—to dance and sing satirical songs. There, they may do the same exactly a month later over the three days of *Buri Diali*—or Hill **Divali**.

In the Buddhist Lahaula tribe's version of this Himalayan variant of the Hindu **Festival of Lights**, held on the full moon of Magha toward February, villagers instead have a lucky snowball fight around their bonfire on what is called there *Sad-halda* ("Searchlight of the Gods").

Across the border in Nepal, women and children carol from door to door on the night of the third day, and men do the same on the night of the fourth day. In the morning, bulls are worshiped as were cows the day before, to ensure their health and safety over the year. It is then that devotees of Krishna everywhere celebrate **Gobhardan Puja** to recall how, as a child cowherd, the incarnate supreme Godhead lifted Gobhardan Hill on his little finger and told his people to take their cattle and find shelter under this giant umbrella when the lesser god Indra tried to drown them with massive rainfall. He had been trying to teach them a lesson because they had refrained from making him their usual offerings for rain, following Krishna's instructions to worship him instead in the guise of the holy hill, as the ultimate source of all bounty—a point that was not lost on Indra, who eventually relented and repented before Krishna. Pilgrims now circumambulate Gobhardan Hill on this occasion, while Krishna's devotees around the world do the same in their temples using a small-scale model embellished with sacred scenes and surrounded by (and largely made from) sweets they will share out in the ensuing festive meal. Nepalese women fashion the sacred mountain and the god lying on it out of cow dung before their men file before it to pay their respects—much as they also do before ordinary dung heaps, since this precious fertilizer and fuel also purifies the home.

That night, household utensils, gardening tools, and farming implements are also blessed during the ancient and purifying household rites of *Mha Puja*—"Worship of One's Person" as divine—along with all other beings and objects ultimately. More specifically, Yama and his messenger Yamadut are thanked for allowing life to be and asked to grant every family member as much of it as possible. This calls for the father to draw a row of mandalas (mystical geometric designs) on the floor—one for each member and for both deities. Everyone sits in his or her mandala and has a long ceremony performed by another family member in a specific order. This ceremony involves heaps of grains and foods (*annakoot*) that are also used in India on this merchants' **New Year** to convey affluence and freedom from debt, before feeding the poor on a large scale.

In Nepal, the traditional **New Year** of the Newars (who consistute a majority of the population) goes back to this date in 880 C.E., when it is said that a man who had come by heaps of magical sand that had turned to gold came to the king of Kathmandu with an offer to pay every debt in the land if a new calendar era was started. In India, when the deposed universal ruler Bali was made king of the lower regions, Vamana promised him that he would be remembered on the first *Pratipada* of Karttika. On this auspicious first day of the **New Year**, people thus take the name of Bali, worship his picture along with that of his wife Vindhyavati, and wave lamps before his idol as they sing: "Let suffering go and let Bali's kingdom come." By this is meant his happy earthly kingdom, which gods thought would make men less mindful of them. This is reminiscent of end-of-year **Saturnalia** in the West, which also bring back the freedom and abundance of Saturn's golden age kingdom before Jupiter overthrew him and took his place as king of the gods.

Fifth Day: Bhai Bij

The fifth and last day of **Divali**, **Bhai Bij**, also called *Bhai Tika*, is the Feast of the Brother, also called *Bhratri Dwitiya* ("Brother's Second Day") and *Yama Dwitiya* (or the "second day of Yama"), because on this day Yama went to visit his sister Yami, and they waved a lamp to each other as a sign of mutual love and respect. Likewise on **Bhai Bij**, sisters wave a lamp to their brothers, and brothers offer gifts to their sisters. In addition, married sisters invite their brothers for meals and wish them a long life as well as health, prosperity, and happiness over the coming year.

Similar rites for brothers' longevity are observed around the same time of year—on the fifth of Shravana (around August) with the tying of an amulet or red thread around a brother's wrist. In southern India, these are known as *Garuda Panchami* and, in the north as *Raksha Bandhan*. The rites ensure the brother will long be able to perform the ancestor-worship rites needed to keep parents out of hell on their death anniversary, the new moon, and during **Pitripaksha**.

In Nepal, it is so important for every man and boy to get this blessing at the close of **Divali** that, when one is without a sister, a close female relative or friend is asked to give it instead, in a ceremony similar to the previous day's *Mha Puja*, with the man sitting in his mandala. The king of Nepal thus receives a yellow tika mark of blessing from his sisters, while a thirty-one gun salute echoes through the Valley of Kathmandu. Throughout his realm, a lunchtime feast soon follows, and the rest of the day is spent in family gambling games.

Holiday Activities

Normally proscribed, gambling was legal in Nepal before 1940 during the five days of **Tihar**, because it is thought to please Goddess Lakshmi, especially when cowrie shells—her favorite plaything and an ancient currency—are used. On the other hand, she forbids all other transactions such as loans and commerce at the risk of being reborn as a mole.

Gambling is encouraged in India, too, on **Divali,** but there it is in remembrance of Shiva and Parvati playing dice at their seat on Mount Kailash. Either way, such games of chance are—as often elsewhere—a **New Year** custom aimed at attracting good fortune. There is plenty of time to play them over the two-to-five day period that government offices, schools, and many businesses remain closed for **Divali**.

About 50 percent Indian, the Pacific archipelago of Fiji also has **Divali** as a public holiday. In South Africa, several Hindu organizations have recently called for **Divali** to be declared one there too, since many of the country's one million Hindus still risk their job if they miss work to observe the feast.

Divali's Meaning to Hindus, Jains, and Sikhs

Beyond the original need to chase the evil spirits of darkness out of the home while the moon is obscured at the end of a year, the deeper meaning of the Hindu **Festival of Lights** is that hearts need to be enlightened with goodwill in view of peaceful coexistence with all creatures. Such enlightenment depends on one's ability to become open to the light of knowledge, which alone can dispel spiritual ignorance.

Similarly, among Jains, the lighting of the lamps on **Divali** is explained as a material substitute for the light of sacred knowledge that passed away with Jainism's founder Mahavira on this day in 527 B.C.E. in Pava, Bihar. Crowds of followers of this religion now appropriately go to Pava on pilgrimage on **Divali**, the special holiday of their merchant caste, which closes the Jain ritual year.

Also well represented among traders, Sikhs likewise incorporated this ancient Hindu festival in their own calendar in the midsixteenth century after their third Guru Amar Das asked them to gather at the seat of the gurus (then Goindval, Punjab) on both **Vaisakhi** and **Divali**. To commemorate the return to Amritsar of the sixth Guru Hargobind from captivity in Gwalior on **Divali** in 1619, the great early apostle of Sikhism Baba Buddha established the practice of illuminating its holy city on that festival. All Sikh homes and temples around the world are then also made bright with the lights of the season.

> ***See also*** Navaratra and Dusshera; New Year (China, Korea), New Year (Japan); New Year (West); Saturnalia; Vaishakha and Vaisakhi

References

Divali Lights: Enchanting Stories and Songs Celebrating the Festival of Lights. (Video; five short films of ten minutes each.) London: BBC, 1994.

Anita Ganeri. *Celebrations: Divali.* Oxford: Heinemann Educational Books—Library Divion, 2001.

James Laidlaw. *Riches and Renunciation: Religion, Economy, and Society Among the Jains.* Oxford: Oxford University Press, 1995.

Mian Goverdhan Singh. *Festivals, Fairs, and Customs of Himachal Pradesh.* New Edition. New Delhi: Indus Publishing Company, 1992.

DJUNGGAWON
See Kunapipi

DODECAHEMERON
See Christmas

DOG DAYS
See Assumption

DOLA PURNIMA, DOLAYATRA
See Holi

DOLL FESTIVAL
See Sekku

DOMINION DAY
See Midsummer, Powwow

▶ DONG ZHI (CHINA)

The twenty-second of the twenty-four periods of China's moon-based agricultural calendar is called **Dong Zhi**, after the day of the winter solstice. As in many other cultures in the Northern Hemisphere, this turning point of the year is marked by family reunions around festive meals of seasonal dishes, as a contrast to the cold.

An Old-Time Winter Family Gathering

This used to be a time when Chinese peasants were struggling against the frost, and many people would even freeze to death near the time of the year's longest night. So the day of **Dong Zhi** became an occasion for families to gather indoors and enjoy a seasonal meal of glutinous flour balls called *tuan yuan*, that symbolized harmony (the word *yuan* meaning "round" or "complete," while *tuan* means "gathering").

Both **Dong Zhi** and **New Year** celebrations have been national festivals in China since the second century B.C.E. In those ancient times, the festive atmosphere of **Dong Zhi** was just like that of the **New Year** a few weeks later, with mutual visits, offerings of incense at daybreak, and businesses closing for the day in some places.

Honoring a Cook's Contribution

Nowadays, certain foods are still associated with **Dong Zhi** by people in southern China on the basis of the story they like to tell about an imperial visit to the construction site of a new sacrificial terrace. Impressed by the fine craftsmanship it displayed, the monarch conferred the title of "master" on the foreman. The head of the carpenters then raised his voice to claim the credit for the special woodwork, and the emperor agreed to give carpenters too the title of "masters." However, the masons then protested that they also deserved it, and then the blacksmiths, the tinsmiths, the goldsmiths, and so on. Seeing this, the generous sovereign

decided to give all artisans the title of "masters." When they heard what was happening, the cooks ran to join the workers and be recognized as masters too, but the others protested that their new title would not be worth much if it was given for such an unskilled job. So that they would be better appreciated, the insulted cooks went on strike, leaving the craftsmen to prepare their own meals. Only then did they come to realize that all they could do was mill about helplessly around the supply of uncooked grain. Alerted to the new development among his workforce, the emperor pointed out to the craftsmen that if with all their skill they were incapable of preparing a simple meal, then cooking must be a special skill after all. Feeling the pangs of hunger already, they were quick to agree. But by then, the head cook was no longer content with being just a master like all the others; arguing that, masters though they were, the latter had no clue about preparing food, and she claimed a title superior to theirs. So she obtained a special distinction above the rest. To prove her worth, she then started to cook *tuan yuan*, won ton, dumplings, and red bean porridge for the whole crew's **Dong Zhi** party the next day. This menu has remained the standard fare at southern Chinese people's **Dong Zhi** dinner ever since.

See also New Year (China, Korea); New Year (West)

References
Goh Pei Ki. *Origins of Chinese Festivals.* Singapore: Asiapac Books, 1997.
Qi Xing. *Folk Customs at Traditional Chinese Festivities.* Tr. Ren Jiazhen. Beijing: Foreign Language Press, 1988.

▶ DORMITION OF THE MOTHER OF GOD
See Assumption

▶ DOUBLE FIVE
See Dragon Boat Festival

DOUBLE NINE
(CHINA, KOREA)

The festival of **Chong Yang** is called thus on account of the doubly auspicious *yang* quality of the ninth day of the ninth month, also called *Chongjiu,* meaning Double Nine. This autumn festival is meant to cultivate good health through such activities as hill climbing, carrying dogwood, gazing at displays of chrysanthemums, and drinking them in infusion.

Averting Pestilence

Double Nine's customs go back to the later Han Dynasty (25–220 C.E.) according to the chronicler Wu Jun. It was at that time that a certain Huan Jing was told by his Taoist spiritual master Fei Zhangfang that on the ninth of the ninth, the God of Plague of Ru River would come out to devastate his native Runan. To escape fatal illness, the villagers were each supposed to carry a little red gauze bag of dogwood attached to their arms and should all take refuge in the mountains to drink chrysanthemum wine until the ominous day was over. They followed the wise man's instructions as transmitted by Huan Jing and were very glad they did. When they came back down to their village, they found their poultry, pigs, and dogs all dead from pestilence. This was the result of autumnal decay, which is said to occur when the wet *yin* principle begins to overtake the dry *yang* principle after the latter's yearly apogee. However, this seasonal hazard is considerably less of a threat on heights, away from human habitation. In addition, dogwood leaves can cure cholera, while dogwood roots repel insects that carry disease. As for the chrysanthemums that blossom that late in the year, drinking their essence in a wine infusion lowers tension, prevents dizziness, and improves eyesight.

Koreans also eat chrysanthemum leaves in pancakes in their version of this festival, which they call **Junggu**.

Chrysanthemum Gazing

While Koreans go picnicking in green valleys, these benefits give the Chinese good reasons to climb hills and drink wine while gazing at a scenery filled with chrysanthemums in bloom. There, they also compose verses in praise of the chrysanthemum—a favorite **Double Nine** custom, dear to emperors and poets from the time of the Tang Dynasty (618–907 C.E.).

Under the Ch'ing Dynasty (1644–1912), there were even special chrysanthemum exhibitions around this date every three, five, or ten years, though the major ones came at the turn of every sixty-year cycle. Such chrysanthemum festivals are still popular in certain parts of China on **Double Nine**, especially in the south, as in Yunnan Province for instance. It remains as ever a fine time to chase away the diseases and depressions of the fall season in the fresh air and fair colors of temperate weather under clear skies.

See also Chiao; Dragon Boat Festival; Midsummer; Sekku

References

Goh Pei Ki. *Origins of Chinese Festivals.* Singapore: Asiapac Books, 1997.

Qi Xing. *Folk Customs at Traditional Chinese Festivities.* Tr. Ren Jiazhen. Beijing: Foreign Language Press, 1988.

DOUBLE SEVEN
(CHINA, KOREA, JAPAN)

See Cowherd and Weaving Maid

DRAGON BOAT FESTIVAL
(CHINA, KOREA)

The **Festival of the Fifth Moon** takes place on the fifth day of that month in the Chinese calendar, toward the summer solstice. It is known as the **Dragon Boat Festival** after the dragon-shaped rowboats competing in regattas in Chinese communities and beyond—both as an invocation for rain and in memory of the national poet-hero Chu Yuan. In Chinese, the Festival of **Dragon Boat**s is called **Duanwu** or **Duanyang** (**Double Five** or **Upright Sun**—a reference to the summer solstice).

The same festival is known as **Dano** in Korea, where it used to mark the end of the sowing season. On this peasants' holiday that now only survives in a few areas of the Korean countryside, women used to wash their hair in a boiled iris concoction to drive away bad luck. They would also play on a swing while the men wrestled in the traditional *sireum* style.

But in China's lunar calendar, this festival remains prominent as one of **Three for the Living** (as opposed to **Three for the Dead**), the other two being the Chinese **New Year** or **Spring Festival** and the **Mid-Autumn** Festival. Like them, it is also known simply as the **Summer Festival**, after the season when it occurs.

Invoking the Dragon for Summer Rain

The festival goes back to ancient tribal sacrifices designed to win the Dragon's favors so that it would rain properly. In some places, if it happened to rain on this day, the water would be collected as a blessing from the Celestial Dragon, to protect the community from disaster and disease. Even today, a Taoist or Buddhist monk awakens the Dragon and makes it present by lighting incense, firecrackers, and spirit money, before painting its eyes on the famous dragon boats that gave the festival its current name.

Having spent the winter in storage, these boats are now ready to be used not just on the fifth day of the fifth month, but over half a year of competitions at sporting events also called **dragon boat festivals**. The shouting and bustle of the **Dragon Boat Festival** proper is meant to scare away the evil spirits that are believed to haunt the river and cause epidemics. This practice, first recorded in the Wu-Yue region, eventually spread all around China.

Exorcising the Evil Month

In earlier times, the entire fifth month was deemed the "Evil Month" because of the hot, muggy weather that favored the spread of infectious diseases and harmful insects. In contrast to the West, where **Midsummer** bonfires emulate the peak of the sun's power, in the East, this fiery, active *yang* energy at its apex around the summer solstice was not to be added to and driven to burning excess by human activities of the same polarity. These included visible fires, the preparation of charcoal and metal, and the handling of weapons to business and government, which therefore used to shut down. On the other hand, wells were dredged so their waters would be renewed and purified (also a concern of Western **Midsummer** customs), thereby strengthening *yin* energy at this vulnerable time. To expel the gods of plague that then took this opportunity to act up as a disruptive form of unbalanced *yin,* people used to hang peachwood or yellow paper strips bearing incantations and the images of animal-shaped deities.

On the fifth of the month, along with these strips, many shops in Beijing would sell images of the "Great Demon-Expelling General" Zhong Kui, a scholar who had been turned down at imperial examinations on account of his ugliness, had committed suicide, and devoted his after-life to slaying the demons tormenting the living. This is how he was bestowed his title by the eighth-century Emperor Ming Huang, when the emperor recovered from a high fever after seeing Zhong Kui in a dream. On the basis of the monarch's description, the image of Zhong Kui was designed and spread through the realm, as in a version showing him eating the "five ghosts." People would likewise eat cakes made in the shapes of the "five poisonous creatures" (all associated with an excess of watery *yin* energy): scorpion, viper, centipede, lizard, and spider, which old women might also cut out of red paper, along with a tiger to imprison all these harmful creatures inside a gourd. On the other hand, girls wore a "fragrant pouch" made from bits of cloth held together by threads of colored silk.

These customs mostly survive in the form of certain local handicrafts. But while mugwort and calamus leaves, along with pungent vegetables like garlic, onions and old cabbages, are still sometimes hung in doorways to avert plagues, the burning of realgar (producing a foul-smelling yellow smoke) to drive away insects, and the use of realgar wine as a drink for health, as an exorcism on male children, and as an offering to the ancestors (along with wheat and fish), have all but disappeared.

Remembering the Virtues of Drowned Worthies

Rationalist historical explanations have long been given to account for many of the festival's colorful practices. Dragon boat races—called *Par Lung Chow* in Chinese—are now supposed to commemorate the people's attempts to recover the body of the great poet Chu Yuan (340–278 B.C.E.), though he only began getting connected to this particular day in the second century. Chu Yuan was a councilor of King Huai who reigned from 328 to 296 B.C.E. over Chu, the largest of the Warring States after which this troubled period of Chinese history is known. Though renowned for his wisdom and loyalty, Chu Yuan was exiled from the capital city of Ying due to court intrigues. When he learned of its fall to the rival state of Chin, which wiped out the dynasty, absorbed the kingdom, and scattered its people, he could not bear to survive the ruin of all he had devoted his life to; so he jumped into the Miluo River with rocks in his sleeves. Fishermen raced in their boats to look for his body, sounding drums all the while in order to scare away the fish and other creatures that would otherwise eat it. Someone also had the idea of throwing rice into the water, so that beasts and spirits would go for it rather than defile the beloved statesman's mortal remains.

Though the search for the body was unsuccessful, it was reenacted out of respect every year from then on. An important addition was made two hundred years later. Under the Eastern Han Dynasty (25–220 C.E.), a certain U Hui met a ghostly civil servant who told him to thank mortals for all their offerings, even though they all went to feed the Water Dragon dwelling at the bottom of the river and causing it to overflow its banks. To prevent this, he suggested that rice be wrapped inside leaves with multicolored threads; this way the Dragon would find them unpalatable and leave some for him. This is how preparing and eating dumplings called *zhung* (cooked sweet rice wrapped in bamboo leaves) became widespread as a way of honoring Chu Yuan on **Duanwu**. Another way to call back his soul was to hang absinthe leaves and iris flowers on doors.

But it is also on that day of the year that, around the same historical period, the mandarin Cao Ding, charmed by the sound of the waves by the river's edge, was carried away by a surging wave when the water spirit chose him as confidant. His daughter Cao-e waited seven days and seven nights by the shore for the body to reappear. By then, she was so distraught that she jumped in the river so as to at least be able to join her father. Their bodies were found together three days later, and Cao-e's filial piety has been remembered ever since by putting her effigy on dragon boats.

Dragon Boat Races

The origins of the dragon boats used today can be traced back twenty-four hundred years, though their festive use in races on the current date did not become widespread until the Tang Dynasty (618–907), and even then, mostly in southern China, where they remain most popular to this day. Less than four feet wide, dragon boats can vary in length from ten to thirty-seven meters, with twenty to a hundred paddlers per boat. The prow is shaped like a dragon's head and the stern like its tail.

Dragon boats are still used in less competitive, more ceremonial versions of the festival by some ethnic groups such as the Hei Miao of central and southern Guizhou Province, who hold their version on the twenty-fourth instead of the fifth day of the fifth month like the majority Han Chinese. Each Hei Miao village along the Qingshui River is represented by a boat carved from three great tree trunks with a splendid dragon's head at its prow. Streamers and banners made of red cloth hang from its horns and maw, and offerings of live ducks and geese for the costumed oarsmen are suspended from its neck at every village where the boat stops on its stately journey, which draws over a thousand spectators on both sides of the river.

In its traditional Han version, the dragon boat is made of teak and can weigh close to six hundred kilograms. The crew includes a helmsman, twenty or twenty-two oarsmen sitting two abreast, often a flag catcher with someone standing up to scan the waters for Chu Yuan's body, and at least one drummer, sometimes with gong players too, to beat out a paddling rhythm that can reach between eighty and a hundred strokes per minute. These long war canoes race two by two over a 640-meter stretch, taking less than three minutes to cross, until a winning team is chosen by elimination. The races are still rowdy, but in the past people would even throw stones at unpopular boats, and it used to be considered good luck if a boat capsized, and somebody drowned.

Such regattas are traditionally held in countless Chinese villages, as well as wherever there are sizeable Chinese communities. Since the late twentieth century, they have even spread beyond them as a fast-growing sport practiced by hundreds of thousands of people of all backgrounds, from Southeast Asia to Northern Europe, on such occasions as the International **Dragon Boat** Race **Festivals** held between May and October in dozens of North American cities and towns, with student, business, ethnic and charity teams in men's and women's categories. They are supposed to be introduced as a demonstration sport at the 2008 Olympic Games in Beijing. Teams already come from all over the world to compete in the International Dragon Boat Championships of Hong Kong or Taipei on the fifth day of the fifth lunar month. But at nightfall, the living leave the river to the dead, as they launch paper lanterns that stand for the wandering spirits of the Buddhist Purgatory, floating downstream to the Pacific Ocean, to rest in peace there.

See also Days of the Dead (China, Korea, Japan); Dionysia; Double Nine; Holi; Midautumn; Midsummer; New Year (China, Korea), New Year (West); Sekku; Spring Dragon; Water-Splashing Festival

References

Anthony F. Aveni. *The Book of the Year: A Brief History of Our Seasonal Holidays.* Oxford: Oxford University Press, 2003.

Pat Barker. *Dragon Boats: A Celebration.* New York: Weatherhill Books, 1996.

International Dragon Boat Federation: www.dragonboat.org.uk.

Marie-Luise Latsch. *Traditional Chinese Festivals.* Singapore: Graham Brash, 1985.

DREAMS (FESTIVAL OF)
See Midwinter

DUANWU, DUANYANG
See Dragon Boat Festival

DUMB WEEK
See Palm Sunday

DURBAR
See Adae

DURGA PUJA
See Navaratra and Dusshera

DZAWUWU
See New Yam Festival

▶ EASTER (CHRISTIANITY)

Whether in terms of nature or spirit, **Easter** is a celebration of the victory of new life over death. For while its folklore perpetuates many pagan rites of springtime renewal, **Easter** (called *Pascha* in Greek and Latin) is the center of the Christian calendar as its oldest annual festival, celebrating the Resurrection of Jesus Christ, believed to have taken place on the third day after his Crucifixion, some time in the third decade of the Common Era. A number of moveable feasts of the church calendar are set in relation to the date of **Easter**, which varies from year to year as well as between the Western and **Eastern** Churches.

The Feast of the Resurrection of Christ

In the West, **Easter** does not enjoy quite the central place in popular piety that it retains in the East. For, even though it is not counted as one of the **Twelve Feasts** of the Church, **Easter** to Orthodox Christians is in a class by itself as "the feast of feasts and the celebration of celebrations." It surpasses all other festivals, as the sun exceeds the stars. This is true not only of human and earthly feasts, but also of those "belonging to Christ and celebrated for Christ," in the words of an **Easter** Sermon (no. 45) by the Church Father Saint Gregory the Theologian (Ouspensky and Lossky, 1982 p. 185), who explained that "it is the day of the Resurrection and the beginning of true life." As such, it is the original **Sunday** on which the weekly liturgies of all other **Sunday**s are based, so much so that in the Armenian Church the melodies are used on **Easter** as on any given **Sunday**. As the feast of the Resurrection of Christ, **Pascha** was celebrated by 120 C.E. throughout the Church, having developed from a weekly vigil service of scripture readings and psalms before the **Sunday** Eucharist into a solemn, annual service. This was meant to be "the foreshadowing of the feast to come," as Pope Saint Gregory the Great maintained to the congregation of the Roman church of Saint John Lateran in a **Quasimodo** sermon (no. 26, 10) on the eve of the Sunday after **Easter** on April 21, 591 (from a French translation by the Benedictine monks of the abbey of Sainte-Madeleine du Barroux, 84330 France, at http://www.jesusmarie.com/gregoire_le_grand_homelies_sur_evangiles.html). He explained: "This is why we celebrate it annually, so that it may lead us to that feast, which will be no longer annual but eternal. When, on a fixed date, we celebrate this feast, we remember better that we must yearn for the other one."

However, determining the date of **Easter** has often been problematic. Initially, different springtime dates were used, which led to bitter quarrels between local churches. Even after these issues were formally resolved at the First Ecumenical (that is, universal) Council of the Church in Nicea in Asia Minor in 325, they lasted another five centuries in some places. The Council favored the first Sunday after the full moon following the spring equinox (usually considered to be March 20), except if this paschal moon fell on the same weekend as the Jewish **Passover** (which **Easter** replaced in the Christian calendar). When Pope Gregory XIV replaced the Julian Calendar (that dated back to Julius Cesar) with the updated Gregorian Calendar in October 1582, the proviso concerning **Passover** was dropped. The new sequence gradually came into universal use, except in Orthodox Churches that still use the Julian calendar when it comes to the date of **Easter** (or even all dates in the many Old Calendar jurisdictions of these Eastern Churches that remain opposed to their partial adoption of the Gregorian calendar). There, **Easter** usually falls later—by one to five weeks—than in the West, where it can fall between March 22 and April 25.

Following a schedule that can be traced back to the third century, the **Easter** vigil service normally begins late on **Holy Saturday** in East and West alike. (Before the practice was restored to its normal time in the 1950s, the Roman Church had fallen into the habit of celebrating the vigil even earlier on **Holy Saturday** —generally on Saturday morning by then.) The service is based on the stark contrast the darkened church provides for the new light from a paschal candle. The flame from this candle is spread to all the other candles in the church at a turning point of the celebrations, and people even try to take it home without letting it go out. This is a custom prevalent in Austria as well as in most Orthodox countries.

In the Ukraine, the same practice applies instead to the candles held by the faithful during the Twelve Gospels service on the eve of **Good Friday**. There too, the aim is to light the candle in the family's icon corner at home and to keep that same flame burning for forty days (or so) until the end of the **Easter** season on **Ascension**—when the paschal candle is extinguished in Catholic churches.

In the East, the distribution of holy fire takes place during the matins, which begin once the embroidered *Epitaphios* depicting Christ's dead body has been removed from the middle of the church (where it had been laid as on a bier for **Good Friday**) to be put on the altar and to remain there throughout the **Easter** season. The Royal Doors of the sanctuary are soon thrown open by the celebrant holding the threefold candle called *trikyrion* in Greek (based on *kyrie,* the Greek word meaning "Lord," for God understood as a Trinity by Christians), while the choir sings, "Come take light from the light without evening and glorify Christ risen from the dead." At the Church of the Holy Sepulchre built around Christ's tomb in Jerusalem, the fire is even said to start miraculously on its own behind the shrine's closed doors just before being distributed to the faithful.

Except wherever local custom dictates a certain order based on gender, age, social, or marital status (as in Greece), the faithful then press toward the priest with their candles to take the new fire from his, spreading it from candle to candle through the crowd and the church to make the candles all shine as the one body of the risen Christ. The faithful then form a procession that will exit the church and circle it to finally gather before its closed door (standing for the fallen world subject to death) to hear the priest's reading from the Gospel of Mark about Christ's empty tomb and the first proclamation that "Christ is risen!" to which the congregation answers that "Indeed He is risen!"—an exchange that will be repeated countless times (and often in several languages) during the service, and as a mutual greeting on every occasion over the paschal season until the **Ascension**.

Next, the procession enters the church to fill it with light and joy as the special matins, called the "Paschal Canon of Saint John of Damascus," are sung for a couple of hours. The singing concludes when the Paschal Sermon of Saint John Chrysostom is read. It invites even latecomers to the seasonal fasting to partake of its joyful rewards at the **Easter** liturgy this saint composed and which follows. Unless the service is scheduled for dawn, it usually goes on well past midnight.

In the West, midnight is about the time the paschal mass would begin if the Roman Catholic missal were followed. It calls for the ancient ceremony of blessing the baptismal font to start before that hour. It normally begins in a darkened church to which fire (often struck from flint as in several such **new fire ceremonies** in other traditions) is brought to signal the Resurrection. This usually emanates from the vestibule rather than from the sanctuary, while the blessing of the **new fire**, as it took shape during the early Middle Ages, occurs in the narthex instead. Similar to the Eastern *trikyrion,* a triple candle is lit. The priest lights each branch in a different location: one in the narthex, one in the middle of the nave, and one in the sanctuary, next to the high altar. This is also where the paschal candle is to be lit, after a cross shape has been imprinted on it with five nails of incense (previously blessed along with the fire) and once the paschal *Praeconium* for its blessing, as well as twelve Old Testament prophecies applying to Christ's Resurrection, have been chanted.

The acolytes then light all the other candles in the church with the flame from the paschal candle before taking it to the baptismal font, where it will be dipped into the water three times. This makes the font fit to bring regeneration to those to be baptized from it shortly and throughout the year. After some of the water has been sprinkled on the congregation, holy oils are poured over it to seal it from the air. The litanies that follow include the baptism of those who are being received into the Church at this point. Halfway through them, the ministers leave the sanctuary to put on their white vestments for the celebration of **Easter** Mass.

The blessing of the font remains an eloquent witness to the ancient and intimate connection between the feast of **Easter** and the sacrament of baptism as the initiation of new believers into the mystery of the Risen Christ. For baptism is the symbolic death in Christ that allows believers to partake of his eternal risen life as members of his body, the Church. Converts used to join the Church during **Easter** night to receive the Eucharist for the first time at the dawn mass. For practical reasons, baptisms came to be celebrated on other major feasts, like **Christmas, Epiphany,** and **Pentecost,** and eventually at any time of the year on a more private basis. As for those who get baptized at Easter, "having descended with Christ into the dark waters and risen again from them, they are now ready to partake of the mystery which represents their identity with the Risen Body— projected out of eternity into time as the Bread and Wine forming human flesh and blood" (Watts 1959, p. 183). The words: "You who have been baptized in Christ, you have put on Christ, Alleluia!" initially aimed at the newly baptized, now echo for all the faithful as they are sung in Eastern rite services on **Easter** and for all the **Bright Week** that follows.

The mass may also begin directly at daybreak, as it does in Poland, where it is preceded by a procession of the Blessed Sacrament (a consecrated host in a monstrance as on **Corpus Christi**) under a canopy that circles the church three times. As at the corresponding point of Orthodox liturgies, church bells then resound, and firecrackers are set off. The latter are actually part of a pagan noisemaking ritual also known on the **New Year.** In northern countries on **Easter,** it includes gunshots as well. The noise is meant to scare off the witches and evil spirits that come out at both these turning points of the year. Similarly, as may also be seen in Tucson, Arizona every **Easter,** Mexico's Catholic Yaqui Indians then burn masks like those of their former pagan gods to symbolize Christ's victory over demons.

Many Protestant bodies have maintained a connection between **Easter** and baptism. While their **Easter** celebrations differ only by a few prayers from the usual **Sunday** worship, in North America they have a custom of holding interdenominational **Easter** dawn services, which are often broadcast live. Unless they are derived from all-night baptismal ceremonies, these may be based on the Gospel account of how, "very early on the first day of the week," it was "still dark, when Mary of Magdala came to the tomb" and found it empty (*Jerusalem Bible* 1968, John 20:1).

The Festival of Springtime Renewal

The old custom, long found from France to the Ukraine, of getting up before dawn on **Easter** morning (as on **Pentecost** in Denmark) to see the sun jump up and down three times as it rose over the horizon may have underscored the point of the feast: that the dark grave of cyclical time could not contain the eternal Light of Christ. Yet it remains true that the visible sun, which emerges every morning out of the darkness of night, is likewise victorious over darkness after the spring equinox, when daytime starts having the upper hand and winter is forced to retreat. And just as in typical celebrations of the sun's eventual triumph at the summer solstice elsewhere, every household in the eastern Dutch provinces was supposed to donate some of the wood for an **Easter** Sunday bonfire, so that it could compete in size and intensity with those of other neighborhoods as all joined hands to dance around them singing hymns. By virtue of the same solar symbolism, Dawn or Ostara was a goddess of spring as the morning of the year for ancient Germanic peoples—an association of ideas that may be traced across the whole range of Indo-European cultures. Likewise, the Sanskrit *usra* and the Latin *aurora* both mean "dawn"—hence the

word "orient" for its place on the horizon, just as the Latvian *aust* for "dawn" also sounds like "east." So the eighth-century Anglo-Saxon chronicler-priest Bede the Venerable could report that his pagan ancestors performed sacrifices to dedicate the paschal month of April to Eostre—which resulted in the English word "Easter." The same goddess was known as Ostara to Germans on the continent, where a prayer to Eostar as earth-mother has been preserved at the Abbey of Corvey in Westphalia, asking her to "make this field grow, expand, blossom, bear fruit," and "protect it so the earth may rest and be fruitful as the saints who are in heaven" (de Benoist 1996).

This helps explain the **Easter** Sunday or Monday custom, known in many parts of Germany (especially in Saxony), of ritual perambulations around fields, sometimes circling back to the point where the sun rises on **Easter** or the spring equinox. They used to involve hundreds of peasants and apprentices, often on horses decorated with ribbons and flowers, just like the ones associated with **Rogations** before **Ascension** at the end of **Easter**tide, juridical as well as magical in purpose. They have eventually been replaced in most cases with a less formal walk through the fields (for which holiday excursions and visits to relatives are current substitutes), called *Emmausgehen* or "Emmaus walk" in parts of Austria, since **Easter** Monday commemorates the Risen Christ's apparition to two of his disciples at Emmaus.

Known in Britain as the "**Easter** Promenade," this rural custom found a new urban setting in North America as the **Easter** Parade, which began on Atlantic City's Boardwalk in 1860. It perpetuated the widespread European practice of wearing new clothes on **Easter**, in keeping with springtime renewal, as old garments would spread the restrictions of winter over the coming year. Americans would likewise make a point of wearing their best finery as they walked all the way to church for the late morning services, so that this became a major social and fashion event, from Detroit's Piety Hill (along a church-lined stretch of Woodward Avenue) to New York's Fifth Avenue (starting at Saint Patrick's Cathedral). The latter's 1912 edition has been immortalized in the Fred Astaire musical *Easter* Parade (1948) with a score by Irving Berlin. Today's **Easter** parades are usually much more informal, sometimes **carnival**-like in tone.

The **Easter** lunch is a family meal where all the good things of the fair season—especially those that have been abstained from during **Lent** and were scarce over the winter—are to be freely enjoyed. Though for a dozen centuries, the main course has often been lamb in Greece, Italy, and France, this symbol of Christ as the Lamb of God sacrificed on the Cross only appears in effigy (made out of butter, cake, or plaster) as the centerpiece of the *swiecone*—the Polish version of the food baskets that are blessed in church after the **Easter** service in Eastern European cultures. In those countries that follow the Eastern rite, the lamb's place is taken by a rich pastry called *paskha*, that also stands for **Passover**. Though the foods included in the **Easter** basket vary according to regional use, each item is accounted for in terms of the Christian symbolism of the feast. Still, in many cases, such **Easter** foods have pagan roots in springtime fertility rituals.

Thus in the West, **Easter** hot-cross buns go back to the Saxons, who ate them in honor of Eostar as part of their moon worship. In this context, the cross stood for the four quarters of the moon, but it made it easy for the bun to gain Christian meaning while it was still used as an amulet, hung in homes and boats over the year for protection against mishaps. Likewise, the mooncakes of China's **Mid-Autumn** festival on the full moon of the eighth lunar month are sometimes kept till **New Year**'s Eve. They honor a female moon deity who regulates fertility and whose pet rabbit is seen on the lunar disc. In Egypt too, as in many cultures across the globe, due no doubt to these nocturnal animals'

thirty-day gestation period, parallel to the phases of the moon and a woman's menstrual cycle, the rabbit or the hare stood for fertility, new life, and the moon, as did the hare as a symbol of Eostre—whose name seems to be echoed in "estrogen"—for pagan Germans, who also saw it in the moon.

The egg was another attribute of Ostara, associated as such with the hare around the first full moon of spring, in relation to which **Easter** was later set. Hence the German custom about the **Easter** Bunny (*Osterhase*) laying **Easter** eggs in nests prepared by children, as first recorded in a medical dissertation in 1682—around the time of the settlement of the Pennsylvania Dutch Country in the United States. Though the custom was not unknown in Britain, such German immigrant communities are credited with spreading it in North America—with the indigenous rabbit standing in for the European hare. Some have even managed to keep or to revive as a collectible handicraft the colorful ribbon-laced **Easter** Egg Tree that was developed from the custom of sticking brown eggs on branches in a bush in Germany and Switzerland. In the latter country until a century ago, it was a cuckoo that was said to lay the eggs that adults would hide through the lawns for children to find at **Easter**. Though the **Easter** bunny was largely dominant as the bringer of the season's gifts in most of Northern and Eastern Europe, it had other regional competitors before its adoption by Americans finished displacing them. Such were the fox and the crane in Westphalia, and in Thuringia, the stork as well as the rooster, which was also present in Belgium's French-speaking and Switzerland's Italian-speaking areas, while the hen was favored in Tyrol and much of Bavaria.

Whether they were laid by unlikely beasts or not, decorated eggs enjoyed a central role in **Easter** celebrations throughout Christendom long before they were recorded as presents for this occasion in sixteenth-century Germany. Indeed, though the techniques and colors employed to make them **Easter** eggs vary greatly according to the region, red eggs are the most prominent overall; they even appeared in ancient Persia and China in the springtime. For the Slavs, as for many other peoples, the egg symbolized both new life and cosmic totality, with the white standing for the moon and the yoke for the sun. Once decorated, it could magically bring happiness, prosperity, health, and protection. Initially attributed to the sun god, such virtues could easily be ascribed to Christ as the Light of the world after conversion from paganism, while old customs were integrated in a Christian guise. Thus, the decorated **Easter** egg, on which batik techniques give a host of elaborate designs that are handed down like family heirlooms, is called *pysanka* from the verb for "writing," in the same sense that icons are said to be written rather than painted. But the Ukrainian legend that the world will go on for as long as there is someone to write them is a reminder of the pagan understanding of the egg as a magic microcosm, standing for the whole.

Pysankas are offered as a token of deep affection, but simple hard-boiled eggs that have been dyed red are used for the egg-tapping games that last through **Easter** week (especially before the **Easter** lunch). In these rituals, two people exchange traditional **Easter** greetings and take turns tapping their eggs against each other until one breaks. It is considered lucky to be the one whose egg lasts longest. Broken eggs are gladly eaten, including the first one to be cracked against a church wall after the service to signal the end of the long pre-**Easter** fast when eggs are forbidden. The fact that there happen to be a large supply of them at this time of year, when they stand for newly accessible seasonal plenty as well as for the abundant gifts of divine grace, has no doubt consolidated the association of eggs with **Easter** in Eastern-rite churches, where dietary restrictions have always been taken seriously. Since the fast comes into effect at the start of **Lent** after **Cheesefare Sunday** (when eggs are still allowed), Greeks have a

saying: "With an egg I close my mouth, with an egg I shall open it again" after the **Easter** liturgy (Megas 1963, p. 71).

Easter Week

The egg-tapping game used to be played on **Easter** Monday in Holland. In Oxfordshire, the day following **Easter** was called "Ball Monday" on account of the many ball games held then. This was probably a variation on the theme of egg games such as "egg rolling," in which **Easter** eggs were rolled down a natural slope, initially as a form of divination as well as entertainment. The egg that rolled the farthest without breaking would bring the most luck or a marriage within the year.

Easter Monday is a festival devoted to such egg games in Tredozio, near Forlì, in northeastern Italy. They have also been known in Greece, Russia, Rumania, Austria, and Switzerland, as well as in parts of Germany, France, and Belgium, and in the north and west of England, in Scotland, and in Northern Ireland. The British custom found a place at the heart of American life as Washington, D.C.'s **Easter** Egg Roll. It was first held on the grounds of the Capitol at the invitation of the wife of President James Madison (1809–1817). And when the boisterous annual event was discontinued in 1878, the children of Washington marched to the White House in protest with their baskets full of the colorful **Easter** eggs they had brought, and President Rutherford B. Hayes's wife prevailed upon him to transfer the custom to the rolling lawns of the official residence instead. Eventually, tens of thousands of eggs were provided for this game, except in wartime. It remains the largest public event held at the White House, where it takes place on its Ellipse and South Lawn. The activities (egg roll, egg race, egg hunt, and the like) are aimed mostly at children ages six and under, who receive commemorative wooden eggs.

In contrast to egg hunts, egg rolling has not caught on in the United States beyond the federal capital. However, Western Slav and Hun-

Kids participate in a rain-soaked Easter Egg Roll event on the South Lawn of the White House, 2004. (Larry Downing/Reuters/Corbis)

garian immigrants long practiced the old country custom known in Poland by the misnomer Smigus Dyngus. *Dyngus* originally referred to **Easter** trick-or-treating, although it came to be associated with the practice of boys drenching girls with water by any means available on "Wet **Easter** Monday." (Girls got their revenge on boys on **Easter** Tuesday.) A related practice once common in western France was that of soaking clerics considered too lazy to wake up on their own that morning, or of dunking the merchants who sold the salted fish Catholics had had to eat during **Lent**—in humorous revenge against the people identified with **Lent**en restrictions that were now over.

This kind of seasonal scapegoating also used to be found in Slovakia, where it focused on Morena, the goddess of winter. She was paraded in the guise of a big white dummy that was carried on a pole by girls to be thrown away in a local stream—a symbolic banishment of cold and death ushering in springtime around **Easter.**

As for the water-splashing custom known there as *polivanja*, though it has now become a free-for-all where young people soak everyone in sight, it too used to follow various gender-based rituals with a view toward ensuring fertility and prosperity (failing which a woman might remain a spinster). These might take the form of just an exchange of **Easter** greetings, gifts of perfume for the girls' hair or of chocolates, painted eggs, cake, or money for the boys. It always featured some form of gentle whipping with a switch or rod usually made of willow—hence the name "**Switching Day**" for **Easter** Monday. This symbolic aggression was supposed to complete the cleansing of any residue of winter's hindrances on health and growth with further stimulation of springtime's regenerative powers, to protect the recipient from harm, and to give her or him vigor and skill over the coming year. Between the afternoon litany at church (following two sparsely attended morning masses) and family visits to the graves of dead relatives, little children would also strike the legs of their aunts and uncles with their own small whips as they recited a trick-or-treating poem that would normally earn them three decorated eggs and honey cakes. In the Finnish version of this custom, the switching still takes place, but it occurs on **Maundy Thursday**, instead of **Palm Sunday**, and the reward is delayed until **Easter** Sunday.

After **Easter** Sunday comes "**White Week**" or "**Bright Week**" as it is called in Orthodox countries; here, the Greek word *lambri* for "bright" is even another name for Easter. In the past, hardly any work was done during this week. It was declared a holiday by the Roman Emperor Constantine soon after he recognized Christianity in 313 C.E. Though the official holiday was eventually limited to **Easter** Monday, there was a long-standing taboo in the Greek countryside on doing any work in the fields or spinning with a white distaff over **White Week**, as this might bring on hail—which is white. It was also thought that hair washed during **White Week** would turn prematurely white.

Today, the usual fasting on Wednesday and Friday is suspended, since the entire week is treated as a succession of **Sundays**, with paschal matins and the Divine Liturgy entirely sung on a different tone every day, along with repetitions of the **Easter** procession around the church and the blessing of water for the faithful. In ancient times, the newly baptized among them, still wearing their white robes and carry-

ing candles (hence the many traces of this kind of light symbolism in the liturgical and folk practices of **Easter**tide), would get tested every day by priests to demonstrate they properly understood the dogmas of their new faith. Greeks still take advantage of these happy days to go for outings in the countryside or to visit relatives in other towns.

New Monday and **New Tuesday** are a direct continuation of **Easter** celebrations. Churches are supposed to stay open day and night to represent the free access to the Holy of Holies after its curtain was torn from top to bottom at the moment of Christ's death. Church bells can be heard all week long in the monastic communities of Mount Athos, but they refrain from announcing the first service of **White Monday** in the rest of Greece; there, the last parishioner who gets to church has to pay a fine, spent on a meal for the congregation. The dancing that follows often rivals **Easter** Sunday celebrations.

In some parts of Greece, dancing takes place as part of a ritual to appease the north wind on **New Thursday** (*Pertei*) so that "it diminishes" (*perti* in Greek). There is always some dancing after the service and procession of **New Friday**, which is dedicated throughout the Orthodox world to the Mother of God as Life-Giving Font (on account of a miraculous fountain in Constantinople on which a church was built in her honor in the fifth century). In other parts of Greece, the weekend sees some continuation of ancient funerary rites such as those of the Roman festival of **Rosaria** or **Rosalia**—witness the traditional songs known as *Roussalia*, sung from door to door by men or children who hold a cross of flowers on a flagpole.

On the following **Sunday of Saint Thomas** (who was not there when Jesus first appeared to the other apostles on **Easter** Sunday and was only convinced of his master's Resurrection at his next apparition eight days later when he touched Christ's wound), Greeks take all the candles left over from **Easter** celebrations to light them in front of the icons. Eastern rite Slavs take home pieces of the *artos*—a loaf of bread standing for eternal life that has been kept on the church's lectern all **Easter** Week and has now been blessed anew by the priest, to be eaten with holy water as a remedy against disease in case of need over the year.

This formal extension or anticlimax of **Easter** Week is known as **White Sunday** in Germany and as **Low Sunday** to English-speaking Christians, except for Catholics everywhere, who call it **Quasimodo** after the first words of its Latin mass—*Quasimodo geniti infantes,* meaning "Like newborn infants," welcoming the newly baptized among the faithful to partake through the Church in the mystery of the Risen Christ's eternal life as the eighth day of Creation.

Next comes **Low Monday** or the **Monday of Saint Thomas**. This is a day of return to everyday routine. It is known to many Greeks as the "Spindle-Resurrection" because, in earlier times, as work in the fields would resume for the men, so the women took up their spindles again. In Athens, they would even dedicate a new spindle to the home icons.

See also Ascension; Carnival; Christmas; Epiphany; Holi; Holy Week; Lent; Lupercalia; Mid-Autumn; Midsummer; Palm Sunday; Rogations; Sunday; Transfiguration; Water-Splashing Festival; Whitsuntide

References

J. James H. Barnett. "The Easter Festival: A Study in Cultural Change," in *American Sociological Review,* Vol. 14, No. 1 (1949), pp. 62–70.

Alain de Benoist. *Les Traditions d'Europe.* 2nd ed. Arpajon, France: Éditions du Labyrinthe, 1996.

Jerusalem Bible. Garden City, NY: Doubleday and Co., 1968.

Rev. Czeslaw Krysa. *Swienconka and Dyngus Day Traditions.* Lewiston, ID: OCO Press, 1986.

George A. Megas. *Greek Calendar Customs.* Athens: [s.n.], 1963.

Venetia Newall. *An Egg at Easter. A Folklore Study.* London: Routledge and Kegan Paul, 1973.

L. Ouspensky and V. Lossky. *The Meaning of Icons.* Tr. G. E. H. Palmer and E. Kadloubovsky. Crestwood, NY: St. Vladimir's Seminary Press, 1982.

Alfred L. Shoemaker. *Eastertide in Pennsylvania. A Folk-Cultural Study.* Mechanicsburg, PA: Stackpole Books, 2000.

Alan W. Watts. *Easter. Its Story and Meaning.* London: Abelard-Schuman, 1959.

▶ EGUBERRI

See Christmas

▶ EID (ISLAM)

The Arabic word *eid* or *îd* (pronounced "eed") means "festival." It refers to the only two festivals ordained as such by the Prophet Mohammed for the Muslim religion he founded. The Minor Festival is *Eid-al-Fitr* (the **Feast of the Break of the Fast** of the month of **Ramadan**) and the Major Festival is *Eid-al-Adha,* or the **Feast of Sacrifice**. On this day, a head of cattle is sacrificed by every head of a household in the Islamic world at the same time as the same sacrifice is performed by pilgrims to Mecca. The two Eids share many similar rites and customs.

Common Features of the Two Eids

When the Prophet Mohammed first came to Medina after the Hegira—his escape from Mecca in 622 C.E., which officially started the Islamic era—one of the things he did to regulate the life of the emerging Muslim community (the *Umma*) was to ban the observance of local pagan festivals. He had just been in Medina a couple of years when he told his followers that God had prescribed only two festivals for them—the Eids. They are referred to as *al-Eidan,* using an Arabic dual number different from either singular and plural to stress that they form a pair. The **Eid**s are an acosmic type of festival, wholly unrelated to the natural cycle of the seasons. They fall at every time of the year in turn, thanks to the purely lunar Islamic calendar. This ensures that the the belief in a transcendent God, free of any wordly association, remains the primary focus of Muslim celebrations.

The two **Eid**s mark the Umma's compliance with two of the five pillars of Islam. For **Eid**-al-Adha, on the tenth of Dhul-Hijja—the last month of the Islamic calendar—it is the completion of the spatial pilgrimage to Mecca, the *hajj.* For **Eid**-al-Fitr, it is the completion of the temporal pilgrimage of the fast begun over three months earlier, starting in the month of **Ramadan** and ending on the first day of the month of Shawwal that follows. Coming upon the fulfillment of God's command of personal discipline and collective worship, both are joyful, yet pious, occasions, when overindulgence is out of place, and a brotherly spirit of peace and forgiveness is called for instead.

Muslims take the opportunity for a fresh start afforded by the three days of each **Eid** to visit relatives and friends, exchange gifts and greetings, and dispel all grudges and ill feeling. Because all of the community must be included, various provisions see to it that the poor are not forgotten and that they get a fair amount of alms from everyone. This is always emphasized especially in the **Eid**-al-Fitr sermon, since the *Zakat-ul-Fitr* seasonal poor-due should have been given by the time it takes place. The breaking of the **Ramadan** fast is also the best time to donate the annual *zakat* in support of underprivileged members of the Umma—a regular act of social solidarity that is another one of the five pillars of Islam (leaving the creed and daily prayers as the remaining two).

As in the Friday afternoon congregational prayer of the weekly **Day of Assembly**, the **Eid** morning prayers at the mosque should be preceded by a bath and attended with clean (often new) clothes. After breakfast, men, women, and children gather at an outdoor prayer meeting, the *musallah,* in front of a white wall adorned with a niche, the *mihraab* pointing in the direction of Mecca (like the one in every mosque). Women are given the option of praying at home—as they mostly do the rest of the year. The prayers consist of two units (*rakat*) plus the six-to-sixteen additional *takbir* recitations of *Allahu Akbar* ("God is Most Great"). These set them apart from Friday prayers, as does the fact that they are followed instead of preceded by a two-part sermon (*khutba*). The **Eid**-al-Adha sermon has the added significance of coinciding with the anniversary of Mohammed's Farewell Sermon to the Umma in Mecca on the ninth of Dhul-Hijja of year 10 of the Hegira. Furthermore, the units are not preceded and followed by the usual invocations, and there is neither a call to prayer (*adhan*) nor a reminder to prostrate (*ikaama*), but only a statement that the faithful are gathered for prayer. This points to the primitive origin of the **Eid**s, as it makes them resemble the prayer (*salaat*) for rain as well as the eclipse prayer. People return home from the musallah a different way from the one they took to get there.

Many local folk customs are common to the two **Eid**s. Thus, in Central Asia, they are the occasion of a famous equestrian contest between teams from several villages, violently fighting for possession of a tied-up sheep. (A form of this sport was taken to the West as polo by British officers who had been introduced to it in India in the third quarter of the nineteenth century.) For Persian-speaking, sedentary Tajiks, as for neighboring Turkic nomads like the Kazakhs and Kirgiz, the **Eid**s have traditionally been a good time for weddings. These have often been decided by a "Love Chase"—a horse race between a girl and her suitors where everything is set up to let her determine who will win it . . . and her.

Eid-al-Fitr, the Small Festival

Eid-al-Fitr is known as the Small Festival—*Eid-al-Saghi,* or *Küçük* **Bayram** in Turkish—which also makes it the feast of little ones. They get new clothes to wear, in addition to various treats, such as little bags of sorghum grain among Swahili-speaking Muslims in East Africa. Hence its alternate name as the Feast of Sweets (*Eid-el-H'lou*) or the Sugar Feast (*Seker Bayrami* in Turkish). But it is mainly called "small" as opposed to *Eid-al-Kabir*, the Great Festival (*Büyük Bayrami* in Turkish) of *Eid-al-Adha*. The latter has independent religious significance, while the former merely marks a well-earned release from the strain of a prolonged ascetic solemnity.

Yet this contrast between the two **Eid**s is not necessarily an accurate reflection of the scale of the celebrations involved—nor of the amount of genuine rejoicing. This enthusiasm erupts spontaneously on the aptly named *Eid-al-Fitr*, the festival of the breaking of the month-long **Ramadan** fast. Still, by then, passions have been so well trained that few unbridled excesses are in evidence at the happy family celebrations of warm community that follow or at the fairground attractions that are set up in some places (as in Turkey, where they include trained bears). Indeed, restored social harmony is on display everywhere over up to three days, with people greeting and congratulating each other in the streets as well as on afternoon visits to relatives, friends, and sick people. Many gifts are offered, particularly to the children of less fortunate families. At home, the family celebrates around a noontime festive meal of, say, *mashwee* (lamb) and couscous in the Maghreb, followed by treats such as sesame oil-fried griddlecakes and almond, prune, or raisin pastries with butter tea in Central Asia. Dead relatives are also remembered as their graves are visited that day.

Eid-al-Adha, the Great Festival

Eid-al-Adha translates as the **Feast of Sacrifice**, which is also known as *Eid-al-Nahr* or as *Bakra Eid* in India and Pakistan, or in Turkish as *Kurban Bayrami* among the peoples of Central Asia, and even in Egypt as just *Bayram*. It is on this day that pilgrims to Mecca sacrifice a sheep, a goat, or a camel to commemorate Abraham's divinely arranged sacrifice of a ram in place of his firstborn son Ishmael, the Arab nation's legendary ancestor, and not of his younger son Isaac, as stated in the Bible.

In the Koran's version of his story, Abraham tells the boy he had with Hagar (the servant of his elderly wife Sara) about a dream he has been having for three nights in a row about sacrificing his only son. Ishmael agrees that the dream must be a command from God, and he volunteers to submit to it. While on the way to the place of sacrifice (Mount Marwah near Mecca instead of Mount Moriah close to Jerusalem) with his father, Ishmael faces three attempts by the Devil to get him to give up his resolution to obey God's unfathomable will at the price of his life. But Ishmael drives away the Tempter (*Shaitan*, in Arabic) with stones. This event is reenacted by pilgrims to Mecca on the morning of the **Feast of Sacrifice**, when they hurl rocks at three stone pillars marking the three stations of Ishmael's ordeal. The point of this may be explained by the imam of any mosque in the world in his *Eid-al-Adha* sermon as being quite the opposite of a human sacrifice or any other kind of sacrifice in atonement for sin or to appease an angry deity. Rather than the giving up of something in order to get something else in return, it is a test from God of a human being's willingness to submit entirely to His will, by sacrificing all self-will, down to one's very self if ever called upon to do so. This makes of Abraham the first and exemplary Muslim, since the word *islam* means just that—submission to God. That is why Abraham was given the Black Stone from heaven by the angel Gabriel and set it in the *Kaaba*. This cubic shrine is thus held by Muslims to be the oldest monotheistic shrine in the world, as well as its very center. They pray toward it wherever they are, and they are expected to go to it on pilgrimage at least once in their lives.

The greatest religious feast of the year is therefore the one when the entire Umma comes

An Afghan man cuts the skin of a slaughtered sheep on the first day of the Muslim holiday of Eid al-Adha in Kabul, January 20, 2005. Muslims all over the world celebrate the three-day Eid-al-Adha festival by slaughtering sheep, goats, cows, and camels to commemorate the Prophet Abraham's willingness to sacrifice his son Ishmael on God's command. (Ahmad Masood/Reuters/Corbis)

Whatever the proportions of this annual slaughter, the Koran (22:37) insists that "it is not their meat nor their blood, that reaches Allah; it is your piety that reaches Him: He has thus made them subject to you, that ye may glorify Allah for His Guidance to you: and proclaim the good news to all who do right" (*Holy Quran*, 1946). The sacrifice of animals is a way to ask God for the forgiveness of sins and somehow partake of His eternity. The sanctity of life is acknowledged by invoking God's name at the moment of taking it, to underscore that this is not an act of wanton cruelty, but a symbol of thanksgiving for the gift of food, which it is all the more meritorious to share as much as possible with fellow humans. Usually, a third of the meat is salted and put in the patio to dry for the future use of the household, one part (some theologians recommend up to two-thirds or even three-quarters) is meant to be distributed uncooked among the poor in the sacred precinct in front of the mosque by the family head after his afternoon nap, and the rest is sent as a gift to relatives and friends.

The sacrifice is performed after the early morning prayer at the mosque, either by the head of the family or by a butcher, following a strict ritual. The beast must be facing in the direction of the Kaaba while its throat is being cut and the slaughterer says the invocation with which every *sura* (chapter) of the Koran begins: "In the name of God, Most Gracious, Most Merciful!" (*Holy Quran*, 1946). Having skinned and gutted the animal, the butcher then takes a bath and dresses up for the occasion of an open-air gathering to praise God. This event starts at eleven in the morning and may last several hours. In places where the division of the beast is not left to the next day, wives stay at home to start sorting and preparing the meat. Thus in the Maghreb, the housewife grills the liver and the heart and consumes them that very morning. While she eats, she enters each room in the house and throws tiny bits of meat in every corner, reciting religious

together at every mosque—either at the same time as in Mecca or on one of the following two days—to celebrate the universal reenactment of the sacrifice of Abraham. The heretical Druze sect of Lebanon and Syria also follows this practice, although it is in memory of the sacrifices of Cain and Abel. Though Turks traditionally regard blood as a forbidden substance they are reluctant to shed, every observant Muslim family head makes a point of properly performing the devotional act. Generally, either a lamb or sheep is sacrificed on behalf of each household, although an ox may be substituted for up to ten people, or a camel for seven households. In every case, the animal must be neither lame nor one-eyed.

formulas in order to drive away ghosts, genies, and the evil eye. She then gives her eldest son the gall-bladder (which is supposed to be Satan's den) and asks him to throw it against the patio's white wall, where it will stick and be left to dry away into dust over a few months. She often insists on going through these superstitious acts even over her husband's disapproval as a Muslim, in order not to break with a tradition (*aada*) that may go back long before Islam, since it has a common root with the Jewish **Passover** in an ancient spring festival of Semitic nomads. Be that as it may, no one will complain about the succulent mashwee she has prepared for the lavish family luncheon. Indeed, in a relatively secularized country like Tunisia, an important segment of the population sees in *Eid-el-Adha* little more than a good excuse to indulge in culinary delights. The day's feasting, singing, and dancing go on until late at night.

Among other typical local customs are those observed in Tajikistan on *Eid-al-Kurban*. They include cleaning up the house and bleaching the walls with wheat flour; or women may greet guests by throwing a pinch of flour on their left shoulder and getting a child to take them inside while holding a sheep on a leash. All this is thought to be conducive to good health and plentiful crops. On the East African coast though, *Eid-el-Adha* is preceded by a nine-day period called *Malimati* in Swahili, during which the dead are commemorated by serving special rice meals in their honor.

See also Day of Assembly; Days of the Dead (West); Passover; Ramadan

References

Aminah Ibrahim Ali. *The Three Muslim Festivals.* Chicago: IQRA International Educational Foundation, 1998.

Gustave Edmund von Grünebaum. *Muhammadan Festivals.* New York: Olive Branch Press, 1988.

Holy Quran. Tr. Abdullah Yusuf Ali. Washington, D.C., 1946. Web.umr.edu/~msnmv/Quran.

Kerena Marchant. *Id-ul-Fitr.* Brookfield, CT: Millbrook Press, 1998.

Edward Alexander Westermarck. *Pagan Survivals in Mohammedan Civilization: Lectures on the Traces of Pagan Beliefs, Customs, Folklore, Practices and Rituals Surviving in the Popular Religion and Magic of Islamic Peoples.* Amsterdam: Philo Press, 1973.

▶ 8 MONKEY (MAYAS)

Some 200 kilometers from Guatemala City, just north of San Francisco El Alto, is a ritual center that is still of major importance for the Maya population. In the hills around Momostenango, altars are set up on mounds of pottery shards that have gathered there over the years. This is where the **New Year** purification ceremony known as "**8 Monkey**" takes place amid a general outpouring of prayer, incense, and liquor.

The New Start of an Ancient Cycle

Actually, **8 Monkey** is the date of the **New Year** in the ritual calendar used by shamans in the village of Momostenango—as in several Guatemalan highland communities, based on the *tzolkin,* the sacred calendar of the ancient Mayas, from which the Aztec *tonalamatl* or *tonalpohualli* calendar was also derived. It consists of a combination of twenty days, each of which is named after its own patron deity, with thirteen numbered days ruled by the divine "lords" of the thirteen heavens. Multiplied by each other, these two "weekly" cycles add up to a 260-day yearly sequence. The function of this divinatory calendar is the regulation of religious acts, which is the responsibility of religious specialists known by the same name as the earth deity: *chuchkajau* or "forebears," or else as *ajk'i,* meaning "masters of the days" in Quiche. The initiation of these soothsayers into the secret art of assigning birthday names and interpreting life's events according to favorable and unfavorable days takes place on the first and most auspicious of them all, when prayers to the earth deity have the greatest efficacy. This is **Guajxaquíp Báts**, which most people in Momostenango translate as "**8 Yarn**," although the esoteric meaning of *báts* is "monkey" and refers to the transformation of Jun Chogüen and Jun Báts into monkeys by Junajpuj and Ixbalanqué. This is an episode described in the Popol Vuh, the sacred book of the ancient Mayas. The fact that their sacred calendar has been maintained and strictly observed so long after the fall of their great city-states in the fifteenth century and the ensuing Spanish domination in the interval is a testimony to the resilience of the oral tradition and indigenous beliefs of their descendants, since it bears no relation to the seasons and begins at all times of year in turn, relying on an accurate mathematical count of purely human conception.

Eve: Church

Guajxaquíp Báts is a religious ceremony where the spirit is purified by the confession of all sins committed and thanksgiving for all the blessings received over the year. The Indians of Momostenango feel they all need to take part and thus come from afar if they happen to be away. Otherwise, they would be exposing themselves to serious illness and even death. In the afternoon of the previous day (9 Dog), they begin to fill the local parish church with their litanies and the glow of hundreds of candles amidst clouds of copal smoke, until nine at night. Then they start going home, having paid their respects to the spiritual powers brought by the Spaniards, before proceeding to honor their own gods the next morning.

Day: Small Broom

For this, the Indians start gathering at dawn at a place called *Chulti-mesabal*, meaning "small broom," one kilometer west of Momostenango. The town's name was given to it by Tlaxtaltec allies of the Spanish conquistadores: it means "surrounded by oratories" in the Mexican

Nahuatl language, which goes to show the continuity of worship at these pagan altars over the centuries. With white handkerchiefs around their head as a distinctive sign, soothsayers officiate in front of groups that number up to a hundred women and twice as many men. As offerings, laypeople place pottery shards to one side of altars that similar shards have served to build from one to three meters high over the years. One or two people at a time approach the chuch kajau to be prayed for by him or her. The chuch kajau first asks their names and the particular objects of the desired prayers, be it the expiation of sins, material or moral well-being, or thanksgiving for a wish the deities have fulfilled. After being paid a symbolic amount of money, the soothsayer burns a small packet of prized *kabagüil* (copal) in a half-meter-wide niche formed to this effect with pottery shards in the altar and decorated with pine boughs for the occasion. The prayer he or she makes to offer the incense is called *sipaj* and is supposed to make the deity well-disposed toward the requests being made on behalf of the supplicants. The ceremony is very long for each of them, as the soothsayer goes through an endless series of all manner of details about their private lives. Sometimes, the soothsayer offers a cup of brandy (*aguardiente*) to the deity, as a way to seal the understanding and communion between them, the same way Indians do between each other. He or she knows from certain signs whether the deity has accepted the offering—which the soothsayer then consumes himself or herself. The soothsayer's own feeling of communion with the supreme deities increases along with the amount of spirits thus absorbed over the day as he or she goes through one offering after another. All the soothsayers' families have their own altars at a separate spot called *Pajá*, in the water on the edge of a brook in a depression to the east of the main altars. There are also smaller, secondary altars for the recently initiated soothsayers, whose services are less in demand.

Night: Big Broom

At dusk, the shamans go a little to the west to pray and to burn incense all night at other altars on a height called *Nim-mesabal,* meaning "big broom." The broom in the name of these holy places is probably a reference to the sweeping away of sins before the **New Year** in the general confession that is a main feature of this festival (also found in old Japanese **New Year** customs), as well as a typical expression of Maya religiosity, meant to remove the spiritual cause of ailments of any kind. Laypeople mostly fall asleep around the altars as the soothsayers are absorbed in prayer, and non-Indians may wander between them unhindered, even though they may have been told they were not welcome in this sacred precinct of native religion. Temporary stands nonetheless mushroom there to provide the 20,000 or so Indian worshippers with all the food, drink, candles, and incense they need over the minimum three days these ceremonies last.

> **See also** Kukulcan; New Fire Ceremony; New
> Year (Japan)

References

Robert M. Carmack. *Rebels of Highland Guatemala: The Quiché-Mayas of Momostenango.* Civilization of the American Indian Series, Vol. 215, Norman: University of Oklahoma Press, 1995.

Garrett W. Cook. *Renewing the Maya World: Expressive Culture in a Highland Town.* Austin: University of Texas Press, 2000.

Antonio Goubaud. *The Guajxaquíp Báts: An Indian Ceremony of Guatemala.* Lecture delivered in Spanish at the Sociedad de geografía y historia de Guatemala on May 3rd, 1935 and published in the quarterly of this institution: *Anales de la Sociedad de geografía e historia de Guatemala,* Vol. XII, No. 1, September 1935. Guatemala City: Centro editorial de Guatemala, 1937.

Barbara Tedlock. *Time and the Highland Maya.* Albuquerque: University of New Mexico Press, 1982.

▶ 8 YARN

See 8 Monkey

▶ ELEUSINIA

See Eleusinian Mysteries

▶ ELEUSINIAN MYSTERIES (GREECE)

In Eleusis, a town in Attica between Athens and Megara, agricultural festivals known as the Greater and Lesser **Eleusinian Mysteries** reenacted the myth of Demeter and Korê. Originally symbolizing the cycle of grain-growing, they gained added meaning for allowing Greeks of all backgrounds to be initiated in a secret cult of personal salvation through participation in renewed life beyond death.

From Tribal Belonging to Personal Freedom

Throughout the Greek world from Alexandria to the Black Sea, there used to be festivals of Demeter. While many of them were derived from those of Eleusis or were even called **Eleusinia** (like the **games** celebrated in that city every odd year of the Olympiad as well as every second year out of four over four days in the middle of the month of Metageitnion toward August), the true **Eleusinian Mysteries** were unique to Eleusis. They started out as a local cult, when initiation in these mysteries was tribal rather than personal, as a kind or rite of passage giving male citizens full membership in the body politic. This all changed when Athens annexed the city in the late seventh century B.C.E. and made the **Eleusinian Mysteries** one of its major religious festivals, so that initiation lost its importance as a way of conferring civic status in Eleusis. At first, every Athenian, and then, with the emergence of an urban, even cosmopolitan, lifestyle (that loosened tribal allegiances and relativized communal roles, making room for voluntary associations and personal commitments independent of social background), virtually every Greek was admitted to the **Eleusinian Mysteries**. Free participation in such religious mysteries in responsible compliance with their rules became a prime example of the new sense of personal liberty, so that those of Eleusis may have given the Greek word for freedom: *elevtheria*. Still, it was partly on account of the spiritual freedom from the bonds of mortality granted by the mysteries that Eleusis (whose name meant "advent") was identified with this cherished ideal of Greek culture.

From Local Clan to National Cult

In ancient times, Eleusis was a day's journey from Athens, since it was located some twenty-three kilometers to the west in the fertile plain of Thria—now an industrial suburb called Lepsina. According to the *Homeric Hymn to Demeter* that probably goes back before the city's annexation by Athens, it was the goddess herself who had instituted the mysteries when she stopped at Eleusis on her search for her lost daughter Korê, who had been taken away as a bride by Hades, god of the netherworld. The people of Eleusis had built a great shrine for her, and she had taught them the sacred rites that would ease her mourning and allow grain to grow again as an embodiment of her daughter, freed to emerge from the depths of the earth for two-thirds of every year before joining her husband back underground in the winter. The entire story of Demeter and Korê was thus painstakingly reenacted in the **Eleusinian Mysteries**.

They were originally the private cult of the noble clan of the Eumolpidae, one of two (along with the Kerikae) from which the clergy still had to be selected, while all initiates were thought of as being adopted into it, becoming sons and daughters of Demeter. The high priest or hierophant made the solemn declaration that opened the Mysteries to Greek speakers (excluding barbarians who might mispronounce the sacred formulas, unless they became citizens), as long as "their hands were not

defiled" by sacrilege or crime. Men and women, citizens and slaves (provided they were of Greek origin) might become mysts (candidates for initiation), coming under the guidance of mystagogues (initiates who led them into the mysteries) and under the surveillance of epimeletes, or overseers. The postulant who had been presented to clerical authorities by a mystagogue and accepted as a myst would then begin to undergo preparations that consisted in a whole series of practices, fasts, and group retreats at different times and in various places, while the mysts of previous years cheered on and other participants looked on.

Lesser and Greater Mysteries

The candidate's mystic journey began in earnest with the Lesser Mysteries, instituted after the annexation of Eleusis by Athens as an adaptation to the new situation and the wider constituency it created. As the first degree of initiation needed to proceed to the Greater Mysteries at Eleusis, they were held at Agrae near Athens six months in advance during that of Anthesterion, just prior to the spring equinox. Presided by the ceremonial king archon of Athens, who was assisted by the clergy and priestly clans of Eleusis, they culminated in a solemn sacrifice to Demeter and Korê, after the candidates had been purified in the waters of the river Ilissos nearby.

The Greater Mysteries were announced in Attica's neighboring states by hereditary heralds, allowing a truce to come into effect before and during them so the participants could gather freely at Eleusis. But first, they went to Athens. For it was from there that young celebrants set out for Eleusis in September—on the thirteenth of Boedromion—to fetch the *hiera*. These sacred objects were brought back the next day in veiled baskets called cists which only female initiates might carry, escorted by ephebes (young men) in a kanephoria, a kind of procession introduced with the annexation to Attica. It was greeted with ritual jeers called *gephyrisms* as it went over the bridge over the Cephisus on its way to bringing the hidden sacramental objects to the Eleusinion Temple in Athens. (There, a meeting of the city's council, called the *Boulē*, was required by law on the day after the Mysteries, by the twenty-fourth of Boedromion.) The people who met these requirements mentioned would be admitted into it after a purification on the fifteenth. This day of meeting (agyrmos) was also named after the opening proclamation (*prorrhesis*) made by the hierophant and the *dadouchos* or "torch-bearer" in the *Stoa Poikile*—the Painted Colonnade. It was up to the mystagogues to make sure that the people present met all these conditions. The sixteenth was called *Halade mustai* after the cry of "To the sea, mysts!" that accompanied their march to the shore to purify themselves and the piglets they carried in the water before making a burnt offering of them to get rid of their own defilements. They went through the procedure several times over, fasting from dawn to dusk for nine days, if they happened to have particularly grave or numerous acts of wrongdoing on their consciences. The mysts wore new clothes and myrtle crowns as they came back to town in a procession for a purifying sacrifice. There was more purification and sacrifice over the next two days with the **Epidauria** in honor of the healing god Asclepius, when mysts who arrived late (as he apparently did from Epidaurus) could still be welcomed.

The Procession of Iacchus to Eleusis

The nineteenth was the most solemn day. It saw the return of the *hiera* to Eleusis in a procession of many thousand people, who first assembled in various points of Athens before lining up in order on the Agora and the Ceramicus to set out from there and through the Dipylon gate on the sacred road to Eleusis. Since they would not get there before nightfall, priests, mystagogues, and mysts, decked

with myrtle and ivy leaves, would carry torches in addition to ears of corn and agricultural implements. The image of Iacchus (that is, Bacchus or Dionysus) was fetched from his shrine along with temple utensils to be placed on a cart with attendants at the head of the procession he was thought to lead in person, having composed the song for it. There were also dances, games played by torchlight (even at the fountain of Kallichoros), sacrifices, and other ceremonies along this protracted journey that stopped at several shrines along the way. Lewd jokes were customary at the festivals of the same earthy gods (like the **Dionysia** and **Thesmophoria**), especially at the Cephisus again. After the statue of Iacchus came the cart bearing the *hiera*, the clergy, the mysts, the citizens lined up by tribe and deme behind their magistrates, the Areopagus and the Council of the Five Hundred, and the whole crowd of those who wanted some part in the famous feast. Rich women used to ride in carriages until the statesman Lycurgus passed a law against this relaxation of traditional decorum in the fourth century B.C.E. The crowds needed some rest and refreshment once they finally reached their destination that night: the Telesterion where the god was installed alongside Demeter. Three thousand people could fill the rows of seats in this initiation hall.

Things Not to Be Revealed

Here the mysteries reserved for the mysts would take place over three days. The first one was a day of fasting, which ended when the mysts and the previous year's initiates—the only ones admitted inside to attend a solemn sacrifice to Demeter and Korê—partook of the meat offered and drank the *kykeon*. This mint-flavored barley gruel or tonic potion was the same one with which Demeter broke her own fasting after nine days of looking for her daughter, enticed by her fellow nurse Baubo, whom she had joined in the service of King Celeus of

Eleusis. That night, the mysts also imitated her wanderings in the area in search of Korê by running with torches in white dresses amidst the coarse jokes of female onlookers. Also known at Demeter's other feasts (for example, **Thesmophoria**) as a way to dispel evil, the latter practice of *aischrologia* echoed the dirty limericks in the iambic meter (named after the king's lame daughter Iambe who had tried to cheer her up with them) that now served to relieve the emotional tension at her mysteries. The mysts also got to ritually manipulate the sexually charged but still unidentified sacred objects of her cult and to sing certain sacred chants under the direction of priests of the clan of the "good cantors" (the meaning of the name of the Eumolpidae's clan).

It was only during the last night that the mysts—or perhaps those initiated the year before—got to the final ceremony of *epoptia*, the "beholding" of the supreme mysteries—whether they were the long hidden *hiera* or some mythological drama. Most likely, the first night introduced the mysts to the first level of the mysteries, having to do with plant fertility; for just as in the myth Korê was carried away to marry Hades (Death) and give birth to Plutus (Wealth), so was grain thrown into the field and buried in the earth to bring forth new life. The second night must have revealed to the new epopts the deeper meaning of a cult of personal salvation, since when a person died, he or she was buried in the earth but could still spiritually partake in the cyclical renewal of life, rather than just fumble in the horrifying shadow and choking confusion of post-mortem dissolution. As the *Homeric Hymn to Demeter* concluded, "Happy is he among deathly men who has seen these things! But he who is uninitiated, and has no lot in them, will never have equal lot in death beneath the murky gloom" (Willoughby 2003). For the rhetorician Themistius, "initiated and made perfect, free, and walking unrestrained, a man can celebrate the Mysteries, a crown on his head; he lives amongst pure and holy men; he sees the crowd of noninitiates on earth, willfully plunging into filth and darkness, and dallying with evil through their very fear of death, instead of believing in the bliss of the life to come" (Flacelière 2002).

Still, "Aristotle is of the opinion that the initiated learned nothing precisely, but that they received impressions and were put into a certain frame of mind" (Synesius, *De Dione* 10, in Willoughby 2003). Oral instructions were given only as pointers to the meaning of something that was shown in the Mysteries in order to be experienced as an inner transformation in a personal encounter with the divine. Both the words and the movements involved constituted *ta aporrheta*—things not to be revealed to the uninitiated on pain of death or an even worse fate afterwards. And despite all the rumors and speculations that have circulated about them, none is really authoritative, and their actual content has remained shrouded in the original mysteries, buried with them forever since they were forbidden by a decree of Emperor Theodosius the Great when he made the Roman Empire officially and exclusively Christian at the end of the fourth century.

See also Dionysia; Games (Greece);
   Thesmophoria

References

Robert Flacelière. *Daily Life in Greece at the Time of Pericles.* Tr. Peter Green. Troy, MI: Phoenix Press, 2002.

Karl Kerényi. *Eleusis: Archetypal Image of Mother and Daughter.* "Bollingen Series" No. 65/4. Princeton, NJ: Princeton University Press, 1991.

George E. Mylonas. *Eleusis and the Eleusinian Mysteries.* Princeton, NJ: Princeton University Press, 1961.

François de Polignac. *Cults, Territory, and the Origins of the Greek City-State.* Tr. Janet Lloyd. Chicago: University of Chicago Press, 1995.

Harold R. Willoughby. *Pagan Regeneration. A Study of Mystery Initiations in the Graeco-Roman World.* Whitefish, MT: Kessinger Publishing, 2003.

► ELEVATION OF THE CROSS (CHRISTIANITY)

To complement the main celebration of the Crucifixion of Jesus in the mournful context of **Good Friday**, another Christian festival on September 14 centers on the discovery of the Cross three centuries later by the Roman Empress Mother Helena. The Cross then symbolizes the victory of Christ, be it through the Church founded as the result of his sacrifice or through the Empire that came to acknowledge him as Lord and God. The feast's various names—**Dedication**, **Invention of the Holy Cross**, **Elevation** or **Raising** or Universal **Exaltation of the Cross**—point to its many aspects.

The Festival of the Dedication

The corresponding stages of development and layers of meaning can be traced by distinguishing the components of a Russian icon of the feast. The church in the background of the icon is a reminder that the feast started out as a yearly temple dedication festival of a type common in the Roman world from pagan times. A few years after giving official recognition to the Christian religion, Emperor Constantine built the Lateran basilica in Rome in 324—an event commemorated since then on November 9 by a minor feast in the Western Church, as the **Festival of the Dedication**. In the Eastern Church though, another **Festival of the Dedication** began to be celebrated soon thereafter on September 14 to commemorate that of the basilica of the Resurrection in Jerusalem, on the site of the Holy Sepulchre where Jesus Christ had been buried after his crucifixion. When it was dedicated in 335 in the presence of Emperor Constantine, for the thirtieth anniversary of his reign, by the bishops who had just gathered at the Council of Tyre, there was no mention of the discovery of the Cross. But by 347, Saint Cyril of Jerusalem could write that "already the whole universe is filled with fragments of the Wood of the Cross" (Ouspensky and Lossky 1982, p. 148). At the century's end, a nun called either Etheria or Egeria who had come on pilgrimage from the Iberian Peninsula would note that, over eight days of processions when all churches would be decorated "as at **Easter** and for **Epiphany**," the dedication of the ones on the Golgotha and on the Holy Sepulchre, along with that of the Temple of Solomon, was "celebrated with the highest honour because the Cross of the Lord was discovered on that day" (*The Pilgrimage of Etheria,* pp. 95–96).

The **Invention of the Cross** is the official Church term for this find, the credit for which was given to Constantine's mother Helena in most accounts from that time onward. But though she had made a famous pilgrimage to the holy sites around 326, bringing them into the limelight of imperial politics and patronage, she had already died of old age by 330. This was a few years before the dedication of basilicas on the Holy Sepulchre and on Golgotha brought with it a renewed interest in the particulars of the death of Jesus, such as its instrument.

The Cross was probably discovered—without Helena—around 340; the anniversary of the **Dedication** was a fitting day to produce it for the first time and to venerate it every year for all time. In 395, Saint John Chrysostom described how Helena had discovered three crosses buried beneath Golgotha—the hill where Jesus Christ was crucified alongside two thieves. His cross was singled out by the trilingual inscription: "Jesus of Nazareth, King of the Jews," mentioned in Gospel accounts of the Crucifixion. Sometimes depicted in the bottom half of the feast's icon, the discovery of three crosses is omitted in the one shown in this section.

The Elevation of the Cross

In the sixth century, Alexander the Monk could refer to the **Festival of the Dedication** and the **Elevation of the Venerable Cross**, but the latter was already beginning to eclipse the former. Nevertheless, the original **Dedication** is still commemorated by the Eastern Church on the eve of the September 14 feast of the **Elevation**. This name refers to the way the Cross was shown to the people of Jerusalem for the first time in the basilica of the Resurrection on the day following the annual commemoration of its **Dedication**. Saint Macarius, the bishop who supposedly had been guided by miracles to find and identify the Cross of Christ (along with Saint Helena), raised it with his outstretched arms in front of the faithful. At this triumphal moment, they started to shout "*Kyrie eleison*" (Greek for "Lord have mercy") over and over again. Their cries are echoed in the sequences of a hundred kyries that now accompany the rite of the **Exaltation** proper (see below). This was the first **Elevation of the Cross**, and it was reenacted in Jerusalem from the time it was discovered there until 614, when the True Cross was seized by the invading Persians.

A Political Side: Imperial Celebration

The festival also commemorates the second great **Elevation** around 630 in Constantinople, after the Roman Emperor Heraclius III recaptured the Cross from the Persians. Patriarch Sergius then carried it in a procession from the church of Blachernes to that of Saint Sophia, where the ceremony was reenacted on a grand scale. Now independent of its original setting in the Holy City of Jerusalem, the festival soon spread to other parts of the Christian Roman Empire. In what was left of it in the West by that time, it was first specifically mentioned in 701 in Rome, its symbolic center, in an obituary for Pope Sergius, and was also alluded to even before in outlying areas of Europe, where it was sometimes set on May 3. In the Eastern Church, the **Holy Cross** is also venerated in much the same way on the first of August and on the third Sunday of **Lent**, known (along with **Palm Sunday**) as **Flower Sunday**, on account of the flowers used to decorate the holy object, and

which the faithful can take away as a blessing. This is similar to what the Sikhs do with the marigolds that have come in contact with their holy book at a **Gurpurb.**

The Roman Empire had initially become the bulwark of Christianity—as the temporal image of the spiritual universality that it claimed—because Constantine was led by clerical advisers to interpret in a Christian key the sign of a cross he saw in the sky before a decisive battle against a rival in 312. The following year, he put an end to the persecution of Christians and started supporting them, so that they in turn interpreted as evidence of the spreading power of the Cross of Christ his later victories and the foundation of a New Rome, Constantinople.

Constantine's sponsorship of the basilica of the Resurrection, where the Cross was first raised after having supposedly been found by his mother Helena (so that both are portrayed as saints on the left-hand side of the corresponding icon), only confirmed this association of spiritual victory and temporal order. This link is therefore celebrated in Orthodox liturgical texts for the festival of the **Elevation of the Cross**—as an ideal if not always as a fact. For in this view, it is the "invincible victory" of the Cross over worldly powers hostile to Christianity that is the "upholder of the universe," as the one sure support for an order reflecting divine goodness amid the turmoil of human history. Thus, it is only by virtue of the Cross that Christian princes can keep at bay the "barbarians" of all kinds who seek to overthrow Christian civilization and can instead extend the latter's sway throughout the world. This was what a Christianized Roman Empire purported to do—in all its varying guises, be it as the so-called Holy Roman Empire founded by Charlemagne in the West in 800 or when Russian czars as "Caesars" ruled a "Third Rome"—Moscow as successor to Constantinople after the fall of this "Second Rome" in 1453.

The Universal Exaltation of the Life-Giving Cross

This political dimension is of course only an outer application of the inner spiritual truth of the festival, summed up in the relevant reading from Paul (I Corinthians 1:25), which proclaims that "God's foolishness is wiser than human wisdom, and God's weakness is stronger than human strength"(*Jerusalem Bible* 1968). For "seeing the Cross raised by the hands of the bishop," the Orthodox Church glorifies in the feast's vespers that "weapon of peace and unconquerable ensign of victory" through which "the curse was abolished, incorruptible life flowered again, earthly creatures have acquired deification and the demon has been decisively overthrown" (Ouspensky and Lossky, 1982, p. 148). The matins that follow thus present Jesus Christ as the New Adam, and his Cross as the Tree of Life by virtue of which a fallen world recovers the incorruptibility of the Garden of Eden. Raised above the earth, the Cross brings heaven within human reach. The outstretched arms of Christ embrace the whole universe from the Cross with which he is raised vertically, while on a horizontal plane its branches also cover the four corners of the world, spreading grace and expelling demons everywhere.

This is the meaning of the rite of the fivefold **Exaltation** that takes place during the Orthodox service of this day of strict fasting, known after it as the **Universal Exaltation of the Venerable and Life-Giving Cross**. A crucifix is adorned either with flowers or with sprigs of sweet basil, because one of these "royal" plants (fit for the King of the Universe since such is the meaning of their Greek name) is said to have sprouted on the spot where his Cross was discovered. It rests on a tray on the altar, which the priest walks around so as to venerate it with incense fumes from all four sides. He then takes the tray on his head in a procession of the clergy out of the sanctuary through the north side door (to un-

Russian icon of the Elevation of the Cross, Anonymous, 19th century. (Heritage Image Partnership)

derline God's self-abasement as a meek man on a cross) to the front of its main Royal Door (named thus because the Emperor would use it as the only layman allowed into the sanctuary, being the image of God on earth). There, he puts the tray on a table in the midst of the people and, facing east, he makes three prostrations. The priest takes the cross with the basil branches, raising it above his head as he loudly says the first of the customary prayers for the faithful. He goes on to make the sign of the Cross with it three times before slowly bending to the ground and slowly rising again to hold it up. He then holds the crucifix at chest level as the choir reaches the end of one hundred *Kyrie eleison*, when he again makes the sign of the Cross with it three times. These gestures are repeated four more times, facing north, west, south, and east in the Greek Church, and south, west, north, and east in the Russian Church. In the latter, bishops alone may perform the five-fold **Exaltation** in cathedrals and monasteries. Ordinary parishes only perform the Veneration of the Cross. In this rite, the faithful prostrate themselves twice before the cross on the table, kiss it, and then do one more prostration—the same way they would venerate any icon, even though this one is more intimately connected to Christ's human nature. This may be why it has the healing properties evoked on the right-hand side of some icons of the feast, where a sick person is being cured, raised up along with the Cross [not illustrated here].

Though this festival is less developed in the West, the cross would traditionally be presented there to the sick, to the clergy, and to the people, who might also take part in processions. The best surviving example is probably the feast of **Santa Croce** in Lucca. In this Tuscan city on September 13, the faithful hold candles as they march from the basilica of San Frediano to the church of San Martino. Here, they venerate an eleventh-century crucifix known as the *Volto Santo* ("Holy Face")—the palladium or protective symbol and fetish that the once proud Republic of Lucca even made its "king." This wooden crucified Christ still wears golden regalia. A fair is held the next day on the Piazza San Michele.

An Autumn Festival

Launched a thousand years ago by Benedictine monks, one of France's largest country fairs also takes place over three days around the **Holy Cross** festival in Lessay, in Normandy. In the Catholic and Anglican Churches, **Holy Cross** Day was normally followed by one of the four **Ember Weeks** of prayer and fasting when the clergy used to be ordained. This is now scaled back to the Wednesday, Friday, and Saturday after the third Sunday of September, and is no longer a fast.

In Greece, the **Exaltation of the Cross** has always been a turning point of the secular as well as of the religious calendar, marking the shift between two seasons in many areas of life. "On the day of the Cross, rest in harbour; on **Saint George**'s Day, rise and set sail again" (Megas 1963, p. 156) goes a saying among Greek seamen about the end of long maritime journeys coinciding with the end of summer. It is also time for everyone to say goodbye to fond summer habits like the midday siesta and the late-night supper: the latter is literally buried in effigy in an ancient ceremony on the Aegean island of Aegina. Peasants bring an assortment of seeds in a dish to be blessed with holy water by the priest at the day's solemn liturgy, and later on they often mix them with the grain they will use for sowing for the following year's crop. Likewise, their wives often prepare fresh yeast with holy water taken from the priest at the end of the service. Thus, on the island of Lemnos, the women first use whatever yeast is left the week before and then take this holy water from the **Raising of the Cross** to make the yeast that will allow their bread to rise over the coming year.

In Ethiopia, this feast—known there as **Masqal**—comes after the heavy rains that make summer a cold season, and functions somewhat like a spring festival. Traditionally, each family prepares a maypole adorned with the yellow wildflowers that then cover the fields, bring it to a central clearing, and lean it against those of other families of the area over the bonfire that is going to be lit in the evening. Before it is ignited, the bonfire has to be consecrated by the priests with the requisite liturgical chants, and then each social group in the hierarchical order (local lord, clergy, lesser nobility, peasant men, women, and finally children) circles the teepee-like structure three times in honor of the Holy Trinity. At night, as the bonfire blazes, young men dance around it singing war chants and playfully throwing burning brands at each other.

See also Conception and Birth of the Virgin
  Mary; Gurpurb; Holy Week; Lent; May Day;
  Palm Sunday; Saint Lucy; Transfiguration;
  Whitsuntide

References

Jerusalem Bible. Garden City, NY: Doubleday and
  Co., 1968.
Donald N. Levine. *Wax and Gold: Tradition and
  Innovation in Ethiopian Culture.* Chicago:
  University of Chicago Press, 1972.
George A. Megas. *Greek Calendar Customs.*
  Athens: [s.n.], 1963.
Leonid Ouspensky and Vladimir Lossky. *The
  Meaning of Icons.* Tr. G. E. H. Palmer and
  E. Kadloubovsky. Crestwood, NY: Saint
  Vladimir's Seminary Press, 1982.
The Pilgrimage of Etheria. Tr. M. L. McLure and
  C. L. Feltoe. New York: Macmillan and
  Ann Arbor, MI: Univeristy Microfilms
  International, 1978.
Louis van Tongeren. *Exaltation of the Cross:
  Towards the Origins of the Feast of the Cross and
  the Meaning of the Cross in Early Medieval
  Liturgy.* Sterling, VA: Peeters, 2001.
Evelyn Waugh. *Helena: A Novel.* London: Penguin
  Books, 1990.

▶ EMBER DAYS

See Elevation of the Cross, Lent, Saint Lucy,
  Whitsuntide

▶ ENTRY OF THE MOTHER OF GOD INTO THE TEMPLE

See Presentation of the Virgin Mary

▶ EPIDAURIA

See Eleusinian Mysteries

▶ EPIPHANY (CHRISTIANITY)

Epiphany is the final day of the **Christmas** season, coming soon after the beginning of the New Year. **Christmas** was actually derived from the Christian festival of **Epiphany**, which is often interchangeable with **New Year**'s Day as a focus of seasonal practices of pagan origin. In the West, it commemorates the coming of the three Wise Men to offer gifts to the newborn child Jesus.

Epiphany is also called **Theophany** in the East, where its name refers to the manifestation of God in Three Persons at the Baptism of Christ. However, there the festival also commemorates his first miracle at the Wedding in Cana.

The Twelfth Day of Christmas

Epiphany was traditionally the **Twelfth Day** of the **Christmas** season, which falls on January 6. Since it is the end of the **Christmas** season, it is known as **Loppiainen** in Finland (from the Finnish word *loppu* meaning "end"). This is one country where **Christmas** trees then come down with a small celebration, involving the eating of edible decorations like apples and candies, in addition to the careful storing of permanent ones.

Epiphany is a kind of second **Christmas** in that it sums up the volatile properties of a holiday season of transition between two yearly cycles. In Ireland, it was even called "**Little Christmas**" or "**Old Christmas**," and people used to light twelve small candles around a large one. The candles were said to stand for Christ and his disciples. However, since the central candle was often replaced by a strange figurine called Old Meg, they more likely represented the reviving sun surrounded by the twelve months of a new year. This might explain the similar English pattern of twelve fires around a large bonfire known until the mid-nineteenth century in Herefordshire, Worcestershire, and the western Midlands as "**Twelfth Night** Fires."

But in Southern German lands (Bavaria, Switzerland, Austria), *der Zwölfer*—the **Twelfth Day**—was also known as *das Grosse Neujahr*—

the **Great New Year**'s Day. There, January 6 was originally the peasants' **New Year**, and the same practices may be observed either on this date or on January 1, depending on the local tradition of a particular town or village. They include various combinations of the following: special lunchtime foods, loud torchlight processions, rowdy competitive games, lively dances and masquerades, and children trick-or-treating and caroling from door to door while carrying stars like the grownup *Sternsinger* (star-singers) of Switzerland. In the Netherlands, young people used to march behind a paper-lantern Star of Bethlehem. Since the fourteenth century, they would dress up as the Three Kings on the eve of their feast, in an outdoor folk version of the liturgical play performed in church since the eleventh century. Noisy activities were meant to frighten the many witches thought to be on the loose during the **Twelve Days** at the turn of the year. **Epiphany** is even called *Perchtentag*—the day of the fairy Berchta or Perchta, an old Germanic deity, on account of witches of her kind who love to cast their spells on spinning wheels. It is believed that these and other weaving tools should therefore be hidden away for the duration of the **Twelve Days** in Austria. In England, distaffs would be burned if anybody used them while they were taboo; January 6 is therefore known as "**Saint Distaff Day.**" Conversely, no **Christmas** greenery is to be kept beyond this date, when all **Christmas** trees are burned in a central community bonfire in some places. Whatever is left of **Epiphany** customs in England is nothing compared to the past revels of this feast, which were at their high point during the Elizabethan era, when William Shakespeare wrote his comedy *Twelfth Night*.

The Italian counterpart of the German witch Berchta owes more of her traits to the Christian story of the Church festival of **Epiphany**, down to her very name: Befana or Pefana. Like the Babushka of Russian **Christmas** folklore, she was an old lady who lived close to Bethlehem when the Three Wise Men came by, asking for

directions to town. At first suspicious, she refused to answer, but then, seized with remorse, ran after them. It was too late: God punished her by making her lose her way, and she has been roaming the earth ever since in search of the place of the Messiah's birth—rather like the Wandering Jew of European folk tales. Except for her appearance as a benevolent witch—with big teeth, black clothes, tattered shoes, and a broomstick to fly on, Befana took on for Italians many of the attributes of **Saint Nicholas** in Northern Europe. On January 6, she flies from roof to roof carrying a big sack on her back. It contains both gifts for good little boys and girls and black coals for those who have been bad, and whose gifts she might take back with her. Nowadays, this sobering possibility is merely hinted at in the candy or chocolate "coals" offered to all children on **Epiphany**, when, unseen to all, Befana goes down chimneys to deliver them. Children used to go trick-or-treating on this day, led by a youngster dressed up as Befana; this was called the *Befanata.*

The Wise Men's visit to the Christ Child is reenacted in typical costumes in some places, as in Tarcento near Italy's northeastern border, where it is part of a torchlight procession up a hill to light a bonfire—the *pignarul*—which gives the signal for other *pignarui* to be lit on surrounding heights. A caravan winds its way through the streets of Madrid too, in the *Cabalgata de los Reyes* (the "Cavalcade of the Kings").

The Wise Men are the feast's main focus throughout Western Europe, where, since the second-century Latin writer Tertullian, they are seen (on the basis of Psalm 72 about the messianic king's universal empire) as three kings from Oriental lands. They also figure prominently in the customs of one of these Oriental lands: the former African kingdom of Ethiopia. They are also known as the Magi, after the Zoroastrian priests of another Oriental land: Persia; it is believed some may have come to Bethlehem looking for the *Saushyant,* the messianic Savior expected at the end of days in their ancient monotheistic religion. It was only natural for such renowned astrologers to be guided by a star to the birthplace of the "King of kings." Persian Magi were famous as king-makers (if not as kings, as in the French *rois mages* for the Wise Men) because of their special ability to forecast from somebody's astrological chart if that person was to be called to the throne. They did this on the basis of the position of the "Little King." This is how the name of the star in question (possibly the star of Bethlehem) in the constellation of Leo translates, whether it is called *Regulus* in Latin or *Basilikos* in Greek.

In Greece, January 1 happens to be the feast of **Saint Basil the Great**, who died on this date in 379 and is thought to visit the earth every **New Year**. He comes down through the chimney to help himself to the food laid out for him in the houses he has come to bless (with special attention to the animals), not unlike Befana or another fourth-century bishop from Asia Minor: **Saint Nicholas**. No less generous than the latter, the well-born Basil, as bishop of Caesarea, distributed his fortune among the poor, the sick, and the orphans during a famine. This is why a priest or the head of the house gets to play his role to distribute gifts to children on **New Year**'s Day, as well as to cut and share out (in a strict order of seniority from the saint in heaven to the poor on earth) portions of the *vassilopita*, the round cake of Basil, whose name means "king." It contains a coin, and whoever gets it in his piece is the lucky winner of a special gift.

As if to underscore the underlying unity of many **New Year** and **Epiphany** customs, this is the way the "King of the Bean" still gets elected in France in the secular setting of family, school, or business on January 6, which is known as the **Fête des Rois**. Traditionally, the "jester" of a "court" where titles were also assigned at random around the table made sure all the guests would then proclaim: "*Le Roi boit!*" ("The King is drinking!"), as they joined him in lifting their glasses just after he found

the bean. The first piece of cake was "God's share," reserved for the poor and assigned by the youngest child of a family. However, in Franche-Comté, children would dress up as the Magi and carol from door to door to claim it, while in Lower Brittany, a poor man dragging a festively decorated horse would likewise do the rounds for "the poor's share." The "twelfth cake" long used in British **Epiphany** customs is clearly the *galette des Rois*, brought from France by the invading Normans in the eleventh century, just when they were also taking over Greek-influenced Southern Italy—along perhaps with the *vassilopita*?

Whether it is on January 1 or 6, the year's orderly cycle yields to blind chance in primal chaos. As games of chance are exceptionally allowed by the Greek Church when children and adults alike gather to play cards on **New Year**'s Eve, social roles too get reshuffled, and a young king can arise out of nowhere to bring order to a new yearly cycle of light and dark. The same **New Year** symbolism of cosmic renewal from humble beginnings seems applicable both to the King of the Bean, randomly selected at **Epiphany** by the same method as the mock king of the Roman **Saturnalia** in December, and to the Christ Child, born among beasts on **Christmas** Night amid rumors of his future kingship, the better to confound the powers that be.

Yet since the Three Kings brought their gifts of gold, myrrh, and frankincense to the Christ Child on **Epiphany**, it is on the **Día de los Tres Reyes** that **Christmas** gifts—especially to children—are offered in Spain, where a silver coin, a bean, or a porcelain figurine is hidden in a crown-shaped fruitcake, the *rosca de reyes*. In Mexican villages, though, families start bringing their small gifts to the central square in a procession called a *posada* ten days before **Christmas**. They pile up there until **Epiphany**, when they are stuffed into large *piñatas*—large and brightly colored papier-mâché or porcelain animals that are then hung up for the children to poke at until they burst and shower them with candies and coins—like a cornucopia, a horn of plenty evoking hopes for a prosperous **New Year**.

The Festival of the Three Miracles

In Northern Italy at the beginning of the fifth century, January 6 was "the **Festival of the Three Miracles**," namely the coming of the Wise Men to Bethlehem, the Baptism of Christ, and the first miracle of Christ's public ministry: changing water into wine at the Wedding in Cana. If the African Bishop Saint Augustine celebrated **Epiphany** as the feast of the Wise Men, his master Saint Ambrose, bishop of Milan, revered it as the feast of Christ's Baptism in the Jordan, following the custom of the Eastern Churches.

The festival had actually originated in the East, where it was second only to **Easter** as the joint celebration of the three starting points of God's "manifestation from on high" (the meaning of the Greek name "**Epiphany**") as Incarnate Word: not only the Baptism of Jesus and the miracle of Cana, but his **Nativity** too. **Epiphany** is thus older than **Christmas**, and was initially more important, commemorating the same event, plus those specific to itself—except for the Wise Men's journey. These mysterious figures, enhanced by legend from sketchy Gospel allusions, rose to prominence in connection with **Epiphany** only after the celebration of the **Nativity of Christ** was detached from it and shifted to December 25. This was done by the popes in the middle of the fourth century, when January 6 first appeared as a feast day in the West. They did this in order to counteract and absorb the winter solstice festivals that were too firmly rooted to be overshadowed—let alone suppressed—by the new Christian religion.

Epiphany was thus gradually demoted over the centuries in the West, to become a mere extension of **Christmas** as the main feast. In the Middle Ages, the celebration of Christ's Baptism was shifted to January 13. (This date is also

the Feast of **Saint Knut**, to which the "**Twelve Days** of **Christmas**" have been extended in Sweden ever since 1131, when the death of King Knut Lavard on January 7 caused the postponement of the normal close of the holiday season. Then in 1972, the Roman Church, in an ecumenical gesture intended to match Protestant usage, made of **Epiphany** a movable feast, to be celebrated on the **Sunday** closest to January 6 and integrating features of both **Candlemas** and the Baptism of Christ.

Such an evolution is unthinkable in the East. There, the celebration of **Christmas** on December 25 had to be imported in the Antiochian Church by Saint John Chrysostom in the last quarter of the fourth century, and even then, chiefly as a way of extending the celebration of **Epiphany** backward! Although Western influence may have contributed to a shift of emphasis toward **Christmas** over time, **Epiphany** retains a very special place in Eastern rites. In the Armenian Church, it still includes the **Nativity of Christ**; this means there is no **Christmas** as such, but instead **Epiphany** celebrations from the eve of January 6 to January 13.

This is because **Epiphany** started out more or less as an Oriental answer to problems similar to those that called for the institution of **Christmas** on Western initiative. For January 6 was the entrenched winter festival in the Near East, not December 25 as in Western Europe. In Greece, this day was already the **Epiphany** of **Dionysus**. On its eve, the god manifested himself through a miraculous wine on the island of Andros. A ritual round cake was eaten, torches and bonfires were lit, and rivers and springs were blessed. In ancient Egypt, the once-dead and resurrected god Osiris, often assimilated to **Dionysus**, also changed the waters of the Nile into wine on the eleventh day of the month of Tybi (now January 6). This festival came on the heels of that of **Khoiak**—the mysteries of Osiris celebrated on December 25 as the solstice—and marked the appearance of a new sun in the dead of winter. A later Egyptian festival held on the same date in Alexandria celebrated the birth of Aion (the Eternal or the World itself and the counterpart of both Osiris and *Dionysus*) to the virgin Korê (an ancient Greek fertility goddess) in a new cosmic cycle every year. It was therefore easy for the new cult of the Sun of Righteousness (as Christ was also known) to take over from these pagan winter festivals the older symbolism of the annual return of the sun through a purifying ordeal.

John's baptism of Jesus by water likewise changed this element into a source of warmth and light. To Christians, water became the wine of Cana as well as the river Jordan at **Epiphany**. But around the year 130, followers of the Gnostic sect of Basilides in Alexandria claimed that Jesus was only born as Christ on the day of his baptism, when God entered his spirit upon testifying from the heavens: "Thou art my beloved Son; this day have I begotten thee!" To these heretics, January 10 (when they observed the feast) would have been the day Jesus was born as Christ—a spiritual birth through his baptism itself. Since Aion figured prominently in their cosmological speculations, they likely were the first to observe the day of a Hellenistic god's virgin birth with Jesus in mind as **Epiphany**.

Orthodox Christians were nevertheless also quick to read their own theology in the Gospel account of the Baptism, commemorated on this day. Assigning a different date to the **Nativity**, as the Roman Church had already done for her own reasons, could only help the Eastern Church underline that Jesus was both man and God from the day he was conceived, so that it was indeed Christ who came to John to get baptized.

The Manifestation of God in Three Persons

As for **Epiphany** itself, Eastern Christians prefer to call it the **Theophany** or "Manifestation of God." For not only does it celebrate the first public manifestations of Christ's ministry—in contrast to the secrecy of his birth in a cave outside Bethlehem, where even King Herod could not find him—above all, it re-creates the first manifestation of God in three Persons, through the two natures of Jesus Christ as Son of God, revealed by the Holy Spirit as fully human and fully divine. In the words of the troparion hymn of the feast's Royal Hours:

> Our God, the Trinity,
> has this day revealed Himself
> to us indivisibly;
> for the Father bore witness to
> His Parenthood with manifest testimony,
> the Spirit descended from the heavens
> like a dove, and the Son bowed His most pure
> head to the Forerunner and was baptised . . .
> (Ouspensky and Lossky 1982, p. 164)

The First Baptism as a Feast of Lights

The **Theophany** is thus also known as the "**Feast of Lights**" because Christ publicly made his appearance in the world as "Light from Light, true God from the true God" (in the words of the Nicean Creed adopted in 325), and even as an actual "great Light" that shone on the Jordan when Jesus was baptized, according to a canonical tradition recorded by Saint Justin Martyr. The trappings of the sacrament of baptism that was instituted by the same token symbolize just such "an immediate perception of God, since the ray that comes from Him invisibly kindles the soul," as the fourteenth-century Greek Orthodox writer Nicholas Cabasilas noted in *The Life in Christ* (Cabasilas 1974, pp. 99–100); for on this occasion, "all things are full of brightness: the torches, the chants, the choirs, the processions, nothing that is not radiant, with the baptismal robes all resplendent and prepared for a spectacle of light." Still, regardless of the joyous light common to the sacrament and the feast, Saint John the Baptist (specifically commemorated on January

7) is always portrayed as recoiling in awe before Christ's request to get baptized in Eastern liturgical texts of the **Theophany**.

The Two Blessings of the Waters

Thus, there is a song in which the Forerunner wonders aloud how the lamp can illuminate the Light and asks to be sanctified along with the waters, and it is intoned at the Great Blessing of the Waters, as part of a prayer almost identical to the one said over the font for the sacrament of baptism. But it then concerns a distinctive rite of the **Theophany**, performed first at church on January 5 (a preparatory day of strict fasting and abstinence), and then outdoors on January 6.

In the First Blessing, as it is called in Greece, a basin of water is blessed after the service, and some water is sprinkled with a sprig of basil by the priest onto the faithful, who can also take some home in a bottle for their personal use. They can either drink it or sprinkle themselves with it, whenever they feel the need for this blessing from what is considered to be the very water of the river Jordan, as it miraculously stood still during the Baptism of Jesus. Bulgarians, who often refer to **Epiphany** as **Saint Jordan's Day**, and who eat a ritual bread on its eve, also think they will be especially blessed if they stay up during the intervening night and happen to witness the skies opening up—a belief found among Orthodox Christians elsewhere about other feasts such as the **Ascension**.

Orthodox priests visit the houses of their parishioners at this time of year to bless them with this holy water. They start right after the First Blessing in Greek villages, going from door to door and through every room with the cross, as well as to the fountains and the fields. This is thought to be the only sure way to drive away the *Kallikantzaroi*—evil spirits who come from underground every year at **Christmas** and make the waters unhallowed for all **Twelve Days**. During the rest of the year, they chip away with axes at the tree supporting the earth;

but just when they are about to succeed in causing the world to collapse into darkness and chaos, Christ is born and the world-tree is replenished. The furious spirits leap to the surface of the earth and try to get back in spite at its inhabitants in every way they can. Feeding on foul things like worms, frogs, and snakes, they like to go down chimneys and soil people's food—much like the spirits of the dead did during the ancient Athenian festival of **Anthesteria**, when Hades opened its gates. The lower jaw of a pig is hung inside the chimney or behind the front door to keep the Kallikantzaroi at bay during the **Twelve Days**. But to purify the earth of their evil presence when their time is up at **Epiphany**, great bonfires are lit in some places, while farmers use candles from the church service to bless their house and their beasts of burden by making the sign of the cross with them. In some Greek villages, people go around wearing horrible masks and jingling bells to frighten away the Kallikantzaroi—or, conversely, to embody them and scare the children, who are often out caroling as on **Christmas** and **New Year**'s Day.

The outdoor **Epiphany** blessing takes place on January 6 beside a body of water. This turns it into a sacramental manifestation of the waters of the river Jordan at the moment when they were transfigured into an eternal sign of salvation by Christ's baptism, and were thus purified of the unclean nature spirits that dwelled in the river's depths. In harsh climates, such as those of Russia or Alaska, a hole is often dug in the ice to dip a cross into the water, or crosses made of ice may be launched into a river. In milder climates—such as around the Mediterranean or, for a century now, at a bayou near Tarpon Springs, a Greek-settled sponge-diving center in Florida—a crucifix is thrown into the sea as doves are set free, and divers often rush into the water after it, vying for the honor and blessing of its recovery. This old Byzantine rite is also still performed in a Catholic setting in Mezzojuso near Palermo in

Sicily. In major Greek towns, state and civic authorities and military and municipal bands are involved in solemn processions of the clergy and faithful under golden banners with the two-headed Roman imperial eagle appropriated by the Church of Constantinople, to carry the cross to the river or the harbor, where all ships have been gathered and decorated for the occasion. Their whistles then sound in unison with the guns that are fired by the warships, and the church bells rung at the moment the crosses hit the water. Only then does it become safe to put to sea again, a reflection of the ancient belief that the waters were treacherous during the **Twelve Days** of **Christmas**. There was even a belief that seawater became fresh and sweet to drink at **Epiphany**, when Greeks still go to the seashore to wash their farm implements and home icons.

Ethiopians wash or renew in advance the white clothes they will wear for "Baptism" or *Timqat,* as the **Theophany** is called in Amharic. That evening, they escort the *tabots* (holy arks partaking of the sacred powers of the holy objects they are meant to contain) from the local church to a stream or pool, to which they will return after supper to spend the night singing devotional chants, sometimes killing an ox for the feast that will follow the pre-dawn service. The chief cleric then blesses the water (sometimes in a large cistern) and throws it onto the frantic faithful, who rush to get some and splash each other; many of them even bathe in it. After a morning rest, the faithful have reconvened at the site of this ritual for noontime, and the tabots are taken back to their shrines by a colorful dancing procession of all the people—the clergy with their umbrellas, the elders with their weapons, children playing with sticks, young men leaping up and down to the rhythm of their chants, and women in their best dresses on their one day of freedom of the year, so that discreet meetings with the other sex can be arranged on the occasion of the festivities that accompany the yearly coming out of the tabots for January 19. This is when the **Theophany** falls when the Julian calendar is used, namely thirteen days after the Gregorian date.

See also Ascension; Candlemas; Christmas; Dionysia; Easter; Khoiak and Heb-Sed; Lent; New Year (West); Saint Nicholas

References
Nicholas Cabasilas. *The Life in Christ* (2:21) Tr. Carmino J. de Catanzaro. Crestwood, NY: St. Vladimir's Seminary Press, 1974.
T. G. Crippen. *Christmas and Christmas Lore.* London: Blackie and Son, 1928.
Fr. Thomas Hopko. *The Winter Pascha. Readings for the Christmas-Epiphany Season.* Crestwood, NY: St. Vladimir's Seminary Press, 1984.
Clement A. Miles. *Christmas in Ritual and Tradition.* London: Fisher Unwin, 1912.
Leonid Ouspensky and Vladimir Lossky. *The Meaning of Icons.* Tr. G. E. H. Palmer and E. Kadloubovsky. Crestwood, NY: St. Vladimir's Seminary Press, 1982.
Francis Xavier Weiser. *Handbook of Christian Feasts and Customs: The Year of the Lord in Liturgy and Folklore.* Colorado Springs, CO: Seraphim, 1999.

EQUIRRIA MARTIS
See Games (Rome)

ETZALQUALITZLI
See Rain Festivals

EVANGELISMOS
See Annunciation

EXALTATION OF THE CROSS
See Elevation of the Cross

FALLING OF FRUIT
See Days of the Dead (West)

FALLING OF THE WATERS
See Rain Festivals

FARJA
See Ashura

FASCHING
See Carnival

FAST OF ESTHER
See Purim

FAST OF THE FIRSTBORN
See Passover

FASTELAVN, FASTNACHT, FAT SUNDAY, FAT TUESDAY
See Carnival

FEAST OF FLOWERS
See Dionysia

FEAST OF FOOLS (CHRISTIANITY)
The medieval **Feast of Fools** is a classic instance of the social inversion long associated with winter festivals. It used to be celebrated on **Innocents' Day** (December 28), **New Year**'s Day, or, to a lesser extent, on **Saint Nicholas**' Day (December 6) and **Epiphany** (January 6).

From Biblical Account to Carnival Figure
The breakdown of social barriers and the temporary reversal of established hierarchies at the end of a year make the **Feast of Fools** a typical **New Year** festival. Yet it found a niche in the Western Christian calendar in connection with December 28, the day of the **Christmas** cycle commemorating all the innocent male children of Bethlehem (aged two and under, and traditionally estimated to have been 14,000 in number) who were slaughtered on the orders of King Herod. For he heard from the Wise Men that a rival new king had just been born in that town: Jesus Christ (Matthew 2:16–18). Recorded as a distinct Church feast since at least the fifth century (having possibly been part of **Epiphany** previously), **Innocents' Day** was also known as **Childermas**. But it eventually gave center stage not only to children and youngsters (to whom parents would even temporarily abdicate authority) but to "innocents," in the medieval Christian sense of mentally ill or retarded people. Hence it got the name "**Feast of Fools**," referring to people who act

like them, having taken leave of all reason. Spaniards play practical jokes on each other that day.

A similar slide from biblical account to **carnival** figure is at the origin of the **Feast of the Ass**, observed mostly in France in the Middle Ages around **Christmas**time. It was supposed to commemorate Joseph and Mary's flight to Egypt on an ass with the child Jesus after an angel warned them of the coming extermination of all the male babies of Bethlehem. But it was the ass who was the actual center of the church feast; honored as a prince, he was taken in procession under a canopy for a mass where the faithful would bray like asses, and the celebrants responded with their own braying noises. The braying song in honor of the ass is quite well known in the medieval repertoire that has come down to us. This was a mild form of the kind of riotous popular satire of the stiff solemnities of the high church and the nobility that was a hallmark of the **Feast of Fools** itself. Likely going back to pre-Christian rituals of festive inversion, it found in churches both a choice target of mockery and an ideal fixed venue at the heart of the community.

Backlash and Persistence

In an early attempt at a crackdown, the ecclesiastical authorities of Nevers in France prohibited the "**Feast of Fools** on **Innocents' Day** and **New Year**" in 1246 (Jones 1978, p. 303). A few years later, the Council of Cognac decreed: "As for the dances which historically take place in certain churches on the Feast of **Holy Innocents**, they are regularly the occasion of brawling and trouble, even during the Holy Office and at other times. We prohibit these amusements on pain of anathema. There will be no bishops created on that feast of **Innocents**; for it is only a pretext for laughter in the Church of God and a derision of episcopal dignity"(ibid.). The election of a provisional "Boy Bishop" by the choirboys was widespread in Europe by that time, being attested in Rouen in Normandy as

early as the eleventh century. He would be provided with episcopal vestments and a miter, could bless the crowd from a balcony, and would have his own clergy of boy chaplains, deans, deacons, and the like, who had the power to conduct levies from door to door and from various authorities in view of their **Innocents' Day** statutory party. They sang the vespers and took part in church services, though masses of course continued to be said by ordained priests. Still, if the boy bishop happened to die between the sixth and the twenty-eighth of December—his last day of authority—he would be buried with all the honors due a real bishop. In monasteries and convents, the youngest monk or nun would act as abbot or abbess on **Childermas**.

The moot services of **Innocents' Day** were too often an occasion for uncontrollable revelry among the lower clergy in the middle of a serious Church holiday season. It was therefore with the aim of toning them down that the festivity had been subdivided and spread out by moving up the election of the boy bishop to **Saint Nicholas**' Day on December 6. This measure had the opposite effect of extending his term of office—with the uproarious disturbances caused by his masked followers—to the intervening weeks, bridging the two festivals and making their folk practices interchangeable.

There were attempts (in Germany especially) on the part of Church and municipal authorities in the late Middle Ages to limit to either a half-dozen feast days, three weeks, or a well-defined month the time when the boy bishop ruled and the **Saint Nicholas** processions roamed. This was because they were turning into a form of vagrancy or even of highway robbery. In 1526, the Council of Xanten decreed that "the parents of the bishop shall not be obliged to donate apples, gloves, and other small presents or to furnish meals" on December 6 (Jones 1978, p. 307). Not only that, but on December 28, the pupils had to invite their schoolmaster to a breakfast of herring, fruits, and nuts with beer. By then, the Protestant Reformer Martin Luther was being less conciliatory, as he thundered that "God has nothing to do with masked persons and Nicholas Bishops!" (Jones 1978, p. 305).

Having severed the Church of England's allegiance to the Roman See in 1534, King Henry VIII legislated against the installation of Boy Bishops in 1541. Then on November 13, 1554, his devoutly Catholic daughter Queen Mary I had the bishop of London issue an edict instructing the parishes of his diocese to elect a Boy Bishop again. However, she failed to appoint a "Lord of Misrule" to organize the **Yuletide** parties (featuring masked balls, parades, and plays) held at court. This had also been done since the late Middle Ages in the houses of great noblemen, in the law schools of the realm's legal societies, and in many colleges of Oxford and Cambridge. At all these functions, the Lord of Misrule would normally preside over a mock court, receiving comic homage from the revelers, like the Boy Bishop from which his office was derived. Both of them soon died out in London under Queen Elizabeth I: the office of Lord of Misrule was never again revived at the English Court, and its Scottish equivalent, that of the "Abbot of Unreason," was suppressed in 1555 by Mary Stuart, the Catholic Queen of Scots.

In France too, there had been an edict against it in Dijon in 1552. Already in 1444, the Faculty of Theology of the University of Paris had recommended curtailing the **Feast of Fools**. Nevertheless, some scholars did grant that the human spirit, like wine fermenting in a barrel, needed to vent a build-up of madness if it was to give a good quality of devotion when the time was right. Such a reasoning might have provided a rationale for the immediate replacement of **Innocents' Day** and the **Feast of Fools**, officially cancelled in Nantes in 1539 (soon after the Breton capital became French in 1524), by a **Carnival** season that began on **Epiphany**

and lasted a couple of months until **Lent**. As if this were not enough, rowdy **Carnival** parades were eventually held on the two Sundays after **Mid-Lent** in this city. We may even see, as a holdover of the role of youngsters around **Innocents' Day,** the fact that the first of these parades was devoted to students in 1880—a custom that was revived over a hundred years later, in 1989. Since then, this local event has become known nationally as an innocent **Children's Carnival**. Also in France at the beginning of the last century, nuns would pretend to listen to schoolgirls when they sat at their desks and let them teach at the great convent of the Congrégation de Notre-Dame in Paris on **Innocent's Day**. At the Franciscan monastery of Antibes on the Riviera, lay brothers would trade places with the clergy—for once confined to work in the garden while they said mass in tattered and reversed vestments.

A more contentious and licentious "adult" version of the **Feast of Fools** on **New Year**'s Day, known chiefly in France between the twelfth and fourteenth centuries, was banned altogether by the Council of Basel in 1434. It involved downright obscene parodies of the mass, including the "Gamblers' Liturgy," the "Drunkards' Liturgy," and the "Will of the Ass," instead of prayers and hymns, and was led by an "Abbott of Misrule," who would deliver a satirical sermon and give ridiculous blessings. Old shoes or even excrement would be burned as incense, and the altars would be used to eat on, while revelers wearing goat and horse masks or clown make up, in church vestments or in drag, would sing and dance lewdly inside the church and through the streets. From the thirteenth century onward, the **Feast of Fools** spilled over to **Epiphany** on January 6, when each town would use lots—in the guise of a bean—to elect its "King of Wine" or "King of Fools" or "Lord of Misrule" for a day. This custom has been echoed in a family setting in places where **Epiphany** is the time to elect as king for a day whoever finds the bean hidden in a special cake: the old English "twelfth cake" or the ever popular French *galette des rois*.

See also Carnival; Epiphany; Lent; New Year (West); Saint Nicholas

References

Mikhail Bakhtin. *Rabelais and His World*. Tr. Hélène Iswolsky. Cambridge, MA: M.I.T. Press, 1968.

Roger Caillois. *Man and the Sacred*. Tr. Meyer Barash. Urbana: University of Illinois Press, 2001.

Harvey Gallagher Cox. *The Feast of Fools: A Theological Essay on Festivity and Fantasy*. William Belden Noble Lectures. Cambridge, MA: Harvard University Press, 1969.

Charles William Jones. *Saint Nicholas of Myra, Bari, and Manhattan*. Chicago: University of Chicago Press, 1978.

FEAST OF INDICTION
See Lent

FEAST OF LIGHTS
See Epiphany

FEAST OF LOTS
See Purim

FEAST OF POTS
See Dionysia

FEAST OF THE ASS
See Feast of Fools

FEAST OF THE DAY OF THE RAT
See Sekku

FEAST OF THE DEAD
See Days of the Dead (West)

FEAST OF THE PITCHERS
See Dionysia

FEAST OF THE SEE OF SAINT PETER
See Caristia

FEAST OF THE VEIL
See Protection of the Mother of God

FERALIA
See Days of the Dead (West)

FERIA
See Games (Rome)

FESTIN DEI COUGOURDON
See Annunciation

FESTIVAL OF COLOR
See Holi

FESTIVAL OF DEVILS
See Days of the Dead (China, Korea, Japan)

FESTIVAL OF DREAMS
See Midwinter

FESTIVAL OF FREEDOM
See Passover

FESTIVAL OF HUNGRY GHOSTS
See Days of the Dead (China, Korea, Japan)

FESTIVAL OF LANTERNS
See Lantern Festival

FESTIVAL OF LIGHTS
See Divali, Hanukkah

FESTIVAL OF NAKED YOUTHS
See Carneia

FESTIVAL OF OSIRIS
See Khoiak and Heb-Sed

FESTIVAL OF PURE BRIGHTNESS
See Days of the Dead (China, Korea, Japan)

FESTIVAL OF THE DEDICATION
See Hanukkah

▶ **FESTIVAL OF THE FIFTH MOON**
See Dragon Boat Festival

▶ **FESTIVAL OF THE FIRST PRINCIPLE**
See Lantern Festival

▶ **FESTIVAL OF THE GATE-HOUSE, FESTIVAL OF THE GREAT-HOUSE, FESTIVAL OF THE MONTH**
See KI.LAM

▶ **FESTIVAL OF THE MOUNTAINS**
See Rain Festivals

▶ **FESTIVAL OF THE SNAKE**
See Sekku

▶ **FESTIVAL OF THE SWING**
See Holi

▶ **FESTIVAL OF THE THREE MIRACLES**
See Epiphany

▶ **FESTIVAL OF THE WEAVER, FESTIVAL OF YOUNG HERBS**
See Sekku

▶ **FESTIVAL OF UNLEAVENED BREAD**
See Passover

▶ **FEST-NOZ**
See Pardon

▶ **FÊTE DES ROIS**
See Epiphany

▶ **FÊTE-DIEU**
See Corpus Christi

▶ **FÊTE NATIONALE**
See Conception and Birth of the Virgin Mary, Midsummer

▶ **FIFTH MOON (FESTIVAL OF THE)**
See Dragon Boat Festival

▶ **FIRST DAY OF THE FIRST MONTH**
See New Year (China, Korea)

▶ **FIRST EASTER**
See Palm Sunday

▶ **FIRST-FRUITS**
See Busk

▶ **FIRST FULL MOON**
See Lantern Festival

▶ **FIRST OF THE FIVE**
See Sekku

▶ **FIRST PRINCIPLE (FESTIVAL OF THE)**
See Lantern Festival

▶ **FLAG DAY**
See Midsummer

▶ **FLORALIA (ROME)**
In Antiquity, the cult of Flora was spread throughout Central Italy: the Sabines named a month after her, and the Samnites worshipped her in conjunction with Ceres, goddess of wheat. Flora had a lot in common with her, being the goddess of the flowering of vegetation, whose name comes from the Latin *flos* for "flower." The **games** celebrated in her honor in Rome, from the original single day of her festival on April 28 until May 3, were the responsibility of the city's plebeian ediles, just like those of **Ceres** held from April 12 to 19. These games were also alike in reflecting the common people's workaday concern for adequate food supplies. Their carefree, often bawdy, festive spirit was also a feature of the Floralia.

The People's Games

Flora had her own *flamine*—a priest attached especially to her service in Rome. She was also among the divinities to which the archaic priestly college of the Arval Brothers sacrificed in their yearly fertility rites of the end of May. Her cult was said to have been introduced by Titus Tatius, the Sabine king who had ruled Rome jointly with the city's founder Romulus. But her **games**, the **Floralia**, were only instituted in either 240 or 238 B.C.E. by the city's plebeian leaders in order to mark the successful outcome of their legal battle against rich landowners who had let their herds graze on the commons without first paying a fee to the treasury for this private use of public property—conquered land made available to the people of Rome. Following an oracle of the Sibylline Books, part of the settlement was used by the common people's victorious representatives to build a temple to Flora near the Circus Maximus, where the sporting events of her games would be held.

Vaudeville and Vegetation

As the festival was expanded and became annual by 173 B.C.E., sports only took up the final day, while the other days came to be devoted to scenic games and plays of a very light, comic, and licentious character. This made it a favorite target of diatribes by early Christian writers such as Lactantius, Saint Augustine, and Saint Cyprian. Prostitutes, who viewed this as their holiday, were hired as mimes and took off their clothes at the prompting of the rowdy audience or participated in mock gladiatorial **games**. According to Valerius Maximus (II, 10:8), the public applauded when the dour conservative politician Cato the Censor (234–149 B.C.E.) discreetly left the theater upon being told his presence was making the audience too shy to call on the actresses to strip. The obscene acts they would then imitate or perform were probably meant to promote the fertility of plants, in the festival's original context of honoring its patron Flora. However, there was also the very down-to-earth reason invoked by the poet Ovid (*Fasti* 5: 351–353, p. 123): "She is neither one of the glum set nor a snob; / She wants her rites open to the *plebs*, / and warns us to use life's beauty as it blooms." Fertility rites may also be discerned in the **Floralia** customs of having marchers throw chickpeas, beans, and lupins at the people (much as in the *setsubun* **New Year** ritual observed in Japan to this day), of lovers picking up blossoming branches along the way to decorate their houses, and of catching deer and rabbits—animals associated with fertility—in specially laid out nets. This was also the right time to wear multicolored clothing, emulating Flora's colorful and richly varied bounty.

Nocturnal Illuminations

The **Floralia** were known for nocturnal illuminations with torches, since their lustful revelries extended late at night, under the appropriate cover of darkness. But this carried its own risks in a big city, which was otherwise without lights and therefore quite unsafe. On the eve of his downfall in 31, the Prefect of the Praetorian Guard Lucius Aelius Sejanus (who, as the scheming and ambitious favorite of Emperor Tiberius, held sway in Rome in his master's absence) was thus able to make himself popular with citizens who had enjoyed the **Floralia** until a late hour by mobilizing five thousand slaves with torches to take them safely home.

See also Games (Rome); May Day; New Year (Japan); Spring Festival of Cybele and Attis

References

Ovid. *Fasti.* Tr. A. J. Boyle and R. D. Woodard. Harmondsworth, Middlesex, England: Penguin Books, 2000.

Valerius Maximus. *Memorable Doings and Sayings,* Vol. I. Tr. D. R. Shackleton Bailey. Loeb Classical Library. Cambridge, MA: Harvard University Press, 2000.

H. H. Scullard. *Festivals and Ceremonies of the Roman Republic.* Ithaca, NY: Cornell University Press, 1981.

▶ **FLOWER FESTIVAL**
See Vaishakha and Vaisakhi

▶ **FLOWER SUNDAY**
See Elevation of the Cross, Palm Sunday

▶ **FLOWER-VIEWING**
See Cherry Blossom Festival

▶ **FLOWERS (FEAST OF)**
See Dionysia

▶ **FOOLS (FEAST OF)**
See Feast of Fools

▶ **FORDICIDIA AND PARILIA (ROME)**
The archaic Roman festivals of **Fordicidia** and **Parilia** came a week apart in April. Ashes from the fertility sacrifices of the former were used in the purifying rites of the latter, aimed at protecting herds from any mishaps due to the overstepping of sacred boundaries by beasts or men.

Fordicidia: Two Cow Sacrifices in One
Coming in the middle of the weeklong **Games of Ceres**, goddess of wheat, the April 15 Roman festival of the earth-protecting goddess Tellus was called **Fordicidia** because it required the killing (*caedo*) of a pregnant (*forda*) cow. As the poet Ovid (43 B.C.E.–17 C.E.) explains, "the herd is now pregnant, seed impregnates the earth; / Teeming Tellus gets a teeming victim" (*Fasti* 4: 633–634, p. 102). Some of the victims were slaughtered on Capitol Hill, and each one of Rome's thirty *curiae* or clan groupings received a cow to be sacrificed by its local priest, the cu-rion. (The only other historically recorded festival under curial responsibility was **Fornacalia** on February 17.) But "when the acolytes have ripped the calves from the wombs / And dropped the sliced guts on the smoking hearths, / The eldest [Vestal] virgin cremates

the calves in the fire / To cleanse folk with this ash on Pales' day" (*Fasti* 4:637–640, p. 102). This occurred on April 21, the date of **Parilia**. The double sacrifice of **Fordicidia** was said to have been inspired in a dream to Rome's wise second king Numa Pompilius while he slept in a wood sacred to the herd god Faunus, the Roman equivalent of the Greek god Pan.

Parilia: Twin Transgressions Among Shepherds
Similarly, it was Pales, the patron goddess of shepherds and their flocks, who was honored a week later at the festival of **Parilia** in rites going back to the very foundation of Rome—an event said to have happened on this very date, when the festival's first known celebrant, the city's first king, Romulus, killed his brother Remus for having overstepped the city boundary he had been tracing with a plow around Palatine Hill. Why this conjunction of an urban anniversary (alternatively known as **Romaia** from the second century to the demise of paganism) with the festival of the goddess of herds? "Is it because the twin brothers were still regarded as the shepherd-chiefs which they had been in their childhood? Is it because through a phonetic consonance, to which modern scholars have been more sensitive than the ancients, Pales was associated with the Palatine, the first settlement of Rome? Is it because a more archaic connection linked Pales not merely with the health of the flocks and the shepherds, but with that of the entire rural society?" Like the historian Georges Dumézil (Vol. II, p. 384), we are left to guess at the reasons for the ceremonies that were continued after the demise of the Roman monarchy, first by the great priest and then by the Vestal Virgins.

On the other hand, the poet Ovid's account of Roman festivals gives us a fairly detailed description of the practices of **Parilia** by the time the Empire was founded. The people of Rome would get from the temple of Vesta the prescribed ingredients for a fumigation that was supposed to purify all it touched. Aside from the ashes of the calves burned earlier at **Fordicidia**, the purifying smoke would be produced with the blood of a live horse combined with bean straw—without the beans (as though their very absence, along with whatever could cause it, was to be burned away following a principle attested in some ancient Indian rituals, as Dumézil has argued). The shepherd himself would purify his herd by splashing the floor of his sheepfold with water and sweeping it with branches, having adorned the room with foliage. Sulfur would be burned in it, along with olive wood, pinewood, Sabine juniper, and bay leaves. A basket of millet was to accompany an offering of millet cakes as the rustic goddess's favorite meal. After sharing it with her and washing it down with lukewarm milk (the way she liked it), the jug would be offered to Pales to invoke her protection from wolves, disease, and famine until the next **Parilia**, as well as to wash away all the past year's trespasses of which the shepherd and his sheep could be guilty, for having overstepped—inadvertently or due to pressing necessity—the boundaries of the sacred grounds of nature deities in brooks and bushes. Such a prayer would be said four times facing the horizon, where the sun was about to dawn. Shepherds would then wash their hands in running water before drinking some milk from a bowl, and in order to complete the process of purification, they would jump through a straw bonfire. An open-air feast concluded these observances.

> ***See also*** Fornacalia and Quirinalia; Games (Rome); Lupercalia; Spring Festival of Cybele and Attis; Terminalia; Vestalia

References

Mary Beard, John North, and Simon Price. *Religions of Rome*. Cambridge: Cambridge University Press, 1998.

Georges Dumézil. *Archaic Roman Religion, with an Appendix on the Religion of the Etruscans*. Tr. Philip Krapp. Baltimore, MD: Johns Hopkins University Press, 1996.

Ovid. *Fasti*. Tr. A. J. Boyle and R. D. Woodard. London: Penguin Books, 2000.

▶ FORNACALIA AND QUIRINALIA (ROME)

On February 17, the ancient Romans festively honored two of the oldest divinities of their pantheon: the war god Quirinus and the wheat oven goddess Fornax, in the concurrent celebrations of **Quirinalia** and **Fornacalia**. Whether this was just a coincidence or on the contrary due to some organic link between the two gods remains a matter of conjecture.

Fornacalia

This date was known as the feast of fools—*stulti,* in the sense of stupid rather than crazy. It got to be called this because February 17 was the deadline for those happy-go-lucky citizens who did not even know which *curia* they belonged to to enjoy one final opportunity to honor Fornax, the goddess of ovens. By then, responsible citizens would have already looked up what day of mid-February had been set aside to do so for each of the *curiae*—these otherwise obsolete clan divisions of the Roman people. The dates applicable to each curia appeared on the corresponding notice-boards put up on the Forum by the Grand Curion, head of the priests of all the *curiae.* This was because there had originally been one oven per curia, and it was there that peasants would lightly roast grains of spelt—a primitive variety of wheat known in Latin as *far,* in order to remove the chaff. Since it was a delicate and hazardous process on which much depended, it was normal that early Romans found a competent deity to turn to for problem-free roasting. But by historical times, better strains and improved agricultural methods had practically removed this once vital concern. Moreover, the curia system to which it was linked had ceased to be a social reality, so that the cult of Fornax was now little more than a ritualistic legacy.

Quirinalia

The **Fornacalia**'s focus on food supplies was thought by Georges Dumézil (1898–1986) to fit in well with the economic function he felt able to ascribe to the very ancient god Quirinus, as the third in a triad with Jupiter and Mars (Jupiter being the god of the first, priestly function, and Mars that of the second, military function) in the threefold ideology common to all Indo-European cultures that the French historian had discerned and saw at play in Roman institutions. But there is little evidence of these supposed early agrarian attributes of Quirinus, and even of the historical rites of **Quirinalia**, the festival devoted to him. The Romans themselves took this god to be their Sabine neighbors' equivalent of their own war god Mars, except that he stood more for peaceable civic life than for aggressively "martial" politics. They thought Romulus, founder of their city, who had ploughed the first furrow in its fields, was actually the son of Mars and that he was deified under the name of Quirinus after he vanished in a thunderstorm, while he was busy carrying out justice on his royal throne. It was suspected that the early senators themselves had put out this story, in order to get away with murdering the king by hiding the body and then conveniently turning him into a god. History (not to mention prehistory) is full of cases of divine kingship being derived from the murder of a founding ancestor, who was then worshipped as a deity—often by the very people who had killed him. This was because they had found the blessings of peace in the collective bond resulting from the sudden violent resolution of the internal conflicts previously fueled by their envy and fear of the father of the nation. The ancient Romans appear to have been sophisticated enough to realize this; after all, their empire had its roots in a similar kind of political-*cum*-ritual murder—that of Julius Caesar in a plot by Republican opponents of his dictatorship, which backfired and made of its victim the tutelary god of the new imperial order.

Yet on February 17, the Romans were still happy enough to turn to their city's deified founder Quirinus as war god. He was said by the historian Livy (59 B.C.E.–17 C.E.) to have once appeared to an ancestor of the deified father of their empire, Julius Cesar, so as to have him deliver to his fellow citizens the prophecy that "it is the will of heaven that my Rome should be the head of all the world. Let them henceforth cultivate the arts of war, and let them know assuredly, and hand down the knowledge to posterity, that no human might can withstand the arms of Rome" (Livius I, 16). A temple was dedicated to Quirinus in 293 B.C.E. on the hill to the north of ancient Rome where Sabine immigrants had established a settlement at the city's foundation; initially called Agonus, this hill has been known ever since then as the Quirinal. The hill has given its name to the palace built on it in the sixteenth century as a summer residence for the popes. It was seized in 1870 by the first king of a unified Italy and became the royal palace until 1946, when the House of Savoy was itself expelled after the Italian Republic was proclaimed. If the Palazzo Quirinale now houses its presidents, it still rests on the age-old foundations of Rome's sacred kingship.

See also Fordicidia and Parilia; Vestalia

References

Georges Dumézil. *Archaic Roman Religion; with an Appendix on the Religion of the Etruscans.* Tr. Philip Krapp. Archaic Roman Religions. Baltimore, MD: Johns Hopkins University Press, 1996.

Titus Livius. *The History of Rome.* Tr. Rev. Canon Roberts. London: J.M. Dent and Sons, 1912, from *Corpus Scriptorum Romanorum. A Digital Library of Latin Literature.* http://www.forumromanum.org/literature/livius/trans1.html.

Adam Ziolkowski. *The Temples of Mid-Republican Rome and their Historical Context.* Rome: "L'Erma" di Bretschneider, 1992.

FOURTH OF JULY
See Powwow, Sun Dance

FORGIVENESS SUNDAY
See Lent

FREEDOM (FESTIVAL OF)
See Passover

FRONLEICHNAM
See Corpus Christi

FUGARENA
See Martinmas

FULL MOON OF THE NEW YEAR
See New Year (Japan)

GADJARI, GADJERI

See Kunapipi

GAHANBAR

See Naw Ruz

GAMES (GREECE)

The most prominent festivals in Greek civilization were games of religious origin. Four of these periodic sets of athletic and artistic contests enjoyed nationwide, panhellenic status: the **Olympic Games**, the **Pythian Games** in Delphi, the **Isthmian Games** at Corinth, and the **Nemean Games** nearby in the Peloponnese.

Panhellenic Games

In ancient Greece, competitive **games**, usually including the performing arts along with sports, were an integral part of certain local cults. As such, they were strictly organized by religious authorities and always preceded by prayers and sacrifices along with banquets and libations. They served as an outlet for the competitive spirit or *agon* inherited from the old aristocracy, whose warrior ethos of honor and valor had spread to all classes even as it lost its exclusive hold on power with democratic reforms. These came along with active military service on the part of all male citizens and, like the contemporary inventions of drama and philosophy, were shaped by the same sporting spirit. Thus, women rarely had their own sports events (such as races that appeared relatively late), except as part of the **games** also featuring two female choirs organized by the "Sixteen"—woman officials—every five years for the **Heraia** winter festival in Elis. Paradoxically, they belong to the same archaic layer from which the **Olympic Games** sprang within the territory of this minor but well-situated city. Its location made it an ideal setting to attract competitors from the entire Greek world, since they could gather on this relatively neutral ground without, at the same time, giving too much power to one important city compared with others. It was thus in Olympia that the records and treaties of all the Greek states were kept, while entitlement to come to the **Olympic Games** was what distinguished Greeks from barbarians.

A similar conjunction of innocuous allegiance and central location allowed three other rural shrines to gain comparable panhellenic significance on account of their games. For there, common Greek values based on competition between cities could find a rare peaceful expression without endangering their independence or interfering in their constant struggles for power. A Sacred Truce even ensured the safe

An illustration of a Greek footrace after a painting by 19th-century German artist Otto Knille. (Bettmann/Corbis)

passage of competitors and visitors in the midst of ongoing warfare, thanks to an agreement not to seize persons or their property on their way to any **Panhellenic Games** and back. It was called a *hieromeny* because it originally lasted one "sacred month," but the **Pythian** hieromeny actually lasted an entire year to allow all the time needed to reach outlying cities, and the hieromenies of the other Games were no doubt comparably long. The expenses involved in such travels and for equipment, as well as the leisure needed for training, helped to restrict active participation to aristocrats of birth or fortune until the fifth century B.C.E. The cities they represented then literally worshipped the winners as heroes, that is as half-gods of a kind customarily revealed by military types of exploits, and guaranteed them a fitting lifestyle. As for losers—no matter the ranking—contrary to the "neo-chivalric" ideal of sportsmanship animating the modern **Olympic** movement, they merely slinked away into shameful obscurity. Winning was truly everything, as a sign of divine favor that brought good fortune to a city; the alternative could not be contemplated with anything but horror and disgust.

Before they were devoted to Olympian gods, all four **Panhellenic Games** had actually been founded as funerary ceremonies in honor of legendary heroes, like those organized by Achilles for his fallen friend Patroclus in the twenty-third song of Homer's *Iliad*. The Dorian invaders from the north who shaped Hellenic civilization thus took over and perpetuated in adapted forms the cults celebrated at these Late Bronze Age shrines by the Ionians before their forced migration to Asia Minor. It was fitting then that both branches of the Greek people would eventually come together around them at the **Panhellenic Games**, on the sites of archaic contests held on a hero's tomb to reactivate his spiritual energy and make its rejuvenated power available to the living. Originally, such funerary **games** were real fights for a nobleman's succession and possessions, but they later became an opportunity for his designated heirs to display the power, wealth, and magnificence of their house. Public **games** of this kind had also been held initially at regular intervals of a king's reign (most often every eight years) to test his fitness for office and sooner or later transfer his charge, privileges, wife, and daughters to the contender who succeeded in defeating him.

In time, the focus of these games shifted to symbolizing and exerting the cardinal virtues of the Greek ethos: the striving for moral excellence and physical perfection in an ascetic struggle to overcome oneself and others so as to prove one's worth or virtue (*arete*) as a man (*aner*). These contests later came to be called *stephanitai* because the only immediate visible reward of victory in this exemplary struggle was a wreath (*stephanos*) of branches from a sacred olive tree at the **Olympic Games**, of fresh celery at the **Nemean Games,** of dry celery at the **Isthmian Games**, and of bay leaves at the **Pythian Games**, where some apples were also thrown in. These were all signs of a glory that ennobled an athlete's family and city—and even endowed him with a kind of immortality. For he would live on in human memory through the choral songs composed about his feats by the greatest poets—as in odes by Pindar that are still part of the literary canon—and through statues like the dozens of centuries-old portraits that the travel writer Pausanias (143–176 C.E.) saw in Olympia and in Delphi—lined up in the original hall of fame.

This said, such glory did bring side benefits—like free meals at public expense for Athens' Olympic champions. Increasingly substantial rewards for victory at the **Olympiads** or the **Isthmian Games** accompanied the gradual professionalization of sports that went hand

in hand with the democratization of Athenian society from the fourth century B.C.E. onward, opening up the games to publicly or privately sponsored athletes of all backgrounds and often modest personal means. Until the Roman Empire, however, they were reserved to Greek citizens who had not committed any major crimes, thus excluding at once slaves and all barbarians, since the practice of athletic sports in a civic gymnasium was a key feature marking off Hellenic culture from all others.

The Olympic Games

Though they had long existed locally and had already gained regional prominence in the Peloponnese, the **Olympic Games** only became truly panhellenic in 776 B.C.E., the date at which the list of victors in the stadium race begins. Their recurrence every four years in late summer was henceforth used to express dates. We thus know that the pentathlon was introduced in 708 B.C.E., chariot races in 680 B.C.E., both riding races and pancratium (combining boxing and wrestling) in 648 B.C.E. The classic lineup of Olympic sports was then essentially fixed—for these **games** at any rate. An increasing number of variations on it necessitated their gradual extension from one to five days—of which the first and last were devoted to public and private sacrifices (to Zeus and from victors and their states), processions (of the sacred embassies from various Greek cities), and banquets (for the victors and their supporters). The contests at Olympia were said to go back to Pelops's arrival to this "island" he named after himself—the Peloponnese—not knowing about the Isthmus of Corinth that actually makes it a peninsula. He was the fourteenth contender for the hand of Hippodamia, daughter of Oenomaos, in a chariot race against this king of Pisa, who rigged it because an oracle had warned him he would be killed by his son-in-law. This turned out to be a self-fulfilling prophecy, since his own daughter, tired of seeing potential husbands lose their lives in her father's false wagers, sabotaged his chariot instead, so that the king died and was replaced by her new husband Pelops. This tale of nuptial elopement has a lot to do with fertility rites as well as the renewal of royal power, like the athletic contests for which it is meant to account.

In 471 B.C.E., however, the small Greek city of Pisa was finally destroyed by its rival Elis. It took over the shrine at Olympia and refocused the worship there on a colossal gold and ivory statue of Zeus, king of the gods, in celebration of this victory, building for it the second greatest Doric temple in Greece after the Parthenon of Athens. The ten judges of a year's **Olympic Games** were chosen among the Eleans—by lots in later times—and they were trained for this delicate task for the better part of each day for ten months beforehand. After the official **games**, public lectures and recitations would help authors promote themselves before a national audience. As at the other **Panhellenic Games**, merchants also took advantage of this gathering for a fair. Solemn announcements of national import were publicly made and recorded on the occasion of the **Olympic Games**. Women were not allowed on the premises and had to remain across the river Alpheus. Inns were built to accommodate visitors who did not bring their own tents, like the sacred envoys.

The Pythian Games

Unlike other major **games**, the **Pythian Games** took place within the sacred precinct of an urban shrine—at Delphi. Even more than to the games, the city owed its panhellenic and even Mediterranean fame to its famous oracle—tied to fumes issuing from a crack in the ground next to the navel (*omphalos*) of the Earth. The nearby sacred brook had been guarded by the serpent Python, son of the Earth-Mother Gaia, until the sun god Apollo defeated him and took it over—as his Dorian worshippers had this aboriginal shrine. As opposed to the yearly Lesser **Pythia** and other festivals of that name celebrated elsewhere, the Great **Pythia** were

held every eight years at first and consisted exclusively of musical contests, based on a hymn to Apollo. Gymnastic and equestrian contests were added when the **Pythian Games** were reorganized on the quadriennial model of the **Olympic Games** and held midway between them by early September from 586 B.C.E. onward. That year, Delphi became the new seat of the Amphictyonic League and transferred to it the appointment of judges and superintendents along with the whole responsibility for the **Pythian Games** and the shrine. That was because the latter's vast treasure was beginning to attract more attention from other states than the city could hope to be able to fend off by itself. The valuable gifts such as tripods that were originally offered were now replaced by wreaths as in Olympia—except they were made of laurel leaves, sacred to Apollo. The victors' chariots were hung from the temple's ceiling among other thank offerings for favors granted, before the altar on which burned the Pythian fire, "common hearth of Greece."

Dating from the fourth century B.C.E., the country's oldest gymnasium ruins include lecture rooms for philosophers and rhetoricians, since scholarly and literary events were featured alongside sports, as in Olympia. A theater was eventually built to hold the musical contests that remained most important at Delphi, centering on the eagerly attended **Pythian Nomos**—a performance reenacting Apollo's fight with the dragon Python (reminiscent of **Saint George**'s fight with another reptilian source guardian). It probably followed the introductory *Trittyes*—a threefold sacrifice to the sun god Apollo, the moon goddess Artemis, and their mother Leto, whom Python had pursued all over Greece while she was pregnant with her children by the sky god Zeus, on his jealous wife Hera's order.

The Isthmian Games

The **Isthmian Games** were held in the pine-grove sacred to Zeus's brother Poseidon near

Corinth, the "city of the two seas"—hence the pine wreaths used to crown victors in Roman times, when musical contests and rhetorical and poetical recitations were introduced beside the original athletic **games**. They took place in April or May every two years—the ones when there were either **Olympic** or **Pythian Games**, once they too became **Panhellenic** in 582 B.C.E. The first temple of Poseidon, god of the seas, running water and earthquakes, had been built in the previous century over the natural crevice in which King Sisyphus of Corinth had buried the drowned Melicertes. This was the child of Ino, who had thrown herself into the sea with him in a fit of madness induced by the goddess Hera and was deified in death as Leucothea, the "White Goddess," watching over seamen (like the Virgin Mary as *Stella Maris* or China's **Matzu** in later eras). Under the name of Palaemon, "the Wrestler," Melicertes was honored in Corinth in a local cult and with funerary athletic **games** in an archaic stadium. Soon, the **Isthmian Games** were especially popular with Athenians. However, they insisted that their own hero Theseus had instituted these contests in honor of Poseidon after ridding the Isthmus belonging to this god of one of the thieves who made its single road unsafe. This is how they justified their privilege of having as many seats of honor in the stadium as could be covered by the sail of the boat that brought over their official delegation. On the other hand, the reason why Eleans were singled out among all Greeks to be altogether excluded remains unknown.

The Nemean Games

The **Nemean Games** were the only ones held—on a national scale since 573 B.C.E.—every odd year in July, about halfway between Corinth to the north and powerful Argos to the south. The latter took them over from the small cities of Cleonae and Phlious in the middle of the fifth century B.C.E. According to ancient chronology, they had started out in 1251 B.C.E. as funerary

athletic **games**, instituted by the Argos-based expedition of the "Seven Against Thebes" to dispel the bad omen of the accidental death upon their arrival of the Nemean king's son Opheltes, henceforth known as Archemoros— "he through whom fate begins." This is why officials at the **games** wore mourning attire. However, the Dorians eventually attributed their foundation in honor of Zeus to the Theban hero Heracles, among whose twelve labors was the strangling of the lion of Nemea.

Equestrian and musical competitions were eventually added to these **games** in the cypress grove of Zeus Nemeios, with a literary emphasis in the Hellenistic era, when the "Guild of Dionysian artists of the Isthmus and Nemea" gained both fame (for its art) and notoriety (for its immorality) as a travelling theater troupe. From the second century B.C.E., the **Nemean Games** were no longer celebrated in Nemea, but at a new shrine of Zeus Nemeios in Argos itself, so that the original one gradually fell into ruins, having never been very rich in the first place. It seems the Roman Emperor Hadrian (76–138 C.E.) may have attempted to revive the site by entrusting Argos with organizing annual winter games there.

Explosion and Decline in an Imperial Era

Departures from the classic *periodos* or four-year cycle of **Panhellenic Games** had started centuries earlier, with the onset of the Hellenistic era in the wake of the conquests of Alexander the Great. His father King Philip II of Macedonia had already taken control of, and credit for, the **Pythian Games** by 346 B.C.E., so as to give legitimacy to his military presence in central Greece. In 278 B.C.E., to celebrate the repelling of a Gallic invasion by the Aetolian League and its allies, the Greek king of Egypt Ptolemy II launched the **Sotiria** in Delphi—in honor of his recently deceased and promptly deified father Ptolemy I Soter ("the Savior"). He had a decree passed by the Aegean League of the Islanders to make these new **games** equal in status to the **Olympiads**. Their panhellenic claims were asserted anew when they were reinstituted in the middle of the century by the Aetolian League, which now controlled the Delphic Amphictyony.

This opened the floodgates for a wave of new biennial or quadriennial festivals vying for recognition from this and other bodies, in view of royal propaganda or in hopes of royal patronage. Down to Roman times, the praise of monarchs in verse and prose thus featured more prominently at these festivals, and their relative importance and prestige in turn became an important stake in international relations. With wreaths of gold and silver as the coveted prizes, they helped foster and maintain Greek identity in a cosmopolitan, imperial setting of relative peace that left no other outlet to the traditional military rivalries between cities, at the root of the agonistic spirit of the games. The more successful ones—above all, the four original **Periodic Games**—remained popular and enjoyed imperial patronage until the end of the second century, while new "sacred" games (often incorporating a fair among the "profane" portion of activities) were instituted by imperial decree but largely funded by private local sponsors. These events now included pantomime from the second century and mime from the third—reflecting their prominent place in late **Roman** scenic **games**. But even the **Olympic Games** may have died out over a century before they were banned by a decree of Emperor Theodosius I against pagan festivals in 393. In 426, his grandson Theodosius II ordered the burning of what was left of the temples at Olympia, and in 521, Justinian banned the Antioch **Olympiads**.

Passing on the Olympic Flame to Modern Times

The term "Olympic Games" was still used about the local contests held in some Greek villages by the time a French educator, Baron Pierre de Coubertin, organized the first "**Olympic Games** of the Modern Era" in Athens in 1896. It had already been used about other attempted revivals, as in Paris on a local scale a century before during the French Revolution, and for Scandinavia in Ramlösa in Sweden in 1834 and 1836, aside from **Panhellenic Games** held in 1859 and 1875—all without lasting success. The tide only turned with the "Congress for the Reestablishment of the **Olympic Games**." It opened at the University of Paris on June 16, 1894, with a performance of the *Hymn to Apollo* just discovered in May 1893, which used to open the **Pythian Games**. Set to music by the composer Gabriel Fauré, it was sung against the evocative classical backdrop of Pierre Puvis de Chavannes's mural painting "The Sacred Grove" at the Sorbonne.

Most of the athletic events included in the program of the recreated **Olympics** were modern ones—even the marathon race, whose dramatic arrival in the Greek capital's recently excavated and especially reconstructed **Panathenaic** Stadium sealed the success of the new games in 1896. It had been invented by classical philologist Michel Bréal on the basis of a spurious literary account of a messenger's race from a victorious battle at Marathon forty kilometers away. Such distance running was unknown at ancient **Panhellenic Games**, which were also traditionally confined to the Greek world, and in no way inclusive of other "barbarian" nations, as the modern **Olympics** purported to be for the first time. Their invented traditions express a need to present them as being in some sort of spiritual continuity with their ancient model, as if they were passing on the flame of classical *agon* and *arete* through time. This is why the Olympic flame (meant to recall the one that used to be kept on an altar for the duration of an ancient **Olympiad**) is still kindled using the sun's rays in a historical reenactment of the rite in the ruins of Olympia's temple of Hera. It is then relayed through space by runners to a new site every four years—often halfway around the globe, which cosmopolitan Western culture now encompasses, as the distant forebear it has in Hellenistic civilization did the classical Mediterranean world.

See also Dionysia; Eleusinian Mysteries; Games (Rome); Matralia; Matzu's Birthday; Panathenaia; Saint George; Terminalia

References

Moses I. Finley and H. W. Pleket. *The Olympic Games: The First Thousand Years.* New York: Viking Press, 1976.

Mark Golden. *Sport and Society in Ancient Greece.* Cambridge: Cambridge University Press, 1998.

Stephen Miller. *Arete: Ancient Writers, Papyri, and Inscriptions on the History and Ideals of Greek Athletics and Games.* Chicago: Ares, 1979.

Tony Perrottet. *The Naked Olympics: The True Story of the Ancient Games.* New York: Random House, 2004.

GAMES (ROME)

Roman **games** were known as *ludi,* from an Etruscan word. In their two types—as scenic **games** of the stage and as arena and circus **games** involving gladiators or animals in fights and races—they were largely adaptations of ancient Etruscan practices to public festivals of a kind that multiplied with Rome's expansion to spread its civilization and sacralize the State. Some of them could even live on in the Christian setting of the Byzantine Empire and find echoes in urban festivals of medieval Italy and early modern Spain that have remained popular to this day.

Religious Rites

While Roman **games** were no doubt spectacles on an ever-expanding scale, they always retained some religious component from their primitive origins. Until the end of antiquity, spectators remained at some level worshippers, who therefore had to wear a formal toga. It was on their behalf that contestants—usually of low birth and often slaves—fought in what outwardly appears to be mere spectator sports meant to please a comfortably seated audience, in contrast to the participative athletic spirit of Greek **games**, which were initially restricted to the sons of the aristocracy, with spectators left standing on the sidelines or sitting on the ground. Reflecting different priorities, the amphitheater is a unique Roman invention—a building designed for the sole purpose of allowing large numbers of citizens to view a spectacle by making two Greek theaters face each other and fuse in the closed ellipse of the "double theater" of its Greek name. But Roman **games** were still in essence ritual displays ensuring joyful communication among human beings and with gods and the world, so that originally, "the slightest offense against the ritual or the most accidental disturbance invalidated the whole performance" (Huizinga 1955, p. 74). Beside the celebrations specific to different scenic or circus **games**, all public **games** also included fairly generic religious rites, be they offerings, sacrifices, prayers, or a procession.

Sacred meals were the most solemn type of offering seen at **games**. Both the **Roman** or **Great Games** (founded in the sixth century B.C.E. in honor of Jupiter Optimus Maximus) from September 5 to 19 and the November **Plebeian Games** (dating back to the fifth century B.C.E. but public since 220 B.C.E.) began with a "banquet of Jupiter" (*epulum Jovis*). In 196 B.C.E., this meal of the magistrates became a meal of the gods themselves, in the guise of a Greek lectistern, in which their statues, seated or reclining, took part in the sacred banquet served before the assembled people. The central location of altars in the circus and the decoration of niches around the building also reflected the ancient need to feed the gods through these **games**. There was no doubt a direct relationship between these circus shrines, often dedicated to Nemesis—divine personification of revenge—and the bloody gladiatorial and animal fights to the death taking place near them, recalling the immolation of prisoners and the suicides of soldiers at funerary **games**.

Prayers of varying length and solemnity were recited or sung, like the one composed by the poet Horace especially for the **Secular Games** celebrated in 17 B.C.E. by the first Emperor Augustus Caesar, a year ahead of their 110-year cycle. Following an Etruscan method of giving the past cycle a proper burial to bring divine blessings on the coming one, they were first observed in 249 B.C.E., to dispel anxiety about the future in the midst of the First Punic War. Augustus sought instead to make them into the harbinger of the new Golden Age prophesied in various quarters about the world-empire he founded. He thus added to the original nocturnal rituals of purification in view of fertility, celebrated beginning on the evening of May 31 at the Terentum underground shrine by the Tiber in honor of the underworld deities Dis Pater and Proserpine, a new set of diurnal sacrifices to sky gods Jupiter and Juno. These sacrifices were made on the third day (after a nighttime sacrifice to Ceres as Earth Mother) to Augustus's patron Apollo Palatine, along with his sister Diana—the sun and moon. It was during that June 3 morning procession from the Palatine to the Capitol of twenty-seven boys and as many girls whose parents still lived that they all sang Horace's *Secular Hymn*. The **Secular Games** were next observed five years early by Domitian in 88, but they were allowed to lapse when they came due in 313, right after the Edict of Milan legalizing Christianity.

This kind of procession often displayed the symbolic ordering of society. Under the reign of Augustus, the Greek historian Dionysus of Halicarnassus described the *pompa circensis* of the **Roman Games** from the Capitol to the Circus Maximus—the "Great Circus" holding 150,000 spectators (a seating capacity only equaled by the great soccer stadiums of the twentieth century). It began with young citizens on foot and on horseback, followed by the competitors—charioteers, horsemen, ath- letes—and then dancers in different age groups doing military dances with weapons, musicians, chorists dressed in goat skins to dance like satyrs in parody of the classical dancers ahead, the carriers of sacrificial instruments, and last but not least, the statues of the gods in the order of the Greek pantheon. These were taken on chariots and stretchers around the circus and onto a ringside tribune called the *pulvinar*, which would later be gradually confused or amalgamated with the imperial box—since the emperor was the Roman god *par excellence* (even as the earthly image of Christ after Rome's conversion). Both he and the gods showed themselves to the crowds to be venerated as such and to receive the people's petitions, thus spiritually cementing by their charisma the political unity of Rome. The dances in the *pompa* all involved *saltatio*— jumping on the ground to shake it up so as to revive plant fertility and animal reproductive powers. If this was pleasing to the gods, laughter and buffoonery were ways of disarming the powers of envy and death as well as of stimulating creative energy—hence the intermingling of feast and farce at **games**.

Scenic Games

According to Book Seven of Livy's *History of Rome*, also written at that time, young men had imitated in free verse farces the improvised magical dances of Etruscan traveling players at a precursor of scenic **games**, performed in 364 B.C.E. to sway the gods in the wake of a plague. This was the kernel out of which Roman theater would grow—though it would take until 55 B.C.E. until a permanent stone theater was built on the Campus Martius. For centuries, performances were given in a circus. After initial exposure to Greek plays, one was first produced in translation by Livius Andronicus in 240 B.C.E. for the **Roman Games** honoring Jupiter. Livy (36:36) also maintains that the first regular scenic games started in 191 B.C.E. with the annual ***ludi** Megalenses* in honor of **Cybele**.

Chariot racing in Rome's Circus Maximus. (Bettmann/Corbis)

That year, an aging Plautus wrote and produced for them his musical *Pseudolus,* when Rome's other great playwright Terence was just a child—one day to write his own groundbreaking comedies of manners for later editions. He thus staged his *Phormio* in 161 B.C.E. for the **Apollinarian Games**, first instituted in 212 B.C.E. at the behest of a soothsayer who had rightly predicted the disastrous defeat of Rome at Cannae at the hands of Hannibal's Carthaginian army in the Second Punic War. People were to offer money donations during these **games** (where plays were normally free), after which two sacrifices were to be made "following the Greek rite"—an ox and two white goats for Apollo, and a cow for his mother Latona. Like many others, these **games** resulted from a vow publicly made in a time of need and crisis—in this case to a Romanized Apollo as bringer of victory. In 208 B.C.E., it was decided to celebrate

his **games** every year on July 13, and the very next year, the tide of war had started to decisively turn in Rome's favor. By the end of the Republic, the **games** had been extended by a week to start on July 6.

Games lengthened and multiplied apace with the Republic's victorious expansion from then on. For this growth brought new resources to invest in them and new tensions to express through them. These tensions were mainly between the various social groups the **games** sometimes specifically catered to, providing them with ways to intervene in political life and the judicial process. **Games** took up to sixty-five days a year by the time Julius Caesar and his successors started to take over the initiative and all the credit for them. Before long, emperors learned how to use **games** to forge a personal link with the masses over the heads of the traditional aristocracy, while bypassing an increasingly disenfranchised citizenry. By the second century, the six great annual **games** alone (**Roman**, **Plebeian**, **Apollinarian**, plus those dedicated to **Cybele, Ceres,** and **Flora** in April) took up fifty-nine days, and all **games** combined probably made up some 200 festive days spread over much of the year. Most were annual, but many only recurred every four or five years, often reflecting pre-Roman regional patterns or extra-Roman influences. Greek influences (not only music and poetry contests, but competitive athletics such as gymnastics—as opposed to Roman paramilitary sports—in addition to horse races) were decried by the old elites when they appeared at the **Actian Games** launched under Augustus to honor Apollo for granting him victory over Antony and Cleopatra at the naval battle of Actium in 31 B.C.E.—and meant to rival the **Olympics**, and especially at the **Neronia**—another set of quinquennial **games** created by Nero in 60, but which was soon abandoned due to the resistance of Roman traditionalists. Yet this imported Greek model of the *certamen* (as opposed to the Roman *ludi*) would triumph at the yearly **games** that Domitian presided over a quarter-century later. These included the **Capitolia** or *Agon Capitolinus,* dedicated to Jupiter, for which he built on the Campus Martius Rome's first and only stadium of the Olympic type (the oblong outline of which has been perfectly preserved in today's Piazza Navona built over it—flanked by the baroque Church of Saint Agnes in *Agone* in the spot where she was martyred in 304), as well as an odeon for musical performances. The Roman **Capitolia** garnered the same athletic fame as the ancient **Panhellenic Games** in their history stretching at least to the mid-fourth century, spawning many imitations. This revival of the agonistic spirit of Greek civilization thus saw the institution of the *Agon Minervae* by Gordian III in 242 and of the *Agon Solis* by Aurelian in 274, not to mention countless *agones* in every corner of the Roman Empire—especially in Hellenized areas, but also in Western centers like Nîmes in Gaul, where athletic associations were founded and sports installations were built for this purpose.

Yet there was something peculiarly Roman about another development that troubled the cultured public: an immoderate taste for sheer spectacle on an ever-grander scale. In a letter (II, I, 182), Horace deplored the fact that even knights joined the plebs in paying less attention to the plot and phrasing of a serious literary text than to the special effects and production values deployed. For a cast of thousands crowded out character development as it marched back and forth with horses and chariots, turning a classic tragedy into a four-hour long war epic. Rome's scenic **games** have tended to privilege the visually imposing depiction of heroic actions and monumental settings in a way that recalls the films of Cecil B. DeMille set in ancient times, and indeed a long line of Hollywood spectaculars, often on historical themes. These have exhibited the basic mass appeal to find a central place in the widest array of cultures and so communicate to them American tastes and habits as a universal norm through a worldwide network of multiplexes. Likewise in the ancient world, entertainment complexes of concert odeons, theaters, amphitheaters, arenas, and circuses in various combinations sprang up in all corners of the Roman Empire up to the third century. Their ruins have often survived as its longest lasting monuments, from Croatia to Tunisia and from Spain to Syria. It was at the theater that Romans became familiar with Greek myths and poetry, that the provinces learned the language and habits of the capital, and that subjugated populations assimilated the conqueror's values to the point of developing a deeply felt solidarity with Roman civilization along with an outer allegiance to Roman institutions.

Thus, in a province like Gaul, which came under Rome's sway during the last two centuries of the Republic, the early appearance, architectural perfection, and sheer number of local theaters has been related by many to the intensity of the process of romanization. The large numbers of seats, even in remote and isolated towns, can only be explained by a large influx of entire surrounding rural populations to sites that, in many cases, were already high places of worship in pre-Roman times. In Gallo-Roman marketplaces and towns, there was often a close physical and functional relationship between theaters and temples, reflecting the need for processions between them on feast days. These included mystery plays. For each Gallic feast was based on an episode in the story of the god or hero whose birthday (or some other anniversary) was celebrated through gatherings, parades, and scenic representations. These different kinds of ritual movements went on simultaneously in a unique combination of the theater with an arena or amphitheater, in which the collective fervor of human beings was expressed in processions, songs, and dances in a circular ground-level area, while on stage the timeless actions of individual supernatural beings from the celestial realm or the netherworld were dramatically displayed as a focus of piety.

This ritual duality of religious spectacle went back to the days of Gallic independence, like certain features of gladiatorial fights there. These were also held on the occasion of feasts, such as the mid-March *Equirria Martis* or "cavalcades of Mars" in Lutetia (present-day Paris), though they had first been instituted in Rome by its founder, Romulus, on the Campus Martius. The fights took place to the musical accompaniment of hydraulic organs (not unlike hockey **games** in North American arenas) and ended with the decapitation of losers by *trinci*—a type of gladiator named after the Gallic word for "cutting" or "slicing." In the second century, many provincial theaters were designed or refitted along the lines of those found in Gaul to accommodate such armored fights as well as *venationes*—animal hunts and fights, which had begun in the circus in the third cen-

tury B.C.E. before moving to the morning portion of the standard program of gladiatorial **games** in amphitheaters. Even in Rome, these, as well as other theater performances, had come to include interludes such as wrestling and bear-baiting alongside magic shows and tightrope acts, gymnastics tournaments, and oratorical contests.

Gladiatorial Games

Under Emperor Augustus, the poet Ovid reported that gladiatorial fights were featured on all but the first of the five days of the **Quinquatrus** festival, ending on March 23 with the purification of the trumpets of war before the military campaign season. It honored Minerva Capta, an idol taken back as a prisoner from Falerii in 241 B.C.E. after the Romans finally destroyed the major Latin center of the cult of this goddess of Etruscan origin, which even belonged to the Etruscan confederation. Gladiators are first known to have fought in Rome's cattle market, the Forum Boarium, in 264 B.C.E., in three pairs as part of funerary **games** for a Brutus. These were of the kind held by such great families as a *munus* or "gift." These *munera* likely followed the principle of Etruscan blood offerings to the dead and to underworld deities such as the demon Phersu, depicted on the tombs of Tarquinia holding a hound on a leash to attack a man. Bear-baiting was another way of shedding blood on a warrior's grave so as to exchange some life-force with the dead, but gladiatorial fights as such were unknown in Etruria until the late fifth century B.C.E. Nevertheless, Roman generals took to putting on such fights and hunts before setting out on a campaign, hoping to boost their battle fortunes by shedding enough of the blood of victims and citizens beforehand to satisfy Nemesis, the goddess of revenge and retribution (to whom many chapels were later set aside in amphitheaters so gladiators could pay their respects before stepping into the arena). In 209 B.C.E., upon taking the Spanish port of New Carthage (present-day Cartagena) in the Second Punic War, the Roman general Scipio the Elder held funerary **games** in honor of his father and uncle, in which some of his men volunteered to fight to the death. These **games** were a new development, using *devotio Iberica*—a local way of saluting a leader's wished for or actual victory (even a foreign one's) by vowing to give one's life for him—to turn traditional ancestor-worship into a ritual glorifying the exceptional man revealed through victory. Gladiatorial fights could now be integrated into votive **games** of the kind promised to a deity if he or she deigned to grant victory in a perilous situation. They drew a following of captivated citizens away from their original religious setting in graveyards into the more secular setting of the forum, at the heart of the public life of the cities of central and southern Italy.

More and more, Roman generals on distant campaigns would pledge to hold such **games** even without Senate approval and thus take personal credit for military victories, over against constituted political authorities, which strictly regulated them so as to limit the number of fights and of gladiators private citizens could sponsor. In 104 B.C.E., gladiatorial fights were first introduced in public **games** on the occasion of the triumph organized to parade and execute the renegade African king Jugurtha by the general and politician Gaius Marius. Instituted by his longtime rival, the **Games of the Victory of Sulla** over the renegade Greek king Mithradates were celebrated on January 27 and 28, 81 B.C.E., right after Sulla became Rome's first dictator for life, and they were observed annually from October 27 to November 1 even after he promptly resigned in order not to create a precedent. But the stage was set for a more successful dictator to institute the annual and quadrennial **Games of the Victory of Caesar** over the Gauls in 45 B.C.E., completing the melding of Rome's victory with her leader's spirit through the blood shed on the arena, as in live battles of infantry and cavalry (including armored elephants), even more lethal than gladiator duels and drawing on armies of untrained condemned prisoners.

Adding a new twist to these all too realistic clashes, amphitheaters (like the Colosseum itself at its inauguration in 80) could now even be flooded for spectacular reenactments of historic naval battles, in which war prisoners and convicts fought each other in galleys (sometimes rigged up for special effects shipwrecks) until one side was destroyed, as in the first one given in 46 B.C.E. by Julius Caesar on an artificial lake built for the occasion on the Campus Martius. As many as a hundred ships manned by 19,000 prisoners already condemned to death were used in the *naumachia* organized on Lake Fucino in 52 by Emperor Claudius—whom they greeted with the famous phrase *morituri te salutant* ("those who are to die salute you"). This was only recorded on the one occasion and was not the standard gladiator motto it has become in the modern imagination. The naumachia (part of the **games** until the fifth century) was a way to appropriate the very history of conquered nations in a kind of mastery of time. A way to display in festive **games** the extent of Rome's domination over nature in space was the use of animals—whether exotic beasts like the elephants and lions introduced in Roman triumphal **games** under Sulla's regime, or the more familiar bulls and boars seen at ordinary provincial **games**, as in Africa, where these hunts were especially popular, since many of the animals used came from there. The Nile's fauna even came to be seriously depleted by the demand for creatures such as crocodiles for live hunts in flooded theaters (also used for artistic swim shows) at Roman **games**. Diana, goddess of the hunt, presided over such *venationes* (which only disappeared in the first half of the sixth century—long after Rome's conversion to Christianity and even its fall), as Mars, god of war, did over gladiators' duels.

The number of pairs of gladiators fighting at **games** in the capital had grown to between 25 and 60 by the end of the Republic. A quantum leap then came when Julius Caesar lined up 320 pairs in silver armor for his father's anniversary funerary **games** in conjunction with the **Roman Games** of 65 B.C.E., demonstrating that their life-giving blood conferred glorious immortality not just to Rome's illustrious dead, but increasingly to their great living descendents. Thus, his adoptive son, Octavian (after he became the Emperor Augustus), as if to crown the process of concentration of authority in the sacred and eventually deified person of a victorious leader, would have 625 pairs on average fight at the **games** over which he presided (the Emperor was exempt from the legal limit applying to private sponsors). Winners were rewarded with palm branches, while the fate of the wounded long depended on the whims of the audience. It thus found itself in a position to drown in the blood of predestined human scapegoats the restless anxiety that came with living in an ever-loosening cosmopolitan community, and to forge social consensus around the imperial symbols of collective victory over the forces of death. This religious dimension, rooted in crowd psychology, was also apparent in provinces like Africa, where the **games** of the amphitheater were tied to the cult of **Dionysus** down to the third century. Women had to be banned from the arena as troublemakers by imperial decree in 200, having first appeared as gladiators under Nero in 63. However, at the **Decennial Games** of Septimius Severus, some of these hefty amazons (also known to have hunted wild animals—as at the Colosseum's inauguration) had dangerously overstepped the boundaries of their role in this microcosm of Roman society by hurling insults at aristocrats in the emperor's box.

Circus Games

Whereas gladiatorial **games** were first held in public fora and then in amphitheaters such as Rome's Colosseum (unsurpassed among them with its capacity of 50,000 spectators), the **games** of the circus proper revolved around equestrian competitions—whose imagery of luck and triumph also found its way in funerary symbolism, especially among the landed aristocracy. Horse races went back to old agrarian and warrior rituals practiced on the Campus Martius (the "Field of Mars"). Mars was the war god to whom the right-hand, outside horse of the winning two-horse chariot in a race held on October 15 used to be sacrificed with a javelin. This has been compared to Vedic India's complex *ashvamedha*, a sacrifice for the enthronement of kings in which a sacred horse was split three ways by a victorious warrior, with the back and front portions going to the war god Indra. In Rome, the people of the Sacra Via and Suburra quarters ritually fought for the head and the privilege of hanging it on each one's most prominent building, that is respectively on the Mamilia Tower and on the wall of the Regia temple (the former royal palace). A runner also had to bring the tail fast enough for some blood to still drip on the temple's hearth, while the head of the **October horse** (*October equus*) was strewn with loaves of bread in thanksgiving for the harvest. This would suggest its sacrifice was at least in part agricultural in nature. Chariot races had a related origin in the cult of Consus (from the Latin verb *condere* meaning "to hide"), the archaic "hidden" god of grain silos in which the harvest was stored. Mules and most horses could then rest and were formally crowned for their recent efforts on the occasion of the summer **Consualia** on August 21 (as opposed to those ushering in winter on December 15, just before the **Saturnalia**). Others ran in chariot and horse races instituted by Rome's first king, Romulus. Thus, the legendary rape of the Sabine women took place during the **Consualia**, when they accompanied their fathers and husbands—enticed by the sporting events—but were kidnapped by Rome's early settlers, in dire need of wives to perpetuate the new race. From the start, Rome's very existence seemed tied up with circus **games** such as the **Consualia**, and Consus remained one of the main gods of the circus. His underground altar was hidden within one of the terminal posts of the Circus Maximus and was only uncovered during races, since horses clearly circled Consus as an offering to him. By stirring up subterranean energies, chariots and horses were supposed to regenerate the forces of the earth and bring humans in harmony with this realm, restoring the *pax deorum* when some transgression caused infectious diseases such as malaria to decimate beasts and humans, or reinforcing the desired "peace with the gods" with thanksgiving whenever they granted military victory. Though more closely tied to its original agricultural focus, this same rationale would later be found in the **Rogation**tide processions and **Ascension** cavalcades of Christian Europe.

In the sixth century B.C.E., under the early Etruscan dynasty of Roman kings, Etruscan horse teams and boxers were featured in victory celebrations on the later site of the Circus Maximus and as part of the ensuing annual **Roman Games**. From the days of the Roman Republic, horse races figured prominently in **games** aimed at agrarian deities, like the **Games of Ceres** or **Cerialia** in April, tied to the awakening of nature with the return of spring. Though the common people was very fond of boxing, wrestling, and foot races, these events were held in the same circus as horse races until the late Republic, when a temporary stadium would be erected for them in the Campus Martium. Horse racing expanded considerably in the Imperial era, when its sacred character was still attested by the ritual of the procession and by the crowded *spina* in the middle of the circus. This marble spine served as a support for a display of altars, victory columns, and obelisks taken from Egypt, representing aspects of imperial domination and the patronage of various (mostly solar) gods. It was the centerpiece of the circus as microcosm—an image of the world in reduction, revolving around its divine Prince. Its circuit was like that of the year; there were twelve chariots by competition—as many as months. They circled the *spina* as their sun seven times—as many as there were days in the emerging planetary week based on the seven celestial bodies of the solar system, and **games** often featured twenty-four races in a day—as many as the hours in it. The *spina* also represented the ocean, and the markers at each end, the rising and setting of the sun—traditionally represented as a charioteer with four horses (as in the standard circus *quadriga*) in Greek mythology under the name of Phoebus Apollo, whose temple overlooked the Circus Maximus as part of the imperial palace. This symbolism extended to the four colors of the different factions of supporters of rival stables, matching those of successive seasons and their dominant elements, each with its divine patron: Jupiter for the wind and winter (Whites); Venus for earth and springtime (Greens); Mars for the fire of summer (Reds); and both Neptune and Saturn for the wetness of autumn (Blues).

The Blues and Greens soon overshadowed the other colors as the focus of partisan passions and social tensions, with the ruling classes supporting the former and the lower classes rooting for the latter soon after they both appeared with the foundation of the Roman Empire. This rivalry was echoed in circuses to its far reaches and reverberated long after Rome's demise in the New Rome that was Constantinople. There, by the seventh century, a system of alliances had gradually emerged between the Reds and the Greens on one side and the Whites and the Blues on the other. But by the fifth century already, these factions or demes had gone beyond their original status as sports associations to become full-fledged political pressure groups that would weigh on the destinies of the Eastern Roman Empire for several centuries, often coming to blows in bloody clashes between Blues and Greens. These conflicts were at their worst in the sixth century.

The escalation of a general obsession with horse races was no doubt linked to the near-disappearance of any other outlet for the agonistic competitive spirit and the sheer bloodlust of the population. Under the rising influence of Christianity, Emperor Constantine had abolished gladiatorial **games** in 325, though with little success, since they were abolished again by Honorius—who became the first Western Emperor in 393. They probably survived in some form until the early sixth century, when the now sole remaining Eastern Emperor Anastasius banned fighting with animals, since such fights often ended badly for their tormentors.

But in Constantinople, as in Rome before, there was still an organic link between imperial authority and public **games**—now predominantly equestrian—and it was reflected in the direct communication between the Palace and the adjoining Hippodrome. Though there were hippodromes in every great city of the Eastern Empire, it was now only at that of the capital that they openly exhibited a religious dimension through their connection with the Emperor. Just as it was the Emperor alone who was victorious in battle through his generals, it was also his personal victory that winning chariot-drivers manifested. In a context where the Emperor was the living image of Christ on earth and the standard-bearer of Orthodoxy in the Church, it was also their victory that winning teams displayed before the world. This is why enemy prisoners were taken to the Hippodrome, so they would witness the triumph of truth over falsehood at the racetrack. The Emperor's authorization thus had to be formally sought two days before all **games**, even those regularly put on in conjunction with major civic celebrations and religious feasts. On some of these occasions, as on the anniversary of the founding of Constantinople, foodstuffs would be distributed to the public present at the **games**. This was in the old Roman tradition of the Emperor giving the people what it wants—"bread and circuses" (*panem et circenses*), in the famous phrase coined by the second-century poet Juvenal in his *Satires*.

The Eastern Roman Emperor in full regalia would go pray from chapel to chapel, and then solemnly accept the homage of guests to his ringside box, before opening the **games** by making the sign of the Cross three times over the people, receiving its acclamations and those of the demes, and throwing into the arena a special embroidered cloth called the *mappa*. Over the centuries, the once factious demes were tamed into a pliant role in the increasingly rigid imperial cult that the **games** had become, so that the races paled in popular appeal before more brutal entertainments provided between them, which grew at least as important. If most went back to Roman times (mimes, jugglers, and wrestling), there was also wrangling in a kind of corrida (reminiscent of the Portuguese style devised in the eighteenth century), in which a horseman would prod and provoke animals with a poker and men on foot would try to lasso it.

The people also demanded more literal displays of the Roman Empire's domination over distant nations, along the lines of the first **games** arranged to present a rich array of interludes by Nicephorus II Phocas. His reign (963–969) saw a resurgence of Constantinople's power against its new Muslim rivals, and this was reflected in exotic attractions featuring Arab jugglers, wandering actors from India, Viking dancers, and performing dogs dressed in various foreign costumes. As for chariots, they had become little more than quaint antiques, and the Hippodrome was falling into ruins by the time Constantinople fell to Western Crusaders in 1204. Even after the New Rome was taken back by its Greek-speaking citizens in 1261, ancient Roman races gave way for good to the medieval sports of European knights, such as dueling, jousts, and tournaments, which prevailed in the imperial capital's **games** down to its conquest by the Ottoman Turks in 1453.

Modern Legacy: Corridas and Palii

Just as horse races were on the wane in the New Rome, they took off in many a city of Northern Italy as a way for its rival quarters to square off in an annual contest, usually in conjunction with its patronal feast, in a way that recalls the obsessive partisanship of colored factions as a lively part of Roman heritage. Many of these urban festival **games** have survived to this day or been revived somewhere along the way. A race of this kind is normally called a *palio*—from the Latin word *pallium* for the precious embroidered cloth that is its trophy (perhaps related to the Byzantine *mappa*). Historical pageants, flag-tossing, and crossbow contests have overshadowed and displaced racing at some so-called *palii*, while others involve donkey racing, like Ferrara's *Palio di San Giorgio,* Querceta's *Palio dei micci* near Lucca, the *Palio degli asini* of Borgomanero near Novara, and that of Alba. Another name may be used for daring horse races like the July *Ardia* of Sedino near Oristano (commemorating Emperor Constantine's victory over his rival Maxentius in 312) or the bareback riding contest between the quarters of Nizza Monferrato at its June Joust, which echoes the classic *palii* of nearby Asti in September and above all Siena on July 2 and August 16.

The **Palio** of Siena was codified in its present form in 1729 as a contest between seventeen *contrade*—quasi-tribal neigborhood units, each represented by a totem animal or symbol that stands for a particular moral virtue. There are no holds barred in this wild race through city streets, where opponents may be struck with whipping crops as part of complex secret tactical alliances between teams, and victory can be earned by a horse without its fallen jockey. For, as in the Mongol **Naadam** cross-country race, the whole emphasis is on the horse, as seen at its church blessing beforehand, recalling the *Blutritt* and other **Ascension**tide equestrian festivals north of the Alps. Siena is said to owe its name to Senus, son of Remus, co-founder of

Rome, and a sixth-century B.C.E. Etruscan frieze found in nearby Murlo already depicts a horse race in similar attire. But it first appears in recorded history in the Middle Ages, when local nobles raced between the Porta Romana and the cathedral on the feast of the **Assumption**. Merchants, craftsmen, and common people were first allowed to compete in 1581, having settled until then for ever more ambitious allegorical float parades, and before that, for ox races, and at first, a **running of the bulls** through the streets—so young men in teams could try to subdue them.

There can be no question of doing anything but one's best to dodge the panicked bulls and steers that are released through the streets of Pamplona, capital of Navarra, on the morning of the eight days of the July 7 feast of the martyrdom of its founding bishop **Saint Fermin**. His late-fifteenth-century wooden effigy is solemnly carried in a procession before mad **Dionysian** excess takes hold of this otherwise conservative Catholic city around the clock while it is host to a couple million tourists. But already on the eve of the feast, the formal procession from the city hall to attend vespers at San Lorenzo parish church also features papier-mâché Giants (kings of various races) and "Big Heads" (caricatures of the ruling classes) of a kind often found at **Carnival**s. First observed officially on October 10, 1324, this particular Spanish **bull run** (made famous largely thanks to Ernest Hemingway's 1926 novel *The Sun Also Rises*) was transferred to July 7 in 1591, and regulated in 1867 in the still current format. In the attempt to outrun and outlive raging bulls on their way to death in the afternoon corrida, runners who have first invoked **Saint Fermin**'s blessings and guidance over their stunt expose themselves to the elemental surge of life's energy as they brush with death in the streets, and the beasts stampede toward the arena, in an 880-meter, four-minute sprint. (At this writing, there have been thirteen fatal gorings since the city started keeping statistics in 1924.) Death is even closer to the matadors (a Spanish word for "slayers") who will face the bulls in a ritualized confrontation of the human spirit with raw animal instinct—in itself a victory over death or the fear of it.

In the case of Pamplona, the bloodshed of the corrida serves to finance the *Casa de la Misericordia,* the senior home for the poor that owns the arena. But the religious significance of the bullfight obviously lies much deeper than this thin veneer of Christian charity. It goes back to the same roots as the combination of Etruscan funerary **games** and Iberian victory celebrations that Scipio the African brought back from Spain as the model for Rome's gladiatorial **games**—spilling blood to commune with spirits of the beyond. Though the first depictions of bull-fighting date back to ancient Crete, it was only in the middle of the second millennium that it openly became the ruling passion of all classes in Spain. It was thus part of every feast and celebration, religious or secular, so that a 1575 papal ban on attendance by the clergy—especially on Church holidays—had to be repealed. It first took the form of the *encierro* or **Running of the Bulls** typified by the Pamplona *sanfermines,* which is also part of the Siena **Palio's** early history around the same time in northern Italy. In the *encierros* of many towns and villages even today, somewhat like the victorious **October horse** in ancient Rome, the bulls are finally killed, cut into pieces, and cooked in large cauldrons, to be eaten outdoors by the entire populace gathered on the town square.

But in the early seventeenth century, young *caballeros* started to run after a bull on horseback and stick long darts in the thick nape of its neck, and the corrida became a favorite pastime of the nobility until a century later. For it then lost favor with the new French dynasty of Bourbon, and this "barbarous" pastime went back to the streets where it came from. This is where the current Spanish style of bullfighting on foot developed, managing to regain its standing in all walks of life in the late eighteenth century. Today, the corrida circuit extends well beyond Spain,

from the far west—Latin America, where for instance **bull runs** called *pamplonadas* significantly take place on October 31 to usher in the joyful funerary celebrations of **Día de Muertos** in Mexico's Michoacan State—to the near east—Provence, whose very name bears witness to its ancient history as a Roman province. There, the blood of bulls and men (or women) still gets mingled in the sand of two of the Roman Empire's best-preserved arenas (both modeled after the Colosseum) in Arles and Nîmes. In the latter city's amphitheater since 1952, bullfights and cavalcades have been drawing a million people annually for a famous **Whitsuntide** *Féria*—named after the old Latin word for Rome's religious feasts, going back to the beginning of the classical culture that shaped Western civilization.

See also Ascension; Assumption; Carnival; Dionysia; Floralia; Games (Greece); Liberalia; Lupercalia; Naadam; Navaratra and Dusshera; Quinqatrus; Rogations; Saturnalia; Spring Festival of Cybele and Attis; Sunday; Whitsuntide

References

Dominique Aubier. *Fiesta in Pamplona.* New York: Universe Books, 1956.

Roland Auguet. *Cruelty and Civilization: The Roman Games.* London: Routledge Publishing, 1994.s

Alessandro Falassi and Giuliano Catoni. *Palio,* with the republication of the essay by Giovanni Cecchini, "Palio and Contrade, Historical Evolution," 1958. Tr. Christopher Huw Evans and Elisabeth Mann Borgese. Milan: Electa, 1983.

Alison Futrell. *Blood in the Arena: The Spectacle of Roman Power.* Austin: University of Texas Press, 1997.

Johan Huizinga. *Homo Ludens: A Study of the Play Element of Culture.* Boston: Beacon Press, 1955.

▶ **GAMES OF CERES, GAMES OF THE VICTORY OF CAESAR, GAMES OF THE VICTORY OF SULLA**

See Games (Rome)

A large clay statue of the elephant-headed Hindu god Ganesha awaits immersion in the Arabian Sea in Bombay. The immersions are carried out as part of a ritual following up to ten days of prayer and festivities during the Ganesha Chaturthi festival. (Amit Bhargava/Corbis)

GANESHA CHATURTHI (HINDUISM)

Possibly of ancient Dravidian origin, this festival marks the birthday of Ganesha, one of India's most popular deities. The elephant-headed god of luck, prosperity, and wisdom is worshipped not only by devotees of his father Shiva, but also by those of the other great god Vishnu. Buddhists and Jains honor him, too.

Regional Patterns

The fourth day of each of the waxing and waning halves of the lunar month is devoted to **Ganesha** in India and Nepal. This is done especially on behalf of a family's favorite son—which **Ganesha** came to be to Shiva. Ganesha's yearly festival is thus held on the fourth (*chaturthi* in Sanskrit) day of the bright half of the month of Bhadra (August–September)—except in Uttar Pradesh, where it falls on the fourth of Magha (January–February). It is celebrated in each of the Ganesha temples to be found in every neighborhood of all the towns and villages of Nepal—where it falls in the midst of the three-to-five-day women's fasting period called *Tij*. It has also been the most popular festival in Maharashtra ever since 1893, when its public celebration was first sponsored as a nationalist statement by Bal Gangadhar Tilak (1856–1920), an early leader of India's independence movement. However, it does not figure in the ritual calendars of some other Indian states—namely Assam, West Bengal, and Bihar in the northeast, Panjab, Jammu, and Kashmir in the northwest, and Kerala in the south. In Tamil Nadu, it is largely a private household ritual, where the head of the family used to ritually mould a clay image of the god.

Idols of Ganesha

Nowadays, in much of India, while student contests reward the best sculpture of Ganesha, people also buy such clay idols of all sizes to keep in their houses as divine guests and pray to for prosperity and good fortune over either one and a half, five, seven, or ten days. These effigies, be they small household models or large elaborate sculptures on a float, are then taken in great ceremony to be thrown into a body of water—well, river, or ocean, so Ganesha can go back to the divine realm. While the idol is being immersed, the people stand in the water to be purified with it, singing a prayer to Ganesha that he come again the next year. In Maharashtra, half the dense population of Bombay (recently renamed Mumbai) turns up on Chowpatty Beach to send off the city's patron deity into the sunset in this fashion.

Among the upper castes of South India, either cowdung or a paste of ginger-like turmeric spice is shaped into a cone to represent Ganesha at the very beginning of any sacred action. Ganesha is actually invoked before any Hindu deity is worshipped, as Shiva ordained for all eternity in order to make up for having unwittingly cut off his new son's head in anger, only to replace it with that of the first animal his servant Gana found asleep with its head facing north (as only the dead are placed): a white elephant.

Moonlight Kleptomania

All the more reason for the moon goddess Chandrama to express her scandal to the creator Brahma that he would fast in the name of the deformed demi-god known as Gajanan ("elephant-face") to ensure that his own creative acts be free of mishaps. Hearing of this, Ganesha put a curse on the Moon: that anyone who caught sight of her would become a kleptomaniac. The other gods fortunately prevailed upon him to forgive the Moon as long as the curse remained in force on the day of his festival. So, people who are out on that night are as-sumed to be robbers, since this is the most auspicious time for them, a measure of their success over the coming year. In Nepal, carrying a talisman such as a citrus fruit or a green chili pepper is thought to reduce the risk of being mistaken for a criminal if one absolutely has to go out. But the only guarantee is to remain shuttered indoors after sunset, to block any opening that moonlight may shine through, and to perform rites such as offerings of sesame, sugar, and radishes—including some aimed specifically at dispelling any criminal inclinations one might feel.

The Remover of Obstacles

A great family feast is then held, after which the beloved tale is told of how Ganesha was "born"—or rather, in the Puranas' mythological account, how he was shaped by Shiva's consort Parvati from a ball of dead skin left from her massage, only to lose his original head by standing in the path of his unknowing and testy "father" before being properly introduced. Having overcome such odds in a spectacular reversal of fortune, whereby Shiva put him at the head of his armies as "Lord of Hosts"—Ganapati—or "army god"—Ganesha, he is thus known as the "Remover of Obstacles" (*Vignaharta* in Sanskrit). His devotees believe that no undertaking will succeed unless he is invoked. That is why his picture is so often found on the doors of houses or printed on wedding cards. All Hindu books have an honorary salutation to him printed on the first page, since Ganesha brings spiritual as well as material success. He is equated in the *Ganapati Upanishad* with the sacred syllable *AUM*, which stands for Brahman as the Supreme Identity of God and man—a unity of macrocosm and microcosm paralleled in the joining of a large elephant head to a small human body. At every level, if **Ganesha Chaturthi** goes by without incident, indicating that the moody elephant-faced god is pleased, this bodes well for the coming year—starting with the upcoming ten-day feast of **Navaratra** and **Dusshera** in the month of Ashvina.

See also Navaratra and Dusshera

References

Alice Getty. *Ganésa: A Monograph on the Elephant-Faced God.* Introduction by Alfred Foucher. Oxford: Clarendon Press, 1936.

K. Gnanambal. *Festivals of India.* Calcutta: Anthropological Survey of India, Government of India, *ca* 1966.

Satguru Sivaya Subramuniyaswami. *Loving Ganesa: Hinduism's Endearing Elephant-Faced God.* Kapaa, HI: Himalayan Academy, 2000.

GANGING DAYS
See Rogations

GANJITSU, GANTAN
See New Year (Japan)

GANNA
See Christmas

GARUDA PANCHAMI
See Divali

GATE-HOUSE (FESTIVAL OF THE)
See KI.LAM

GATHERING FESTIVAL
See Mid-Autumn

GAURA PURNIMA
See Holi

GEEREWOL (WODAABE)

The **Geerewol** ceremony is celebrated by the Wodaabe nomads of Niger when the rainy season subsides. This festival is famous as a series of dance contests that serve as beauty pageants for young men and as a great opportunity to start new love affairs.

Desert Dandies

Originally from Senegal, the Fulani or Peul family of peoples, now some seven million strong, has been scattering eastward across West Africa ever since the fifteenth century, along a band stretching south of the Sahara all the way beyond Lake Chad. The tribes that went past the Niger River and have by and large managed to remain faithful to their nomadic lifestyle are called the Bororo Peuls—a term derived from the Fulfulde word *mborooji* for the zebu they herd and applied to them derisively by sedentarized Peuls. If they look down on the Bororos as half-heathens on account of their lax adherence to the precepts of Islam, they are also viewed by them as Fulanis who have lost their way. Bororos who have kept to their nomadic lifestyle and remained faithful to the traditional code of conduct called *pullaaku* (based on reserve, discernment, loyalty, and resignation) can in turn be divided into two groups of cultures on the basis of typical ceremonies. The semi-nomadic Bush Peuls practice *soro*—the beating of young men with sticks on a voluntary basis, as a test of endurance that earns them prestige with their peers and the admiration of girls. These rewards are gained in a more direct, more peaceable manner in the male beauty dance called *geerewol* that is common to the Hontorbe, the Hanagamba, and the Wodaabe—its classic exponents.

The Wodaabe's name is the Fulfulde phrase for "People of the Taboo." Numbering about 45,000, they are among the last fully nomadic pastoralists in Africa, and they pride themselves on their strict adherence to the rules and taboos of *pullaaku*. For this code frames the birthright they hold from their mythical ancestors Adam and Adama: a knack for beauty and its social expression, epitomized in the **Geerewol** celebration. It takes place around September, at the end of the rainy season, that is at the crest of the wave of new life that has just transfigured their steppe habitat of central Niger, otherwise desolate and dry for nine months of the year.

For seven to ten days, as many as a thousand men may then take part in a series of dance contests-*cum*-beauty pageants. Also central to the Greek ideal, male beauty used to be judged in contests as part of the ancient festival of **Panathenaea**. But among the Wodaabe, it is three of the most beautiful unmarried girls who serve as judges, while in the audience, both sexes are on the lookout for new romantic affairs or even love marriages. Called *teegal,* these marriages can be begun and ended at will—up to a limit of three wives between the fifteen lineages, as on occasions like markets or above all **Geerewol**, when lovers can meet, as long as the single permanent *kobgal* marriage arranged at birth between cousins within one's own lineage is not put into question.

The Ruume Circle Dance
The celebration begins with the *Ruume* circle dance—a dance welcoming the hundreds of guests that arrive the first two days and a dance of seduction the first night. Wearing turbans, with painted faces, the men move rhythmically counterclockwise around the old people in the middle, clapping in unison as they sing the praises of the grace and beauty of women—who amble around them admiringly with their umbrellas. One of them may respond by approaching a dancer from behind and running her fingertips along his back, which he will pretend not to notice. However, he may later wink at her upon catching a glimpse of her averted eyes. If she is indeed the right person, they are not fully downcast—as modesty requires. This furtive eye contact once established with some certainty, the man she covets will then subtly twitch the corner of his mouth to point to a bush behind which they can later meet up.

The Yakke Charm Dance
Starting the late afternoon before the second night, the *Yakke* charm dance is a personality contest and a well-known occasion for roman-tic affairs. In preparation for it, men spend the day wrapping the twelve-feet-long turbans they will wear under conical hats, applying the same makeup (so no one has an unfair advantage): pale yellow powder to lighten the face, black kohl borders to highlight the whiteness of teeth and eyeballs, a painted line from the chin to the shaved hairline to elongate the nose and heighten the forehead—all of which are the main ingredients of physical beauty or *bodem.* But even more important perhaps is charm or *togu,* and to enhance it, they also collect fresh *maagani*—the kind of medicinal potion used to cure physical and psychological conditions, for which the Wodaabe are famous throughout West Africa. They will put some in a small perfume bottle to be hidden inside their elaborately embroidered tunics as they dance, trusting the charmed fragrance will make their own charm irresistible to the female judges. They also wear leather talismans holding excerpts from the Koran as protection from evil spirits and jealousy, to be more desirable to women, and to be able to escape detection—through sheer invisibility—when eloping with another man's wife at night. In the dance itself, they stand shoulder to shoulder in a long line as they quiver forward on tiptoe to emphasize their height and take on a variety of wildly exaggerated facial expressions to bring out their charm and personal magnetism. For instance, they pout their cheeks as they give out short puffs of breath, purse, part, and quiver their lips, flash their teeth, and roll their eyes—even one at a time if they can—which will help them stand out in the lineup and beguile the judges. For there is a Wodaabe saying that the strength of the eyes is what makes marriages. At the height of the dancing, an elder woman may run up and down the line to make fun of dancers and criticize them in order to egg them on to better performances, which she will acknowledge by dashing toward an exceptional dancer, yelling "*Yeeeee hoo!*" to gently butt her head on his chest.

Wodaabe men present themselves for view at the annual Gerewol festival—in which male beauty is the subject of contests and celebrations, Sahel Desert, Niger. (Tiziana and Gianni Baldizzone/Corbis)

The Geerewol Dance Proper

It is during the *Geerewol* dance proper, held on afternoons and evenings over five days, that the selection of the most handsome men takes place. Again, they wear similar clothes and makeup—red ochre this time—to make it easier for the judges to assess their merits fairly. But to bring out their own beauty, some dancers rely on milk-based potions of bark and grasses, which the hypnotic chant of the men as they dance shoulder to shoulder is supposed to "awaken," causing them to "rise to the heart and show themselves in the blood." In groups of at least fifty, the dancers bend their knees and sink down, letting their arms gracefully swing forward and turning their heads to show off the whiteness of their eyeballs and their teeth as they smile broadly. To display their strength and endurance, in addition to this, they also jump up and down frenziedly and stamp the ground martially, for a couple of hours at a time. On the last day, the final contestants are crowned with horsetail plumes in their turbans (without conical hats this time), which they wear in the chorus line of the grand finale. The elders bring out one by one the unmarried girls they have chosen for their beauty to serve as judges. Each one kneels modestly to observe the dancers with lowered eyes, eventually rising to indicate her choice of a favorite by slowly going over to point him out with a graceful swing of the arm. The pride of victory, the admiration of their peers, and the adulation of women are prize enough for the winners who are crowned in the glow of a huge bonfire that night, as couples slink off into the darkness for many a tryst.

A Women's Art Show: Worso

Likewise, pride is the main reward of the women who put on display their elaborately decorated prize calabashes (as opposed to those they use everyday) during the three-day period called *Worso* within **Geerewol** celebrations. Along with the found objects mixed in with them, they have no utilitarian purpose beside their part in this brief annual exhibition, after which they are packed up for another year of nomadic wanderings. As a teenage Wodaabe girl called Jaro once explained to a researcher:

> Everyone must have charm and beauty. Men show their beauty in the dances. Women show their beauty by their displays of calabashes and the many beautiful things they put on them. We seek beauty everywhere. It is the Wodaabe way—grace and elegance in all things. (Maybury-Lewis 1992, p. 164)

See also Panathenaea

References

Carol Beckwith. "Geerewol: The Art of Seduction," in Michael Feher, ed. *Fragments for a History of the Human Body.* New York: Urzone/MIT Press, 1989, pp. 200–216.

Carol Beckwith and Marion Van Offelen. *Nomads of Niger.* New York: Harry N. Abrams, 1983.

David Maybury-Lewis. *Millennium: Tribal Wisdom and the Modern World.* New York: Viking Penguin, 1992.

▌ GENERAL SALVATION

See Days of the Dead (China, Korea, Japan)

▌ GENESIA

See Days of the Dead (West)

▌ GHOST MONTH

See Days of the Dead (China, Korea, Japan)

▌ GION FESTIVALS (JAPAN)

Kyoto's **Gion Festival**, stretching over all of July, is probably the most popular festival in Japan, where it has provided the model for a number

An ornate float is drawn through Kyoto during Gion Matsuri. (Frank Leather/Corbis)

of other local summer **matsuri**s. Its essential feature is a parade of over thirty floats depicting scenes from ancient times.

A Typical Summer Festival

The **Gion Festival** owes its name to the Gionsha Shrine, even though it is now based at the Yasaka Shrine. In 869, a Shinto priest from that shrine led a memorable religious procession of the people, carrying sixty-six halberds on a portable shrine to the Shinsen-en sacred pond in the center of Kyoto. There, the weapons were immersed in a purifying ritual meant to put an end to the plague that had been besetting the imperial capital, since such conventionalized phallic symbols were associated with the deities that prevent pestilence—the Sahe-no-Kami. Since this seemed to work, the **Gion Festival** has since then honored the spirit of the emperor (who successfully interceded with the god) by means of a parade that takes place on July 17 to commemorate the original procession. *Gion*

Matsuri is actually typical of Japanese summer festivals—called *natsu* **matsuri**—in its concern for the safety and purity of the water supply. For the hot weather and long rainy season used to cause water to go bad and insects to proliferate, giving rise to epidemics and disease in people, animals, and crops.

An Extravagant Float Parade

Coming in the middle of a month of street fairs and games when people eat lots of festive treats, like *takoyaki* (battered octopus nuggets) and *tomorokoshi* (ears of corn with soy sauce), the ritual procession involves—like many a **matsuri**—the carrying of sacred palanquins by teams of white-clad, sandal-shod men. It has gradually developed into a spectacular parade through downtown Kyoto, the *Yamahoko Junko*. Though its original purpose has been nearly forgotten by now, it is still clearly echoed in the very tall halberd-like poles carried by large wheeled shrine floats (up to twenty-four meters high and twelve tons in weight), along with other symbols of the *kami* or Shinto deities. Among these are statues and mechanical dolls, spears and precious textiles (such as centuries-old Turkish and European tapestries), in addition to countless paper lanterns and musicians playing in the special *Gion-bayashi* style. While these giant *hoko* floats are pulled with ropes by large teams of men, there are also smaller shoulder-borne wheeled floats—also known in China as *yama*—on which scenes from Japanese history and mythology are enacted by performers striking poses in *tableaux vivants*. The floats have fixed wheels and can only turn corners by being pivoted on wood blocks in a delicate maneuver.

Gion Festival Spin-Offs

The thirty-two or so *yamaboko* (as both kinds of floats are called together) are assembled on the streets during the festival, when people may even visit them. But they are kept, maintained, and refurbished over the year by the respective neighborhood groups sponsoring them, so they can vie with each other in the colorful designs and inventive concepts of their creations. The competitive yet civic spirit expressed in such parades of brightly decorated floats was originally referred to by the word *furyu*, which was later applied to certain folk performances. Being infectious, this unique festive spirit has generated yamaboko parades on the pattern of Kyoto's elsewhere, beginning in the smaller provincial cities, where there were local branches of the Gionsha Shrine, from the seventeenth century onward.

In many cases, such an event is even called "**Gion Festival**" too, like the one held between July 20 and 27 at the Yasaka Shrine of the small fortified city of Tsuwano in the Sanin district. Very faithful to its Gion model, it is mostly known for the graceful Heron Dance (*Sagi-mai*) learned by the Tsuwano clan in Kyoto just before it disappeared there in the seventeenth century. In 1954, it was reintroduced as part of the original Gion Festival after Tsuwano performers taught it to their Kyoto colleagues. When the sun goes down over either **Gion Festival**, the Heron Dancers, in their wide-spanned white paper bird costumes, silently move into position in front of Yasaka Shrine's main sanctuary, to the sound of the flutes and drum that accompany an austere, yet elegant choreography going back over 400 years. It has recently spawned a playful offshoot in the Heron Chick Dance, conceived especially for Tsuwano's children, who dance through the streets in flocks of about a hundred heron chicks, wearing diminutive versions of the stately Heron Dancers' costumes.

Another example of a **Gion Festival** spin-off is the **Sugô Festival** of Okazaki in Aichi Prefecture, held on July 19 and 20. There, a tall halberd, similar to the ones crowning shrine floats in Kyoto, towers over two boats coupled together with rope and adorned with hundreds of shining paper lanterns to sail up and down the river. Likewise at the **Tennô Festival** of Aichi

Prefecture, held on the fourth weekend in July, such lantern-bearing boats are set afloat on a pond. They are joined on Sunday night by floating reeds, deposited there in a quiet ceremony. This ritual was originally carried out on the Tennô River itself as a purification by water that could help drive away plagues.

See also Matsuri; New Year (Japan)

References

Kodansha Encyclopedia of Japan. New York: Kodansha International, 1983.

Bill Logan, ed. *All-Japan: The Catalogue of Everything Japanese.* New York: Quarto Marketing, 1984.

Sokyo Ono, with William P. Woodard. *Shinto: The Kami Way.* Rutland, VT: Charles E. Tuttle Co., 1991.

GION OKERA FESTIVAL
See New Year (Japan)

GIRLS' DAY
See Sekku

GIVEAWAY
See Powwow

GOBHARDAN PUJA
See Divali

GOELAOUST
See Lugnasad

GOLDEN WEEK
See Cherry Blossom Festival

GOOD FRIDAY
See Holy Week

GORU BIHU
See Vaishakha and Vaisakhi

GOULAOUST
See Lugnasad

GOURD DANCE
See Powwow

GREAT GAMES
See Games (Rome)

GREAT HOSANNA
See Sukkot

GREAT-HOUSE (FESTIVAL OF THE)
See KI.LAM

GREAT NEW YEAR
See Epiphany

GREAT PEACE CEREMONY
See Busk

GREAT WEEK
See Holy Week

GREATLY PRIZED CEREMONY
See Midwinter

GREEN CORN CEREMONY, GREEN CORN DANCE, GREEN HARVEST FESTIVAL
See Busk

GREEN SUNDAY
See Palm Sunday, Whitsuntide

GREEN THURSDAY
See Holy Week

GREENERY DAY
See Cherry Blossom Festival

GROSSE NEUJAHR
See Epiphany

GROUNDHOG DAY
See Candlemas

▶ GUAJXAQUÍP BÁTS

See 8 Monkey

▶ GUIJIE

See Days of the Dead (China, Korea, Japan)

▶ GULES OF AUGUST

See Lugnasad

▶ GUNABIBI

See Kunapipi

▶ GURPURB (SIKHISM)

Gurpurbs are anniversary commemorations of crucial events in the lives of the eleven successive Gurus who laid the foundations of the Sikh faith between the fifteenth and eighteenth centuries in Punjab—an area now divided between India and Pakistan. These festivals are specific to Sikhism and differ in this respect from others, such as **Vaisakhi**, **Divali**, and **Holi**, borrowed and adapted by this monotheistic religion from the Hindu tradition. The main **gurpurb**s are those devoted to the births of the first Guru Nanak and of the tenth Guru Gobind Singh, and to the **martyrdom**s of the fifth Guru Arjan and of the ninth Guru Teg Bahadur.

Birth, Accession, and Death of Gurus

Counted among the eleven gurus is the Sikh holy book itself, designated by the tenth Guru as the "Eternal Guru" for future generations of Sikhs. This was done in order to prevent further disruption of the spiritual lineage of Sikhism, since human gurus had proven to be easy targets for Islam's persecution of this indigenous creed—its rival as a nonritualistic, egalitarian alternative to Hinduism. Guru Gobind Singh had lost all four of his young sons and heirs apparent in this way; one Gurpurb commemorates the **martyrdom** of the elder two on December 21, and another commemorates their juniors on December 26. Yet another Gurpurb on October 20 marks the day (on October 6,

1708, which was the eve of his death, commemorated on October 21) when Gobind Singh made of the Adi Granth—the "First Book" of the faith—his successor for all time as the Guru Granth Sahib. The holy book had already been installed in Amritsar's Golden Temple in 1704 by its editor, the fifth Guru Arjan—an event now commemorated on September 1 as a Gurpurb, just like the installation of the ten human Gurus.

Aside from their accession, the birth and death of particular gurus also provide obvious occasions for **gurpurb**s. **Guru Gobind Singh's Birthday** in 1666, celebrated on January 5, is an occasion for young Sikhs of Amritsar in warrior costumes to perform the *gatka* dance, which is derived from an ancient martial art. The **martyrdom** of Guru Gobind Singh's father Guru Teg Bahadur—for refusing to convert to Islam—is commemorated on November 24. Though widely observed elsewhere, the latter **gurpurb** is centered on two Delhi gurdwaras (as Sikh temples are called): Sis Ganj, which is built on the spot where Teg Bahadur's head was cut off on November 11, 1675, and Rakab Ganj, which was erected where the rest of his body was clandestinely cremated by a disciple, who put it in his own hut and set it on fire.

Guru Nanak's Birthday

The founder of the faith Guru Nanak was born on April 15, 1469—a first of Chet in the Hindu calendar that was used by Sikhs until March 2003, when they officially replaced it with their own Nanakshahi calendar in fixed relation to the Gregorian year. It is dated from that day, so that they know the anniversary initially chosen for the calendar to come into force on March 14, 1999, as 1 Chet 1 Nanakshahi. **Guru Nanak's Birthday** is celebrated on a spectacular scale in Delhi. There, Sikhs decorate the streets over fifteen kilometers on the path of their procession, itself three to four kilometers long. On the many similar **gurpurb** processions that take place in major Indian cities, some floats are

Indian Sikhs perform Gatka, a traditional martial art, during a religious procession near the Golden Temple in the northern Indian city of Amritsar on November 25, 2004. The annual procession takes place in the region to commemorate the martyrdom of the Sikhs' ninth Guru Teg Bahadur in 1675. (Munish Sharma/Reuters/Corbis)

decorated with garlands of marigolds that have first been put on the Granth Sahib in the gurdwara. The flowers are handed over to the faithful along the way, as a kind of blessing from the holy book as Guru.

Festive Demonstrations

At some **gurpurb**s, the Adi Granth is itself part of a parade headed by five armed guards carrying the Sikh flag (as on **Vaisakhi**), that also includes bands to perform religious music, as well as marching schoolchildren. All Sikh festivals are preceded by *akhand path*—a continuous, complete reading of the Granth Sahib over three days at the gurdwara. Its end on the festival day marks the culmination of up to three weeks of early-morning hymn-singing processions around town; sweets and tea are offered by pious Sikhs when such a *pheris* passes their homes. Houses and temples remain illuminated by countless lamps throughout the celebration. *Kirtan* sessions of religious singing are the centerpiece of special activities at the gurdwara, where free sweets and *langar* community lunches are offered to all visitors—irrespective of religious faith—by volunteers, for whom this is an act of *seva* (service) and *bhakti* (devotion). Many commercial fairs take place at such Sikh religious gatherings. Called *melas,* they also feature sporting and equestrian competitions, military displays, live entertainment, fireworks, and community meals.

Commemorating Martyrs

The atmosphere is somewhat more sober on the **gurpurb** in memory of the fifth Guru Arjan on June 16. He is the one who first compiled the sacred scriptures of the Sikh faith and later became its first martyr on May 13, 1606, shortly after the death of the enlightened Moghul ruler Akbar Shah, whose tolerant religious policy was reversed by his fundamentalist successors. The anniversary of this event also commemorates all the Sikhs who were to suffer for their faith from then on. This **gurpurb** is second only to **Guru Nanak's Birthday** in importance and features the distinctive practice of setting up booths called *chhabil,* where volunteers offer sweetened cool water to passersby.

> **See also** Divali; Elevation of the Cross; Holi; Vaishakha and Vaisakhi

References

W. Owen Cole and Piara Singh Sambhi. *The Sikhs. Their Religious Beliefs and Practices.* New Delhi: Vikas Publishing House, 1978.

The Living Festivals (video series), *Part 2 (Sukkot, Divali, Guru Nanak's Birthday).* Exeter, UK: Pergamon Educational Productions in association with RMEP, 1987.

Gurbachan Singh. *The Sikhs—Faith, Philosophy, and Folk.* New Delhi: Roli Books, 1998.

GURU NANAK'S BIRTHDAY, GURU GOBIND SINGH'S BIRTHDAY
See Gurpurb

GUY FAWKES DAY
See Samhain

GWYL AWST
See Lugnasad

GYMNOPAIDIAI
See Carneia

HADAKA MATSURI
See Naked Festivals

HAG, HAG HA'ASIP
See Sukkot

HAG HAAVIV, HAG HAHEROUT, HAG HAMATZOT, HAG HAPOSAH
See Passover

HAG HA-QAZIR
See Shavuot

HAG HASSUKKOT
See Sukkot

HALLOWEEN
See Days of the Dead (West), Samhain

HAMESHANDAS
See KI.LAM

HANA MATSURI
See Vaishakha and Vaisakhi

HANA TAUE
See Matsuri

HANAMI
See Cherry Blossom Festival

HANSHI
See Days of the Dead (China, Korea, Japan)

HANUKKAH (JUDAISM)
Hanukkah is a minor and relatively recent Jewish festival. As the **Festival of Lights** though, coming shortly before the winter solstice, it often tends to vie with **Christmas** nowadays, both in its customs and in relative scale. **Hanukkah** actually commemorates a victorious second-century B.C.E. uprising against an attempt by a Syrian ruler to assimilate the Jews forcibly into cosmopolitan Hellenistic civilization, with its pagan religion.

History
Hanukkah is one of two "**good days**" established during the Second Temple period of Israel that have survived and even increased in festive emphasis to our day, the other being **Purim**. Like **Purim**, **Hanukkah** calls for a ritual narration of the miracle it celebrates, both in the *Amidah* prayer and the grace said after meals, as well as for the *Hallel* prayer in complete form, as on the **pilgrim festivals** of **Shavuot** and **Sukkot**.

Since **Sukkot** is the ancient **Festival of the Dedication**, the part of it that involves the kindling of lights in the Temple is the direct source

Lighting the menorah candles during the Jewish festival of Hanukkah. (Richard T. Nowitz/Corbis)

of the Lights after which **Hanukkah** came to also be known as *Urim*. This festival goes back to the rededication of the Temple after Jerusalem was won during the Jewish rebellion against the Seleucid king Antiochus IV's hellenizing policy, which called for pagan sacrifices on its altar. It was on the third anniversary of his sacrilegious edicts, on the twenty-fifth of the month of Chislev in 164 B.C.E., that the eight-day rededication ceremony took place. It was based on King Solomon's original dedication of the Temple, still evoked in the Torah readings for **Hanukkah**. It also included **Sukkot**'s Temple-bound observances, since the Jewish partisans away in the field had been unable to carry them out at their regular date a couple of months earlier that year. Upon restoring the kingdom of Israel, their victorious leader Judah Maccabee decreed that these eight

days of rejoicing were also to be observed by later generations on the same date. The custom of kindling lights on **Hanukkah** at home and in the streets spread to towns and villages outside Jerusalem. Yet it gradually fell into disuse at the Temple itself, to the point where people no longer realized that it was on its account that **Hanukkah** was called the **Festival of Lights**.

By the beginning of the Common Era, facing new trials with the destruction of the Temple, the Jews made a point of kindling **Hanukkah** lights. However discreetly they might do it when they were in danger, this was meant to "publicize the miracle" of their earlier victory as that of the few over the many, and of the spirit against force. A pious legend was spread by the rabbis to convey this miracle as that of the **Hanukkah** lights themselves: the flames were said to have been fed over the eight days of the original celebration from a remaining supply of undefiled oil only sufficient to last for one day. To recall the makeshift candelabrum in the devastated Temple, an eight-branch menorah, the *hanukkiyah*, was developed to hold the lights that stand for the eight days. They are kindled at the rate of one a day, until the whole row is burning. It is considered preferable to burn olive oil.

Domestic Rites

Neither the light nor the lamp may serve any utilitarian purpose—even to light one branch from another. An extra light called the *shammash* (Hebrew for servant) therefore has to be used to kindle each one in turn; but first blessings are said on the day that it starts—one for the light and another for the miracle, plus one more on the **Hanukkah** season itself. A short prayer immediately follows the lighting of the lamps. Sephardic Jews then recite Psalm 30, while Ashkenazi Jews sing a special hymn from thirteenth-century Germany, "Mighty Rock of My Salvation." Ashkenazis often eat pancakes at this point, but doughnuts are usually preferred in Israel. *Latkas* are probably the most typical **Hanukkah** treat; they can be made from a variety of local ingredients, ranging from fruits and vegetables in Israel, to potatoes in the United States and Canada. The seasonal rationale is that the oil used to fry the food fits in well with the oil symbolism of miraculous Lights in the Temple. **Hanukkah** feasting has long been customary for Jews everywhere.

A Children's Festival

On this and other counts, **Hanukkah** has tended to emulate the general pattern of **Christmas**, especially in the Reform communities of places like North America where this holiday has grown into an important family celebration. Leaving aside the fact that the **Hanukkah** and **Christmas** seasons both begin on the twenty-fifth day of the first winter month of their respective calendars, this convergence of emphasis was favored on the one hand by the triumph of light in both **Hanukkah** and the pagan winter solstice, and on the other by the place of children in the two festivals. Jewish children have long received **Hanukkah** money and played with a seasonal top called either a *dreidel* or a *sevivon*. Books are also a traditional gift on this students' holiday, which marks a break in the rabbinical and secular school-years. In Sephardi communities, children have even been the focus of special feasts and junior competitions. These have taken on a civic dimension in Israel, in the yearly torch relay race from Modi'in, where the Hasmonean priestly clan of the Maccabees started its revolt and now lies buried. Giant **Hanukkah** lamps are also lit atop Israel's public buildings.

See also Christmas; Purim; Shavuot; Sukkot

References

Hersh Goldwurm, with Meir Zlotowitz and Nosson Scherman. *Chanukah—Its History, Observance, and Significance: A Presentation Based Upon Talmudic and Traditional Sources.* Brooklyn, NY: Mesorah Publications, 1981.

Philip Goodman, ed. *The Hanukkah Anthology.* Philadelphia, PA: Jewish Publication Society, 1992.

Rev. Oliver Shaw Rankin. *The Origins of the Festival of Hanukkah. The Jewish New-Age Festival.* Edinburgh: T. and T. Clark, 1930.

▶ HARVEST FEAST

See Shavuot

▶ HARVEST MOON FESTIVAL

See Midautumn

▶ HEB-SED

See Khoiak and Heb-Sed

▶ HEGIRA (DAY OF THE), HIJRA NEW YEAR

See New Year (Islam)

▶ **HERAIA**

See Games (Greece)

▶ **HIDRELLEZ**

See May Day

▶ **HILLULA DE-RABBI SHIMON BAR YOHAI**

See Lag ba-Omer

▶ **HOL HA-MO'ED**

See Passover

▶ **HOLA**

See Holi

▶ HOLI AND VASANT PANCHAMI (HINDUISM, SIKHISM)

Coming in February or March on the full moon in the middle of the last month of Phalguna, **Holi** seems to have begun as a fertility festival in ancient times. This Hindu festival may be compared to both springtime and year-end festivals in the West. Like **May Day**, it features phallic maypoles and bonfires, aside from street dancing to loud drums, and horns with obscene gestures and lewd remarks, among various forms of social inversion that are reminiscent of Rome's mid-December **Saturnalia**, as well as of **Carnival**, since there too, various substances are thrown at people. Except among some devotees of Krishna, specifically religious observances like fasting or worship tend to be absent on this day, in contrast to about forty days earlier, when the first signs of the coming spring and its festival of **Holi** appear on **Vasant Panchami**—a feast honoring the goddess Sarasvati. Its myths, rites, and customs involving the ceremonial burning of some minor deities are spread out in a way that bridges the forty-day interval between **Vasant Panchami** as the minor spring festival and **Holi** as the major spring festival, which can be seen respectively as the initiation and the consummation of a single spring festive cycle.

Indian women play with colored powder and liquid on the eve of Holi, the festival of colors, in Calcutta on March 6, 2004. Holi marks the beginning of spring and is celebrated across India by about March 7. (Heta Das/Reuters/Corbis)

Vasant Panchami as a Herald of Holi

Falling on the fifth (*panchami*) of the month of Magha in early February, this festival is considered the first day of spring—*Vasant*. It is the equivalent of the Chinese **New Year** or even **Candlemas** in the West, which occurs around the same time. Hindus all over the world celebrate **Vasant Panchami** with gusto as Sarasvati's birthday. Temples are full of activity when Sarasvati is dressed in yellow garments and worshipped there as well as in all educational institutions, since she is the goddess of learning. Young children (ages five and seven in Nepal) are taught to write the alphabet or their first words as an auspicious beginning to learning, while their elders clean their pens and inkwells but abstain from reading and writing. (Similar observances are typical of

New Year customs from Rome to Japan.) People try to wear yellow clothes and prepare saffron rice as part of the yellowish sweets they offer each other, since this is the color of prosperity and love.

In Nepal, Sarasvati's shrines are filled with food offerings so she can join her worshippers in breaking the day's fast in her honor. Her blessings are sought on this most popular day of the year for weddings so they too can start on the right foot. Spinners seek to increase their skills by adorning their shuttle with one of the balls from a cottonwool garland they have offered to the idol of Sarasvati.

There is a common custom in India of putting a log in a prominent public place. On it is set a combustible image of the fireproof demoness Holika with a noncombustible image of her devout nephew Prahlada in her lap. That is because on **Holi**, the sister of the demon king Hiranyakasyapu will try to kill this child devotee of Vishnu by holding him as she sits on a pyre and sets it ablaze. Holika will then get burned to ashes while Prahlada remains unscathed. In the meantime, people keep throwing twigs and any combustible material on the log, which grows to sizable proportions between **Vasant Panchami** and the night of Holi. It is then lit as mantras from the *Rig-Veda* are recited to ward off all evil spirits, and coconuts and coins are thrown into the fire. The next morning, the consecrated ashes are collected and smeared on people's limbs, and the roasted coconuts are eaten. This calls to mind the **Yule** log of European folklore, whose charred remains can cure beasts and humans as its ashes protect the fields.

On **Holi**, some households eat a mixture of mango blossoms and sandalwood paste as *prashad*—the portion of a sacred offering that returns to humans as a blessing from its divine recipient. In this case, this comes after simple backyard worship of an image of Kamadeva (from Sanskrit *kama*, meaning lust), the Indian Cupid who impudently threw his flower darts at a meditating Shiva to arouse his desire to unite with his wife Parvati and restore the earth to creativity. His awakening from deep, sleep-like absorption is celebrated on the morning after the "Great Night of Shiva"— **Mahashivaratri**. But Kama was instantly reduced to ashes by fire shooting out of the irate god's third eye of inner realization beyond duality. His wife Rati pleaded with her father Shiva that Kama be allowed to live for two days a year, after which she would join him on his funeral pyre at the climax of **Holi**. This was granted after Rati's severe penance of some forty days—corresponding to the interval between **Vasant Panchami** and **Holi**, and comparable in length and timing to the West's **Lent**en season of ascetic repentance between **Carnival** and Christ's Passion and Resurrection at **Easter**.

Holi as a Spring New Year Festival

In southern India and many western regions, **Holi** is known as the "Great Festival of Kama"—*Kama-Mahotsava* in Sanskrit—on account of this story and focuses on the burning of Kama. Since this festival is of special importance to the shudra or peasant caste, it is acted out in a pantomime among the lower castes of some districts of the Madras area. This is followed by ten days of mourning. Then the altar erected to him in the village common is set on fire, along with sugarcanes representing this cupid's bow. The next day, two men dressed as Kama and his wife Rati go around collecting money amid great rejoicing.

Uninhibited joy and revelry characterize this festival in all classes and most regions of India. In the north and to the east, it is called *Holikotsava* or the "Festival of Holika," since she is the one who gets burned in a great bonfire there. As *Holika*, it is mentioned in very early religious texts such as Jaimini's *Purvamimamsa-sutra* and *Kathaka-Grhya-sutra* around 400 B.C.E. It seems to have begun as a special rite performed by married women for the happiness and well-being of their families in honor of the full-moon deity Raka.

In those days, the lunar month was counted from the full moon instead of the new moon as today. The full moon of Phalguna was therefore the last day of the year, and the New Year started the next day with the spring. Holika was at once New Year's Day and *Vasanta-Mahotsava*—meaning the "Great Festival of Spring" in Sanskrit, or *Kaman Vila*—Early Spring of Kama—in Tamil.

There were thus two powerful reasons for it to gradually become a festival of merrymaking, when social order dissolved with the old year and liberated chaotic irrational forces, both as a joyful harbinger of spring and as dangerous pent-up instincts. These were allowed to play themselves out for a while but were soon burned in effigy to clear the air for new beginnings—such as the rebirth of Kama as the full restoration of the fruitful tension between vital desire and an impassible godhead, regenerating the world.

A Hindu Carnival

In the state of Andhra Pradesh, active preparations for the local version of **Holi**, called **Kamana Panduga** in Telugu, begin after **Mahashivaratri.** Though all castes are involved, brahmins, silk traders from the vaishaya, or merchant, caste and a rising segment of the peasant caste vie for prominent roles in the organization and sponsorship of the festival, under the leadership of the family of the elected member of the Legislative Assembly. They like to immortalize their young men in photographs, where they wear their silk costumes for the *tableaux vivants* they are cast in on the various groups' respective floats in a **Kamana** procession of gods and heroes. They mostly represent the ones important to Vaishnavas, as the wealthy families that have taken on both the prestige and the responsibility of putting on this festival of Shiva are among such followers of Vishnu. It is thus held largely in temples of

this rival focus of devotion in modern Hindu piety.

There, the paper idols of **Kamana** and Kamamma (as Kama and Rati are known locally), dressed in silk with flowers, garlands, and jewels, are not consecrated and do not receive any worship or offerings. On the first night, and again on the second, more boisterous one, when few women are seen, lower caste men, drunk on country liquor, dress up as wild animals and dance up and down between each higher caste house, until every one is given his traditional half-rupee's due. Their own ceremonies precede the final procession of **Kamana** and Kamamma that sets out by two o'clock in the morning to go through merchant and brahmin quarters before returning near its point of departure to be burned in a joyful bonfire. All around town, bonfires are fed with old pots, mats, tools, old furniture and cots—which all have to be ceremonially broken first and replaced by new ones. Old people may once have been thrown along as well to make way for youth, since groups of young men now lay them in a cot they rush to throw into the fire—having dropped the startled passenger at the last moment.

Holi may be said to be the year's last, but not least *parva* or joint, as such festive turning points are known in the Hindu tradition. For just as the human body would be stiff and lifeless without joints to articulate its form and allow its limbs enough play for motion, so human societies would collapse if they did not have festivals as joints to articulate their cyclical unfolding in tune with the world's seasonal energy shifts and allow social ties to be relaxed and renewed.

This is why the usual restrictions of caste, gender, age, and status are suspended in this joint between two yearly cycles, when celebrations are often marked by risqué language and lewd behavior and people throw colored water and powder on each other, shouting "*Holi hai*!"—"It's **Holi**!" Between men and women, the traditional use of large phallic syringes called *srngas* (often replaced today by *pishkari*, or squirt guns made out of bicycle pumps) to spurt loads of colored fluids such as musk (from the Sanskrit word *muska* for testicles)—when they do not smear each other with it—is an obvious expression of sexual playfulness. Yet this represents a taming of the initial practice of throwing mud, earth, and dust that long prevailed in the earlier days—among peasants especially. From these roots as a fertility ritual, it evolved into more innocuous aesthetic forms, just as in the **Carnival** customs of Europe, fruits, eggs, flour, and plaster were gradually displaced as projectiles by more gentle substitutes, such as confetti, which were invented in Nice for this very purpose. And as in Portuguese and Brazilian palaces and manors during such a **Carnival** *Entrudo, Rung Khelna* or playing with color used to be popular, even among the wealthy and official classes of the kingdom of Nepal, on the pattern of many ancient Indian courts. However, there, as elsewhere on the subcontinent, it has since lost some favor with the introduction of nonwashable suits and Western forms of entertainment. Laws have now been passed there to restrict the throwing of *gulal* (now mostly synthetic ochre, green, or vermilion powder) and colored water balloons to willing victims. If young men still boldly serenade maidens, the indiscriminate use of foul language has all but disappeared. In Nepal as in India, it used to be explained by stories where pranks and abuse were the secret weapon of children against a fiend that persecuted them—be it the ogress Dhundhi among followers of Shiva (Shaivas) or the demoness Holika for devotees of Vishnu (Vaishnavas). In Andhra Pradesh, the main object of color-throwing is to violate respect relationships in the kin group, as exemplified in the local version of the story of Kama. For there, he is seen as the grandson of Shiva, yet tries to seduce the latter's wife Parvati—an act equivalent to mother-son incest that causes him to be reduced to ashes by the god's righteous wrath.

Krishna Devotion

Vishnu's beloved eighth avatar or incarnation Lord Krishna is also said to have held a **Festival of Color** to entertain the 16,000 milkmaids of Brindaban in Uttar Pradesh, who used red fruit from local trees to make crimson powder. It is now called **Phalgun Krishna Pratipad** by worshippers of Krishna, and its frivolity is considered to be in imitation of his play with these *gopis* in Braj Bhoomi—the land of cowherding—where he lived until age seven near Mathura in the same state. In that area, **Holi** is just the culmination of a week of pilgrimages, devotions, and wild fairs, where spirits are raised and tongues are loosened under the influence of hemp-based *bhang*—the spiced fruity drink then consumed day and night. The boys of Nandgaon, where Krishna lived, first come to Barsana, birthplace of his favorite *gopi* Radha, to playfully harass the women amid increasing rowdiness. Gopis get their revenge for Krishna's brother Baldev's improper addressing of Radha at the *Lathmar* **Holi**, in which the women of Barsana get to pummel the men of Nandgaon with *lathi* sticks (otherwise used mostly by the police nowadays) as the latter protect their heads with leather shields. The women can thus relentlessly beat them up until nightfall. Five or ten of them may gang up on one man amid general laughter, in stark contrast to traditional Hindu women's customary subservience to their husbands as their gods. The men of Barsana go to Nandgaon the next day to receive the same treatment from its women, and the scene is repeated by female lynch mobs in several remote villages of the region. Children ransom processions through the countryside, as part of which boys and girls go two by two splendidly dressed up as Krishna and Radha and receive offerings of coins, candies, and flower collars. In Phalen during **Holi** night, a pundit who has been preparing with meditation for a month immerses himself in the sacred pond Pralad Kund before running through an eight-meter-wide flaming pyre and emerging on the other side unscathed. The next morning in the soon very slippery marble courtyard of the Baldev temple outside Mathura, all the colors of powders and perfumed water poured by the gallon from the terraces by the men mix together in the soggy pandemonium of a general battle of the sexes, and it escalates to the point where women tear their male opponents' shirts off to use these wet whips against them.

Marking the birth in 1485 of the mystic saint Shri Krishna Chaitanya, this day is also celebrated as **Gaura Purnima** in Puri in Orissa, where he died in 1533, as well as in the Vaishnava holy places of Mathura and Brindaban and throughout his native Bengal. Most of his followers there consider him an avatar of Krishna, as do the many converts this movement has recently found around the world through ISKCON—the International Society for Krishna Consciousness (which is how the name of Krishna Chaitanya translates). In this atypically devotional guise, **Holi** is thus observed as an important festival by the highly visible Hare Krishna sect in the West. In Bengal generally, in contrast to the wild revelry seen elsewhere in India, **Holi** is observed in a quiet and dignified manner as *Dolayatra*—the **Festival of the Swing**. Also known as *Dola Purnima* or **Swing Full Moon**, it actually begins the day before and lasts between three and five days. King Indradyumna of Brindaban is said to have instituted this celebration in honor of Agni—the fire god to whom grain and stalks from new fruit rites are offered there and elsewhere in north India, as well as to worship Govinda—that is, Krishna—in effigy on a swing. The fire is kindled on the first day and is to be maintained until the last day, when the decorated swinging platform is to be rocked twenty-one times to the accompaniment of special songs.

Ascetic Adaptations and Military Maneuvers

In northwestern India, many people take an opium drink from each other's palm on auspicious occasions such as **Holi**, when the Rabari pastoral nomads of Rajasthan reel under the drug's influence as they perform the *dandi*—a stick-waving dance. The austere Jains of Gujarat to the south celebrate **Holi**, too—as much as they might in principle frown upon the kind of unbridled excess often indulged in by their Hindu neighbors. They decorate their temples and are also supposed to fast on the full moon of Phalguna.

The Sikhs of Punjab to the north also had reservations about **Holi** revelry, so in 1700 their tenth Guru Gobind Singh devised for them a less frivolous, more purposeful observance of the coming of spring for the next day. It is called *Hola mohalla,* from the Punjabi word *halla* meaning "attack," hence *mohalla* for the place of attack—the fort of Holgarth in Anandpur, which would be attacked and defended by two renowned war chiefs while the Guru judged their performance. This was his way of preparing the Khalsa (the community of Sikh warrior-saints he had established the previous year) for the armed struggles it would keep on facing in the future, by giving his followers this opportunity to drill and hone their military skills through competitions in wrestling, archery, close combat with sword and shield, dagger play, fighting on horseback, and the like.

As observed today, the Sikh festival of **Hola** has lost its original military function but not its martial flavor. Members of the quasi-monastic military order of the Nihang Sahibs, created in the seventeenth century to fight off Muslim incursions into Sikh areas of Punjab, wear their blue and yellow military uniforms with a full array of traditional weapons as they congregate at Anandpur in colorful processions for displays of horsemanship and mock-combat—such as *gatka* contests to practice fighting with a mace. There, **Hola** is thus essentially a fair or *mela* with an historic military meaning and traces of the original peasant **Holi** such as playful mutual aspersions of red

Dressed in costumes from the Heian Period (794–1185), participants march in the Imperial Procession during Kyoto's annual Aoi no Matsuri, or Hollyhock Festival in English. The procession begins at the Imperial Palace and ends at Shimokamo Shrine. (Michael S. Yamashita/Corbis)

powder. But this festival is also observed elsewhere in Punjab among Sikhs, albeit on a more modest scale.

See also Candlemas; Carnival; Christmas; Easter; Lent; Mahashivaratri; May Day; Navaratra and Dusshera; New Year (China, Korea); New Year (Japan); New Year (West); Saturnalia; Vaishakha and Vaisakhi

References

Leona May Anderson. *Vasantotsava: The Spring Festivals of India. Texts and Traditions.* New Delhi: D.K. Printworld (P) Ltd., 1993.

Jane M. Christian. "The End Is the Beginning: A Festival Chain in Andhra Pradesh," in Guy R. Welbon and Glenn E. Yocum, *Religious Festivals in South India and Sri Lanka.* New Delhi: Manohar, 1982, pp. 243–267.

K. Gnanambal. *Home Life among the Tamils of the Sangam Age.* Madras, India: Central Press, 1947.

Sunil Kumar Nag, ed. *Popular Festivals of India.* Calcutta: Golden Books of India, 1983.

▌ HOLLYHOCK FESTIVAL (JAPAN)

The most impressive ceremony of the imperial calendar of **annual events**—(*nenchu gyoji*), the **Hollyhock Festival**, or *Aoi no Matsuri,* was often referred to simply as "the Festival" over 1,000 years ago in Japan. The use of hollyhock (*Asarum caulescens*) to adorn people, buildings, and carriages on the Second Day of the Bird of the fourth month was ordained by the god of the Upper Kamo Shrine in Kyoto. It is still observed today in the May 15 reenactment in Heian-period costume of the courtiers' procession to offer the plant's leaves at the Lower Kamo Shrine, in order to prevent thunderstorms and to promote a plentiful rice harvest.

As records of the festival from 667 onward show, after ancient dances at the Emperor's Palace in the morning, his envoys, selected from the Guard, would proceed through crowds of people and rows of ox-drawn carriages to offer his gifts to the gods at this shrine. There, Shinto ceremonies of purification and thanksgiving were performed. On the previous day, the Great Vestal would have taken part in ceremonial washing rites in the Kamo River, along whose banks the procession followed her to the Upper Shrine to carry out further rituals and sacred dances. The Great Vestal's return on the next day called for a repeat of these observances and then for a great banquet at her palace.

See also Matsuri; Vestalia

References

Hideo Haga. *Japanese Festivals.* Tr. Don Kenny. Osaka, Japan: Hoikusha Publishing Co., 1981.

Ivan Morris. *The World of the Shining Prince. Court Life in Ancient Japan.* New York: Knopf, 1964.

▶ HOLY CROSS

See Elevation of the Cross

▶ HOLY INNOCENTS (FEAST OF)

See Feast of Fools

▶ HOLY WEEK (CHRISTIANITY)

In the Church calendar, **Holy Week** is the one preceding **Easter** Sunday as the feast of Christ's Resurrection from the dead after his Crucifixion on **Good Friday**. The events leading up to his Passion and death are evoked on the corresponding days of **Holy Week** as a timeless sacred drama that is to be inwardly relived by devout Christians. For in the words of an Orthodox **Good Friday** hymn: "God our King from before the ages has worked our salvation in the middle of the world," suspended between heaven and earth on the Cross on Golgotha—the "Place of the Skull" of the archetypal first man Adam in the central, holy city of Jerusalem.

Origins

The term "**Holy Week**" is first found in the fourth century, when the Church of Jerusalem organized dramatic ceremonies during the week before **Easter** at the original sites of Christ's Passion. The expression "**Great Week**" is also used, sometimes concurrently as in the Orthodox Church's full name for it, which is "Holy and Great Week." When early Christians began celebrating **Easter** Sunday, at first they observed only the previous Friday and Saturday as holy days. Wednesday then appeared as a day marking Judas's plot to betray Jesus, and the three other weekdays were added by the start of the third century. By the fourth century, processions between the holy places in Jerusalem on the Sunday before commemorated the triumphal entry of Jesus Christ, with children waving palms.

Holy Monday, Tuesday, Wednesday

Holy Week is counted as part of **Lent** in the West but not in the East, where the **Lent**en season proper ends on the eve of **Lazarus Saturday** before **Palm Sunday**. Since the Eastern Church still follows the Jewish usage of counting days from sundown to sundown, the morning service of any given day is often sung on the evening of the previous day while the evening service may be celebrated in the morning. This is why **Holy Week** begins in the evening of **Palm Sunday** in the East, with special matins known as the Service of the Bridegroom. Repeated with variations on **Holy Tuesday** and **Holy Wednesday**, it centers on Gospel parables and episodes calling on the soul not to fall asleep as its Lord may appear at any moment of the night (and will come in full power at the end of time), expecting it to be ready to serve Him as master of the house. The faithful are thus enjoined to take full advantage of the few days remaining before **Easter** and spare no ascetic effort to ready themselves for the coming of God in the bridal chamber of his tomb and in their own souls as the Passion of His Son unfolds during **Holy Week**. They also ask for mercy for their shortcomings.

The Orthodox Royal Hours of the first three days include Bible readings from the Books of Ezechiel, of Exodus, and of Job that are thought to announce the way of Christ's sufferings, death, and saving Resurrection. On **Holy Monday** and **Holy Wednesday**, they precede the evening Liturgy of Presanctified Gifts consecrated the previous Sunday, as is also done on Wednesdays and Fridays during **Lent** in the East and on **Good Friday** only in the Catholic Church. There, the Passion stories according to Saint Mark and Saint Luke are read on **Holy Tuesday** and **Wednesday**, respectively, while excerpts from Saint Matthew are mostly used in Orthodox services to follow the order of events leading up to Christ's Passion.

The theme of **Holy Wednesday** is introduced Tuesday night during the Bridegroom service in a hymn by Greek princess Saint Cassiana that contrasts, on the one hand, the repentance of a public sinner, the prostitute Mary Magdalen, pouring perfume on the head of Jesus, who took it as an anticipated embalming of his corpse, with, on the other hand, the hypocrisy of Judas, the so-called disciple who complained the perfume could have been sold for charity, when he only wanted to help himself to the proceedings and was already plotting to sell his master Jesus to his enemies. It is on account of this song in which Mary Magdalen laments being "in the night of burning lechery, in the love of dark sin," that, in Greece's urban centers, prostitutes make a point of attending the **Holy Tuesday** evening service. In seventeenth-century Spain, there also was a **Holy Tuesday**

procession of prostitutes from Valladolid's Magdalen Church as their one chance of salvation, but their pimps kept threatening them along the way to make sure they would not seize it. As for Judas, Polish youngsters enjoyed hurling his effigy from a church steeple and dragging him through the streets, beating him up along the way to the nearest body of water, into which they dumped what was left of him.

By analogy with Mary Magdalen pouring perfume on the body of Christ—which is Jesus' Greek title as the "Anointed One" of God on the model of Biblical kings, anointing with oil features prominently on **Holy Wednesday**. In the East, the sacrament of the Holy Unction, aimed at the sick, is administered to all, since there is no sharp distinction between bodily and spiritual sickness. This is an ideal preparation for all the faithful to receive Holy Communion the next day, when penitent sinners used to be allowed to partake of it again, or for the first time in the case of converts. In Albanian Orthodox parishes, an old lady prepares the bread for the Eucharist of **Maundy Thursday** from a bowl of flour in which the flask of oil for Holy Unction has been put; part of this bread is reserved to give communion to the sick over the year.

Maundy Thursday

It is on **Maundy Thursday** that the oil used for this and other sacraments (like last rites to the dying, called the "Holy Chrism") is blessed each year in the major church of every Catholic diocese during the Chrismal Mass. This is also done on some years in the centers of the various Orthodox Churches during Saint Basil's Liturgy.

This **Maundy Thursday** liturgy is the most solemn and elaborate one of the Eastern rite, since this day celebrates the institution of the sacrament of the Eucharist, the Holy Sacrifice of the Mass or Divine Liturgy at the heart of Christian worship and life. This is why **Lent**en mourning recedes for a day: white vestments replace purple ones, and in the Catholic

Church the "Gloria" can be sung, while bells ring out for the last time until **Easter**. Hence the folk belief in Latin countries, which goes back to the general implementation of this rule at the end of the twelfth century, that all the church bells flew to Rome to get the **Easter** eggs that would soon be found in people's gardens. In their absence, Western European children would go through the streets with rattles, clappers, and various noisemakers, to announce the special services of the solemn *triduum* comprising **Maundy Thursday**, **Good Friday**, and **Holy Saturday**. Such ceremonial racket may have something to do with archaic methods of chasing away storms and other evils.

The Gospel reading for the **Maundy Thursday** vesperal liturgy is the longest of the year in the Eastern Church. Later that evening, there follows the **Good Friday** reading of twelve excerpts from the Gospels of Saints Matthew, Luke, and John that relate the events surrounding Christ's Last Supper. Before the sixth reading, in the Greek use (as opposed to the Slav use), the priest carries a large cross from the sanctuary and sets it up to be venerated by the faithful in the middle of the church, symbolically representing the middle of the world. This ceremony originated in the Syrian Church of Antioch and was only adopted by the Greek Church of Constantinople in 1824.

In certain cathedrals and monasteries in East and West and in some parish churches in the West, the **Maundy Thursday** service proper is followed by an old, dramatic foot-washing ceremony (*pedilavium*), in which the bishop, abbot or priest takes the part of Christ in washing and kissing the feet of twelve priests or poor people representing Christ's disciples. This is accompanied by the singing of the antiphon (a verse repeated during the liturgy): "A new commandment I give you: that you love one another, as I have loved you, says the Lord," which, in the Latin translation of the Bible, begins with *Mandatum novum do vobis*. This is the origin of the English phrase "**Maundy Thursday**." It no

doubt arose under the impact of seeing this ceremony performed by the British monarch or other dignitaries, who would often proceed to give out clothing, food, or money. All that is left of it in the United Kingdom nowadays is the distribution of **Maundy** money. The annual number of recipients of this symbolic gift to the poor has matched the sovereign's age since the reign of King Henry IV (1399–1413). Special silver coins with a face value in pence equal to it were first issued in 1662. In 1689, the Glorious Revolution put Mary II on the British throne, jointly with her Dutch-born husband King William III; balking at the prospect of washing the feet of twelve elderly subjects, he delegated the unsavory task to his chaplain, and the practice eventually lapsed.

The full royal foot-washing ritual was performed until the twentieth century in Austria, as well as in Spain. There, a few prisoners used to be released (as the Gospel says was the custom at **Passover** in Roman-occupied Jerusalem) in earlier times in Valladolid, after the **Maundy Thursday** prisoners' procession with its songs to the Virgin and her suffering Son.

In the Indian state of Kerala, Christian families mark Christ's Last Supper at their own evening meals by cutting a cross-cake into pieces, each of which is dipped in sauce and handed over to every member in due order. In Greece, **Maundy Thursday** is known as **Red Thursday**, because it is the day when **Easter** buns are baked and **Easter** eggs are dyed the lucky color red, widely favored for this throughout Eastern Europe. Germans and Western Slavs also know the day as **Green Thursday**—a term said to derive from the early practice of giving penitents a green branch as a token of their completion of the **Lent**en journey of repentance. In folklore, it is mostly a day to eat greens such as spinach in specific combinations (often involving nine kinds). But the Pennsylvania Dutch (actually *Deutsch* for "German") traditionally just eat a big fresh salad. Like the eggs laid that day in parts of Austria, these green dishes are thought to have curative properties. Western Slav homemakers vie with each other in the thoroughness of their spring cleaning on this day, since it keeps all harm at bay for the next year.

Good Friday

By contrast, until the middle of the twentieth century, there were many folk taboos about housework on **Good Friday**, as well as about lighting fires and daily tasks such as plowing. The latter was tantamount to digging one's own grave or was believed to make the earth bleed, like the flesh of Jesus on this day of his execution. For the Church, the commemoration of the Crucifixion makes **Good Friday** a day for mourning and for strict fasting. Some Greek villagers and most of Kerala's churchgoers, in their desire to participate in spirit in the Divine Agony, go so far as to consume distasteful vinegar concoctions, in memory of the vinegar-soaked sponge Jesus Christ was offered when he complained of thirst on the Cross.

In the Eastern Church, **Good Friday** has been beginning with the morning hours based on messianic Psalms and prophesies since the fifteenth century at the earliest. This service includes the symbolic removal of Christ's body from the Cross. Then his funeral is celebrated at the matins of **Holy Saturday** following vespers (toward noon on **Good Friday** in the Greek practice or in the late afternoon in the Slav tradition) with a procession of the *Epitaphios*. The latter is a painting or goldthread embroidery on a stiff piece of cloth depicting Christ's burial. While it is being venerated by the faithful, the clergy throws incense smoke on it continuously. Later on, rosewater is sprinkled both on it and on the people. The symbolic bier is then taken to the altar standing for Christ's tomb, where it will remain for forty days until the **Ascension**. The procession often takes place outside the church—and even all around town in Orthodox countries—accompanied by a band playing funeral marches and by represen-

tatives of civil authority. This protracted and solemn service is based on the singing of Psalm 119 (the longest one in the Bible) interspersed with and followed by many other poetic texts like the Eulogies of Saint Cassiana. These texts largely deal with the Harrowing of Hell—Christ's intrusion into the land of the dead to rescue from its shadows the righteous of all ages by granting them eternal life in communion with him as their deathless God. Orthodox Christians often pass under the Epitaphion at some point to receive its blessing. They may take the candles home as curative talismans and some of the spring flowers used in large quantities to adorn it, since these objects have thereby acquired a miraculous power to keep death and disease at bay.

In Catholic Poland and Slovakia too, it is a life-size figure of the dead Christ lying in a specially made coffin that the faithful venerate on **Good Friday** and above all on **Holy Saturday**. Parishes compete in the arrangement of Passion scenes around the Blessed Sacrament (a consecrated host from the mass) draped in a filmy veil.

Indeed, most religious symbols, including crosses, used to be covered on **Good Friday** in Catholic churches—literally shrouded in black. This transformation would have begun the previous night as part of a *triduum* service, which is still celebrated in monastic settings. It was also very popular with the laity in early modern France, when no other entertainment was allowed during **Lent**, and the music was provided by the best composers and opera singers of the age. This office is called *Tenebrae* (Latin for "darkness"), since the church grows darker with the blowing out in turn of fifteen candles set in two seven-branch candelabras representing the twelve disciples minus the traitor Judas plus the three Marys with a separate extra candle for their Master. It extends over the course of three nocturns of three psalms, three anthems, and three readings, interspersed with the singing of the Lamentations of Jeremy over the Hebrews' Babylonian captivity. Near the end of the cycle, all other lights in the church are put out, and only one last candle is left to represent Christ, deserted by his disciples and given over to the forces of darkness during the night of **Good Friday**. Even that single light is finally taken out and hidden behind the altar (like Jesus in the tomb and God in his humanity), leaving the church in total darkness until the *strepitus* (a sudden sharp noise) is heard. This is the signal for the candle to be brought back to its place on the stand. For Christians believe Jesus Christ is "a light that shines in the dark, a light that darkness could not overpower," according to his beloved disciple John at the beginning of his Gospel (*Jerusalem Bible* 1968, 1:5), from which the Passion story is taken during the Catholic and Anglican **Good Friday** Mass of the Presanctified. This is the only remaining Western occurrence of a type of service still widely used during fasting periods in the Eastern Church, except for this day when no liturgy is held at all. This ancient mass has other Eastern features, like the Greek *Trisagion* prayer ("Holy God, Holy Mighty, Holy Immortal, have mercy upon us!") that has always been in daily use in Orthodoxy. Here, it punctuates the Reproaches of the Messiah to the people of Israel for failing to recognize him after all the wonders the Lord did for it in the Old Testament. This is sung after a great wooden crucifix has been gradually unveiled, and while it is being venerated by the faithful as the wood of the Cross—the Tree of Life that heals the wounds brought on by eating forbidden fruit from the Tree of the Knowledge of Good and Evil in the Earthly Paradise, which is said to have caused the Fall of Adam and Eve into sin, corruption, and death.

But now the choir can sing the *Vexilla Regis* hymn praising the Cross as the triumphal banner of the King, while the host consecrated on **Maundy Thursday** is being taken out, and then held up for the adoration of the people by the priest. (From the thirteenth to the mid-twentieth century, the priest was the only one to receive it, but since 1955, there is a general communion at this point.) The mass then ends in silence, with all lights extinguished. The doors of the tabernacle holding the Blessed Sacrament are thrown wide open, just as the veil of the Temple of Jerusalem was rent from top to bottom at the moment when Christ is thought to have died on the Cross around three o'clock on the afternoon of **Good Friday**.

At that time in churches in the Rhineland, children still make lots of noise with stomping, whistles, and other instruments, to evoke the earthquake and the sudden darkness said to have simultaneously occurred in Jerusalem. After the morning Mass of the Presanctified, Catholics and Anglicans follow the interdenominational Protestant use of holding three hours of meditation on Christ's death—from noon onward (in order to match the Gospel timing reflected in their observance in Jerusalem as early as the late fourth century), focusing on the Seven Last Words or sayings Christ uttered from the Cross. In many American cities until the last quarter of the twentieth century, most businesses would even close between noon and three o'clock.

Since the Catholic Counterreformation, the fourteen Stations of the Cross have retraced meaningful incidents on the way to Golgotha, the place of execution to which Jesus was made to carry its instrument himself. They are marked by pictures around the nave of Catholic churches, so that the devout can meditate and pray in front of each in sequence. They may also be reenacted outdoors in a procession, as through the streets of Paris or Montreal, not to mention the original sites along the Way of the Cross in Jerusalem.

Holy Week and especially **Good Friday** processions are most popular in southern France, Italy, Portugal, and above all in Spain and Latin America. The procession held every day of **Holy Week** in Antigua Guatemala, the most important one in the New World, allows women to carry the *Virgen Dolorosa*. But as a rule, such processions are organized and performed by lay brotherhoods that arose from the eleventh century onward for mutual help and the expiation of sins by mortification and penitence. These brotherhoods all have their distinctive colored robes, often with pointed hoods covering the head so that participants can preserve their anonymity and refrain from taking any personal credit or suffering public shame for the penance they are doing for their sins. Sometimes, this used to involve a good deal of bloodletting by self-flagellation and other means: certain Spanish processions even left a trail of blood on the streets. Such excesses have led to their toning down from the late eighteenth century onward. Likewise, the medieval "mystery plays" performed in front of churches on **Holy Week** disappeared in the sixteenth century, for similar reasons.

Yet Passion plays soon reappeared in the context of the Catholic Counterreformation, and some fifty of them still thrive in much of Europe in secular settings, though they tend to be performed after **Easter**, around **Pentecost**. Aside from the very popular church square Passion plays called *cenaculos* (extreme, literal forms of participation in Christ's Passion) persist in the Philippines; every year, many men and women volunteer to be flogged, or even crucified, on **Good Friday**.

Holy Saturday

In Sweden and Finland, children trick-or-treat for money as **Easter** witches with pussy-willow wands adorned with feathers of many colors on **Holy Saturday**. For this is when these evil beings take advantage of the absence of Christ from earth to come out for their annual meeting with the Devil at the fairy-tale Blue Mountain. This custom spread from the western coast of Sweden in the nineteenth century but has been considerably toned down since the days young people would do pranks such as toppling

carts, knocking on the walls of houses, and throwing ashes at the windows. Though it may be an equivalent of **Halloween**, it is nonetheless receding due to the latter's fashionable new arrival from the United States.

Greeks think of **Holy Saturday** as an auspicious day to die, since the deceased are then in the company of Christ walking among the dead. Evil is then expelled in the shape of a straw dummy of the traitor Judas that is often burned in a great bonfire either Friday night or on the morning of **Holy Saturday**. Following a custom borrowed from the Church of Jerusalem, the day's vespers held at the latter time are punctuated by loud, boisterous responses and the scattering of laurel leaves whenever the priest shouts, in anticipation of the Resurrection: "Let God arise, let his enemies be scattered" (*Jerusalem Bible* 1968, Psalm 68:1). The phrase "Let God arise!" has thus become proverbial in modern Greek to denote a loud noise or a scene of uproar.

The vespers are followed by the Liturgy of Saint Basil, called the "First Resurrection" by Greeks, among whom black mourning vestments make way for the white of Paschal joy. After this morning service and a meal marking the end of the day's strict fast for Catholics and its beginning for the Orthodox, Eastern Europeans turn to the preparation of **Easter** festivities: women bake, and some of the men kill lambs.

Holy Saturday is thus characterized by the appearance of many joyful harbingers of the next day's **Easter** services, in the midst of the continuing contemplation of the awesome mystery of God's self-abasement to share mankind's condition in the person of Jesus, down to this extreme point of his seeming disappearance in the abyss of death and oblivion. In the Orthodox Church, this dual character of **Holy Saturday** is due to the long-term trend to start **Easter** celebrations always earlier, so that by now they usually begin in earnest late that night at the Sunday matins of the Resurrection

with the exultant proclamation that "Christ is
Risen!"

   See also Ascension; Ashura; Days of the Dead
     (West); Easter; Lent; Palm Sunday; Passover;
     Samhain; Whitsuntide

References

G. C. Barker. "Some Aspects of Penitential
   Processions in Spain and the American
   Southwest," in *Journal of American Folklore*,
   Vol. 79, No. 276 (1957), pp. 137–142.

Eileen Elizabeth Freeman, ed. *The Holy Week
   Book.* San Jose, CA: Resource Publications,
   1979.

*Holy Week: The Greatest Week in the Life of the
   Church.* (CD-ROM). Salisbury, MD: Regina
   Orthodox Press, 1999.

Alexander Schmemann. *Holy Week: A Liturgical
   Explanation of the Days of the Holy Week.*
   Crestwood, NY: St. Vladimir's Seminary Press,
   [*s.d.*].

Jerusalem Bible. Garden City, NY: Doubleday and
   Co., 1968.

HOMOWO
See New Yam Festival

HONNONOUAROIA
See Midwinter

HORSES' EASTER
See Lent

HOSHANA RABBA
See Sukkot

HOUSE OF WHISTLING
See Sun Dance

HUARACHICU
See Inti Raymi and Huarachicu

HUEYMICCAIHUITL
See Days of the Dead (West)

HUI
See Chiao

HUNGRY GHOSTS (FESTIVAL OF)
See Days of the Dead (China, Korea, Japan)

HYPAPANTÍ, IMBOLC
See Candlemas

I

IMMACULATE CONCEPTION

See Conception and Birth of the Virgin Mary

INDEPENDENCE DAY

See Midsummer, Powwow, Sun Dance

INDICTION (FEAST OF)

See Conception and Birth of the Virgin Mary

INNOCENTS' DAY

See Christmas, Feast of Fools

INTERMEDIATE DAYS

See Passover

INTI RAYMI AND HUARACHICU (INCAS)

For the Incas of Peru, **Inti Raymi** was a solar solstice festival that came in two versions: in the Southern Hemisphere's summer as the greater, Capac **Inti Raymi** nevertheless overshadowed by the concurrent **Huarachicu** rites of passage of December, and in the winter as the lesser **New Year** festival of **Inti Raymi** proper in June. Though these complementary festivals both had a pastoral element consisting in llama sacrifices, they were in fact primarily agrarian festivals. The great harvest festival of the lesser **Inti Raymi** had a more basic and ancient claim to

Women in traditional dress carry bowls in a procession at Sacsayhuaman, where the celebration of Inti Raymi is held annually. Inti Raymi, an Incan festival, commemorates the winter solstice and honors the sun god. (Ric Ergenbright/Corbis)

Andean peasants' allegiance than other ceremonies of the Inca Empire. It thus managed to survive the Spanish Conquest under the guise of the Catholic festival of **Corpus Christi**, and was even revived in a large-scale reenactment from the middle of the twentieth century onward.

Huarachicu and Capac Inti Raymi

In the Inca capital Cuzco, Capac **Inti Raymi** was celebrated around December 22 as the summer solstice: the longest day of the year, when the sun was mature and the moon full. In that city, it happened to coincide with the climax of the process of initiating boys into manhood in a **Huarachicu**. Held in different months according to the place, this annual ceremony can be compared to the putting on of the virile toga through which adolescents became Roman citizens on the day of the festival of **Liberalia.** Like its Roman equivalent, it involved leaving behind the attributes of childhood—in this case, the *rutuchicu,* the name every child was given upon his or her first birthday. Similarly, once girls had had their first menstruation, after fasting for three days, they underwent a family ritual known as *Quicuchica,* in which they were washed, were given their adult dress and sets of ceremonial clothes (consisting of the *acso* wraparound skirt and the *liquilla* square shoulder cloth), had their hair plaited, and received a new name. Because exclusively male Spanish chroniclers had no access to this February ceremony (possibly overlaid by one of the two Church feast days of the Virgin of Copacabana —the **Purification of the Virgin Mary** on the second of the month), much less is known about the women's initiation that seems to have followed a largely parallel sequence to that of men's; just as in Coricancha, the cult of the Sun was carried out side by side with that of his consort, the Moon, which was entrusted to women.

In contrast to the largely domestic women's rituals, the **Huarachicu** was an elaborate public festival. During the first eight days of the month of Capac Raymi, a boy's relatives would be very busy getting his special attire ready— not only the *huara* breeches made from aloe fiber and the sinews of llamas that gave the festival its name, but all the other sets of ceremonial clothes corresponding to the different stages of the initiation, such as the black tunics and white cloaks they would wear on their pilgrimage to Huanacauri, where they also had their heads shaven. This mountain, whose name means "rainbow," about three miles from Cuzco, was where Ayar Uchu, one of the mythical founders of Inca rule, had turned to stone, making it the most venerated of *huaca*s (sacred objects and shrines of local deities). His last request was to be honored as a father by all young noblemen who came to be initiated in a **Huarachicu.** That morning, the youths had first been taken to the great square of Cuzco by their relatives and were joined there by princely young maidens bearing vases of the *chicha* maize liquor. They all gathered around the images of the deities that were brought out before the Inca himself came forth to give the youths permission to sacrifice to Huanacauri. They then proceeded to the sacred mountain, taking a llama each to sacrifice at a sacred spot on the foothills at dawn. Still fasting, they climbed up the mountain to pray to Huanacauri that the Creator, the Sun, the Thunder, and the Inca enjoy eternal youth, committing themselves into his hands and those of the Creator.

It is only then that the boys would be given their *huaras.* They were marched straightway to the ravine Quirirmanta, where their relatives awaited them for a severe flogging, meant to test their endurance. They would do the Huari dance that the Creator had taught Manco Capac, the eldest of the four Ayar brothers. When the young men were done, the entire party returned to Cuzco's great square to repeat the flogging publicly. In the ceremony that followed, heralds blew through seashells, a shepherd brought the white *napa* (a llama draped in red cloth with golden earrings), the imperial insignia were displayed, and a dance was performed. The youths then went home with their families to feast upon the roasted meat of the llamas killed in sacrifice.

The initiation continued all through the month of Capac Raymi. The next stage was a great footrace to Huanacauri from another hill two leagues from Cuzco, called Anahuarqui. In the morning, five lambs were sacrificed to the Creator and to the Sun. Several hundred runners, each holding a *tupac yauri* staff mounted with gold or bronze, would then stand in a row, waiting for a splendidly attired official to drop his own staff to start leaping across the plain. At the finishing line of a grueling marathon stood noble maidens with vases of chicha to quell the thirst of the exhausted runners, egging them on with the refrain, "Come quickly, youths, we are waiting for you!" (Markham 1910). Singing and flogging would conclude the event. Then all would follow the insignia and the golden llama in a grand evening procession back to Cuzco.

The aspirants would spend the night two miles away from Cuzco, in Yavira, at the foot of a hill where the huaca called Raurana stood. It consisted of two falcons carved in stone and set on an altar. In the morning, its priest would offer sacrifices and prayers that they should become brave warriors, and, with faces smeared with llama blood, they would in turn swear allegiance to the Sun and to the Inca in the presence of the latter; once the *haylli* victory anthem had been sung, the monarch would signal the priest to present each of the youths standing in rows before him with breeches called *huarayuru*, golden earrings, red mantles with blue tassels, red shirts, plumed diadems called *pilco cassa*, and gold and silver pieces to hang around their necks. Later, on Cuzco's Haucaypata square, the young knights, wrapped in gold-festooned puma fleeces as a sign of courage, would parade and get to do the Yaqauyra dance: they held one end of the cable *huascar*, while women held the other, and so they all went in circles into the night, to form and then unwind the spiral shape of a shell.

After a thirty-day fast, during which their elders chanted in honor of the Sun, the young men bathed in the spring Calizpuquio in the ravine of the Huatanay, a mile behind the fortress of Cuzco. They could then come to the main square in their finest tunics, to be solemnly presented with their weapons: the sling, the club, the axe, and the shield, in a ceremony that ended with prayers and sacrifices.

Once they were back home, they were made drunk with chicha in order to have their ears pierced, which allowed them to wear the ear spools that set apart Inca nobles from the common folk; hence the word *orejones* ("big ears") by which they would come to be known by the Spaniards. The next day, that of Capac **Inti Raymi**, the **Huarachicu** concluded with a public feast after a mock battle in Haucaypata, where the young men used slings to pelt each other with prickly pears. They were no longer boys, but were recognized henceforward as fully equipped noble warriors of the Inca, entitled to bear arms and to run his domain. In this capacity, at the end of one last series of fasts and sacrifices, they would be seen six months later accompanying their sovereign in various functions at the **New Year** and harvest festival of the winter solstice: **Inti Raymi** proper. Stretched between these two alternating versions of **Inti Raymi**, the initial stages of human life were thus closely correlated with the sun's celestial journey.

Inti Raymi Proper

The winter **Inti Raymi**'s high point came around June 22, in conjunction with the reappearance (after two months below the horizon) of the Pleiades, a constellation worshipped in Peru as the "Seven Kids." This festival was meant to honor the Sun and all huacas, to give thanks for the past harvest, and to make supplication for harvests to come. In August 1550, shortly after the Spanish Conquest, in partial reenactment of these rites, the Indians were seen entering the former imperial capital Cuzco after they had gathered the harvest, carrying digging sticks and maize straw, and merrily singing their old seasonal songs.

The full cycle of imperial ceremonies of the lesser **Inti Raymi** had been carried out for the last time in 1535. It included many instances of harvesting and plowing with golden digging sticks, beginning in a field called Sausero, a holy place near Limapampa, where the Incas sang to the Sun. It belonged to the mummy of Mama Huaco, the first Inca Manco Capac's consort who, according to legend, had found arable land around Cuzco for her wandering people by throwing two golden rods into the air. The rod that sank deep into the ground where it fell down identified the site as fertile, so that the incas laid claim to it. This is why Mama Huaco's field was the first to be harvested and plowed, followed by other sacred fields belonging to the Creator, the Sun and Moon, the Thunder, Huanacauri hill, the living Inca, and his deceased predecessors. Their crops provided for the cultic and personal needs of their respective owners.

Among these needs was that for chicha, consumed on this day in Mama Huaco's honor, and drunk by the Inca (monarch) with the other huacas; for the sun was small and weak during the winter solstice and needed to be strengthened with sacrificial chicha. Some was also given to drink to the *napa*, a white llama wearing the same ornaments as humans, as he represented the first llama to emerge with them after the flood at the start of the current cosmos. It was displayed on Cuzco's Haucaypata Square for a month at the beginning of the lesser **Inti Raymi**, during which time it was expected to kick over the chicha vessel; the spillage became an instant sacrifice that was supposed to help the maize form grains. Once this ritualized accident had taken place, a procession would dance down the street running south to Limapampa.

Llamas were burned at every stage of the main day of this solar festival, when the singing of the people, led by the monarch, varied in intensity as the sun first rose, then stood almost still overhead, and eventually set, apparently following the path marked along the mountainous northern horizon by massive stone pillars; the chanting was thus barely audible at dawn, at its height at noon, and fading away in the evening. The people made offerings of clothes and of both live sheep and their miniature gold and silver effigies to entreat the sun to come at the appropriate time for planting, while the Inca spent much of the festival inside an elaborately carved sun-watching complex north of the city. It had its counterpart to the south in the one centered on a pair of pillars indicating the sun's position at the summer solstice in December, so that the capital city's twin moieties or kinship groups, divided between its southern and northern portions, could each feel responsible for encouraging the sun along half of its journey, on Capac **Inti Raymi** and the lesser **Inti Raymi**, respectively. The sites for the latter festival's sacrifices also shifted from East to West with the sun's course. The first sacrifice of the day was for Huanacauri, the sacred hill southeast of Cuzco, and was accompanied by the prayer: "Creator, Sun, and Thunder, may you always be young, may the peoples multiply, and may they live in peace" (Markham 1910). The people offered similar prayers for the Inca and his consort on this turning point of the Sun as his celestial counterpart, when all fires were extinguished in the capital in order to be relit later that day from the fire ignited by the sun's rays on a piece of cotton batting; an overcast sky, requiring the kindling of the **new fire** by friction methods (as in many **New Year** festivals of the Northern Hemisphere), was therefore a bad omen. But if all went well, after the sun had reached its zenith, the Inca would reflect its rays in a golden disk all around the courtyard of his palace, the Qoricancha or "Golden Enclosure," after being paraded around the city by the people gathered on the main square, along with mummified ancestors, dressed like him in golden finery.

Among many other ceremonies of the day, 200 young women, walking in files of five, brought jars of chicha and baskets of coca leaves for the Sun that morning. At midday, a llama was sacrificed on the patio of the Qoricancha, a sacred enclosure where a crop was grown especially to be distributed throughout the empire as a sign of fellowship and communion. Llamas were also let loose in the streets of Cuzco for the people to help themselves and catch them. This free-for-all created a disturbance in the day's solemnities, causing aristocratic onlookers (since the city center was ordinarily reserved for officials, nobles, and their retinues) to burst into laughter. When the sun was close to setting, however, a sad mood overtook the participants' singing and bearing, to give way to expressions of outright grief upon its disappearance, as they meekly worshipped it. They then took down the trappings of the celebration for the night, to take them out again on each of the following eight or nine days it lasted.

Harvest Rituals

Aside from the images of the Creator, the Sun and the Thunder that were placed on golden altars, the most prominent among these ceremonial trappings were sacred ancestral figures (whether they were mummies or statues is not clear) from the shrines of Cuzco. The major ones were splendidly clothed and set under elaborately worked feather awnings, attended by servants and chosen women, to line an avenue where the nobles also stood. They would accompany their lord the Inca at the end of this week that concluded the maize harvest, to initiate the plowing of the land for the next crop. For the young men newly knighted at the preceding December's **Huarachicu**, this would have been their first public function in their adult estate of warriors and administrators of the Inca.

They all went first to Sausero, then to other sacred fields before those of the Inca and his officials; the reaping of the fields of the common people brought the harvest to a close. As they harvested, they sang *aravi*—the mournful dirges of Andean villagers about absent loved ones or the hope for adequate maize supplies. When they went on to plowing with their golden digging sticks, they interspersed their aravis with *hayllis*—triumphal songs of conquest of the enemy or of the soil. In that spirit,

they returned to Cuzco's main square–Haucaypata—in tunics they had won in warfare. About that time, a pilgrimage was made to various huacas, such as that of the Inca to the northeast, the direction of the rising solstice sun, to Lake Titicaca, birthplace of both the Sun and the Incas.

Once the harvested maize was ready to be shelled, to conclude the celebration of the lesser **Inti Raymi**, the Inca led a procession to Matucalla Hill that excluded women (except for the ones who had prepared the chicha). But it did include two sacred images of women clothed in superb textiles, as well as four life-size images of llamas, two in gold and two in silver, dressed up in fine tunics and borne on the shoulders of noblemen, in memory of these animals' common origin with humans after the cataclysm that set in motion the present cycle of time—as another was set to end it in the fullness of time. Like the mix of joyful and mournful songs during plowing, this was but one more reminder that the beginning was found in the end and the end in the beginning, in an alternation of light and darkness where the two solstices echoed each other in every respect. Hence the many common elements of **Inti Raymi** proper and Capac **Inti Raymi**, such as the role of the primordial napa llama—the object of a sacrificial procession to Huanacauri in the latter December festival.

From Underground to Revival

The lesser **Inti Raymi** ended towards August on Mantocalla Hill after a period of feasting and rejoicing. During that time, human effigies, sculpted in the same *quisshuar* wood out of which digging sticks were made, were dressed in beautiful clothes before being burned. It is understandable then that Andeans would find something familiar in the religious statues brought out in procession by their Spanish conquerors around the time of **Inti Raymi**, on the June festival of **Corpus Christi**, with their naturalistic design, lifelike glass eyes, blushing cheeks, and bejeweled attire. This resemblance allowed them to see these figures as the huacas and mummies of the Christians, on a par with their own sacred objects, only foreign, and fit only for the Spaniards. For their own purposes of confessing and sacrificing to them so the Pleiades as "stars of disease" (*Oncoiqoyllur*) would spare their crops from seasonal frost, they could thus take the liberty of putting their own huacas next to images of saints. This way, they were able to revere them as was due at **Inti Raymi** under a thin veneer of Christian devotion. Similarly, when the people of Cuzco scattered coca leaves, flowers, and many-colored feathers on the path of the **Corpus Christi** procession of the consecrated host—ostensibly a triumphant display of the European Counter-reformation's social hegemony, they were reenacting the homage traditionally paid to the Inca as he returned to the capital from Mantocalla Hill, in the closing rite of the **Inti Raymi** festival. It had used to give the signal to irrigate the land, taking advantage of a pause in the yearly round of festivals, as had been ordained in the mid-fifteenth century by the great legislator Pachacuti for the Inca Empire. But after the latter's demise and Spanish colonization, the festivals that endured in Andean people's lives (however covertly) were the ones having directly to do with the success of the crops on which peasants depended, like **Inti Raymi**.

Yet this one left such a mark that, since the middle of the twentieth century, it has been openly revived in a large-scale reenactment that is second only to the Rio **Carnival** as a tourist event in South America. Over 200,000 people come each year to witness the reenactment of **Inti Raymi** by a cast of several hundreds in gold and silver ornaments on June 24—the feast of **Saint John the Baptist**, who otherwise takes the place of honor once held by the Inca and his retinue. Amid the open-air eating of roasted guinea pig and drinking of *pisco*, countless other events surround this one, such as parades, exhibitions, and street activities in daytime and nighttime

outdoor concerts on the Plaza de Armas, the square between the legs of the puma-shaped city of Cuzco. It is at the head of the puma that the festival itself is staged, in the setting of the archeological complex of Sacsayhuamán, also called the "Sacred House of the Sun." But it starts on the Avenida del Sol in front of the Qoricancha, also known as the Santo Domingo, after the church and monastery built on the remains of the imperial palace and Temple of the Sun. It is there that, standing on top of its perfectly shaped granite wall, the Inca and high priest give their solemn orations in Quechua—the original language of the Incas, still spoken in wide areas of the surrounding Peruvian highlands. Another highpoint of the festival, after the procession of the Inca impersonator on a replica of the emperor's famous golden throne, is the sacrifice of the white llama at the fortress of Sacsayhuamán. Since 1997, as a result of protests, the sacrifice is only make-believe–though the heart the high priest holds up above him looks real enough. At sunset, big campfires are set all over the fortress, and people start dancing around them in honor of the god of fire.

Since 1998 especially, thousands of Indians and Mestizos from all over South America also gather at the pre-Inca ruins of Tiahuanaco, outside the Bolivian capital La Paz, around the June 22 date of the Incas' **Inti Raymi**, to proclaim their faith in a renewed ascendancy of the native peoples of the continent.

See also Candlemas; Carnival; Christmas; Corpus Christi; Liberalia; Midsummer; New Fire Ceremony; New Year (Japan); Samhain; Situa

References

Anthony F. Aveni. *The Book of the Year. A Brief History of Our Seasonal Holidays.* Oxford, UK: Oxford University Press, 2003.

Carolyn Dean. *Inka Bodies and the Body of Christ: Corpus Christi in Colonial Cusco, Peru.* Durham, NC: Duke University Press, 1999.

Nicholas Griffiths. *The Cross and the Serpent. Religious Repression and Resurgence in Colonial*

Peru. Norman: University of Oklahoma Press, 1997.

Sir Clements Markham. *The Incas of Peru.* London, UK: Smith, Elder and Co., 1910.

▶ INVENTION OF THE CROSS
See Elevation of the Cross

▶ IRIS FESTIVAL
See Sekku

▶ ISTHMIAN GAMES
See Games (Greece)

▶ IZCALLI (AZTECS)

Taking its name from the eighteenth and last month of the Aztec solar civic year (*xihuitl*), the Izcalli festival was poised on the cusp between continuing cosmic order and the fearful possibility of its collapse into chaos. In order to favor a positive outcome, rites of passage, ceremonial hunts, human sacrifices, and a sacred court dance were performed. The Nahuatl word *izcalli* means "stone house" and refers to the building where maize used to be dried and roasted at this time of year (between mid-January and mid-February). The whole month was therefore devoted to fire.

Baptism by Fire

As one of the oldest deities in the Mesoamerican pantheon, the God of Fire actually looked his age, with his deep wrinkles, and his back curved under the weight of an incense burner. He was most often referred to as Huehueteotl—"the old god." He was also known as Otontecuhtli—"the Otomi Lord," because even before the coming of the Aztecs from the North, the ancient Otomi people of the highlands where Mexico City now stands had worshipped a primordial couple of Old Mother and Old Father. The latter deity was already identified by the Otomi both with Fire and with

the Sun. Since turquoise was a symbolic equivalent of fire for Aztec priests, they had yet another name for this god: "the Turquoise Lord"—Xiuhtecuhtli. A small fire was permanently kept alive at the sacred center of every Aztec home in honor of Xiuhtecuhtli, as the earthly representative of the Creator Ometecuhtli. This is why the ritual piercing of the ears of Aztec children when they were formally introduced to the Fire God as part of the year-end rites of Izcalli may be seen as a kind of "baptism" into the domestic service of this divine protector, as well as into the larger community of all the family groups who were bound to it.

The Lordly Dance of the Luminaries

Ceremonial hunts were a regular feature of the public celebration of the Izcalli festival, along with human sacrifices. Every four years, these sacrifices took on an added dimension, as the victims were dressed up to impersonate the Fire God. Every eight years, the solar year and the 584-day cycle of the planet Venus were completed on the same day. It was feared the world might end if the sun and Venus did not start again on their respective courses. A solemn "Lordly Dance" would then be performed during Izcalli after the sacrifices. In it, the empire's highest nobles imitated the stars, the moon, and the sun—which the other celestial bodies were always so jealous of that they tried to stop it in its tracks when it was born anew every day, so that it needed regular infusions of human blood in order to overcome all obstacles to the completion of its course.

This Lordly Dance was a magical method for encouraging the heavenly bodies to go on with their usual rounds. Wearing his turquoise diadem, the emperor led his court in the dance; all participants were in full ceremonial dress, and each bore a small red-and-white stick along with a paper bag of incense. As they came out of the temple, they circled the courtyard together four times. "And when they had danced, they dispersed and went away, and thereupon all entered the palace in proper order," according to the Spanish chronicler Bernardino de Sahagún (Townsend 1979, p. 47).

Extra Days of Doom and Gloom

But there was no guarantee that the celestial bodies would cooperate and that the world would not collapse. This is why the five *nemontemi* intercalary days—"blank" days separating the last month **Izcalli** of one year from the first month **Atlcaualo** of a hypothetical new year—were considered highly inauspicious. They were spent in the shadow of doom and gloom. Most everyday pursuits ground to a halt, and all religious activity was suspended. Nothing was supposed to have its start during these extra days after **Izcalli**. No trip was undertaken, nor was any marriage celebrated. It was thought that the unfortunate child who happened to be born in this in-between time was sure to have a disastrous destiny.

See also Rain Festivals

References

Bernardino de Sahagún. *Florentine Codex: General History of the Things of New Spain*. Tr. Charles E. Dibble and Arthur O. Anderson. Salt Lake City: University of Utah Press, 12 vols., 1950–1975.

Richard Fraser Townsend. *State and Cosmos in the Art of Tenochtitlán*. Washington, DC: Dumbarton Oaks, 1979.

Robert Wauchope, gen. ed. *Handbook of Middle American Indians*. Austin: University of Texas Press, 1964–1976, Vol. VI (M. Nash, ed.): *Social Anthropology*.

JANMASHTAMI (HINDUISM)

The birthday of Lord Krishna ("the Dark One" in Sanskrit) is celebrated on the eighth day of the waning, or "dark half" (*krishnapaksha*), of the lunar month of Shravana (July–August) or of that of Bhadra (August–September) in an alternate reckoning of the months, depending on the region. It remains one of the few fixed feasts to be performed at the same time throughout the Indian subcontinent as one of a number of festivals occurring around this time in the monsoon season.

Place in the Calendar

Krishna's birthday can be celebrated on one or both of two consecutive days. That is because he is said to have been born as the eighth child of Devaki while the moon was passing through the asterism (constellation segment) named after his father Vasudeva's other wife Rohini on the eighth, which it does not do every year. If Rohini is crossed on the eighth day of the month, the festival is called *Krishna Jayanti* (birthday); if not, it is still held mostly on the eighth, or *ashtami*, and it is thus called simply *Krishnashtami.* Nevertheless, the name *Janmashtami* (from *janma,* which is Sanskrit for "birth") is the one most often used in both cases for this feast honoring the eighth and most glorious of the ten numbered incarna-tions, or avatars, of the god Vishnu, the Pre-sever in the *trimurti* or Hindu triad (alongside Brahma as Creator and Shiva as Destroyer). He takes birth in this capacity whenever the cosmic law, or *dharma,* needs to be reaffirmed in times of confusion and corruption. In Krishna's case, it is supposed to have occurred at midnight, so that his devotees (especially women—for this "primal male" was always known as a seducer) keep a vigil and fast twenty-four hours until that time. The image of the infant Krishna—born blue-skinned and lotus-eyed in a yellow silk robe with a crown of jewels—is then bathed in water and milk, dressed in new clothes, placed in a cradle, and worshipped with offerings of food, money, and flowers. Still, devotees of Shiva wait until sunrise on the eighth to worship the newborn avatar of Vishnu.

Krishna's Story as Spiritual Path

Regardless of sectarian preferences, this festive occasion is celebrated with classical as well as folk songs and dances all over Northern India. The state of Uttar Pradesh is especially known for the *raslila* (play of delight) genre of solo and group dancing combined with chanted recitation to instrumental accompaniment—with audience participation to sing refrains and mark the beat by clapping hands, reenacting episodes from the life of Krishna, above all his love affair with Radha. She stands for the human soul in its playful love relationship to Krishna, as do the *gopis*—cowherds' wives who joined him in amorous dances in a forest clearing. Little girls dress up as gopis to dance around a teenage Krishna in city crossroads and village squares. As for Krishna, his devotees see him as the Supreme God on the basis of the sixth book of the Bhagavad Gita. In this classic section of the vast *Mahabharata* epic, which is also viewed as the cream of the metaphysical wisdom of the Upanishads, Krishna reveals the secrets of His true nature and of man's place in the scheme of things (that is, disinterestedly following God's will in the performance of worldly duties) to his friend, the warrior-king Arjuna. This restores the latter's resolve to face his relatives and many good people in the great battle of rival divine clans at Kurukshetra, 160 kilometers north of Delhi.

It is, however, from the tenth book of the South Indian Bhagavata Purana, dealing extensively with Krishna's childhood, that devotees draw in preparing small images of the god, human characters, and animal figures for elaborate representations of his birthplace, the North Indian kingdom of Mathura, on the banks of the river Yamuna, over which he was carried out of reach of the usurper Kansa's massacre of innocent newborns (including all but one of Krishna's older brothers), and of Gokul, the refuge where he grew up among cowherds.

Remembering Krishna as a Young Cowherd

If **Janmashtami** is the major yearly event in all Krishna temples, it is observed with special splendor in Mathura and Vrindavan, the respective scenes of Krishna's birth and childhood in what is now Uttar Pradesh. There, as in Maharashtra state, the celebration is also called **Dahihandi**, after the practice of tying an earthen pot (*handi*) filled with butter, milk,

curd, or *jvari* (parched grain) from a high rope or tall poles in the streets, and having young men or children climb upon one another in a human pyramid to break it with a hammer. While girls swarm and dance around the young "Krishna" who delivered the blow, the pot's spilled contents are eaten as *prashad* (an offering of the god's favor) amidst acclamations of "*Govinda!*"—another name for Krishna as cowherd. That is because, as a child, he was known, in the mischievous pranks he indulged in along with his cowherd playmates, to steal butter and curd from earthen pots placed beyond their reach by their mothers. At home as in the temples, shrines are decorated with leaves and flowers, and sweetmeats are offered to Krishna before being distributed as *prashad* to all family members. The women are thus kept busy beforehand preparing them, as well as milk products such as butter, which was Krishna's favorite food as a child. Many different kinds of fruits are also offered on this day.

All the way to Nepal, Krishna's image is everywhere to be seen, from the effigies displayed amid flowers and jewels in shop windows to the posters on the walls of houses, bazaars, and temples that recall the many colorful stories of his adventurous life and loves. Pundits also read them to passers-by from cloth-covered benches set for them along the streets and on temple grounds.

Celebrating Krishna Around the World

The joy of these stories and that festival is in the very nature of Krishna, as the mere mention and remembrance of his divine name brings joy. Witness the converts of many backgrounds who are known for chanting it through the streets of all the great cities of the world as members of the International Society for Krishna Consciousness (ISKCON), commonly referred to as the Hare Krishna movement. They, too, gather in their Krishna tem-

An Indian artisan gives finishing touches to idols of Hindu deity Lord Krishna in the northeastern Indian city of Siliguri. The idols are being prepared for Janmashtami, a Hindu festival celebrating the birthday of Lord Krishna. (Rupak De Chowdhuri/Reuters/Corbis)

ples (a major new one being Bhaktivedanta Manor—the stately house and gardens bequeathed to them in his will by former Beatle George Harrison in Watford, Hertfordshire) for **Janmashtami** celebrations that are sometimes very elaborate. These often feature traditional dance and new devotional plays before the late-night prolonged anointing (*abhisheka*) in milk of the small figures of Radha and Krishna, followed by flower offerings by all the guests and a countdown to midnight. In the darkened temple, the curtains of the shrine are then reopened to reveal the large images of Krishna and Radha in radiant glory, and a plate of lamps is taken from it among the faithful, who take the warmth of the blessed flames with their hands and "wash" their faces with it.

But the devotees of this highly visible sect also have further cause to extend seasonal celebrations in that **Janmashtami** tends to fall near the **Appearance Day of Srila Prabhupada**—as they like to call their guru A. C. Bhaktivedanta. Born on September 1, 1896, he brought this otherwise somewhat marginal Bengali current of enthusiastic *bhakti* (devotion) to Boston in 1965. It was already firmly established in the Americas and Europe by the time of his death on November 14, 1977. His movement's "evangelical" style of Vedic fundamentalism has kept gathering new devotees for Krishna there and wherever rampant materialism has left many people begging for the restoration of moral law and inner joy. This is what this god has always stood for in India and what is now celebrated the world over on his birthday.

See also Holi

References

A. C. Mukerji. *Hindu Fasts and Feasts.* Calcutta, India: Macmillan, 1916.

Paul Michael Toomey. *Food from the Mouth of Krishna: Feasts and Festivals in a North Indian Pilgrimage Centre.* Delhi, India: Hindustan Publication Corporation, 1994.

Devi Vanamali. *Sri Krishna Lila: The Complete Life of Bhagwan Sri Krishna, Taken from the Sreemad Bhagavatham, Sreemad Mahabharatam and the Wealth of Oral Tradition.* New Delhi: Aryan Books International, 2000.

JIDAI MATSURI
See Matsuri

JINJUTSU, JOMI, JOSHI NO SEKKU
See Sekku

JOYDAY
See Days of the Dead (West)

JUDGMENT DAY
See Rosh Hashanah

JUHANNUS
See Midsummer

JUNGGU
See Double Nine

JUNGWON
See Days of the Dead (China, Korea, Japan)

K

KADJARI
See Kunapipi

KAG BALI, KALI CHAUDAS
See Divali

KALENDS OF JANUARY
See Saturnalia

KALI PUJA
See Navaratra and Dusshera

KALLIGENEIA
See Thesmophoria

KALWADI
See Kunapipi

KAMA-MAHOTSAVA, KAMANA PANDUGA, KAMAN VILA
See Holi

KAMUI OMANTE
See Bear Festival

KANTO
See Sekku

KARNEIA
See Carneia

KARNEVAL
See Carnival

KARWADI
See Kunapipi

KASUGA FESTIVALS (JAPAN)

On March 13 in Nara, a ceremony is held that is said to have remained unchanged since the ninth century, when Kyoto replaced that city as capital of Japan. According to the imperial court calendar of **annual events** (*nenchu gyoji*), it then took place on the Second Day of the Monkey of the second lunar month, at the Kasuga Shrine, which has given its name to a certain type of Shinto shrines.

Acknowledging the Power Behind the Throne

Located in the midst of an old forest famous for its deer, the original Kasuga Shrine is dedicated to the god of the Fujiwara clan of statesmen, which was in those days becoming ever more closely allied to the throne, even by marriage—so much so that an imperial messenger would come to make offerings to this family shrine on the monarch's behalf. The Fujiwara clan continued to provide Japan with all-powerful regents and classic writers until the twelfth century, when gradual encroachments on its lands by neighboring warrior families ate away at its power base. The **Kasuga Festival** proper is now mostly known for the ritual dance called *yamato-mai*, performed by eight young girls holding evergreen branches.

Revival and Pageantry around a Branch Shrine

The decline of the clan did not prevent a syncretic salvation cult involving the Buddhist and Shinto gods of the Kasuga shrines from reaching its height between the twelfth and fourteenth centuries. That was largely due to the fact that, at the twilight of its glory, the illustrious clan had been able to launch yet another festival, also observed to this day at a branch of Nara's Kasuga Shrine: the Wakamiya Shrine dedicated to the clan founder's eldest son. His spirit, symbolically held within layers of white silk cloth, is ceremonially taken to this tiny subsidiary shrine by Shinto priests late on the night of December 16. The next morning, performers form a parade to pass through the main Kasuga Shrine's huge *torii* gate on their way to a stage in front of an ancient pine, which is also depicted on its backdrop. This day is mostly devoted to a program of dances, featuring Okina dances and Dengaku pogo-stick dancing. Like sword juggling, the latter is a remnant of a form of circus entertainment brought over from China and called *sangaku* in Japan. These performances would go well into the night and were meant as an offering to the deity.

Nowadays, the **Kasuga** Wakamiya Grand **Festival** is celebrated on December 15–18. There are still performances of Japanese classical music and Noh theater, following a procession of people dressed as courtiers and warriors of the period.

The Kasuga Grand Shrine holds an **On-Matsuri** Festival every year. The highlight is a gala procession of people masquerading as courtiers, retainers, and wrestlers of these distant medieval times.

See also Matsuri New Year (Japan)
References
Hideo Haga. *Japanese Festivals.* Tr. Don Kenny. Osaka, Japan: Hoikusha's Color Books Series, 1981.
Ivan Morris. *The World of the Shining Prince. Court Life in Ancient Japan.* New York: Knopf, 1964.
Susan C. Tyler. *The Cult of Kasuga Seen Through Its Art.* Ann Arbor, MI: University of Michigan Center for Japanese Studies, Michigan Monographs in Japanese Studies, 1992.

KATCHINA FESTIVALS
See Shalako

KATHINA (BUDDHISM)

In Asian countries where the ancient Theravada tradition of Buddhism prevails, an annual retreat (*vassa*) is observed by monks during the rainy season on the recommendation of the Buddha, during which time they instruct lay followers in his doctrine of awakening, called the *Dhamma* (the Pali form of the Sanskrit word *Dharma* more generally used elsewhere in the world). It starts in June or July on the full moon of the month of Asalha and ends three months later in October, after the full-moon *posadha* (the monks' bimonthly general confession to their peers), with a festival known as **Kathina**—after the ceremonial robe that is offered to the monks among other gifts such as food, fabrics, and clothing, in a lively procession of the people. For the laity, this is one of the best opportunities to earn spiritual merit through acts of generosity (*dana*).

The Festive Close of a Buddhist Lent

A common feature of **Kathina** is the illumination of all sacred places, and even of private homes and public buildings, for as long as three consecutive nights. Since this feast closes three months of **Lent**en abstinence and privation to honor the Buddha, along with the monks during their retreat, the general population of a country like Laos comes out in droves and fills every city's streets, tearooms, and fairgrounds. At night, people from the four districts of the former royal capital Luang Prabang march in a parade around their respective candlelit floats, made of rice paper mounted on bamboo sticks. In the current capital Vientiane, regattas are held on the Mekong River between pirogues propelled by fifty oarsmen each.

The Five Buddhas of Lake Inle

On Burma's Lake Inle, the crews of native "Sons of the Lake," or Intha, are also fifty strong, but they stand upright on their long, ultraslim craft as they use their legs to hold the oars in a competition for cash, clothing, and silver prizes, amid generalized—if illegal—betting on the outcome. Prior to the races, the same boats tow an ornamental barge featuring a gigantic gilded prow figure of the mythical *karaweik* bird, emblem of Burma's former royalty. It is the centerpiece of a spectacular boat procession in this part of the land through which the "Way of the Elders"—called *Theravada* in the Pali language (close to Sanskrit) of the Buddhist canon in South India—spread from its early stronghold on the island of Sri Lanka to Thailand, Cambodia, and Laos. This event may serve as a fine example of the kind of popular piety and colorful folklore surrounding the close of the monks' yearly retreat in a Southern Buddhist nation such as Burma.

The **Kathina** festival of Phaung Daw U Temple lasts about eighteen days, from the new moon of the Burmese month going from mid-September to mid-October to the third day of the waning moon. Its main focus consists in five foot-high wooden statues that can no longer be identified as this or that Buddha or disciple under the countless layers of gold-leaf annually laid on them by worshippers; some have grown quite abstract in the process, like

bulging butter balls. If entire families come to prostrate before them while they are on display, because female beings are thought of as ritually impure, only men may touch them to apply gold leaf—as is also the practice at Kyaik-tiyo, the famous hanging rock held on the edge of a cliff by a hair of the Buddha in Thaton, 150 kilometers southeast of Rangoon. Yet according to legend, it is a female ogre who found the wood in which the statues were carved and offered it to Alaungsithu, third king of Pagan, around 1120. She did this out of gratitude for the Dharmic monarch's miraculous rescue of her little one, whom she had dropped in the water, transfixed as she was by the appearance of the king on his barge on Lake Inle while he was touring his kingdom with his retinue of wives, ministers, and generals. Thagyamin, king of the Nat protecting spirits, sculpted the five statues out of the odorous wood, so as to benefit all beings by spreading Buddhism. The human king then put them on the prow of his barge and took them to the foot of a mountain. Though it is more likely that he brought the sculptures from Malaya, the name of the temple now housing them is said to refer to these legendary occurrences: *Phaung* as the barge, *Daw* in honor of kings and monks, *U* for the prow.

Thagyamin had set relics in his sculptures, and they behaved accordingly—with awe-inspiring unpredictability. In most cases, a Buddhist reliquary is put on the back on an elephant that is then released into the jungle, and a temple to house it is built wherever the animal stops. In this case though, the statues were set on two rafts—since the fifth one did not fit with the others on just one raft. This Buddha went on beyond the first raft and was finally given to a village monastery, while the other four were only found in 1359 in a cave near Nyaungshwe, north of Lake Inle, by a local chieftain of the Shan hill people. All five Buddhas were only reunited in 1615 in a specially built temple, which burned down in 1771. The same thing happened in 1951 to the temple

Festival raft with bird on prow, Inle Lake, Burma, 1986. (Christophe Loviny/Corbis)

they had finally come to in Nanhu in 1881 after decades of moving around, but it was soon rebuilt more solidly.

Peril came from another direction in 1965 in the guise of a violent storm that hit the ceremonial barge carrying the four statues for **Kathina**, making them fall into the lake, though they were fortunately recovered in less than an hour. It had been after a series of similar misadventures that people finally gave up trying to bring along the fifth statue. In the strangest one, the barge sank in a storm, and only four statues could be found at the bottom of the lake, despite the gold covering that should also have signaled the fifth. As concern was growing that it was actually lost, somebody spotted it in its usual place in the temple—covered with mud and algae. It finally had to be admitted that the fifth Buddha—ever independent-

minded—just did not care to join the others in their procession.

So, over a couple of weeks, only four statues—shaded by four white parasols with the Buddhist flag flying and a soldier on ceremonial guard—are taken through this lake country of ethnic Mon on a nineteen-stop itinerary of villages and temples by a bird-shaped silver coach overland and by a bird-shaped golden barge on water, before joining up again with the fifth statue in Phaung Daw U Temple across the lake from Nyaungshwe. To commemorate their first journey on King Alaungsithu's barge, they are taken down the narrow channel, surrounded by a flotilla of canoes holding monks, notables, mountain people, women wearing their best *longyi* skirts around their waists, maidens singing from *sutta* scriptures (or *sutras* in Sanskrit) lying open on their laps as they kneel in rows, not to mention heaps of fruit and flower offerings.

The station at Inthein is the occasion for a local fair and bazaar, full of attractions and bargains that bring down tribesmen from the surrounding mountains. There, as elsewhere, the statues are taken off the barge one by one to a chariot waiting under a portal decorated with flowers and streamers. It will slowly take them up to the temple, to be covered with gold leaf by the same crowd that presses against this vehicle to the point of appearing to lift it, showering the Buddhas with rice to the accompaniment of gongs and strident reed instruments. But at the last stop of the year in Nyaungshwe, the people are called upon to actually pull the silver coach themselves: lined up along two long ropes, they slowly progress on a petal-strewn road to the shrine for the culmination of this festival of Buddhist devotion.

See also Lent; Vaishakha and Vaisakhi

References

Alan Houghton Brodrick. *Little Vehicle: Cambodia and Laos.* London: Hutchinson, 1949.

Manning Nash. "Ritual and Ceremonial Cycle in Upper Burma." in Manning Nash et al., *Anthropological Studies in Theravada Buddhism.* New Haven, CT: Yale University Press, 1966.

John Powers. *A Concise Encyclopedia of Buddhism.* Oxford, UK: Oneworld Publications, 2000.

KATHODOS

See Thesmophoria

KÄYRI, KEKRI

See Samhain

KENPO KINEN HI

See Cherry Blossom Festival

KERMIS (CHRISTIANITY)

In the Low Countries, the annual commemoration of a church's consecration and dedication to a particular saint on his or her feast day is called a **kermis**, from the Dutch words *kerk* for "church" and *mis* for "mass." It is also the occasion for a usually weeklong outdoor fair with folk entertainment—or fairground attractions nowadays.

"Let the Peasants Have Their Kermis!"

Among the first depictions of the life of common people for its own sake in Western art, **kermis** pictures began being made by German printmakers around 1530, when the Flemish painter Pieter Bruegel the Elder was born. He would follow their example in making the **kermis** a favorite subject of his paintings and engravings. He portrayed in loving detail the peasants' boisterous merrymaking with folk dancing, games and plays, drinking, eating, and love-making, right next to the sparsely attended church flying its patron saint's flag on his or her feast day. On such **kermis** images, the following legend often appeared—on the flag of an inn for instance: "Let the peasants have their **kermis**!" This may have been the slogan of a protest against an edict by Holy Roman Emperor Charles V (1500–1558) limiting the **kermis** to a single day on account of the notorious drunken excesses associated with it—leading to sometimes fatal scuffles.

From Religious Feast to Secular Fair

In the Middle Ages, in the Low Countries as in much of Europe, merchants had soon begun to take advantage of such religious holidays as a **kermis** to temporarily set up shop on church grounds and sell their wares to the crowds of prospective customers temporarily gathered in one spot. It was not long before commerce overtook religion as the main attraction at these fairs—a secularization process furthered in the Netherlands by the Protestant Reformation and its banning of the cult of saints. Yet profane entertainment continued unabated at the annual, or even biannual, **kermis** held over

Kermesse by David Teniers the Younger (1610–1690), Pushkin Museum of Fine Arts, Moscow. (Scala/Art Resource)

a week, or up to three weeks, in every Dutch town or village of any significance. Until around 1660, the most honored among **kermis** performers were the *rederijkers,* or rhetoricians. The *rederijker* society of one town would invite its counterpart in another town to its own **kermis**. The *rederijker* chambers from all the Low Countries (at least before the independence wars with Spain split the rebel North from the loyal South) used to gather in a different city each year for a contest called the *landjuweel,* or "land's jewel," instituted by Philip the Good, Duke of Burgundy (1419–1467). Among the best-loved oratorical performances, both there or at a **kermis**, were comic morality plays known as *sotties* and seemingly derived from the **Yule-tide Feast of Fools**, where actors played the fools before finishing their satirical or nonsense skits with music, song, and dance.

See also Feast of Fools; Lent; Pardon

References

Svetlana Leontief Alpers. "Bruegel's Festive Peasants," in *Simiolus—Netherlands Quarterly for the History of Art,* Vol. VI, Nos. 3 and 4 (1972–1973), pp. 163–176.

———. "Realism as a Comic Mode: Low-Life Painting Seen Through Bredero's Eyes," in *Simiolus—Netherlands Quarterly for the History of Art,* Vol. VIII, No. 3 (1975–1976), pp. 115–144.

Paul Zumthor. *Daily Life in Rembrandt's Holland.* Tr. Simon Watson Taylor. Stanford, CA: Stanford University Press, 1994.

▶ KHITROI

See Dionysia

▶ KHOIAK AND HEB-SED (EGYPT)

From the twelfth to the thirtieth day of the month of **Khoiak** (the fourth and last month—falling around November—of the season of Flood, or Akhet), as the waters of the Nile receded to expose silt-covered fields fresh for sowing, certain rites of the ancient Egyptian mystery cult of the murdered man-god Osiris celebrated him in his triple aspect: as dead—under the name of Khenti-Amentiu (Ancient Egyptian for "first of the Westerners"—that is, "chief of the departed" into the sunset); as dismembered—under the name of Osiris-Sep; and as reconstituted by the union of his scattered limbs—under the name of Sokaris. The next day was the winter **New Year** and would be marked after thirty years of a Pharaoh's reign by the ancient **Heb-Sed** jubilee festival in honor of Sokaris and his son Horus.

The Cult of Osiris in Ancient Egypt

The month of **Khoiak** was named by early Christian Copts after an eighteen-day sequence of festivals that had previously used to be celebrated at all the main Osiris temples in Egypt, to commemorate various episodes of the life, death, and resurrection of the god. They are best known from the account provided by the Greek historian Plutarch (who lived from about 46 until after 119 of our era) in his book *On Isis and Osiris*. By then, there was a central shrine of Osiris in each of the forty-two nomes, or regions, of Egypt. It was called a *Serapeum*, or the place where Serapis was worshipped, because Osiris Khenti-Amentiu was identified with Serapis, a dead Apis bull god immortalized as an Osiris. The variety of such aspects under which Osiris was worshipped goes to show to what extent the original attributes of the god had become blurred over time as he absorbed a number of local deities, so that he came to be identified with the sun, the moon, the air or sky, the Nile, or with any kind of life-force manifesting the mysterious power of spontaneous self-renewal of which he was the ultimate source. (This is conveyed in the original Ancient Egyptian form of the comparatively late Coptic word *Khoiak*: (*ka-her-ka*, meaning "sustenance-upon-sustenance.") This evolution eventually allowed him to become the focus of a mystery religion of personal salvation through initiation in divine life. At base though, common views of Osiris were still largely the same as those current when the Pyramid Texts, found in the tombs of Old Kingdom rulers from the middle of the third millennium B.C.E., were meant to ensure with magical incantations their immortality through identification with Osiris. Such beliefs and practices probably had their roots as far back as prehistoric times.

A much later inscription from the Ptolemaic period (between Alexander's conquest and that of Augustus) describes the funeral rites of Osiris, as they were observed in **Khoiak** at his great festival in sixteen shrines, each of them the reputed burial site of one of the sixteen members of the body of Osiris (other counts for these body parts and the corresponding reliquaries range from fourteen to forty-two—one for the Serapeum of every nome): his head, the souls of his feet, his bones, his arms, his heart, his innards, his tongue, his eye, his fist, his fingers, his back, his ears, his loins, his trunk, his (ram-faced) head, and his hair. The finding of each body part was celebrated on its own day of the festival. Engraved on the walls of the god's temple at Dendara some sixty kilometers north of Thebes, this text also contains alternate counts of fourteen members and towns, and indications of the variations in local usage between many of them, as well as detailed instructions about the materials to be employed in the rituals. Among them were sixteen amulets: four figures of the children of Horus, one of Horus himself, one of Thoth, two bulls, two lapis lazuli utchats (the famous "Eye of Ra"

The Serapeum at Saqqarah, Egypt, is a tomb for the holy Apis bulls, which Egyptians believed were manifestations of Osiris, god of life after death. (Roger Wood/Corbis)

or "Eye of Horus" design), and six pillars—four of lapis lazuli, two in carnelian—shaped like the hieroglyph *Tet* or *Dad* for Osiris.

Agricultural Rites

On the twelfth day of **Khoiak**, ceremonies began with the **Festival of the Ploughing of the Earth**—with a black copper plowshare harnessed to two black cows by a tamarisk yoke. The chief celebrant recited the ritual chapter on the "Sowing of the Fields" while a boy scattered the seed: barley on one end of the field, flax in the middle, and spelt (an archaic variety of wheat) on the other end. There followed on the fourteenth the **Great Festival of Peret**—meaning "germination"; this was the name of the second of three seasons in the agricultural calendar, about to begin with the winter **New Year** upon the festival's end as that of the "Flood" season of Akhet.

The sixteenth of **Khoiak** was the **Festival of Osiris Khenti-Amentiu**. The dead Osiris was thus named after the local jackal god of Abydos in the lower desert, whose cult he had gradually absorbed into his own at the reputed site of his main tomb, held to contain his head. Abydos

was perhaps only rivaled by Busiris, capital of the ninth nome in the Nile Delta, as a "holy place of the cult of Osiris," since this phrase for any shrine of the god, *P-usiri*, gave its name to the city where his cult may have originated in prehistoric times in that of the local god Andjty, so that he was known as "the One who dwells in Andjet," as Busiris was also called. This was one place where, by the twentieth of **Khoiak**, sand and barley were put in the god's "garden"—some kind of large flowerpot (much like the pot of basil or corn derived from the ancient "gardens of Adonis" in the **Midsummer** folklore of southern Italy)—in the presence of a gilded sycamore statue of the cow goddess Shenty containing a headless human figure. From then on, fresh floodwater was poured from a golden vase onto both the goddess and the "garden." This caused the barley to grow over the ensuing weeks—as a tangible equivalent of the resurrection of Osiris after his burial in the earth, manifesting the same spontaneous and unfathomable divine power of self-renewal. At his great shrines like Dendara and its Sacred Lake, at the eighth hour on the twenty-second of **Khoiak**, the images of Osiris and many other gods were made to carry out a mysterious symbolic journey in thirty-four tiny papyrus boats illuminated by 365 lights, which took until the twenty-fourth of **Khoiak**.

Fashioning a Dead God

By that day, a half-meter-tall image of the god was fashioned in sand or top soil with an assortment of grain and some water, to which incense and finely ground precious stones were sometimes added—as they were to the sacred tar-based ointment prepared concurrently for the anointment of idols over the coming year. The image of Osiris was cast in a mold of pure gold, representing the god in the form of a mummy, with the white crown of Upper Egypt on his head—corresponding to the underworld. His face was painted yellow and his cheekbones green, and he may well have had, as in two paintings on the walls of his inner sanctum at Abydos, an erect phallus, to display his power to rise up from death with overflowing, self-renewing vitality (just like the obscene Adonis that was often depicted on Italian **Midsummer** pots of corn). This molding was the task of the "lord of the mystery"—an initiate acting out that of the god's life-giving death, so that it was no mere mortal, but Osiris himself, who gave shape to his own image in the secrecy of a portable chapel called the "room of the bed" in the temple workshop and inner sanctum, itself known as the "Duat House" after a common name for the land of the dead. This part of a shrine was also associated with the king's *ka*—his spiritual double, whose vital link with the body was loosened by death but carefully maintained through appropriate funerary rites such as mummification. Given a body in this effigy that was only outwardly manmade, once it had been exposed to the sun on a golden pedestal and aspersed with sacred water and frankincense for a few days, Osiris received just such a royal burial.

Sky Burial

The first meaning of *Duat* is actually the night sky, which is depicted on the star-studded inside of the god's coffin, known both as *ift sheta,* "mystery chest," and *itrty,* "chest of the two parts of the world," which to the Egyptians meant the north and south of the kingdom, corresponding respectively to heaven and earth. Detailed instructions are given for the making of this funeral chest, modeled on the one that had carried the god down the Nile to the papyrus swamps in its Delta. There, it had landed among the branches of a willow tree, which had grown to the point of enclosing it within its trunk. The local king was struck by this majestic tree and had it cut down to make a pillar for the roof of his house. It is this tree-trunk which is referred to by the hieroglyphic sign *tet* often used for Osiris in Egyptian texts. His wife Isis managed to cut the chest out of the tree and

take it back to Upper Egypt. But his murderer Seth stumbled upon it and was able to cut the god's body into fourteen or sixteen pieces, which he scattered across the land to prevent Osiris from being revived. (To punish Seth, the ass included as a magic substitute for him in the funeral procession of Osiris—initially as Sokaris on a sacred *mefekh* sled taken around the walls of the old capital Memphis where the custom is first recorded for the twenty-sixth of **Khoiak**—was bludgeoned before being put to death by the Pharaoh himself.) Undaunted, Isis then used a papyrus boat to go and collect all the pieces in order to give them a proper burial; her prayers and those of her sister Nephthys, wife of Seth, to the gods Rê, Thoth, and Anubis, allowed her husband Osiris to live forever in the beyond as the benevolent god and king he had been on earth. In older texts, the role of Isis is interchangeably given to the sky goddess Nut, depicted as a starry dark woman stretching over an earth god lying on his back, just like the coffin's cover over Osiris—as a dead vegetation god for Sir James George Frazer (1854–1941) or a symbol of "the concealment and disappearance of water" for Plutarch (*De Iside et Osiride* 366D, 20, p. 179).

It was likewise after nightfall that the mulberry wood coffin was buried. At the ninth hour of the night of the twenty-fourth, the dried-up effigy that was made the previous year would be removed from its own tomb, refreshed, adorned, placed on sycamore boughs, and carried by four men standing for the four sons of Horus to a secret corner of the necropolis for its final reburial, before the newly embalmed effigy was also laid on sycamore boughs for its own "sky burial" above ground. On this occasion, as Plutarch explains (*De Iside et Osiride* 366E, 1–6, p. 181), "the things mourned for are four: first, the dwindling and receding of the Nile; secondly, the cessation of the north winds through the complete domination of the south winds; thirdly, the day's getting shorter than the night; and above all the denudation of the earth together with the stripping of the plants which at this time lose their leaves." For on the "divine morning" of the twenty-fifth of **Khoiak**, the approaching solstice (at least in early times when the unadjusted and gradually advancing official calendar was devised) marked the lowest ebb of the Nile's water as well as of the sun's light (so that Sokaris was called "Little Sun"), without which all plants withered in the dry desert wind of the Egyptian winter.

Earth Burial

According to the Dendara text, the god would lay in state—his body slowly sprouting shoots (hence his usual depiction with green skin in a white shroud as well as the homemade versions of this "vegetating Osiris" peasants would make from the Nile's silt and some corn if the river's flooding had produced enough)—during the remaining week of the year, until a new spring began, that is for "the seven days of Osiris' stay in the womb of his mother Nut, when she was pregnant with him. A day stands for a month: the sycamore boughs represent Nut" (Kristensen 1961, p. 168). Then the coffin would be taken from this "above-grave," or "above-Duat," in "above-Busiris" for its "earth burial" in the underground "below-Duat." This might be a grave freshly dug under a sacred *ashd* tree as part of the "great mystery of the ploughing of the earth" celebrated on the first day with the slaughter of sacrificial animals. Such were perhaps the ox and ass herds with which the Pharaoh and his people are depicted circling the walls of Memphis on a tomb at Kheryaf near Thebes. "Below-Duat" could also be a permanent subterranean stone chamber under a grove of these *Persea* trees such as was found at all sites where parts of Osiris's body were said to be buried, also holding his *ba*, or spiritual personality, in the afterlife. This replica of the underworld would have seven doors—since it had seven gods, and like the sun in its journey under the horizon from sunset to sunrise, the

pallbearers would enter it through the western door and come out through the eastern door, having reverently laid the dead god on a bed of sand. On this thirtieth and last day of the month when the divine members of Osiris were brought, his *Tet* or *Djed* pillar was raised—hidden under a cloth as depicted in the inner sanctum of Abydos: with the large royal family, helped by a priest, pulling the ropes as shown at Kheryaf, to make the pillar stand for the god's burial among the dead and his arising in eternal life, since it is connected to the backbone of Osiris and of any deceased person in Chapter 155 of the Egyptian Books of the Afterlife. Some also liken it to the nilometers used to detect and measure signs of flooding, while it also clearly symbolizes the stability, continuity, and harmonious order of a divine cosmos.

Victory Over Death

This victory of life over death and of light over darkness, sometimes assimilated to the sun god Rê's killing of Apap (the snake of chaotic primordial waters—enemy of light and order) under the *ashd* tree in the eastern sky, was then represented as the revenge of Osiris over his enemies, through ritual drama—often taking the form of an archaic funerary contest. The climax of the mystery plays at Abydos took place by the river, when the crowds assembled to witness them at this earliest known pilgrimage site cheered the return of the resurrected Osiris to his temple in the kind of ceremonial boat known as *wetes neferu* ("which holds up the beauty" of a god like the throne of his resurrection and its very power), guided by the statue of the jackal god Upuaut as demon-chaser and psychopomp, or leader of souls to the afterlife. The abovementioned Theban grave from the fifteenth century B.C.E. shows a reenactment of the cosmic struggle of Osiris by fifteen men in teams, going through the motions with sticks and their bare fists. A thousand years earlier, a text relates how the gods—played by such stand-ins—hurry over to Osiris to fight for him and win him eternal life. According to the Egyptian Books of the Afterlife, it is precisely when his *Tet* pillar is raised that Osiris becomes *ma-kheru*, "blessed after death," as opposed to his hapless enemies. From around 1600 B.C.E., the "wreath of he who has been declared just over against his enemies," like the wreath laid on mummies for the afterlife, was woven from leaves of the sacred *ashd* tree growing over the grave of Osiris (or even holding his coffin like the *Tet* or *Djed* in some accounts), and given to participants in the feast in a victory ceremony. For there would be no such funerary combat over their own graves; to them, victory over death was wholly a function of their partaking of the god's own timeless victory through the mystery of this feast of resurrection. That is why, at the conclusion of this pilgrimage the Egyptians simply called the **Festival of Osiris**, before leaving Abydos to return home, they would give votive offerings in gratitude to the god who gave them a new lease on life beyond death, like a miniature model of his *henu* processional boat. Such were also the majestic temples built on this site by Pharaoh Sety I and his son Ramses II in the thirteenth century B.C.E. And yet, this was a time when the once vital pilgrimage was increasingly becoming optional, as its depiction on the walls of tombs could be given the same efficacy as the act itself with the proper charms and magic formulas, allowing the virtual representation to gradually displace the actual performance of this religious duty.

A common Egyptian tombstone inscription was: "May I be among the retinue of Osiris-Sokaris on his great festival"—the **Night of Onions**, or *Netjeryt* (likely meaning "making divine"). First dedicated to Sokaris as the local god of Memphis when it was the capital of the Old Kingdom in the third millennium B.C.E.— during which he became assimilated to Osiris, this festival kept on being celebrated on the twenty-sixth as it then spread throughout the land. In Thebes when it was the capital of the New Kingdom of the second half of the second millennium B.C.E., such tombstone inscriptions often mention "tying onion collars during the divine night" before that morning, in order to then "follow Sokaris with onions around the neck" or in wreaths. The onions were to be offered to this solar falcon god as his earthly, snake-repellent fertility symbols, as well as to departed relatives in connection with a festive memorial version (with family members and friends playing the parts of the various deities involved) of the funerary Ritual of the Opening of the Mouth—opening access to the afterlife in keeping with the distinctive original functions of Sokaris, and purifying the mouth of the deceased with onions, viewed as a new set of white teeth (like those of the child Horus born of dead Osiris) that brightened their faces and allowed them to regain their senses. According to the Book of *Am Duat* (after which the whole collection of Books of the Afterlife is named), the third hour of the night—devoted to the dead Osiris Khenti-Amentiu like the sixteenth of **Khoiak**—was the "fighting ground" of the god's champions against his enemies, where he could be joined after death by his devotees as "mysterious souls." For the time and place of the god's murder and revenge were then one—and the same as those of his victory over death, to be shared in by the mortals who ritually went through it. Similarly, Christians have their own pillar of victory in the Cross on which their god was executed—going through the underworld only to rise again after three days so as to give them access to his own divine life through the mystery of **Easter**.

The mysteries of Osiris too brought divine blessings in this life as well as the next. But in view of the latter, just as Christians from late Antiquity to the high Middle Ages sought to be buried *ad sanctos*—next to the saints who were known to be already deified, in the hope of being carried along by their spiritual energies into the resurrected life, ancient Egyptians also tried their best to be buried as close as possible to the recognized tomb of Osiris in Abydos. They would be taken to their own tomb nearby in the same *Neshemt* boat as Osiris, as it was supposed to fight for them the same good fight against the dark powers of chaos and death that was already won for him beyond time. Thousands of stelae were also set up there by those who could not afford this burial fit for a god. They are inscribed with the name of the departed and a prayer to the god. But grain-stuffed figures of Osiris have been found in graves throughout Egypt, "bandaged like mummies with patches of gilding here and there, as if in imitation of the golden mold in which the similar figures of Osiris were cast at the festival of sowing" that Sir James George Frazer mostly saw in the mysteries of **Khoiak** (Frazer 1935, p. 91). However, it now seems these figures and their agricultural symbolism are probably later additions to the royal myth of Osiris as slain by his rival sibling to become judge of the dead and immortal king of the netherworld.

Heb-Sed: A New Year Coronation Festival

As for the living, in the person of the pharaoh, they were ruled by Horus himself as the son, alter ego, and eternal avenger of Osiris. After thirty years of rule and every three years thereafter, the divine monarch was entitled to take this occasion to secure at once his harmony with the cosmos, the unity of his kingdom, his long reign, healthy life, and glorious afterlife as an Osiris, in the **Heb-Sed** jubilee festival held just after the god's eternal life had been reactivated as that of nature with the raising of his pillar on the last day of **Khoiak**. This was also a good opportunity for pharaohs to raise new obelisks—quadrangular pillars tipped with a golden *pyramidion* to recall the stone on which the sun god Rê alighted after first rising at the mythical time of origins.

On this first day after the solstice (initially at least), days grew longer and plants were already sprouting as spring began with the winter **New Year** in the "season of coming out," or Peret,

when Egyptians, rarely more than once or twice in a lifetime, might have the privilege to witness this grandest and oldest of festivals. Like all others, it started and ended with an imposing procession. Sculptors would have reproduced the shrines of the local deities of all the land to show the extent of the king's authority on behalf of Osiris. As the Pharaoh renewed his ties with the gods, his officials and the country's nobles renewed their allegiance to him in the course of ancient ceremonies that reenacted both his own coronation and the unification of Egypt as a kingdom by Menes in Memphis 5,000 years ago. A Pharaoh might also take this opportunity to enact new annual state endowments to various temples and their clergy. In later times, as a way to reassert Egypt's claim to rule all corners of the world, the Pharaoh, acting out the part of Horus in his father's battles, would shoot four arrows to the four directions as a way to frighten off evil powers. Many centuries after the final passing of this ancient empire, halfway around the world, a similar purification ceremony called *Tsuina* would also play a role in **New Year** customs at Japan's Imperial Court.

See also Beautiful Festival of the Valley; Christmas; Easter; Eleusinian Mysteries; Epiphany; Games (Rome); Midsummer; New Year (Japan); Spring Festival of Cybele and Attis; Thesmophoria

References

E. A. Wallis Budge. *Osiris and the Egyptian Resurrection.* New York: Dover Publications, 1973.

Émile Chassinat. *Le Mystère d'Osiris au mois de Khoïak.* Cairo: Institut français d'Afrique orientale, 1966–68.

Sir James George Frazer. *The Golden Bough. A Study in Magic and Religion. Part IV: Adonis Attis Osiris. Studies in the History of Oriental Religion.* Vol. II. 3rd ed. New York: Macmillan, 1935.

Wolfram Grajetzki and Stephen Quirke. "The Festivals of Khoiak" webpage of *Digital Egypt*

for *Universities* (www.digitalegypt.ucl.ac.uk/
ideology/Khoiak.html). London: University
College, 2003.

E. O. James. *Myth and Ritual in the Ancient Near
East: An Archaeological and Documentary Study*.
London: Thames and Hudson, 1958.

W. Brede Kristensen. *Symbool en werkelijkheid:
Godsdiensthistorische studiën*. Zeist,
Netherlands: W. De Haan and Arnhem,
Netherlands: Van Loghum Slaterus, 1961.

Plutarch's De Iside et Osiride. Tr. J. Gwyn Griffiths.
Cardiff: University of Wales Press, 1970.

▶ KI.LAM (HITTITES)

One of the most accurately reconstructed festivals of the Hittite Empire, which ruled over
much of Anatolia (in the Asian part of present-
day Turkey) and beyond between 1700 and
1200 B.C.E., is known only by its cuneiform logogram KI.LAM.

Character and Timing

The title of the main document devoted to the
KI.LAM festival characterizes it as the one
"When the king takes his seat three times in
the gate-house." This has been interpreted as
evidence that its name means the "**Festival of
the Gate-House**," and that it lasted three days.
In relative brevity, it compares to the three-day
long **Festival of the Month** and two-day-long
Festival of the Great House, in contrast to the
twenty-one-day **Nuntariyashas** harvest festival, the thirty-eight-day **Hameshandas** (also
known by its word-picture, or logogram,
AN.TAH.ŠUM^{SAR}) spring festival of the **New
Year**, or the long **Purulli** festival of the Hattian
weather-god of Nerik in honor of his slaying of
a dragon as the supposed cause of springtime
renewal—a seasonal ritual which took thirty-
two tablets to describe.

On each of the three days of KI.LAM, a royal
procession would stop at the gates of various
buildings of the Hittite capital Hattuša, in particular those of the royal storehouses of sup-

plies from subject cities, with their respective
"overseers" (a term phonetically pronounced
abarakku for the logogram AGRIG) standing in
front of them to pay homage to the king. (They
also provided wine and beer for the celebrations.) The point of the festival may well have
been precisely to reaffirm the bond between
such public officials–and possibly the people at
large—and their sovereign, and a fall date after
the harvest would have been a good time to do
this, while the storehouses were full. On the
other hand, the omission of certain common
features of the three-day ceremony on its second day may have been due to the need to
squeeze into the proceedings an extra festival in
honor of the grain goddess Halki, as mentioned
in an oracle text. Her temple was also visited
during the AN.TAH.ŠUM^{SAR} festival, which
makes it possible that KI.LAM had a spring
date. It may even have been held on both dates:
once in the fall as the "regular" KI.LAM festival
described in one incomplete series of tablets,
and again as the "great festival" evoked in the
other one devoted to it, which might have been
abridged on the second day to incorporate a
spring festival for Halki.

Distinctive Features

On the other two "standard" days of KI.LAM,
the king, after preparing himself in the palace
and being presented a ceremonial iron spear
by the foreman of the smiths, would leave
through the palace gate. So-called "comedians" greeted him at the gate of the queen's
treasurer. They provided musical entertainment as he sat on some sort of ceremonial
stand to review the procession of the "masters
of the words," or wizard-priests, and the "animals of the gods" (ritual standards including
golden lions, silver leopards, wolves, bears and
boars—some of the latter in lapis lazuli instead), preceded by "spears" and "copper
fleeces" and followed by "dog-men," gold and
silver "stags," and unidentified ivory objects.
This "animal" procession of cult images marks

off **KI.LAM** from most other Hittite festivals. So does the ceremony of the AGRIG's that follows it in the vicinity of the gate of the temple of the grain goddess (the probable "gate-house" of this festival's name) after the king and queen have been driven there in their respective chariots. Introduced by a herald with the native Hattic name of the town for which he was responsible, each AGRIG would offer to the king some produce brought over from its storehouse in the capital.

The Great Assembly

The ritual proceeds with the offering ceremonies customary at Hittite festivals and takes place first at the temples of various deities inside the city and then outside of town at the "Great Assembly" (*šalli ašeššar*) in a "ceremonial tent" near the *huwaši*—of the weather-god—possibly the rock sanctuary at Yazilikaya near present-day Bogazköy where the ruins of Hattuša are to be found. Over forty different deities—mostly Hattian—were worshipped there "sitting," except for the deified "Day," the weather god, who was bowed to by the king, and the sun goddess, who was not. This was done by "drinking to" them, to the accompaniment of music, dance, and recitations in Hattic, with unknown ceremonies in between these "toasts," and wine and bread offerings afterwards. Then incense from the royal mausoleum (literally: the god's "stone house") was burned before the king. This meant it was time for one ceremony of the "Great Assembly" that has often been discussed: the foot race of the ten runners—one of them naked—who had earlier figured in the procession (separated from the royal chariots ahead by ceremonial oxen carts and from the "animals of the gods" behind by the priests of KAL, god of hunting). According to the longer Old Hittite account of the race, "the runner who wins takes from the hand of the king two *wagada*-breads and one mina of silver," while a later version says both the winner and the runner-up receive a tunic—a much

less impressive prize. This has prompted the expert on **KI.LAM** to ask: "Might this not have value to scholars of the history of sports?" (Singer 1983, p. 104).

It was the runners who brought in a large gold or silver vessel called *kalti*, or *galdi*, to place it by the throne, where it was filled by the "wine-suppliers." After taking a sip from it, a "comedian" said a Hattic recitation and handed it over to the king, who poured wine into the hands of the assembled dignitaries of the imperial administration's upper echelon. Low officials, high officials, princes and princesses, SANGA-priests, and the king himself would then leave the tent in that order, the reverse of that in which they had entered. The royal couple went by a number of city gates again before disappearing through that of their palace. If the standard celebrations in honor of a long list of gods were carried out on the second day as on the first and third, it is precisely those features of **KI.LAM** that were of a less solemn, more "secular" nature that appear to have been dropped: at least the "animal" part of the procession, the giving of a "ceremonial dress" to the "dignified dog-men" in it, the singers, the runners, and the ceremony of the *kalti* libation vessel.

References

Oliver Robert Gurney. *Some Aspects of Hittite Religion.* Oxford, UK: Oxford University Press for the British Academy, 1977.

Hans G. Güterbock. "Some Aspects of Hittite Festivals," in André Finet, ed., *Actes de la XVIIe Rencontre assyriologique internationale.* Ham-sur-Heure, Belgium: Comité belge de recherches historiques, épigraphiques et archéologiques en Mésopotamie, 1970, pp. 160–170.

Itamar Singer. *The Hittite KI.LAM Festival.* Wiesbaden, Germany: Otto Harrassowitz, "Studien zu den Bogazköy-Texten, Heft 27," 1983.

▶ KNEELING SUNDAY

See Whitsuntide

▶ KNUT

See Epiphany, Saint Lucy

▶ KOKUZAHN (VOODOO)

The Voodoo religion, with 50 million followers in West Africa alone (from whence it spread to the New World through the slave trade), owes its name to the word for "god" or "spirit" in the Fon dialect of Ewe—the language of the Ewe people that co-originated Voodoo alongside Benin's Fon and Ghana's Ga. Two and a half million strong, the Ewe are also found in these two countries as well as sandwiched between them in Togo. Most Ewe are devout believers in Voodoo and may therefore attend some of its great initiation festivals, held at intervals of several years. One example is **Kokuzahn**, which, for seven days in May every three years, draws coastal devotees to a clearing by a beach outside Aflao, near Ghana's border with Togo, for a spectacular display of the gods' powers in the superhuman feats performed by the mortals they then possess.

From War God to Healing God

The cult of the warrior god Flimanu Koku was brought from Benin over a century ago by Ewe elders, along with his fetish, a calabash containing fourteen sacred knives, each with a small gourd filled with magic potions tied to its handle, and covered with sacrificial blood. This arrangement reflects the dual, shifting focus of the god's action. On the one hand, he was once known for the protection—even invincibility—he brought warriors in battle, with the power to strike from a distance, as the sacred knives still do when devotees point them at a live chicken balanced (like William Tell's apple) on a child's head two meters away: it then gasps and collapses within seconds—to be cooked in a dry calabash that somehow does not burn in the fire. On the other hand, Koku is now better known as a healing god, for the protection he brings to bear against witchcraft and other evil influences thought to be at the root of many diseases. The medicinal contents of the sacred calabash are thus so filled with spiritual power that believers nearly collapse under its weight as they carry it for public display—cloaked in white cloth—out of the "male" shrine where a priest guards over it. An Ewe has to carry it once in his or her lifetime before being considered a *Kokushi*—a devotee of Koku. The same thing happens when Azizan is taken out of the "female" shrine—being the feminine counterpart of the Koku fetish: a calabash holding pieces of termite mounds with healing powers.

Ritual Purity

Believers often fall into a trance after carrying either fetish for a while and always do when they see Koku's calabash opened before them, becoming possessed by the god. They take a concoction of ground nuts and seeds in water early in life for protection against evil spirits into old age, and Kokuzahn is supposed to boost its effects—provided one obeys the requirements of ritual purity set by the gods. Thus, for two weeks before the festival, participants must abstain from goat meat and sex, but above all, neither steal nor commit adultery, nor kill anyone, in order to have a clean heart. If any of these rules has not been strictly observed, it will show, since the gods will not fully extend their protection to people they possess. But when all the rules have been respected, the gods direct the unconscious actions of their followers and tell them what medicines to take in order to avoid being harmed by the ordeals they put them through, in order to demonstrate their power to counteract evil and inflict punishment.

Under the Spell of Voodoo Gods

Generally speaking, the devotees, barefoot on the natural arena's hallowed ground, work themselves into a trance by increasingly frenzied undulating and whirling dances to the sound of Voodoo drums and songs of rapture. They are protected from harm by smearing a mixture of palm oil, maize flour, and herbs, and by wearing *alatsi*-tree fiber skirts. Still, friends may need to intervene when a possessed devotee attempts to repeat a dangerous feat such as walking along the branch of a palm tree. But then again, they may also slam a pestle into a wooden mortar laid on a man's chest, just so he can get up unharmed and demonstrate how he can blissfully proceed with his dancing. Similarly, women may throw sand into their own open eyes without blinking, just as men may cut their own skin with glass shards without bleeding, or else lick a red-hot knife, or swallow a burning branch without their tongue even getting red. No pain is felt by the devotees who perform these stunts, nor do they have any memory of them after they emerge from their trance, but for the utter bliss of what is to them the highest state a mortal can reach: being possessed by a deity. When they are fully under its spell, it is possible to tell which one inhabits them by the direction in which their irises have rolled behind their eyeballs to leave a telltale, ghost-white stare. For instance, their rolling upwards makes it the look of the thunder god Hebioso (alter ego of the Yoruba god Shango). By then, it is probably time to carry the stiff-limbed, half-paralyzed devotee inside the shrine, so the priest can douse him or her with a potion that allows her or him to slowly awake from these drug-free altered states.

See also New Yam Festival; Òsun Festival

References

Carol Beckwith and Angela Fisher. "The African Roots of Voodoo," in *National Geographic*, Vol. 188, No. 2, August 1995, pp. 102–113.

———. *African Ceremonies.* New York: Harry N. Abrams, 1999.

Nadia Lovell. *Cord of Blood: Possession and the Making of Voodoo.* London: Pluto Press, 2002.

▶ KOSHOGATSU

See New Year (Japan)

▶ KREUZMONTAG

See Rogations

▶ KRISHNA JAYANTI, KRISHNA'S BIRTHDAY, KRISHNASHTAMI

See Janmashtami

▶ KUKULCAN FESTIVAL (MAYAS)

Before the Spanish Conquest, one of the major festivals of the Maya civilization of Central America was held by mid-December on the sixteenth day of Xul—the sixth of eighteen months of twenty days each, adding up to a 360-day solar year (plus five between each one and the next) in the agrarian *haab* calendar—as opposed to the *tzolkin* sacred calendar. On account of this celebration, the whole month was dedicated to the god **Kukulcan**, a feathered serpent who came to prominence in the Mayas' Postclassic period (900–1500) as a borrowing from Mexico, where he was known as Quetzalcoatl and was the patron of Aztec rulers. The **Kukulcan** festival was first observed by Maya ruling families—like those claiming Toltec descent—all over the Yucatan peninsula. But after the fall of the last great Maya urban center Mayapan to the Xiu clan in 1441, it was only held in its new capital Mani, while other provinces sent their gifts—such as four or five splendid featherwork ceremonial banners.

Gifts to the Gods

The many pilgrims who came to Mani for the feast of **Kukulcan** would have been preparing for the occasion with a period of fasting and abstinence. In the first evening, a procession set out from the house of the lord sponsoring the event to make its way to the Temple of **Kukulcan**. It was made up of lords, priests, commoners, and the clowns after which the festival seems to have also been "clown-named"—the meaning of the Quiche term *chic kaban*. The feather banners were flown atop the gaily decorated pyramid temple as people arranged their personal wooden and clay idols in the court-yard in front in the midst of prayers and exorcisms. Incense was burned after the kindling of a **new fire**. The food offerings that followed had to be unsalted and free of chili pepper, while they were accompanied by a beverage made from ground beans and squash seeds.

On the fifth and final day of the festival, **Kukulcan** himself was thought to come down from heaven to accept the offerings made over the course of the festival. Banners and idols could then be taken back to the house of the festivities' sponsor. However, many other worshippers actually stayed at the temple for the remainder of the month to pray, make offerings to their idols, and perform sacred dances, while the clowns made the rounds of wealthy households to entertain them with their antics and to collect gifts that were later shared between lords, priests, dancers, and the clowns themselves. It may be noted that clowns played a similar role in ancient Persia's springtime **Naw Ruz** celebrations.

See also 8 Monkey; Naw Ruz; New Fire Ceremony

References

Sylvanus G. Morley and George W. Brainerd. *The Ancient Maya.* Stanford, CA: Stanford University Press, 1983.

J. Eric S. Thompson. *Maya History and Religion.* Norman: University of Oklahoma Press, 1970.

Alfred Marston Tozzer. *Landa's Relación de las cosas de Yucatán, A Translation.* Cambridge, MA: Peabody Museum of Archaeology and Ethnology Papers, Vol. 28, 1941.

▌ KUNAPIPI (AUSTRALIA)

The mother-goddess of the Aboriginal tribes of northern Australia, who gave life to all human and nonhuman creatures, is called either **Kunapipi** or **Gunabibi** (since the actual pronunciation falls somewhere in between), as is the ritual sequence held during the dry season to call on her fertilizing powers.

The New Cult of the Old Mother

In the Northern Territory (particularly in Arnhem Land) as well as the southern Kimberleys of Western Australia, certain secret cults, maintained by local Aborigines to initiate young men into tribal tradition about the Dreamtime of sacred beginnings, only came to the attention of researchers in the middle of the twentieth century. They actually spread to tribe after tribe of that whole area over the course of these decades, at the same time as they came under increasing pressure from modern civilization, so that they now mostly survive as syncretistic mixtures of three basic ritual complexes that can still be made out, called **Ngurlmak**, **Djunggawon**, and **Kunapipi**. The latter is perhaps most representative of an emphasis on sexual symbolism and fertility rites reflecting the primacy of female Primordial Beings—a fairly recent innovation which sets them apart from the religious patterns found in central and southeastern Australia. It may be a result of Melanesian influence coming from the sea through the Gulf of Carpentaria's coastal areas. It caught on because, in these tropical regions, life and fertility depend on the regularity of rainfall.

This was already the focus of the pan-Australian myth of the bisexual Rainbow Serpent who controls it, and who now became an assistant or manifestation of **Kunapipi** as the "Old Mother." Her name is also said to mean "Whistle-Cock," with reference to the unique practice of subincision of the urethra (as opposed to the more widespread circumcision of the foreskin) of the penis, adding a uterus-like incision to the phallic image of a now bisexual snake. But **Kunapipi** is mostly known as "Fertility Mother" throughout the Northern Territory, where she has often absorbed the local mythology and rituals of the two Wauwalak Sisters, making them into embodiments of her power as well. If many ceremonies in the area deal with Fertility Mothers and Rainbow Snakes in a number of combinations and outer expressions, there is a recognizable cluster of them that is common—

albeit in just as many variations—to all versions of **Kunapipi** proper.

Snake Swallows Sisters

They of course share a belief in **Kunapipi** as the eternal fount of the life and reproduction of all creatures, identifiable with both the earth that supports it and the cycle of dry and wet seasons that sustains it. The ritual sequence enacting her creative mysteries thus usually takes place during the dry season, after the monsoon that ends by April, when people are reaping the benefits of previous ceremonies in the form of plentiful food. Messengers first go out to notify neighboring groups that it is about to begin. Taking anywhere between two weeks and several months to complete, it starts out in the main camp, with women dancing as the men sing the "outside" version of the Wauwalak and **Kunapipi** songs, as well as more secular clan songs. Then, to the accompaniment of swinging bullroarers as the thunder-like voice of the Great Serpent Yurlunggur/Julunggul (or Muit) —which the women and **Kunapipi** leader answer with the same cries as the Wauwalak Sisters when he/she (given its ambiguous gender) came to swallow them, the young postulants, smeared with red ochre, are taken to the triangular secret-sacred ground prepared in the bush as **Kunapipi**'s womb, to be swallowed up in it as an equivalent offering to this Python. Upon hearing of this from the men back in the main camp, the women lament the fate of the postulants. While the older women stand aside to call the names of foods forbidden to them at this time, the others then crouch under *ngainmara* conical mats and blankets as the men dance around them. They imitate Yurlunggur's coiling around the hut built by the Wauwalak Sisters to escape the rain he spouted as he emerged from the sacred well Muruwul near the Arafura Sea, attracted by the smell of the elder sister's blood after she gave birth to an incestuous child.

When the two sisters had first arrived by the well, all the animals they tried to cook had jumped from the fire into the well. At the sacred ground that night, men dance the part of one species each as they reenact this event by jumping into the *nanggaru* rectangular hole dug at one end to represent the well—some of them simulating intercourse as they do. "As the men perform the ceremonies the 'shades' or spirits of the natural species perform their own increase rites in the spirit world" (McCarthy 1957, p. 131). These performances may go on for weeks before a large crescent-shaped *kanala* trench is dug as a symbol of **Kunapipi**'s uterus, with an image of Yurlunggur etched on its sand walls. At some point, the novices will go down into it and be covered with bark, and intercourse will again be simulated there.

One or two four-to-seven-meter high *jelmalandji* (or *yemerlindi*) poles, a python drawn in blood on each, are later erected by the edge of the sacred well, to represent either Muit with **Gunabibi** or a palm tree—or a couple of snakes. They are given voice by bullroarers as men dance in front of them wearing conical hats covered like the poles with white feather-down snake designs. The bark is removed from the well to allow the boys to gaze at the double Python rising from it toweringly. The snakes' lightning will now strike them in the guise of firebrands thrown over the trench where they still lie. The dancers then reenact the swallowing of the Wauwalak Sisters in their hut— which to their way of thinking suggests both its phallic penetration by the Snake and a return to their Mother's uterus. After sprinkling blood from their arm veins on each other and into the trench, as the blood of the devoured sisters, participants push over the *jelmalandji* and fill in the *kanala* with earth and sand, using their dancing feet. This closes the main section of the **Kunapipi** rituals, which may well appear in varying order or with some omissions at the totemic leaders' discretion.

Ceremonial Wife-Swapping

The first of two concluding ritual sequences, rarely carried out in Arnhem Land, centers on the *kurangara* wife-swapping ceremony on the **Kunapipi** ground. Men bow their heads as they sing before the now sacred women, smeared in ochre and wearing feathered headbands to do the *ngamamali* dance. In between two sessions, they use a *Kitjin*—that is a post of bound paper-bark representing Yurlunggur—to strike a pole standing for a tree so that pieces of stringy bark fly off, symbolizing the lightning flashed by the Python as he/she circled the Wauwalak Sisters' hut. Women form a dancing line before the men as they finish the *ngamamali,* and are approached with presents of food, string, or ochre from their assigned partners in the ritual, which they may pass on to their husbands. This is the occasion for a lot of lewd joking with obscene gestures, and some of the men and women have intercourse on their way back to camp, even though they are not supposed to until the last night in the sequence, when it follows a repeat of the other dances. But first, maidens are ritually deflowered with a *galiwali* boomerang, either for real or symbolically for those who are no longer actual virgins and who just get the tip introduced into their vaginas. (This counterpart for girls of what the sub-incision rite is to boys is absent like it in north-eastern Arnhem Land.)

Stimulated by days of anticipation, a woman prides herself on the number of men she has sex with. After she is finished with one, her husband will come to rub his sweat on the man's limbs to prevent the illness that would otherwise result from such transgressive behavior, sanctioned in this exceptional ritual setting by the Primordial Beings and **Kunapipi** herself. This potentially perilous though light-hearted sexual activity is said to be done in imitation of the Wauwalak Sisters' incestuous relations with men of their clan but ultimately has more to do with the life-giving symbolic fructification of the Fertility Mother. Coming at the climax of weeks of religious activity, it offers emotional release and reinforces social bonds, being conducive to general goodwill and fellow feeling.

Snake's Belly and Mother's Womb

The last ritual sequence begins the next morning and focuses on the *djepalmandji*—the Wauwalak Sisters' hut, made from boughs hanging from a horizontal pole connecting two upright forked posts. Novices crouch under the boughs' shelter while two men sitting face to face in the womb-shaped forks cry ritually like the Wauwalak child, since this setup refers to childbirth. Bullroarers are swung and dancing women and children call in answer, smeared in red ochre. They surround the *djepalmandji* and then sit together a few meters away, covered with bark and *ngainmara* mats, in the manner of the Wauwalak. Dancing men, who had been hiding in the bush some forty meters away, then come out in single file to surround them all in turn and prod them with spears. The dramatic exchanges between the two gender groups allude to the stealing of the sacred rituals and fertility symbols of the Wauwalak Sisters by the men, which explains their prominent role in the festival of a mother-goddess. "This is because all the Dreaming business came out of women—everything; only men take 'pictures' for that Julunggul. In the beginning we had nothing, because men had been doing nothing; we took these things from the women," assuming they never got wise to the tricks played on them, as an informant candidly admitted in a "man-to-man" talk with an ethnographer (Berndt 1951, p. 55).

When the djepalmandji's covering is thrown aside, the novices emerge from it smeared in red ochre as the men call out to the women: "See those young men covered with the saliva of that Snake?" They then add what is officially supposed to be a secret to women: "but really, they are covered with spring blood"—that of the Wauwalak. The novices are taken to camp after the knocking down of the djepalmandji, and the men sing "outside" **Kunapipi** songs as they dance around the boys and lead them in single file to the sacred ground, where their handbands are removed for use in future rituals of **Kunapipi**. If, in the myth, the first people went straight from her womb to a "ring place," men who enter this secret-sacred ground return to her womb and emerge from it revivified after the rites are completed. Both there and at the main camp, the Rainbow Serpent's outline is traced in the red ochre smeared in bare outline on everybody's back "so that you can't see it," as a ceremonial purification called "baptizing." Before all decoration signs are finally washed off, it will take place on alternate nights with this singing on the pattern of the first rituals for a week or two, as a precaution against sickness in Yirrkalla near Cape Arnhem by the Gulf of Carpentaria (Berndt 1951, p. 56).

Big Sunday

Other names used for the same ritual complex include **Kalwadi** (or **Karwadi**) and **Kadjari** (or **Gadjeri**). Among the Waibiri of the central west of the Northern Territory, the latter is known as **Big Sunday** in aboriginal-English, although its full name is *Mamandabari-maliara*, after that of two Dreamtime characters in the myth and the term *maliara*, for circumcised or *Gadjari* novices. **Gadjari** is also called **Big Sunday** among tribes farther north, where it was forbidden near wartime Army Settlements because such large ceremonies disrupted the normal work routine. The few that were still carried out at a safe distance away were drastically shortened and largely reduced to an occasion for sexual promiscuity for its own sake, for recreational as well as religious purposes. There were

further crackdowns on the spreading abuse of taboos to appropriate certain objects, or to secretly declare semi-public areas off-limits to women on pain of punishment unless they paid in kind, sexual favors being the preferred currency. Yet far from the capital Darwin and places where such distortions brought on State or Church repression, in North-Eastern Arnhem Land Aboriginal Reserve for instance, **Kunapipi** rites have long endured in certain outlying areas. There, "people have come together to renew their faith, to refresh themselves spiritually, and to ensure that the continuity of the seasons is maintained, as well as the continuance of the life they know and appreciate. The pervading influence of the Great Mother is, to them, a reality" (Berndt 1951, p. 207).

See also Sunday

References

Ronald M. Berndt. *Kunapipi. A Study of an Australian Aboriginal Religious Cult.* New York: International Universities Press, 1951.

Frederick D. McCarthy. *Australia's Aborigines. Their Life and Culture.* Melbourne, Australia: Colorgravure Publications, 1957.

Mircea Eliade. *Australian Religions. An Introduction.* Ithaca, NY: Cornell University Press, 1973.

Roger Peterson Sandall. *Gunabibi—An Aboriginal Fertility Cult.* (53 ½-minute 16-millimeter film of phallic songs and dances from the Kunapipi initiation ceremonies of the *dua* and *jiridja* moieties at Maningrida Settlement, Arnhem Land, Northern Territory). Canberra, Australia: Australian Institute of Aboriginal Studies, 1966.

KURBAN

See Eid

LABA (CHINA)

Laba is an ancient Chinese harvest festival that has become mixed with some Buddhist monastic customs over the centuries, by way of seasonal offerings of a special porridge.

Archaic Roots of an End-of-Winter Festival

On the eighth day of the twelfth lunar month, "when the drum beat of **Laba** can be heard, the grass begins to grow," goes an old Chinese saying about this festival. This is because peasants used to drive away plagues and calamities by making lots of noise while disguised as gods. Though these come up as Buddhist deities in historical records, **Laba** seems to have archaic roots in a ceremonial hunt for victims to sacrifice to the ancestors for the **New Year**, as the word *la* (meaning "hunt") in its name suggests.

By the late Imperial time of the *Annals of Yanjing*, "on the eve of the Festival of **Laba**, fruits have to be peeled and washed. Then, the porridge is cooked until the next morning. Once the offerings of porridge have been made to the ancestors and the Buddha, the rest is distributed to family and friends. The distribution has to be over by noon" (Qi Xing 1987, p. 68). The more kinds of porridge there are, the better.

Porridge for the Buddha

This has been the basic pattern of **Laba** for over a thousand years, ever since the Buddhist monks of China started eating this porridge of the Seven Treasures and Five Flavors after a reading of the sutras in honor of the Buddha's Enlightenment. They thought it had taken place after he feasted upon the humble porridge that a shepherdess gave him when she found him unconscious, exhausted from his ascetic exercises and wanderings through what is now Bihar State in India. Having come to his senses and shed the excesses of mortification as being just as much of a dead end as those of indulgence, Prince Shakyamuni then bathed in a river and sat down to meditate under the Bodhi tree, (that is, the spot where he eventually became fully awakened as the Buddha).

From the great monasteries of the Sung Dynasty's capital Dongjing, the custom of eating this virtuous porridge spread to lesser ones, as well as to the Court. There, the Emperor, the Empress, and the princes would offer it to ministers, to generals, and to handmaidens, giving rice and fruits instead to the monks. The common people started to imitate this practice, to the point that under the Ch'ing Dynasty, from the middle of the seventeenth century, preparing the **Laba** porridge had become a regular part of the celebration of the harvest. In and around modern Beijing, however, **Laba** is the time for putting cloves of garlic inside glass jars filled with vinegar. They will be opened a few weeks later during **New Year** celebrations to provide two favorite seasonal treats for the price of one: vinegar-tasting garlic and garlic-tasting vinegar!

See also New Year (China, Korea)

References

Annual Customs and Festivals in Peking as recorded in the Yen-ching Sui-shih-chi by Tun Li-ch'en. Tr. and ed. Derk Bodde. 2nd ed., rev. Hong Kong: Hong Kong University Press, 1965.

Wolfram Eberhard. *Chinese Festivals.* London: Abelard-Schuman, 1958.

Qi Xing. *Les Fêtes traditionnelles chinoises.* Beijing: Éditions en langues étrangères, 1987.

▶ LABOR DAY

See May Day

▶ LAG BA-OMER (JUDAISM)

The **Omer** period of semi-mourning is named after the offerings of barley sheaves that used to be made at the Temple of Jerusalem on the second day of **Passover**, at the start of this count of forty-nine days until **Shavuot**. But the normal mourning prohibitions are lifted on **Lag ba-Omer**—as the thirty-third day of counting is known in Hebrew. Falling on the eighteenth of the month of Iyyar, this minor festival sees many weddings and all kinds of entertainment. Ashkenazis may then shave and get haircuts, but Sephardis have to wait for the next day. **Lag ba-Omer** is held to be the day when manna first fell for the people of Israel. In the State of Israel, it is a school holiday; children light bonfires as college campuses hold **Students' Day**.

Festive Relief in a Period of Trial

This holiday goes back to the lively **Scholars' Festival** of medieval rabbinical schools, to mark the alleged date of the end of a plague that claimed 24,000 disciples of Rabbi Akiva ben Joseph (50–136). This great master of the Mishnah (the oral tradition of Jewish law) was the soul of Bar Kokhba's revolt against the Romans. Some see this as a more likely occasion for his students' death, and the source of the custom of children playing with bows and arrows (also symbols of the rainbow) on **Lag ba-Omer**, as if to recall their desperate armed struggle. Others suggest that the epidemic was the result of an inability to live up to the spiritual demands embodied in the journey of **Omer** from **Passover** (as the Exodus from Egypt through the desert of the Sinai) to **Shavuot** (as the Giving of the Torah). In the students' case, this would have been shown by their lack of respect for one another.

The potential for outer danger—rising with that for inner growth—over the **Omer** period is illustrated by several other sad events of Jewish history that took place at this time of year. Among them are the massacres of entire Jewish communities in Germany during the First Crusade, and then in the Ukraine in the mid-seventeenth century. This is why the **Omer** period has become one of semi-mourning in which weddings or festivities, as well as creature comforts like shaving and getting a haircut, would normally be out of place. But since the plague came to a halt on the thirty-third day, **Lag ba-Omer** is the exception that confirms the rule: a day of celebration in the midst of restraint, like manna falling from heaven to sustain Israel in its journey through the wasteland.

What **Lag ba-Omer** is meant to celebrate is particularly the fact that the Torah was brought back from the brink of extinction through the death of specialists in its lore, not only to find a new beginning in a precious few survivors, but also to reach new inner depths in an esoteric reading. For after the decimation of his students, Rabbi Akiva, the last remaining master of the Torah, made his way to the rabbis of the south to give them his knowledge. On **Lag ba-**

Hassidim dancing at the tomb of Rabbi Shimon Bar Yohai during the Lag ba-Omer Festival. (David Rubinger/ Corbis)

Omer, he began to instruct these rabbis, his last five disciples. It is in their honor that bonfires are now lit all over Israel, to symbolize the new spreading of the light of the Torah throughout the land from these five sparks.

From the Light of the Torah to the Fire of the Kabbala

The best of Rabbi Akiva's students, Simeon Bar Yohai, hid in a cave for thirteen years after the martyrdom at the hands of the Romans of his master of thirteen years. He is regarded by Kabbalists as the author of their chief esoteric text: the *Zohar*, meaning literally "The Shining Light"—that of the hidden wisdom which he revealed to them on the day of his death and mystical **ascension**, thought to have taken place on the thirty-third day of **Omer**. To them, if the Torah is represented by light, the esoteric, hidden Torah they see in the Kabbala (a Hebrew

word for tradition or oral transmission) should be seen as an even more intense light, one that burns like the fires of **Lag ba-Omer**. They are all the more symbolic since the Kabbalistic practice of "releasing the sparks of holiness" present throughout Creation finds a striking analogy in fire as the conversion of matter into energy.

Pilgrimage to Meron

As if to underscore the esoteric view of all material objects as nothing but temporal reflections of spiritual reality, Kabbalists even have a custom that flies in the face of the received wisdom of Jewish ethics about the avoidance of needless waste. They throw bags of clothing in the fire, especially on the big bonfire they light with leftover oil from **Hanukkah** lamps in the Galilean village of Meron near Safed, where Bar Yohai is said to be buried. Whether Sephardic or Hasidic, they are heavily represented among the tens of thousands who honor the anniversary of his death on this very spot, as *Hillula de-Rabbi Shimon bar Yohai.* On this occasion, three-year old boys get their first haircut (leaving the sideburns to grow into *peyes*, the trademark side curls of the Hasidim worn in compliance with Leviticus 19:27), as their proud parents offer wine and sweets. There is much dancing and singing around the bonfire at night, featuring the special hymn for Bar Yohai, with its ten stanzas that correspond to the ten *sefirot* of the Kabbalistic Tree of Life (power points corresponding to levels of the unfolding of reality out of God). On the way to the gravesites of the many Talmudic sages buried there, makeshift stands sell pastries, editions of the *Zohar,* or amulets offering protection against the evil eye. Inside the tombs, men and women are segregated as they turn to God, relying on proximity to the remains of the righteous (*tzaddik*), with the access it brings to their merit (*zechut*), to give an extra boost to their prayers and make the Almighty look on them with favor. It must be stressed though that they do not pray to the holy person the way Christians would, but to God alone directly.

On **Lag ba-Omer**, Meron becomes a giant campground, where many come mainly to bask in the festive atmosphere, amid the smoke of barbecues. The devout make a point of roasting a lamb for a **thanksgiving** meal, called *seudat hodayah* in Hebrew; a makeshift butcher station is on hand for those who need a kosher slaughter in accordance with Biblical commandments. People find spots on high places hours before sunset to make sure they have a good view of the spectacular bonfire. But this is also the highpoint of the day all across the land. Children rival each other in the height and extravagant architecture of the pyres they have been preparing by collecting all kinds of objects to use both as fuel and building blocks. When flying over Israel in a plane that night, it is possible to see the myriad fires of **Lag ba-Omer** dotting Jewish-populated areas of the Holy Land.

See also Easter; Hanukkah; Seven-Five-Three; Shavuot

References

Yehudit Chana Rosenthal, ed. *We March as One: Lag B'omer Parade, 5747.* Brooklyn, NY: Merkos L'Inyonei Chinuch, 1987.

Hayyim Schauss. *Jewish Festivals. A Guide to their History and Observance.* Tr. Samuel Jaffe. New York: Schocken Books, 1996.

LAILAT-UL-QADR
See Ramadan

LAKSHMI PUJA
See Divali, Navaratra and Dusshera

LANSARA
See Midsummer

LAMMAS
See Lugnasad

LANTERN FESTIVAL (CHINA, KOREA)

The celebrations of the Chinese **New Year** come to a close with the full moon on the fifteenth day of the first lunar month: the day of the **Festival of Lanterns**. At least 3,000 years old, it is still very popular. It features the famous Dragon Dances and others about the Chinese astrological sign of the new year. The old year is burned in effigy, fireworks are launched, but above all, lanterns of all shapes, sizes, and styles are hung up and lit everywhere to evoke the light and warmth of spring. This is known as the **Children's Festival** since lanterns are also meant to invite newborns into this world. It is also called the **Festival of the First Principle (*Shangyuan*)** or **Night of the Principle (*Yuan Xiao*)**, when young and old eat *yuanxiao* (glutinous rice balls) and recall the story linking them to lanterns, which serve to guide ancestors' spirits home for the family reunion and back to the beyond when it is over. On this day

Sky lanterns are released to celebrate the traditional Chinese Lantern Festival on the first full moon of the Lunar New Year in Taipei, capital of Taiwan, on February 5, 2004. The lanterns are released in the belief that they will bring good luck and blessings over the coming year. (Simon Kwong/Reuters/Corbis)

they call **Daeboreum**, Korean families also prepare special dishes from seasonal produce to chase away bad luck and wish for a good year, as farmers pray for good harvests, and fishermen, for good catches.

Dragon Dances

The **Festival of Lanterns** is observed with great pomp in Taiwan's capital Taipei. The population gathers on Chiang Kai-Shek Square to witness dances evoking ancient springtime agrarian rites—first those of the island's aborigines and then the classic ones of the mainland Han as known in every Chinese community in the world: the Dragon Dances. In these, the mythological serpent, standing for the cycle of water between earth and sky, is shown running after a ball representing the sun, so as to bring about the desired meeting of the two elements needed

for agriculture to start again. Other dances will illustrate a legend associated with the particular symbolic animal of the **new year**. The old year is burned in the giant effigy of its own astrological animal that night in a grand finale, just after the **New Year** Presidential address. (In Korea on **Daeboreum** Eve, a straw effigy called a *jeung* used to be thrown into a stream as another way to expel bad luck that also has many parallels in European folklore.) Dozens of lantern-shaped hot-air balloons are then launched from the city's public squares into the moonlit sky.

To explain the identification of the Dragon with the hydrological cycle as the origin of the main dance, there is a traditional story about a snake that had been captured near the Lingxi river to be sold as meat to a restaurant. The magistrate of Jinhua County in Zhejiang Province, which flourished thanks to his irrigation projects, noticed that the snake had tears in its eyes and bought it as a pet. Oddly, it liked to eat grain products. There was a drought that summer, and the river dried up. When the magistrate prayed Heaven for an end to the people's suffering, it was the county's earth deity that appeared to him in his sleep to say there would be rainfall if he put the snake in the dry riverbed. He did, and enough rain came to save the new crops. To thank the snake and to obtain another good harvest the next year, the peasants threw big sacks of grain into the river. But the weather deteriorated, and the snake appeared to the magistrate to explain that these wasteful offerings had actually offended the Jade Emperor in Heaven. If he was to relent from his planned punishment of a two-year drought, the people were to offer only pure water in the future. Unfortunately, in thanks for the returning rain, someone insisted on offering animal products. The Jade Emperor vented his wrath on the Dragon of Mount Qiling—the same one he had previously banished to earth as a snake for disobedience, and who had again let him down by failing to prevent humans from acting badly. So they suddenly noticed that the rain had turned red and then found the scattered remains of the slain dragon in the riverbed. In their remorse, they created the Dragon Dance, with each performer holding up a segment of the serpent with a stick. Together, they were able to evoke its live motion. In this way, people thought it might come to life again.

Yuanxiao

This is but one typical custom of a festival that has evolved many more over its 3,000 years of history. It soon became very popular with everyone for bringing a temporary relaxation of the normative social strictures of time, space, and class. In the face of public resentment at the early breaking up of the festivities—in compliance with the strict curfew enforced from the time of the Western Chou Dynasty

(1000 B.C.E.)—later regimes exceptionally lifted it on this and other such nights. The day's original sacrifice to the Eastern Emperor, god of the sun, had evolved into a dusk-to-dawn ceremony for the Celestial Emperor by the Han Dynasty. Emperor Wen Ti (180–157 B.C.E.) then made the popular celebrations official as the **Yuan Xiao** Festival, from *yuan* meaning "first (month)" and *xiao* for "night." He had liked to join in them during his years of struggle against usurpers.

The best-loved story about the origin of the feast's Chinese name is that of a Court handmaid, called Yuanxiao. In northern China, her name stuck to her culinary specialty: the glutinous rice ball known in the South as *tuan yuan*. Today the *yuanxiao* symbolizes family harmony and union on her account—another reason the **Festival of Lanterns** is often called **Yuan Xiao**. As the story goes, Yuanxiao was saved by Dongfang Shuo, councilor to the Han Emperor Wu Ti (147–87 B.C.E.), when she was about to throw herself into a well out of desperation at not being allowed to rejoin her family for this special holiday. Taking pity on her plight, Dongfang Shuo had Yuanxiao pass for the Fire Goddess bringing a decree from the Jade Emperor, in which he declared he wanted to witness the burning of the capital Chang'an when he would come to its southern gate that evening. When Dongfang Shuo was asked for advice about this impending doom, he pointed out that the fire deity was very fond of *tuan yuan*, and that Yuanxiao made the best ones around. If she was ordered to make some to be sacrificed to this divinity, and all the land's households were to do the same, it might appease the Fire Goddess. The deity might then turn back, if she was also given the impression that the city was already burning; this could be achieved by lighting lanterns and setting off fireworks everywhere. Instructions to this effect were given. Yuanxiao herself was sent to meet the fire deity by the city gates. She was followed by Dongfang Shuo, who urged her to raise the red lantern she was carrying with her name on it. She then heard familiar voices shout: "Sister Yuanxiao! Sister Yuanxiao!" Her loved ones had come from the provinces for the general gathering to light up the city and had seen the two characters on her lantern.

Lanterns

Just as the *yuanxiao* rice balls now come in all sorts of regional variants, so do seasonal lanterns. They are said to have been invented by the carpenter Lu Ban while building a royal palace during the era of the Warring Kingdoms (475–221 B.C.E.). Made from all manners of materials in a vast array of shapes, colors, and sizes, they depict animal, floral, mythological, or literary designs, often combined to form charades since the third century Wei Dynasty. It is under the Southern and Northern Dynasties (420–589) that the custom of hanging lanterns on all buildings became widespread, as the focus of intense emulation at every level of Chinese society. In 713, the Tang Emperor Hsuan Tsung had a 60-meter-high portal erected in front of the Imperial City to bear 50,000 lanterns, as a way to invite the common people in to gaze at the lavish lantern displays of its temples and noble houses. They were entertained with song and dance by a thousand Court handmaidens, as well as young ladies of the imperial capital, who were mobilized for the duration of the three days to which the civic holiday had been extended—long the only time they were allowed to get out of the house. In classic Chinese literature, many a love story therefore begins on this day of the year's first full moon, when the old Moon Minister of Marriage matches baby boys and girls so they will fall in love when they later meet on that night.

This new formula for the public illuminations was kept, and it was even enlarged upon by the emperors of the Sung Dynasty (960–1279). As a further incentive to come and admire their ever more spectacular lantern displays, they had a cup of wine offered for free to everyone who showed up within the now five-day holiday. Later, Hung Wu doubled its duration to ten days, in order to secure popular support for the Ming Dynasty he founded in 1368. Under his successors and the alien Manchu emperors of the last Ch'ing Dynasty, theater performances featured more prominently in the celebrations. Shadow plays put on from inside big revolving lanterns are still popular.

Seasonal Customs

Other typical pastimes of the **Festival of Lanterns** include fireworks, swings, stilts, the dragon-lantern game, and the Boat Dance. In Chinatowns across North America, this is also a normal time for the **New Year**'s parade that concludes the festive season. This is the case for the oldest and largest Chinatown in San Francisco. Since its inception in 1958, the San Francisco Chinatown **New Year**'s parade has been held on the Saturday closest to the full moon. It now attracts millions of spectators and television viewers, especially for the 201-foot-long golden dragon called Gum Lung, its twenty-nine segments carried by a hundred men as it winds its way through the streets of San Francisco amid the crackle and smoke of firecrackers.

The **Festival of Lanterns** also used to be called the **Children's Festival** because, on that day, children would dress up and run around on the streets of towns and villages, singing and dancing. Afterwards, they would bring the magnificent lanterns especially made by their parents to school. This was so their teacher would light a candle inside each one, as an auspicious sign that the pupil holding it would also shine in his studies over the coming year—ushered in with a bang on the final day of **New Year** festivities.

Because this is a day when the Sea Goddess accepts mortals' wishes, Chinese people toss various offerings into rivers, such as apples (for their fragrance) to get a wife, oranges (symbolizing prosperity) to get a husband, longan fruits to have children, pebbles for a house, coins for treasures, and red dates for all good things.

As part of their *sesi* seasonal customs for **Daeboreum**, on the morning of the fifteenth day of the first moon, Koreans used to drink wine to "clear the ear" so as to hear good news in the year just starting and "crack nuts" such as chestnuts, walnuts, pine nuts, or gingko nuts in order to prevent ulcers. To have strong legs, avoid getting footsores, and generally remain in good health, it was common on the previous evening and even afterwards to "tread on the bridge" for as many times as one had lived years. The one ahead would bring abundance if cows brayed or the weather was clear on this day and/or the lunar **New Year**. Comparable to **Yuletide** mummers' plays or the **Carnival** *Fastnachtspiel* in the West, Korea's more elaborate and stylized satirical mask dance-dramas would traditionally be performed on this festival of the **First Full Moon**, and/or on the **Dano** and **Chuseok** festivals (which correspond to China's **Dragon Boat** and **Mid-Autumn** festivals, respectively) as well as on **Buddha's Birthday** on the Eighth of the Fourth Moon, in addition to state occasions and rain rituals.

> **See also** Anna Perenna; Carnival; Christmas; Dragon Boat Festival; Matzu's Birthday; Mid-Autumn; New Year (China, Korea), Purim; Spring Dragon; Vaishakha and Vaisakhi

References

Derk Bodde. *Festivals in Classical China: New Year and Other Annual Observances during the Han Dynasty, 206 B.C.–A.D. 220.* Princeton, NJ: Princeton University Press, 1975.

Choe Sang-su. *Annual Customs of Korea: Notes on the Rites and Ceremonies of the Year.* Seoul: Seomun-dang, 1983.

Burton Wolf. *Gatherings and Celebrations. History, Folklore, Rituals and Recipes for the Occasions that Bring People Together.* New York: Doubleday, 1996.

▶ LARENTALIA

See Days of the Dead (West)

▶ LAZARITSA, LAZARUS SATURDAY

See Palm Sunday

▶ LEMURIA

See Days of the Dead (West)

▶ LENAEA

See Dionysia

▶ LENT (CHRISTIANITY)

Owing its name to the Middle English word for spring, **Lent** is a forty-day season of fasting and penance in preparation for the central Christian festival of **Easter**.

Two Ancient Fasts Converge at Easter

The first nucleus of **Lent** was the total fast observed in the second and third centuries on **Holy Saturday**, and often on **Good Friday** as well. For these were the two days of Jesus Christ's absence from the world of the living, between his death on the Cross and his Resurrection at **Easter**. He had foretold this as the time when the Bridegroom would be taken away; not until then were his friends to fast (Matthew 9:15). By the middle of the third century, the fast had been extended to part, or all, of the six days preceding **Easter**, which however were not yet individually associated with specific stages of Christ's Passion, as in today's **Holy Week**. This Paschal Fast in preparation for the **Easter** Eve vigil service is not identical with **Lent** and is not even counted as part of **Lent** in the Eastern Church, though seasonal ascetic prescriptions apply all the more then.

Lent is a forty-day fast that first appeared in the third century and became the general norm in the fourth as a period of intensive training and instruction for catechumens—candidates to be received in the Church through the sacrament of baptism that had by then come to be administered chiefly at **Easter**. (**Epiphany** had initially been favored for this as the commemoration of Christ's own baptism, preceded by a couple of days of fasting—now down to one day of strict fast.) The baptized faithful joined them in prayer, abstinence, and special services in order to renew their own dedication to Christ on the same occasion and to collectively support them by sharing their experience as the Church—in which there is traditionally no such thing as merely "personal" salvation. Baptized Christians eventually got into the habit of doing this for its own sake, so as to be able to partake of the joy of **Easter** as though for the first time. For baptism is precisely an initiation into the mystery of the Crucifixion and Resurrection of Jesus Christ, originally relived as one on **Easter** night, instead of being spread between Friday and Sunday over a three-day **Pascha**. **Lent** as we know it was born of the natural convergence around the same end-point at **Easter** of the weeklong Paschal Fast and of a generalized forty-day baptismal fast.

The Meaning and Reckoning of the Forty Days

The forty-day figure was meant to call to mind several Biblical precedents for this fast: Jesus Christ's forty-day fast in the wilderness, where he was tempted by the devil before setting out on his ministry; Noah's forty days adrift on his ark during the Flood; Elijah's forty-day abstinence from food as he journeyed to Mount Horeb; and Moses' forty-day fast on Mount Sinai before he received the Ten Commandments, as well as the forty years he spent leading the people of Israel from slavery in Egypt through the wilderness to the Promised Land.

In the East, the forty days of **Lent** are counted continuously, but not from **Easter**, as they exclude **Holy Week**, **Palm Sunday**, and the preceding **Lazarus Saturday**. In the Roman Church, however, all these days are included except for **Palm Sunday**, since **Sunday**s do not count as days of fasting; this results in six weeks of six days each, to which four extra days have

been added in order to give forty. For this reason, while in the East, **Lent** starts on the Monday after **Forgiveness Sunday**, in the West, **Ash Wednesday** was instituted as its beginning in the ninth century. It was created by generalizing a rite that had been performed until then to prepare grievous sinners to be accepted again for communion in the Eucharist on **Holy Thursday**. Having confessed their sins by the last day before **Lent**—**Shrove Tuesday**—they could then be sprinkled with ashes, following Biblical practice. Likewise, on **Ash Wednesday**, the faithful receive an application of the blessed ashes of the palms used on the previous year's **Palm Sunday**. The priest traces the sign of the Cross on everybody's forehead, reminding each that "dust thou art, and unto dust thou shalt return," as the choir sings: "Let us change our garments for ashes and sackcloth: let us fast and lament before the Lord: for our God is plenteous in mercy to forgive our sins" (Watts 1959, p. 140). In some parts of France, there is an **Ash Wednesday** custom of baking pretzels, since their shape echoes the folded arms of penitents as they receive ashes.

In the Eastern Church, the first Sunday in **Lent**, coming a full week into the full fasting season, is the **Sunday of the Two Saints Theodore**, otherwise known as **Horses' Easter** among Slavs after prayers said for their health to their patron Saint Theodore Tyro, sometimes followed by horse races. More importantly, it is also the **Sunday of Orthodoxy**, a feast celebrating the triumph of right doctrine and practice with the final restoration of the cult of holy images at the Seventh Ecumenical (that is, universal) Council of the Christian Church in Constantinople in 842—after a century of iconoclastic agitation in the Eastern Roman Empire to ban it as idol worship. A special vesper service was then instituted, based on the public reading of the *Synodikon,* a lengthy liturgical text commemorating the defenders of the Orthodox Christian faith and anathematizing as heretics all those who failed to recognize all the teachings of the first seven ecumenical Councils of the Church (plus some later decrees of the synod of the Patriarchate of Constantinople). In North America, since the end of World War II—which had given Orthodox servicemen of different ethnic backgrounds the opportunity to worship together and realize their unity in the faith—this has taken the form of Pan-Orthodox Vespers. On this occasion, for once in the year, the Orthodox faithful of different Church jurisdictions in the same city step beyond them to worship together at a church belonging to each one in turn.

In the Roman Catholic tradition, the corresponding first Sunday after **Ash Wednesday** used to be followed by one of the four special **Ember Weeks** of fasting and prayer set aside over the year for the ordination of the clergy. Although it is only the thirty-sixth day of **Lent** counting backwards from **Easter**, this first Sunday is called *Quadragesima* (the Latin word for "fortieth") and all of the **Lent**en season is named after it in Romance languages, be it as Italian *Quaresima,* as Spanish *Cuaresma,* or as French *Carême.* In Savoy and Burgundy, and in many other parts of Europe as well, thorns, hedge cuttings, and all the dead wood that seemed to stifle new growth would be burned on that night until the mid-twentieth century (except for a few feeble survivals to this day). Young men took firebrands and ran with them through the orchards, threatening each tree with the same fate as dead wood if it did not give fruit over the coming year, before throwing them into the air to frighten the evil spirits of winter. Trees were also protected from the frost and insects by fumigation with the **Lent**en fire's smoke, and by spreading its ashes, in a pagan variation on **Ash Wednesday**'s penitential theme.

Pre-Lent

By analogy with *Quadragesima* rather than by exact count, the three preceding **Sunday**s used to be known in Latin as *Quinquagesima* (meaning "fiftieth"), *Sexagesima* (or "sixti-

eth"), and *Septuagesima* ("seventieth"), forming a pre-**Lent**en season that was abolished by the Catholic Church in 1969—soon after the end of the fasting of **Ember Weeks** in 1966. In Eastern Christendom though, the three **Sunday**s before the start of seasonal fasting are still known after their respective themes as the **Sunday of the Last Judgment** (or **Meatfare Sunday** because it ends the last week when meat is allowed), the **Sunday of the Prodigal Son**, and the **Sunday of the Publican and the Pharisee**. They were introduced in the Orthodox Church in the same reverse order of the calendar between the sixth and the eleventh centuries. Between the last two **Sunday**s mentioned, a period considered as the first week of **Carnival**, no liturgy is held, nor are the regular weekly fasts observed—no doubt in order to give the faithful a break before they embark upon the long, arduous journey of **Lent**.

No liturgies are celebrated either during **Cheesefare Week**—a modified pre-**Lent**en fast when eggs and dairy products are allowed. **Cheesefare Week** arose by the seventh century to accommodate the Palestinian practice of counting eight weeks of pre-**Easter** fasting with five fasting weekdays each, in a fifty-six day season including breaks, while the Greek Church knew only seven continuous weeks of fasting, for a total of forty-nine days. This extra week of build-up just before the actual start of **Lent** now culminates at the vespers of **Forgiveness Sunday** (or **Cheesefare Sunday**) in a moving practice to be seen in many Orthodox parishes. There, the faithful line up to perform a full prostration before everyone present in turn, and embrace him or her while asking for their forgiveness for any sins—whether conscious or unconscious—they may have committed against them. It is on the same occasion that a church's liturgical ornaments and the clergy's vestments are all changed, to leave only the mourning colors of black and purple for the duration of **Lent**. Such a seasonal color scheme was regulated in the Christian West under Pope

Innocent III in the early thirteenth century, but it has also influenced Orthodox usage, above all in the Russian Church by way of Catholic Poland in the seventeenth century. Yet, if the Roman Catholic Church refrains from singing "Glory" and "Alleluia" over **Lent**, the Orthodox Church does not shy away from these triumphant outbursts even then, as it feels that this would be like ignoring the fact the Resurrection has already taken place.

The Rules of Fasting

From **Cheesefare Week** on, the dietary prescriptions of **Lent** take effect. The ground rule still observed in the Christian East is that animal substances are forbidden, as is oil on Wednesdays and Fridays, while fish and wine are in a gray area, being allowed on certain festive occasions such as the **Annunciation**. However, invertebrates such as seafood and snails may be consumed, the rationale being that they hardly count as sentient creatures. For the purpose of avoiding animal foods during **Lent** is not only personal asceticism, but also reconciliation with the whole of God's creation, human and nonhuman alike, as a way to make up in some way for the intrusion of predation and death in its midst as a consequence of the Fall of the first man Adam in the Garden of Eden, before time, as we know it, began. The dietary aspects of **Lent** are thus but one very obvious point of application of the general attitude of detachment from carnal desires, of moral penitence, and of spiritual purification to be maintained by Christians in all areas of life, so as to refocus thoughts and deeds on the person of Jesus and on his demands—as hunger and thirst for God. The Church Fathers often insisted on the value of alms in this respect. Since the Vatican II Council, the Catholic Church has echoed this message in laying special emphasis on the distribution to the needy of whatever has been saved as a result of **Lent**en austerity, and on humanitarian social action generally. The discipline of the early Church also prescribed marital abstinence and forbade participation in feasts or attending performances. Up until fairly recently, these recommendations had a deep, if varied, impact on the social life of Orthodox and Catholic cultures alike.

In Spanish cities, where theater was a daily event by the seventeenth century, actors would suddenly find themselves out of work for nearly seven weeks—unless that is they were called upon for the Passion plays (*autos*) in which the lean season culminated. Through most of Spain, there would be a marked decrease in the number of weddings, but this was nothing compared to the impact on weddings and births that the **Lent**en and **Advent** seasons had in France or Poland.

For **Advent** is another, lesser period of fasting of several weeks in preparation for **Christmas**. Orthodox tradition even speaks of the Great **Lent** before **Easter**, as opposed to the **Christmas Lent** (also known as **Saint Philip**'s **Lent** after his November 14 feast as its starting date) and two smaller "**Lent**s"—the two-week **Dormition** Fast (Our Lady's **Lent**) before this August 15 Marian feast and the **Apostles' Fast** or **Lent** lasting one to six weeks before the June 29 feast of **Saints Peter and Paul**, depending on the date of the end of the fast-free week following **Pentecost** when this fast starts.

Exceptions to the Rule

The same ascetic directives apply in principle to all these **Lent**s, but aside from not performing weddings while they last, the Eastern Church has usually left it to the conscience of the believer to adapt them to his or her own personal circumstances. For one thing, it lacked the central authority that could enact detailed rules and special exemptions from them, as the Pope of Rome often did. The general rule began to be relaxed in the West in the ninth century by allowing the single meal of the day to be had at noon instead of in the evening, when a second light meal soon appeared. Eating fish became accepted in the Middle Ages, and then even meat—on Saturday only at first, and eventually on all weekdays but Friday, until today, when fasting and abstinence are required of Roman Catholics only on Fridays, **Ash Wednesday** and **Holy Saturday**.

Still, there was strict enforcement of whatever rules applied in the Catholic world, just as there were also carefully negotiated exceptions to these rules. For instance, a medieval papal bull gave Spanish crusaders the special privilege of eating eggs and dairy products during **Lent**, which was later sold to private persons in the name of financing the struggle against the Muslims. Spaniards were even granted a "Meat Bull" during an eighteenth-century war against England, so that meat could be eaten four days a week. Such cash-based dietary indulgences were beyond the means of the vast majority of Spaniards, who instead ate lots of cheap fish like cod and sardines at that time of year. But there were still many who found medical excuses to escape dietary restrictions.

Mid-Lent and Saint Joseph's

Another general exception to **Lent** was the **Mid-Lent** break, when the fast used to be suspended for a day of **carnival** on the Thursday of the third week in Italy, Spain, France, and French Canada. Instituted by Pope Innocent III in 1216, it allowed young apprentices who had been sent away to learn their trade to go back to their families for the fourth Sunday of **Lent**. Not unlike the **Spring Break** in the North American school year of today, **Mid-Lent** was a time for feasting and fooling around at parties, dances, and fairs, and more specifically for float parades and dressing up—often in horse costumes. In Italy, the most famous **Mid-Lent carnival** surviving today is that of Forlimpopoli in Romagna, called the **Segavecchia** after the burning of an old witch in effigy.

In Poland, the March 19 feast of **Saint Joseph** used to fulfill the same function as a temporary relaxation of the fast in order to allow the many people named after Mary's husband to properly celebrate their name-day. This also holds true today for the many Italian towns and quarters which have Joseph as a patron saint. For instance, in the Tuscan city of Siena, there is a float parade in the Torrita quarter and a rice fritter and toy fair in the Onda quarter on the feast of **San Giuseppe**.

A Secular Philanthropic Offshoot: Mothers' Day

In Great Britain, the fourth Sunday of **Lent** used to be **Mothering Sunday**, which commemorated the miraculous Feeding of the Five Thousand by Jesus with five barley loaves and two fish (John 6:1–14) by bringing loaves of bread to all mothers. In 1907, this old custom was reinvented by the Philadelphia social activist Anna Jarvis in honor of her mother Anna Reeves Jarvis, who had organized mothers' days during the Civil War, when they would care for the wounded and call for improved sanitary conditions. In 1915, President Woodrow Wilson recognized her efforts by declaring the second Sunday in May to be **Mothers' Day**, in honor of all mothers, both living and dead.

Lent as Personified in Folklore

At some level, while being generally observed, **Lent** was also resented by the population of France and Spain, judging by its common depiction in folklore: a skinny old lady made of cardboard or paper who personified winter hardships. In her Madrid version, like the "nun" calendars traditionally used by children for a **Lent** countdown in parts of France and Greece, she had seven legs when she triumphantly escorted King **Carnival** to his grave, but lost one with every week of fasting that went by, until her head was cut off on **Holy Saturday**. In a disturbing variant, the old lady might be replaced by a dummy (as in Greece) or an actor impersonating Judas, who would be tried, condemned, and executed during **Holy Week**—sometimes for real when things got out of hand; such was the power of a realistic scapegoating ritual known in Spain until the mid-twentieth century.

Liturgical Observances

By then, the Roman Catholic world was about to be dramatically changed by reforms that would, among other things, relax the observance of **Lent** to the point of its virtual disappearance from social life. It seemed to make little difference that liturgical reforms restored the moveable **Lent**en cycle of masses for each day (reflecting the fact that during **Lent** a so-called "stational mass" was originally supposed to be celebrated by the Pope in every church of Rome in turn) to give it prominence over the cycle of fixed feasts for **saints' days**, which it had lost in the course of the Middle Ages.

By contrast, the **Lent**en cycle was always paramount and has even tended to absorb the sanctoral calendar in the Eastern Church. Fasting also remains a cornerstone of Orthodox piety, observed in some form all year round—though with more flexibility regarding exceptional circumstances than used to be the case in the Catholic Church. Since the third century, there is fasting almost every week on Wednesday (in remembrance of the betrayal of Jesus by Judas) and Friday (to mourn for Christ's death). During Great **Lent**, on those two days of the week in Slavic Churches and on Wednesday evenings only in others, the Liturgy of Presanctified Gifts (taken from the previous **Sunday**'s Eucharist) is offered after vespers, since a full, triumphant celebration of the Eucharist would clash with the spirit of austerity to be maintained on weekdays; in this, it is like the Catholic **Good Friday** Mass. On Friday evenings (except in Slavic Churches) comes a recitation of part of the *Akathist* Hymn to the Mother of God, named thus in Greek because "no sitting" is allowed while it lasts. Originally composed in the sixth and seventh centuries in order to thank Mary for saving the Eastern Roman Empire from the threats of Persians and Arabs, as well as for the March 25 fixed feast of the **Annunciation** celebrating the conception of Jesus by the Blessed Virgin, this masterpiece of Greek religious poetry, attributable in part to **Saint Romanos the Melodist**, is now read in its entirety on the Friday (or the Saturday in the Slavic use) of the fifth week of **Lent**. On Wednesday or Thursday, as well as on the stricter first four days of **Lent**, it is the turn of the Great Canon of Saint Andrew of Crete, a lengthy cycle of odes contrasting human frailty with divine mercy.

In Eastern rite churches, great complines are read every weekday but Friday. On Sundays, the longer Divine Liturgy of Saint Basil replaces the usual one of Saint John Chrysostom, moved to Saturdays. At evening services and at home before going to bed, the **Lent**en prayer of Saint Ephraim the Syrian (intercut either with prostrations on weekdays or deep bows on weekends) asks God for deliverance from idleness, discouragement, vain talk, and the urge to dominate, praying instead for the gifts of chastity, humility, patience, charity, and the grace of judging oneself instead of others.

See also Annunciation; Assumption; Carnival; Christmas; Easter; Elevation of the Cross; Epiphany; Holi; Holy Week; Martinmas; Palm Sunday; Paryushana and Dashalakshana; Protection of the Mother of God; Ramadan; Saint George; Saint Lucy; Saint Nicholas; Sun Dance; Sunday; Whitsuntide

References

Gillian Feeley-Harnik. *The Lord's Table: The Meaning of Food in Early Judaism and Christianity.* Washington, DC: Smithsonian Institution Press, 1994.

Hermann Franke. *Lent and Easter—the Church's Spring.* Tr. Benedictines of St. John's Abbey, Collegeville, MN. Westminster, MA: Newman Press, 1955.

A. Allan McArthur. *The Evolution of the Christian Year.* London: SCM Press, 1953.

Jack Santino. *All Around the Year: Holidays and Celebrations in American Life.* Urbana: University of Illinois Press, 1994.

Fr. Alexander Schmemann. *Great Lent: Journey to Pascha.* Crestwood, NY: Saint Vladimir's Seminary Press, 1969.

Alan W. Watts. *Myth and Ritual in Christianity.* London: Thames and Hudson, 1959.

▶ LIBERALIA (ROME)

The public festival of **Liberalia** was celebrated in Rome on March 17 in honor of Liber and Libera, an unmarried couple of ancient Italic divinities who represented procreation. The day was marked by a number of fertility rituals concerning in particular liquid forms of seed and including the boys' coming of age ceremony: the taking of the virile toga.

Fertility Rituals

With the goddess Ceres, Liber and Libera formed a Latin triad of fertility gods, which was integrated in the state religion of the Roman Republic in the early fifth century B.C.E. It was also identified early on with the Hellenic triad of gods of the underworld: Demeter corresponding to Ceres, her daughter Korê to Libera as Proserpine, and Dionysus to Liber Pater as Bacchus. Though Father Liber was originally distinct from Bacchus—a composite of Asian, Greek, and Roman divine traits—as an indigenous agrarian deity, he became specialized as the patron of wine, was thus gradually assimilated to Bacchus as the god of wine, and eventually to his Greek counterpart Dionysus—masks of whom hung on the trees during this festival, as mentioned in Virgil's **Georgics** (II, 385–396). Wearing ivy crowns like Bacchus, old ladies sold honey cakes called *liba* on the streets on **Liberalia**; they would offer them in the buyer's name on small portable altars. Liber Pater was said to have discovered honey and invented apiculture, when bees were attracted to the noise of his cymbals, and he caught them in a hollow tree. The god's name is thought to refer to germination, birth, and growth, in the vegetable, animal, and human realms. This is why wine was also offered in his honor; for as Saint Augustine would later explain (*The City of God* VII, 21), Liber had responsibility over "liquid seeds, and therefore not only over the liquors of fruits, among which wine holds, so to speak, the primacy, but also over the seeds of animals." He was thus an object of the ancient phallic cult widespread in many forms throughout the Mediterranean basin.

> For during the festival of Liber this obscene member, placed on a car, was carried with great honor, first over the crossroads in the country, and then into the city. But in the town of Lavinium a whole month was devoted to Liber alone, during the days of which all the people gave themselves up to the must dissolute conversation, until that member had been carried through the forum and brought to rest in its own place; on which unseemly member it was necessary that the most honorable matron should place a wreath in the presence of all the people. (*Christian Classics Ethereal Library,* http://ccel.org/fathers)

As in similar Greek processions in honor of Dionysus, this *phallophoria* was thought to keep away disease and other disasters that could affect crops at this time of year when they were germinating.

The Taking of the Virile Toga

March 17 was also the day when boys matured into young men who could marry. Those who were seventeen would put on the *toga libera* or virile toga (probably named after Liber) for the first time in their lives, in an important coming-of-age ceremony. Leaving behind the *bulla* amulet worn around the neck and the purple-lined *toga pretexta* denoting childhood, they would go up to the temple of Jupiter on Capitol Hill and offer a sacrifice to deified youth—*Iuventas.* Liber too happened to be depicted as an eternally young man. Yet the main idea of putting on the virile toga on that day was that one took on the responsibilities of a full-grown adult and was granted the political liberties of a citizen. The idea of liberty thus became associated—however fancifully—with the name of the concurrent festival of **Liberalia**. The poet Ovid, who mentions this linguistic link in his *Fasti*, also suggests that in the distant past, peasants had used to come up to Rome for special games in honor of Liber on this occasion. But by his time, Liber was no more than a second fiddle at the April **games** in honor of Ceres. She had largely replaced Liber as a focus of the common people's affection and of their interest in plentiful crops. His association with the taking of the virile toga had become so remote in the second century, when the Christian writer Tertullian denounced most Roman social customs as idolatrous, that he spared this one as a purely civil affair, that was therefore not offensive to a jealous God.

> **See also** Apaturia; Dionysia; Games (Rome); Inti Raymi and Huarachicu; Spring Festival of Cybele and Attis

References

Christian Classics Ethereal Library. http://ccel.org/fathers/NPNF1–02/Augustine/cog/t37.htm#t37.htm.4.

Georges Dumézil. *Archaic Roman Religion, with an Appendix on the Religion of the Etruscans.* Tr. Philip Krapp. Baltimore, MD: Johns Hopkins University Press, 1996.

Ovid. *Fasti.* Tr. A. J. Boyle and R. D. Woodard. London: Penguin Books, 2000.

H. H. Scullard. *Festivals and Ceremonies of the Roman Republic.* Ithaca, NY: Cornell University Press, 1981.

▶ LIGHTS (FEAST OF)

See Epiphany

▶ LIGHTS (FESTIVAL OF)

See Divali

▶ LILLE JUL, LITTLE CHRISTMAS

See Saint Lucy

▶ LITTLE CHRISTMAS, LOPPIAINEN

See Epiphany

▶ LITTLE NEW YEAR

See New Year (Japan)

▶ LORD'S DAY

See Sunday

▶ LOSAR

See New Year (China, Korea)

▶ LOTS

See Purim

▶ LOW MONDAY, LOW SUNDAY

See Easter

▶ LUCIA

See Saint Lucy

▶ LUDI

See Games (Rome)

▶ LUDI PESCATORII

See Vestalia

▶ LUGNASAD (CELTS)

By early August throughout the Celtic world, an important festival marked the end of summer and the beginning of autumn. Called **Lammas Day** in English, it is best known from its Irish version as **Lugnasad**. It featured agricultural fairs, competitive games, and joyous celebrations—that were nonetheless also very serious in ancient times, as all of Celtic society came together as one around the king on the site of an archaic sacrifice.

The Gules of August

Lugnasad has given its name to the month of August in modern Irish (as *lúnasa*), but its local survivals go by about a hundred denominations in either Gaelic or English, the chief one in the latter language being **Lammas** Day. It is a contraction of the ninth-century Anglo-Saxon expression *Hláf mæsse*, "from the hallowed bread [*hláf*—hence "loaf"] which is hallowed on **Lammas** Day" (Toller 1976, p. 540), that is, at the mass of the feast of **Saint Peter in Fetters** (commemorating his arrest and miraculous deliverance from prison as related in Acts 12:4–20), to be offered to the four corners of the house as **first-fruits** in **thanksgiving** for the ripe corn harvest. This first day of the month was called the **Gules of August**—from the Latin *Gula Augusti* for "the mouth of August," which also gave *goulaoust* in French, with the variant *goelaoust* in Brittany, where the Breton word *gouel*, otherwise coming up only before the name of saints, makes this translate as "Saint August." This would suggest that this significant date of the Celtic calendar was deliberately Christianized (in name at least) throughout Roman Gaul, especially in view of the parallel case of **Gwyl Awst** that subsisted in Wales until about a century ago. **Gwyl Awst** was a day for fairs, for hillside picnics, and for pilgrimages to Little Van Lake in the hope of catching a glimpse of the Lady of the Lake, on the first Sunday in August in modern times, but initially on August 1.

In England, though it was frequently assimilated into the August 15 feast of the **Assumption**, **Lammas** used to be celebrated on the first Monday of August (still a bank holiday throughout the British Isles) in Chalford in Gloucestershire, while in other places its observance was switched to August 13—after thirteen days of the year were skipped with the introduction of the Gregorian calendar in the United Kingdom and its colonies in 1752. This was the case of the York **Lammas** fair as well as of the Coventry **Lammas** riding, a horseback perambulation to the sound of band music and church bells (a frequent feature of **Lammas** customs), reminiscent of **Rogation**tide bound-beating processions. Yet the aim here was to

mark the point at which certain lands used by their owners to grow wheat and other crops were to be thrown open for common pasture and public use until the return of spring. In Colchester in Essex and in several towns around what is now the Greater London area (namely Epping, Newbury, Staines, Ware, and Watford Fields), these ancient rights of pasture usually applied to so-called "half-year lands" from **Lammas** on August 1 (or 13 as Old **Lammas**) until **Candlemas** on February 2, when the fences were put up again. These were also the dates when half-yearly agricultural rents were due in Westmoreland, a former county of England's Lake District. Coming six months apart, these two dates opened the fourth and second quarters of the Celtic year, respectively, when its sacred cycle hinged on two of its four major festivals: **Lugnasad** and **Imbolc**.

Yet the modern Welsh version of the **Gules of August** remains the closest counterpart of Ireland's ancient **Lugnasad**. There, several townships at a time would celebrate the new harvest on a hilltop or a prehistoric site (initially by offering a sheaf of the new corn to Lug before burying it there and coming back after the meal to see the god's impersonator banish the monstrous figure of famine), with song and dance, games and competitions, feasts and matchmaking, aside from produce, horse and cattle fairs, and often pilgrimages under the protection of a saint—such as Patrick himself. Ireland's patron and early Christian saints were able to maintain these and other observances of a pagan festival because, unlike the yearly observances of **Beltane** (**May Day**) and **Samhain** (**Halloween** —the Celtic **New Year**), they were not as overtly religious and did not include sacrifices but undeniably had a high moral tone and a civilizing social role.

The Royal Assembly of Lug

Like these other Celtic festivals however, **Lugnasad** (meaning the "Assembly of Lug" in his capacity as divine protector of the realm) required the participation of every segment of the people around the king as Lug's human agent: the druids or *filid* assisting him, the warriors—from whose midst these priests elevated the king to rule above all, and the craftsmen and peasants—not just as providers of the general wealth at his disposal, but as beneficiaries of his generosity. For the king was called upon to demonstrate it on this occasion by rewarding everyone according to the quality of their performance in the day's various contests. If he was remiss in his seasonal obligations of hospitality, he failed the crucial test of fitness for his office, and it was thought he would have to suffer the consequences of his greed: overweening pride and premature aging.

The monarch who neglected to celebrate **Lugnasad** properly was the very type of a bad king, who reduces his subjects to poverty with excessive taxes, and eschews the crucial royal function of the liberal gift—made possible at this time of the year by the harvest just brought in. This material plenty was conducive to the peace and friendship that ought to prevail at **Lugnasad**. Some political and legal questions having to do with the distribution of wealth and responsibilities might also be settled during the compulsory general assemblies held on this festival—from three to fifteen days before and after, depending on its importance and on its annual or triennial periodicity. But while they lasted, a strict military truce was observed, along with a ban on legal proceedings—even as oratorical contests and sporting events engaged the same competitive skills in peaceful ways. Thus, by much the same means as the North American **potlatch** halfway around the world, this ancient Irish fair or *oenach* helped to strengthen the consciousness of tribal unity and tribal connections as "various enactments were adopted or confirmed, especially in regard to the dues of various tribal chiefs" (Gwynn 1913, p. 470). No one was allowed to break away, even to take a meal; for although eating was generally far from absent, this feast of obli-

gation actually counted as a fast. It was never to be allowed to degenerate into an orgy; the desired moral propriety was enforced through formal separation of the sexes on different portions of the fairgrounds.

Games on Goddesses' Graves

The fact that the site was always adjacent to the burial mounds of mythological or pseudo-historical characters helps to account for these sober undertones of the celebration of **Lugnasad**. For these assemblies always originated in, and revolved around, ritual commemorations of a woman of royal blood and divine stature who ordained them, promising general prosperity as long as they were faithfully observed. But over the centuries, other Irish worthies would get buried near her so as to also be able to get their yearly share of the spiritual benefit of the collective lamentations accruing to her, and of the funerary **games** in her honor (which are thus closer to Roman **games** than to the Greek **Olympiads** Irish chroniclers liked to compare them to). These inviolate graves may be compared to the princely tombs left by continental Celts. What is for sure is that, like all Irish capitals—such as central Tara, the **Lugnasad** fairgrounds had as eponymous (name-giving) founders fairy queens who had suffered tragic deaths. If there are few details on the fairgrounds of Colman and Cruachan, this is made up by the prose and metrical *Dindshenchas*—the "Lore of Places"—when it comes to those at Carman and Teltown, as Tailtiu is known in English.

The famous fair of Tailtiu, recorded since the sixth century, continued to be held regularly until 927—not counting sporadic attempts to revive it in the eleventh and twelfth centuries. It was the most important fair in Ireland because it was sponsored by the king of Tara, the head of the mighty confederation of O'Neill dynasties. Based in Tailtiu, in the ancestral homeland of their northern clans, it took place on or around August 1—possibly from the first Monday of the month. It was said to have been instituted by Lug, king of the divine race of the Tuatha Dé Danann, in honor of his nurse Tailtiu, a princess of Spain (since this country was part of the Other World in ancient Ireland's sacred geography), who had been the wife of Eochu, the last Fir Bolg king of Ireland, before becoming the wife of another Eochu from the new divine dynasty. Being a mother-figure before belonging to any particular lineage, Tailtiu thus stands for the earth as the ground of the wealth of the realm that the king commands and distributes and must not be confused with the sovereignty of Ireland, always symbolized by the king's young bride. As for Carman, she is said to have died a hostage as the mother of invaders who had been ravaging Ireland, to guarantee that they would not return. Indeed, the remains of a young woman showing signs of having been buried alive were uncovered in 1944 at a dig in County Kildare, on a possible site of the assembly of Carman. Such a sacrifice might have been understood at some point as the price of Ireland's peace and prosperity. Still, as related by the eleventh-century bard Fulartach, the fair broke up at the signal of a formal Christian blessing on "the fortunate ever-joyous host:/ may there be given to them, from the Lord,/the earth with her pleasant fruits!" in the name of national and regional patrons Patrick, Brigit, Caemgen, and Columcille, "the saint[s] of the compact" guaranteeing the truce— no deceitful blessing—"/above the hallowed water of Carmun, devoutly,/mass, genuflection, chanting of psalms" (Gwynn 1913, p. 23, verses 269–276).

From Lug to Caesar to Christ

On the continent in Antiquity, the Assembly of the Gauls would meet in August on a site dedicated to Lug where the waters of the river Saône flowed into those of the river Rhône. It is known only in the romanized form of the *Concilium Galliarum* of Lugdunum, present, day Lyon. Born there in 10 B.C.E., Emperor Claudius, who was an able historian and a skilled linguist, must have realized the political interest of promoting the conversion of a pan-Celtic August festival of the king's peace into a celebration of the universal *Pax Romana* under the aegis of an imperial dynasty founded by a *divus Augustus*. But before very long, a further conversion—turning the focus upward still from a divinized universal monarch to a God made man as heavenly Prince of Peace—was destined to have a more lasting impact on the ancient seat of the continental Assembly of Lug; also born there, the French Church is headed to this day by the bishop of Lyon as Primate of the Gauls.

See also Assumption; Busk; Candlemas; Games (Greece); Games (Rome); May Day; Midsummer; Potlatch; Rogations; Samhain

References

D. A. Binchy. "The Fair of Tailtiu and the Feast of Tara," in *Ériu*, Vol. XVIII (1958), pp. 113–138.

Anna Franklin and Paul Mason. *Lammas: Celebrating Fruits of the First Harvest.* St. Paul, MN: Llewellyn Publications, 2001.

Edward Gwynn, ed. *The Metrical Dindsenchas*, Part III. Dublin: Hodges, Figgis and Co., "Todd Lecture Series" Vol. X, 1913 (reprint Dublin Institute for Advanced Studies, 1991).

Ronald Hutton. *The Pagan Religions of the Ancient British Isles: Their Nature and Legacy.* Oxford: B. Blackwell, 1992.

Máire MacNeill. *The Festival of Lughnasa. A Study of the Survival of the Celtic Festival of the Beginning of Harvest.* London: Oxford University Press, 1962.

T. Northcote Toller, ed. *An Anglo-Saxon Dictionary.* Oxford: Oxford University Press, 1898, reprint 1976.

▶ LUPERCALIA (ROME)

Tracing its roots to the very origins of Rome, the February 15 festival of **Lupercalia** proved to be the city's most resilient one. It survived the fall of the Empire long enough for Pope Gelasius I to have to crack down on attempts at a full-fledged revival at the end of the fifth century. He thus instituted both **Candlemas** on February 2 and the yearly commemoration of Roman cleric **Saint Valentine**'s martyrdom on February 14, 269. By contrast to the sentimental affair the latter festival has become, the ancient **Lupercalia** of February 15 were an unromantic—if colorful—fertility ritual, involving a race in which women were slapped by the runners with leather strips to purify them of obstacles to childbirth.

Dead Ancestors and Future Descendents

The **Lupercalia** fell toward the beginning of **Parentalia**, an end-of-year novena (nine-day religious observance) to appease dead relatives. The *Luperci*, or wolf-priests, may have stood in for the dead and acted as advocates for the living. They gave the blessing of new life to the women they met on their race around Palatine Hill, who offered their backs and limbs to be slapped with strips of skin from billy goats just sacrificed. These strips were known as *februa* for their purifying properties. The month of February was named after them.

Romulus and Remus

Everyone on the way was slapped with these sacred whips by the two groups of runners—young boys from the Quinctii and Fabii families, descended from Romulus and Remus respectively. They came from the Lupercal, the cave to the southwest of the Palatine where the city's twin founders were said to have been suckled by a she-wolf, after they were abandoned at birth on the orders of a usurper uncle. Once the goats had been sacrificed there, as if to celebrate the fact that Romulus and Remus had been fed with milk instead of being just eaten up like stray sheep, two boys—one from each noble clan—were brought to the Lupercal to play the part of their mythical ancestors. Some priests would touch their foreheads with the

bloody knife used for sacrificing the animals, and other priests immediately wiped them with milk-soaked wool. The two boys, like miraculously rescued victims, were supposed to laugh out loud on the spot, as if to dispel the thought of the peril just averted. They could now join the race of the Luperci, wearing only goatskin loincloths. It was as one of them that, in 44 B.C.E., Mark Antony took this opportunity to offer a royal diadem to Julius Caesar, which he turned down—though the incident still fuelled rumors he wanted to restore the monarchy and become king himself.

Lupercus: the Faun as Wolf God

"A peculiarity of this festival is that the Luperci sacrifice a dog also," adds the Greek chronicler Plutarch (50?–125?, in *Romulus* XXI, 6), who points out its name "has the meaning of the Greek 'Lycaea' or *feast of wolves*, which makes it seem of great antiquity" and Arcadian origin (XXI, 3, in Plutarch's *Lives*, Vol. I, pp. 156–159). The dog probably stood in for the wolves that the wolf god Lupercus was supposed to keep at bay as a protector of herds. The poet Ovid (43–17) knew this god only as Faunus, whose name means "the strangler." He identified him with the goat-footed Greek god Pan; hence the *panic* running of the naked Luperci. Ovid (*Fasti* 2:424, p. 39) was aware though that under this name of Pan, "Lycaean Faunus has Arcadian shrines" in Greece, where the equivalent of the Luperci was named after Mount Lykaios—that is, "wolf-mountain." All this points to the identification in a single divine figure of the threat of canine predators and of the herds of sheep requiring protection from them. Human beings, in the form of Luperci, could relate to the wolves and to the sheep, both as victims and as victors, like the defenseless babies Romulus and Remus adopted by a she-wolf as her own cubs.

Rumina's Fig Tree

The spot of this miracle was known as the original site of the fig tree Ruminalis (moved since by another miracle), sacred to Rumina, goddess of suckling. This function, along with a similar-sounding name, caused her to be associated with Romulus and his legend. Such a link between milk-feeding—both animal and human—and the infant twins who, against all odds, would grow up to found Rome, may well explain why the race of the Luperci promoted childbirth, through the women's contact with the goat-leather whips wielded by youths who had just received aspersions of milk from a piece of raw wool.

From Juno Lucina to Saint Valentine

But the reason Ovid (*Fasti* 2:441, p. 40) gives to account for the **Lupercalia**'s focus on women's fertility is the following command issued by the goddess Juno Lucina from her sacred grove—*lucus*—on Esquiline Hill: "The sacred goat must penetrate Italy's mothers." These words were reportedly heard coming out of the bush a little after Rome was founded in 753 B.C.E., when the kidnapping of Sabine women by Romulus as wives for his subjects failed to have the desired effect on the fledgling settlement's birthrate. A temple was dedicated to Juno as goddess of childbirth on the Esquiline in 375 B.C.E. on the first of March. Two weeks after **Lupercalia**, this date (which had long been that of the **New Year** until the religious reforms attributed to Romulus' son King Numa Pompilius) would henceforward be celebrated as the festival of **Matronalia**, in honor of the institution of marriage as well as of the peace secured by the early marriages between Roman men and Sabine women.

But it was on the former eve of **Lupercalia** — **Saint Valentines**—that Juno, the goddess of marriage, would keep on being honored for centuries by the drawing of the names of girls from lots by boys (and eventually vice versa), sometimes pairing them as friends until **Easter**, for a year, or even for life as spouses. Hence the custom of picking **Valentines** on the feast of a saint known for performing secret weddings for young men who sent him notes stating they would rather make love than war (since Emperor Claudius II had temporarily outlawed marriage as a ground for avoiding the draft). The old pagan association of this date with fertile unions was reinforced by its medieval interpretation as the start of mating season for birds, when swallows made their appearance as the first harbingers of spring—not unlike **groundhogs** on **Candlemas** twelve days earlier.

See also Candlemas; Days of the Dead (West); Easter; Games (Rome); Matronalia; New Year (West)

References

Alberta Mildred Franklin. *The Lupercalia.* New York: [s.n.], 1921.

A. W. J. Holleman. *Pope Gelasius I and the Lupercalia.* Amsterdam: Adolf M. Hakkert, 1974.

Ovid. *Fasti.* Tr. A. J. Boyle and R. D. Woodard. Harmondsworth, Middlesex, UK: Penguin Books, 2000.

Plutarch's Lives in Eleven Volumes. Tr. Bernadotte Perrin. Cambridge, MA: Harvard University Press, 1948.